AF512911

Leadership and Change Management

Leadership and Change Management

Ashim Gupta

RANDOM

RANDOM PUBLICATIONS

NEW DELHI (INDIA)

Leadership and Change Management

ISBN 978-93-5111-240-2
© Reserved

All Rights Reserved. No Part of this book may be reproduced in any manner without written permission.

Published in 2014 in India by

RANDOM PUBLICATIONS

4376-A/4B, Gali Murari Lal, Ansari Road
New Delhi-110 002
Phone : +91-11-43580356, +91-11-23289044
e-mail: randomexports@gmail.com, sales@randompublications.com, info@randompublications.com

Reprint 2023

Type Setting by : Keystoneprintads, Delhi-110051
Digitally Printed at: Replika Press Pvt. Ltd.

Preface

The world is experiencing and encountering immense cultural, social, political, and organizational transformation which creates challenges as well as opportunities for organizations. Leadership in organizations requires an overall understanding of the fast-paced changes of both the external and internal environments to be able to respond effectively. Leadership is essential for any system to begin to respond adequately to the present and create future needs to review, reanchor, and recalibrate with the present realities. Today's leaders need to depart from earlier modes of providing directions. They require tools for understanding self and understanding others and the knowledge and understanding of strategy. They also require skills in diagnosis and analysis. This workshop will provide an ideal platform for leaders to explore these issues to be able to make strategic choices anchored in the vision of the organization and for understanding of self and others.

Leadership has been described as "a process of social influence in which one person can enlist the aid and support of others in the accomplishment of a common task", although there are alternative definitions of leadership. For example, some understand a leader simply as somebody whom people follow, or as somebody who guides or directs others, while others define leadership as "organizing a group of people to achieve a common goal". Studies of leadership have produced theories involving traits, situational interaction, function, behavior, power, vision and values, charisma, and intelligence, among others.

Change management is an approach to transitioning individuals, teams, and organizations to a desired future state. In a project management context, change management may refer to a project management process wherein changes to the scope of a project are formally introduced. Organizational change is a structured approach in an organization for ensuring that changes are smoothly and successfully implemented to achieve lasting benefits. In the modern business environment, organizations face rapid change like never before. Globalization and the constant innovation of technology result in a constantly evolving business environment. Phenomena such as social media and mobile adaptability have revolutionized business and the effect of this is an ever increasing need for change, and therefore change management. The growth in technology also has a secondary effect of increasing the availability and therefore accountability of knowledge. Easily accessible information has resulted in unprecedented scrutiny from stockholders and the media. Prying eyes and listening ears raise the stakes for failed business endeavors and increase the pressure on struggling executives. With the business environment experiencing so much change, organizations must then learn to become comfortable with change as well. Therefore, the ability to manage and adapt to organizational change is an essential ability required in the workplace today. Due to the growth of technology, modern organizational change is largely motivated by exterior innovations rather than internal moves. When these developments occur, the organizations that adapt quickest create a competitive advantage for themselves, while the companies that refuse to change get left behind. This can result in drastic profit and/or market share losses. Organizational change directly affects all departments from the entry level employee to senior management. The entire company must learn how to handle changes to the organization

I thank all members of my team who have helped in the preparation of the book. My special thanks go to "Random Publications" who have published the book.

– Ashim Gupta

Contents

1

Leadership

INTRODUCTION

The sales manager's role has two important elements to it:

- To achieve sales targets (in line with the company's business objectives)
- To manage and develop their sales people.

How can sales managers get a high performance from their team, in order to succeed in their role and achieve the above objectives? One key aspect will be the manner in which they lead.

In this chapter we will look at the practical steps sales managers can take to:

- Demonstrate leadership skills (to help sales people exceed their targets)
- Use different communication styles (to help people with different levels of ability and experience)
- Develop skills through delegation (to encourage sales people to contribute to the team and meet their personal goals).

UNDERSTANDING LEADERSHIP

In this section we will define leadership and distinguish it from management.

If a sales manager is also a good leader they will bring three main benefits to the sales team:

- A positive attitude that encourages loyalty and a desire to perform.
- A good working atmosphere.
- Better working relationships – by having clearly defined goals and levels of expectation.

DEFINING LEADERSHIP

Leadership means providing consistent, clear direction to your team.

As a sales manager you will be judged on results. This will test your ability to:

- Assess (and interpret the challenges facing your sales team)
- Communicate (these challenges and find ways to overcome them)

- Create the right atmosphere for the sales team to perform
- Support your sales people.

There are many ways for a sales manager to be an effective leader.

Some characteristics that are commonly seen in leaders are:

- *Vision and anticipation*: How you see the sales team developing and anticipating what might happen in the future.
- *Integrity and honesty*: Representing the principles that your team will respect
- *Self-belief*: Encouraging other sales people to believe in themselves
- *Being objective*: Being realistic and fair (completing tasks, admitting any mistakes you make and correcting them)
- *Innovation*: Looking at ways of doing things better and trying new ideas
- *Listening and communicating*: Involving the team, communicating with them regularly and incorporating their suggestions

DIFFERENCES BETWEEN SALES LEADERSHIP AND MANAGEMENT

It is the combination of leadership and management that creates a successful sales manager. What is the difference between leadership and management?

- Management means organising the activities of the people who directly report to you

The focus is more on the task – getting the job done.

- Leadership is about creating an environment where people can get results

The focus is more on the people – encouraging the right behaviour. Management and leadership are both about getting results. Managing a sales team means that you need to lead it too. There is pressure in sales management to meet and exceed company targets.

A good sales manager will ensure that he/she:

- Focuses on *how* they lead their team
- Manages the tasks in order to meet the target.

How you manage your team will affect their success in meeting the overall sales targets. A measure of your leadership style will be your ability to balance the focus on the task with your focus on the people you manage.

CONTEXT, CHARACTER AND ATTITUDE

The starting point for effective leadership in sales management is to address:

- The context (of the situation you face)
- Your character
- Your attitude.

Let us look at each of these three characteristics individually.

Context

Looking at the context of a situation will include a number of elements.

It will depend on whether you:

- Follow the company's sales plan properly
- Regularly assess the effectiveness of the sales team (to fit in with the plan)
- Look at current market forces to assess realism of sales forecasts.

Sales people can work more effectively if they understand some of the areas that affect their sales performance. A sales manager needs to interpret the company's sales plans and communicate relevant information to the team.

This can be used to address different aspects of performance, for example:

- Factors affecting sales targets (and what needs to be done)
- The impact of any developments on customers
- The way sales people are working internally with other parts of your company.

Character

Character is about self-knowledge and understanding what principles are important to you.

It covers issues like:

- What you value most in being effective at work
- Honesty
- How good you are at keeping to your commitments
- Being structured and well organised.

Elements of your character will be noted and copied by your sales team. A leader sets the standard for others to follow. You should be aware of what fundamental issues you agree with so that you can communicate these to the members of your team. This will help create respect for your role and give people a high standard of behaviour to follow.

Attitude

Attitude is about how you think and behave. It is affected by how you feel.

This, in turn, can affect how you manage your sales people and what you say to them. Your attitude will determine:

- What you say
- How you say it
- How you respond to the needs of others
- What mood you are in.

Your attitude is what defines you today. It is about the type of person you are and about other people's perception of you. The context of your existing situation, your character and your attitude towards the people that you manage are important elements to consider as a leader. By being aware of these three leadership areas you should find it easier to manage your sales people.

SELF-DEVELOPMENT

One way to develop your own style of leadership is to think about the qualities you have and to list them. Although this is subjective it will give you the opportunity to focus on what your strengths are. This can be looked at in more detail in the following way:

Step 1

List as many qualities as you can that you would associate with a successful leader. Think of people you know and admire, historical or contemporary. Note what you admire about them and which qualities you see as effective.

Step 2

From this, you may then want to decide which three leadership elements of your own character to focus on. For example, you might decide to be more patient, helpful or assertive.

Step 3

By being aware of the leadership characteristics you want to adapt you can measure yourself more easily in different situations. This will give you focus and help you to be more aware of how you deal with people. These qualities will form a key element to you using your influence and authority effectively.

This will come essentially from a combination of three sources:

- Status: your position in the company
- Knowledge: your level of experience
- Attitude: being positive/personal attributes.

While status and knowledge are important, it is the third element that will make you a role model to your sales team. If you are consistent and positive in your communication to others your colleagues will find it easier to work with you. This will give them a reason to respect you and your style of leadership.

An important leadership challenge many managers face is to understand the connection between:

- What you want – (results)
- How you want to manage – (behaviour).

Understanding your own leadership qualities and aspirations will make you more aware of when and how you use them successfully.

LEADERSHIP STYLES

Effective leadership in the sales management role is often about good communication skills. We will now consider how a sales manager can lead in a way that will help sales people to produce the results they aim for. There are different ways to lead the sales team.

In this section we will:

- Identify the range of leadership styles to use
- Establish which one to use (depending on the situation).

Your leadership style will be influenced by the type of person you are and the circumstances you face. Your effectiveness will be determined partly by how well you are able to adapt your style of leadership.

THE FOUR LEADERSHIP STYLES

We will describe four leadership styles and look at which one you could adopt depending on the sales situation you face.

There are two extremes to consider:

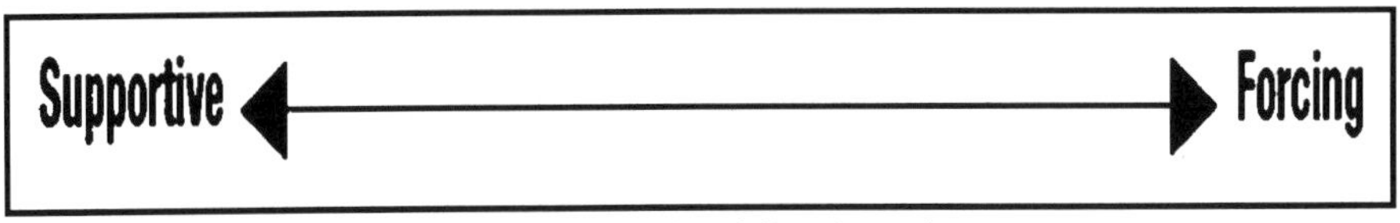

The Supportive style incorporates the following elements:

- Praise and encouragement
- Being helpful and providing suggestions
- Listening and understanding
- Allowing the individual to make their own decisions.

The Forcing style makes clearer demands. It requires:

- Control, structure and being decisive
- Direction and guidance
- Written communication
- Regular monitoring (to ensure that any agreed actions are completed).

There are times when a manager will not need (or feel comfortable using) the extremes of these styles. Most of the challenges they face require a style that is somewhere between the two. You will also need to take your own personality into account when deciding upon a correct course of action.

If you are a strong willed person you may want to balance this with a more supportive approach. Someone with a naturally supportive style might want to be more assertive where appropriate. These more moderate communication styles can be divided into two categories below.

Supportive – Forcing

Focuses on the same areas as supportive but requires elements of the forcing style.

Forcing – Supportive

Focuses on the same areas as forcing but requires elements of the supportive style. The four leadership styles are illustrated below:

Supportive ⟷ Supportive - Forcing ⟷ Forcing - Supportive ⟷ Forcing

A sales manager might use one style as opposed to another depending on:

- The type of person he/she is
- The type of person he/she is communicating with
- The current situation
- Directives from senior managemen
- How well the sales targets are being met.

INTERPRETING THE STYLES

It is difficult to indicate the right style to use for every sales situation. However, in the table below we describe the four leadership styles and provide some examples of how they can be interpreted. This will depend on the individual and the context of the situation.

Supportive

Communication Style

Less time spent with person, regular acknowledgement, and goals with long timeframes.

Objective

Your aim is to give the sales person a certain amount of freedom. This allows them to perform without instruction from you.

Examples of when to Use

- The sales person is experienced and performing well. He/she is demonstrating the right effort and selling skills.
- The sales person may be under-performing but you have a good knowledge of their ability. You have given them a task that he/she should be able to achieve.

Supportive – Forcing

Communication Style

Some time spent with the sales person, regular acknowledgement and follow-up with longer timeframes.

Objective

Your aim is to remain flexible with the sales person while introducing an element of guidance. Advice is given from you on how a situation might be solved.

Examples of when to Use

- The sales person may be performing well but you have identified an aspect of their behaviour (skill, effort, and attitude) that needs improving.
- The sales person is under-performing and you wish to provide guidance and advice to help them.

Forcing – Supportive

Communication Style

More time spent with the sales person. Regular acknowledgement and follow-up with shorter timeframes.

Objective

Your aim is to deal with an issue using a more direct approach. This may be combined with instruction, guidance and positive co-operation.

Examples of when to Use

- The sales person is performing well, but may not have implemented your previous suggestions properly.
- The sales person is under-performing and you are taking corrective action. You are communicating what is needed and how it can be done.

Forcing

Communication style

More time spent with the sales person; written objectives; regular meetings and short timeframes.

Objective

Your aim is to confront, control, direct and demand action with no flexibility.

Examples of when to Use

- The sales person is performing well, but is setting a bad example to other members of the team.
- The sales person is under-performing and has failed to implement your previous instructions.

FLEXIBILITY OF STYLE

The challenge you face is to assess how to handle different combinations of performance. This can be managed well if you begin by setting standards of acceptable sales behaviour. This will show that you are consistent and flexible in most situations.

The chart below is designed to provide you with further guidance on the choice of styles:

- If you have someone consistently meeting his/her sales target with a positive attitude, you might allow greater flexibility in your style.
- Conversely, poor performance and lack of commitment may require a more disciplined, direct approach. This might include specific, targeted areas for improvement and supervision.

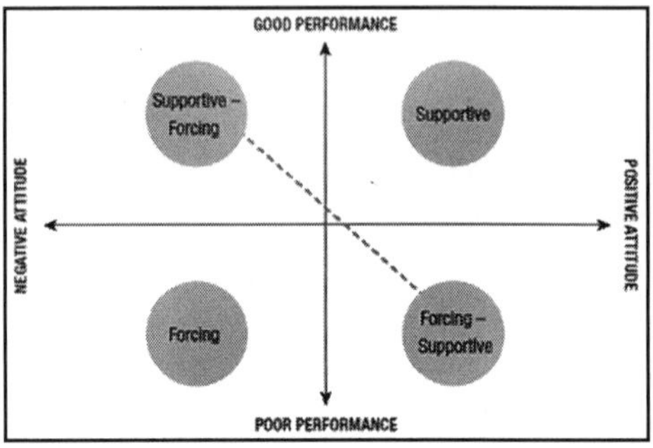

Fig. Choosing a Leadership Style

As a sales manager you will need to monitor a sales person's attitude/motivation and performance to be able to set the correct standards. The benefit of doing this is that it will encourage you to be consistent and to use the extreme leadership styles for the right reasons. Using the Forcing/Supportive styles can occur because of your mood and this might affect the attitude of your sales team.

A sales manager's main goal is to be able to move from one style (up/down) to another depending on the situation. If you are supportive in your style at the beginning and it is not working, move up to the next style. This illustrates your desire to solve the problem and shows your strength of commitment. We have looked at different forms of communication a sales manager can adopt to suit individual circumstances. Which style you use, and how you communicate with members of your sales team, will influence their level of motivation. This will depend on the attitude of your sales people and of yourself. It will also depend on how well they are performing.

LEADING THE TEAM

Adopting the right team leadership style will differ depending on the context of the situation. A sales manager's intuition also plays a part in this. There are a number of elements that will affect the outcome.

For example:

- The sales manager's level of interaction with the team
- His/her experience
- The strength of the personalities in the team.

With proper thought and planning you can demonstrate good leadership skills. Above all, it is your behaviour that will inspire your team.

TEAM ASSESSMENT

The leadership styles (Supportive through to Forcing) we looked at earlier can be easily applied to a group of sales people as well as an individual. A sales manager will need to assess which leadership style is appropriate to the team.

This will depend on a number of factors, including:

- The current state of motivation and attitude of the team.
- The level of effort and application (being shown by each team member).
- The trend of recent sales results.
- The gap between expected and actual results.
- The stability and experience of the team.
- External factors (changes in your market, mergers and new competitors).

By reviewing each description the manager builds an objective view of the state of their team. This can help them to select a leadership style, that they believe will best suit their purpose. In this example, a manager might conclude that this is a below average performance from a team that has the potential to exceed the sales target.

- Morale is fair
- The correct effort is being shown and results are moving in the right direction
- The gap between actual and expected is still of concern
- The low maturity of the team requires strong leadership.

The sales manager might select a Supportive – Forcing style, recognising the team's efforts and pointing out that results are moving in the right direction.

An increase in effort and the setting up of specific objectives are needed to achieve this:

- The Supportive element takes into account the effort being shown
- The Forcing element focuses the team on the challenge ahead.

A sales manager must be sensitive to the level of motivation within the team. At times this can be difficult to assess. An objective analysis of the situation can help you to decide on the correct course of action.

DELEGATION

A measure of the effectiveness of your leadership style will also be reflected in your ability to develop your sales people. Delegating certain tasks will form an essential part of this and will have the following benefits:

- Motivating the team (by helping to make them more effective)
- Developing leadership skills
- Getting the team to interpret your company's strategic goals
- Helping them to fulfill their role as a team member and take responsibility.

Delegation can be defined as giving someone the authority and responsibility to complete a task or action. This will be a time saving for you so that you can concentrate on managing the task rather than actually doing it. As we have mentioned, delegating some managerial tasks can provide an opportunity for personal development.

However, people should not be given so much to do that:

- It stops them performing their primary sales role
- It stops you from performing yours.

When to delegate to someone, and how much to give them, are therefore important factors in this decision.

HOW TO DELEGATE

Delegating tasks to people can create more work to begin with, as many tasks need regular review. Questions may be fed back to you and this will require more of your time.

Therefore, in order to build your confidence and to delegate effectively, consider the following points:

- Ensure that you delegate tasks that provide an element of decision-making and responsibility.
- Where possible allow the individual to decide how they will implement the task. This encourages initiative and self-confidence.
- Avoid giving tasks that might de-motivate someone. This could mean that they avoid doing them in the future.

The following steps can help you to decide whom to delegate responsibility to:

- *Step 1:* Select an individual who will benefit from a combination of:
  - Gaining experience.
  - Improving their leadership skills.
  - Adding an interesting challenge to their job.
- *Step 2*:
  - Ensure that you explain the task fully, including why you are delegating it to the individual.
  - Discuss the importance of the task and how it will develop the person. The aim is to motivate them to do it.
- *Step 3*:
  - Focus on the anticipated results and state that you require a deadline for the task to be completed.
  - Decide whether to explain how a task was dealt with on a previous occasion. You can also use the opportunity to encourage the person to suggest their own plan of action.
  - Let the individual get on with the task and encourage them to take the initiative.
- *Step 4:* Plan a way to monitor the individual's progress.
- *Step 5:* Emphasise your availability to provide help and support when your sales people need it. This can be done by agreeing specific

times in the day (or during the week) when you will be available for questions. Your focus should be on providing support, not apportioning blame. Your role is to resolve problems and to reinforce success with praise.

DIFFERENT WAYS OF DELEGATING

How you monitor a task will depend on:

- The nature of the task
- The individual's level of experience
- Your preferred leadership style.

There are four ways to decide how to delegate a task. These are:

- *Option 1*: We discuss – We decide – You act – You report back
- *Option 2*: You decide – We discuss – You act – You report back
- *Option 3*: You decide – You act – You report back – We discuss
- *Option 4*: Your task – You report back as agreed

The above options give you the opportunity to plan the delegation steps appropriately. They allow you to increase the individual's level of delegated responsibility, depending on their experience, ability and success. As someone becomes more proficient you can move from Option 1 through to Option 4.As their level of control increases so will their confidence.

This provides a valuable learning opportunity for them in a leadership role. It also helps that person to accept a level of responsibility so that you are not doing their job for them! A sales manager can strengthen the team's motivation and performance by helping sales people to develop themselves in their role. Effective delegation is a good leadership skill for a sales manager to acquire. It requires patience, planning, trust and a good monitoring process.

SUMMARY

In this chapter we have looked at 'Leadership'.

This included:

- Understanding leadership
- Leadership styles
- Leading the team
- Delegation.

Effective leadership is about setting clear standards and adapting your approach to suit the differing needs of the individual and the sales team. This requires a sales manager to be objective about their own role and leadership style.

2

Change Management: An Introduction

CHANGE MANAGEMENT DEFINED

FOUR BASIC DEFINITIONS

In thinking about what is meant by ¯change management, at least four basic definitions come to mind:

- The task of managing change.
- An area of professional practice.
- A body of knowledge.
- A control mechanism.

THE TASK OF MANAGING CHANGE

The first and most obvious definition of ¯change management is that the term refers to the task of managing change. The obvious is not necessarily unambiguous. Managing change is itself a term that has at least two meanings. One meaning of ¯managing change refers to *the making of changes in a planned and managed or systematic fashion.* The aim is to more effectively implement new methods and systems in an ongoing organization.

The changes to be managed lie within and are controlled by the organization.1 However, these internal changes might have been triggered by events originating outside the organization, in what is usually termed ¯the environment. Hence, the second meaning of managing change, namely, *the response to changes over which the organization exercises little or no control.* Researchers and practitioners alike typically distinguish between a knee-jerk or reactive response and an anticipative or proactive response.

The task of managing change also includes managing its impact on people. For many managers, this aspect of the task of managing change is complicated by the fact that they have to help their people cope with change and the managers also face their own coping challenges.

AN AREA OF PROFESSIONAL PRACTICE

The second definition of change management is "an area of professional practice."

There are dozens, if not hundreds, of independent consultants who will quickly and proudly proclaim that they are engaged in planned change, that they are change agents, that they manage change for their clients, and that their practices are change management practices. There are numerous small consulting firms whose principals would make these same statements about their firms.

And, of course, most of the major management consulting firms have a change management practice area. Some of these change management experts claim to help clients manage the changes they face – the changes happening to them. Others claim to help clients make changes.

Still others offer to help by taking on the task of managing changes that must be made. In almost all cases, the process of change is treated separately from the specifics of the situation. It is expertise in this task of managing the general process of change that is laid claim to by professional change agents.

A BODY OF KNOWLEDGE

Stemming from the view of change management as an area of professional practice there arises yet a third definition of change management: the content or subject matter of change management. This consists chiefly of the models, methods and techniques, tools, skills and other forms of knowledge that go into making up any practice. The content or subject matter of change management is drawn from psychology, sociology, business administration, economics, industrial engineering, systems engineering and the study of human and organizational behaviour.

For many practitioners, these component bodies of knowledge are linked and integrated by a set of concepts and principles known as General Systems Theory. It is not clear whether this area of professional practice should be termed a profession, a discipline, an art, a set of techniques or a technology. For now, suffice it to say that there is a large, reasonably cohesive albeit somewhat eclectic body of knowledge underlying the practice and on which most practitioners would agree — even if their application of it does exhibit a high degree of variance.

A CONTROL MECHANISM

For many years now, Information Systems groups have tried to rein in and otherwise ride herd on changes to systems and the applications that run on them. For the most part, this is referred to as ¨version control and most people in the workplace are familiar with it. In recent years, systems people have begun to refer to this control mechanism as ¨change management. Moreover, similar control mechanisms exist in other areas. Chemical processing plants, for example, are required by OSHA to satisfy some exacting requirements in the course of making changes. These fall under the heading of Management of Change or MOC.

To recapitulate, there are at least four basic definitions of change management:

- The *task of managing change*
- An *area of professional practice*
- A *body of knowledge*
- A *control mechanism*

CONTENT AND PROCESS

Organizations are highly specialized systems and there are many different schemes for grouping and classifying them. Some are said to be in the retail business, others are in manufacturing, and still others confine their activities to distribution. Some are profit-oriented and some are not for profit. Some are in the public sector and some are in the private sector. Some are members of the financial services industry, which encompasses banking, insurance, and brokerage houses. Others belong to the automobile industry, where they can be classified as original equipment manufacturers or after-market providers.

Some belong to the health care industry, as providers, as insureds, or as insurers. Many are regulated, some are not. Some face stiff competition, some do not. Some are foreign-owned and some are foreign-based. Some are corporations, some are partnerships, and some are sole proprietorships. Some are publicly held and some are privately held. Some have been around a long time and some are newcomers. Some have been built up over the years while others have been pieced together through mergers and acquisitions. No two are exactly alike.

The preceding paragraph points out that the problems found in organizations, especially the change problems, have both a content and a process dimension. It is one thing, for instance, to introduce a new claims processing system in a functionally organized health insurer. It is quite another to introduce a similar system in a health insurer that is organized along product lines and market segments. It is yet a different thing altogether to introduce a system of equal size and significance in an educational establishment that relies on a matrix structure.

The languages spoken differ. The values differ. The cultures differ. And, at a detailed level, the problems differ. However, the overall processes of change and change management remain pretty much the same, and it is this fundamental similarity of the change processes across organizations, industries, and structures that makes change management a task, a process, and an area of professional practice.

THE CHANGE PROCESS

THE CHANGE PROCESS AS "UNFREEZING, CHANGING AND REFREEZING"

The process of change has been characterized as having three basic stages: unfreezing, changing, and re-freezing. This view draws heavily on Kurt

Lewin's adoption of the systems concept of homeostasis or dynamic stability. What is useful about this framework is that it gives rise to thinking about a staged approach to changing things.

Looking before you leap is usually sound practice. What is not useful about this framework is that it does not allow for change efforts that begin with the organization in extremis nor does it allow for organizations faced with the prospect of having to ¯hang loose for extended periods of time. In other words, the beginning and ending point of the unfreeze-change-refreeze model is stability — which, for some people and some organizations, is a luxury. For others, internal stability spells disaster. A tortoise on the move can overtake even the fastest hare if that hare stands still.

THE CHANGE PROCESS AS PROBLEM SOLVING AND PROBLEM FINDING

A very useful framework for thinking about the change process is problem solving. Managing change is seen as a matter of moving from one state to another, specifically, from the problem state to the solved state. Diagnosis or problem analysis is generally acknowledged as essential. Goals are set and achieved at various levels and in various areas or functions. Ends and means are discussed and related to one another. Careful planning is accompanied by efforts to obtain buy-in, support and commitment. The net effect is a transition from one state to another in a planned, orderly fashion. This is the planned change model.

The word—problem carries with it connotations that some people prefer to avoid. They choose instead to use the word—opportunity. For such people, a problem is seen as a bad situation, one that shouldn't have been allowed to happen in the first place, and for which someone is likely to be punished—if the guilty party can be identified. We will set aside any cultural or personal preferences regarding the use of —problem or—opportunity. From a rational, analytical perspective, a problem is nothing more than a situation requiring action but in which the required action is not known.

Hence, there is a requirement to search for a solution, a course of action that will lead to the solved state. This search activity is known as—problem solving. From the preceding discussion, it follows that—problem finding is the search for situations requiring action. Whether we choose to call these situations—problems or whether we choose to call them—opportunities is immaterial. In both cases, the practical matter is one of identifying and settling on a course of action that will bring about some desired and predetermined change in the situation.

THE CHANGE PROBLEM

At the heart of change management lies the change problem, that is, some future state to be realized, some current state to be left behind, and some structured, organized process for getting from the one to the other. The change problem might be large or small in scope and scale, and it might focus on individuals or groups, on one or more divisions or departments, the entire organization, or one or on more aspects of the organization's environment. At a conceptual level, the change problem is a matter of moving from one state to another state. Moving from A to A′ is typically accomplished as a result of setting up and achieving three types of goals: *transform, reduce,* and *apply*. Transform goals are concerned with identifying differences between the two states. Reduce goals are concerned with determining ways of eliminating these differences.

Apply goals are concerned with putting into play operators that actually effect the elimination of these differences. As the preceding goal types suggest, the analysis of a change problem will at various times focus on defining the outcomes of the change effort, on identifying the changes necessary to produce these outcomes, and on finding and implementing ways and means of making the required changes. In simpler terms, the change problem can be treated as smaller problems having to do with the how, what, and why of change.

CHANGE AS A "HOW" PROBLEM

The change problem is often expressed, at least initially, in the form of a ¯how question. How do we get people to be more open, to assume more responsibility, to be more creative? How do we introduce self-managed teams in Department W? How do we change over from System X to System Y in Division Z? How do we move from a mainframe-centered computing environment to one that accommodates and integrates PCs? How do we get this organization to be more innovative, competitive, or productive? How do we raise more effective barriers to market entry by our competitors? How might we more tightly bind our suppliers to us?

How do we reduce cycle times? In short, the initial formulation of a change problem is means-centered, with the goal state more or less implied. There is a reason why the initial statement of a problem is so often means-centered and we will touch on it later. For now, let g″s examine the other two ways in which the problem might be formulated ◎ g″ as ¯what or as ¯why questions.

CHANGE AS A "WHAT" PROBLEM

To frame the change effort in the form of ¯how questions is to focus the effort on means. Diagnosis is assumed or not performed at all. Consequently, the ends sought are not discussed. This might or might not be problematic. To focus on ends requires the posing of ¯what questions. What are we trying to accomplish? What changes are necessary? What indicators will signal success? What standards apply? What measures of performance are we trying to affect?

CHANGE AS A "WHY" PROBLEM

Ends and means are relative notions, not absolutes; that is, something is an end or a means only in relation to something else. Thus, chains and networks of ends-means relationships often have to be traced out before one finds the ¯true ends of a change effort. In this regard, ¯why questions prove extremely useful.

Consider the following hypothetical dialogue with yourself as an illustration of tracing out ends-means relationships:

- Why do people need to be more creative?
- I'll tell you why! Because we have to change the way we do things and we need ideas about how to do that.
- Why do we have to change the way we do things?
- Because they cost too much and take too long.
- Why do they cost too much?
- Because we pay higher wages than any of our competitors.
- Why do we pay higher wages than our competitors?
- Because our productivity used to be higher, too, but now it's not.
- Eureka! The truc aim is to improve productivity!
- No it isn't; keep going.
- Why does productivity need to be improved?
- To increase profits.
- Why do profits need to be increased?
- To improve earnings per share.
- Why do earnings per share need to be improved?
- To attract additional capital.
- Why is additional capital needed?
- We need to fund research aimed at developing the next generation of products.
- Why do we need a new generation of products?
- Because our competitors are rolling them out faster than we are and gobbling up market share.
- Oh, so that's why we need to reduce cycle times.
- Hmm. Why do things take so long?

To ask—why questions is to get at the ultimate purposes of functions and to open the door to finding new and better ways of performing them. Why do we do what we do? Why do we do it the way we do it? Asking—why questions also gets at the ultimate purposes of people, but that's a different matter altogether.

THE APPROACH TAKEN TO CHANGE MANAGEMENT MIRRORS MANAGEMENT'S MINDSET

The emphasis placed on the three types of questions just mentioned reflects the management mindset, that is, the tendency to think along certain lines depending on where one is situated in the organization. A person's placement in the organization typically defines the scope and scale of the kinds of changes with which he or she will become involved, and the nature of the changes with which he or she will be concerned. Thus, the systems people tend to be concerned with technology and technological developments, the marketing people with customer needs and competitive activity, the legal people with legislative and other regulatory actions, and so on. Also, the higher up a person is in the hierarchy, the longer the time perspective and the wider the range of issues with which he or she must be concerned.

For the most part, changes and the change problems they present are problems of adaptation, that is, they require of the organization only that it adjust to an ever-changing set of circumstances. But, either as a result of continued, cumulative compounding of adaptive maneuvers that were nothing more than band-aids, or as the result of sudden changes so significant as to call for a redefinition of the organization, there are times when the changes that must be made are deep and far-reaching. At such times, the design of the organization itself is called into question.

Organizations frequently survive the people who establish them. AT&T and IBM are two ready examples. At some point it becomes the case that such organizations have been designed by one group of people but are being operated or run by another. Successful organizations resolve early on the issue of structure, that is, the definition, placement and coordination of functions and people. Other people then have to live with this design and, because the ends have already been established, these other people are chiefly concerned with means.

This is why so many problem-solving efforts start out focused on means. Some organizations are designed to buffer their core operations from turbulence in the environment. In such organizations all units fit into one of three categories: core, buffer, and perimeter. In core units, coordination is achieved through standardization, that is, adherence to routine. In buffer units, coordination is achieved through planning. In perimeter units, coordination is achieved through mutual adjustment.

People in core units, buffered as they are from environmental turbulence and with a history of relying on adherence to standardized procedures, typically focus on ¯how questions. People in buffer units, responsible for performance through planning, often ask ¯what questions. People in the perimeter units are as accountable as anyone else for performance and frequently for performance of a financial nature. They can be heard asking ¯what and ¯how questions. ¯Why questions are generally asked by people with no direct responsibility for day-to-day operations or results.

The group most able to take this long-term or strategic view is that cadre of senior executives responsible for the continued well being of the firm: top management. If the design of the firm is to be called into question or, more significantly, if it is actually to be altered, these are the people who must make the decision to do so. Finally, when organizational redefinition and redesign prove necessary, all people in all units must concern themselves with all three sets of questions or the changes made will not stand the test of time.

To summarize: Problems may be formulated in terms of ¯how, ¯what and ¯why questions. Which formulation is used depends on where in the organization the person posing the question or formulating the problem is situated, and where the organization is situated in its own life cycle.

- How questions tend to cluster in core units.
- What questions tend to cluster in buffer units.
- People in perimeter units tend to ask ¯what and ¯how questions.
- Why questions are typically the responsibility of top management.

In turbulent times, everyone must be concerned with everything.

SKILLS & STRATEGIES

Managing the kinds of changes encountered by and instituted within organizations requires an unusually broad and finely honed set of skills, chief among which are the following.

POLITICAL SKILLS

Organizations are first and foremost social systems. Without people there can be no organization. Lose sight of this fact and any would-be change agent will likely lose his or her head. Organizations are hotly and intensely political. And, as one wag pointed out, the lower the stakes, the more intense the politics. Change agents dare not join in this game but they had better understand it. This is one area where you must make your own judgments and keep your own counsel; no one can do it for you.

ANALYTICAL SKILLS

Make no mistake about it, those who would be change agents had better be very good at something, and that something better be analysis. Guessing won't do. Insight is nice, even useful, and sometimes shines with brilliance, but it is darned difficult to sell and almost impossible to defend. A lucid, rational, well-argued analysis can be ignored and even suppressed, but not successfully contested and, in most cases, will carry the day. If not, then the political issues haven't been adequately addressed.

Two particular sets of skills are very important here:

- Workflow operations or systems analysis, and
- Financial analysis.

Change agents must learn to take apart and reassemble operations and systems in novel ways, and then determine the financial and political impacts of what they have done. Conversely, they must be able to start with some financial measure or indicator or goal, and make their way quickly to those operations and systems that, if reconfigured a certain way, would have the desired financial impact. Those who master these two techniques have learned a trade that will be in demand for the foreseeable future.

PEOPLE SKILLS

As stated earlier, people are the sine qua non of organization. Moreover, they come characterized by all manner of sizes, shapes, colours, intelligence and ability levels, gender, sexual preferences, national origins, first and second languages, religious beliefs, attitudes towards life and work, personalities, and priorities — and these are just a few of the dimensions along which people vary. We have to deal with them all. The skills most needed in this area are those that typically fall under the heading of communication or interpersonal skills. To be effective, we must be able to listen and listen actively, to restate, to reflect, to clarify without interrogating, to draw out the speaker, to lead or channel a discussion, to plant ideas, and to develop them. All these and more are needed.

Not all of us will have to learn Russian, French, or Spanish, but most of us will have to learn to speak Systems, Marketing, Manufacturing, Finance, Personnel, Legal, and a host of other organizational dialects. More important, we have to learn to see things through the eyes of these other inhabitants of the organizational world. A situation viewed from a marketing frame of reference is an entirely different situation when seen through the eyes of a systems person. Part of the job of a change agent is to reconcile and resolve the conflict between and among disparate points of view. Charm is great if you have it. Courtesy is even better. A well-paid compliment can buy gratitude. A sincere ¯Thank you can earn respect.

SYSTEM SKILLS

There's much more to this than learning about computers, although most people employed in today's world of work do need to learn about computer-based information systems. For now, let's just say that a system is an arrangement of resources and routines intended to produce specified results. To organize is to arrange. A system reflects organization and, by the same token, an organization is a system. A word processing operator and the word processing equipment operated form a system. So do computers and the larger, information processing systems in which computers are so often embedded. These are generally known as ¯hard systems.

There are ¯soft systems as well: compensation systems, appraisal systems, promotion systems, and reward and incentive systems. There are two sets of systems skills to be mastered. Many people associate the first set with computers and it is exemplified by ¯systems analysis. This set of skills, by the way, actually predates the digital computer and is known elsewhere as ¯systems engineering. For the most part, the kind of system with which this skill set concerns itself is a ¯closed system which, for now, we can say is simply a mechanistic or contrived system with no purpose of its own and incapable of altering its own structure. In other words, it cannot learn and it cannot change of its own volition. The second set of system skills associated with a body of knowledge generally referred to as General Systems Theory and it deals with people, organizations, industries, economies, and even nations as socio-technical systems—as—open, purposive systems, carrying out transactions with other systems and bent on survival, continuance, prosperity, dominance, plus a host of other goals and objectives.

BUSINESS SKILLS

Simply put, you'd better understand how a business works. In particular, you'd better understand how the business in which and on which you're working works. This entails an understanding of money — where it comes from, where it goes, how to get it, and how to keep it. It also calls into play knowledge of markets and marketing, products and product development, customers, sales, selling, buying, hiring, firing, EEO, AAP, and just about anything else you might think of.

FOUR BASIC CHANGE MANAGEMENT STRATEGIES

Empirical-Rational

People are rational and will follow their self-interest — once it is revealed to them. Change is based on the communication of information and the proffering of incentives.

Normative-Reeducative

People are social beings and will adhere to cultural norms and values. Change is based on redefining and reinterpreting existing norms and values, and developing commitments to new ones.

Power-Coercive

People are basically compliant and will generally do what they are told or can be made to do. Change is based on the exercise of authority and the imposition of sanctions.

Environmental-Adaptive

People oppose loss and disruption but they adapt readily to new circumstances. Change is based on building a new organization and gradually transferring people from the old one to the new one.

FACTORS IN SELECTING A CHANGE STRATEGY

Generally speaking, there is no single change strategy. You can adopt a general or what is called a "grand strategy" but, for any given initiative, you are best served by some mix of strategies.

Which of the preceding strategies to use in your mix of strategies is a decision affected by a number of factors.

Some of the more important ones follow:

- *Scope and Scale*. This can vary from the minor—tweaking of a process within a unit to the complete transformation of the entire organization. The larger the scope and scale, the more likely a broad mix of strategies will be required with Power-Coercive playing a central role.
- *Degree of Resistance*. Strong resistance argues for a coupling of Power-Coercive and Environmental-Adaptive strategies. Weak resistance or concurrence argues for a combination of Empirical-Rational and Normative-Reeducative strategies.
- *Target Population*. Large populations argue for a mix of all four strategies, something for everyone so to speak.
- *The Stakes*. High stakes argue for a mix of all four strategies. When the stakes are high, nothing can be left to chance.
- *The Time Frame*. Short time frames argue for a Power-Coercive strategy. Longer time frames argue for a mix of Empirical-Rational, Normative-Reeducative, and Environmental-Adaptive strategies.
- *Expertise*. Having available adequate expertise at making change argues for some mix of the strategies. Not having it available argues for reliance on the power-coercive strategy.
- *Dependency*. This is a classic double-edged sword. If the organization is dependent on its people, management's ability to command or demand is limited. Conversely, if people are dependent upon the organization, their ability to oppose or resist is limited.

ONE MORE TIME: HOW DO YOU MANAGE CHANGE?

The honest answer is that you manage it pretty much the same way you'd manage anything else of a turbulent, messy, chaotic nature, that is, you don't really manage it, you grapple with it. It's as much a matter of leadership ability as it is one of management skill.

- The first thing to do is jump in. You can't do anything about it from the outside.
- A clear sense of mission or purpose is essential. The simpler the mission statement the better.—Kick ass in the marketplace is a whole lot more meaningful than—Respond to market needs with a range of products and services that have been carefully designed and developed to compare so favourably in our customers' eyes with the products and services offered by our competitors that the majority of buying decisions will be made in our favour.
- Build a team.—Lone wolves have their uses, but managing change isn't one of them. On the other hand, the right kind of lone wolf makes an excellent temporary team leader.

- Maintain a flat organizational team structure and rely on minimal and informal reporting requirements.
- Pick people with relevant skills and high energy levels. You'll need both.
- Toss out the rulebook. Change, by definition, calls for a configured response, not adherence to prefigured routines.
- Shift to an action-feedback model. Plan and act in short intervals. Do your analysis on the fly. No lengthy up-front studies. Remember the hare and the tortoise.
- Set flexible priorities. You must have the ability to drop what you're doing and tend to something more important.
- Treat everything as a temporary measure. Don't—lock in until the last minute, and then insist on the right to change your mind.
- Ask for volunteers. You'll be surprised at who shows up. You'll be pleasantly surprised by what they can do.
- Find a good "straw boss or team leader and stay out of his or her way.
- Give the team members whatever they ask for— except authority. They'll generally ask only for what they really need in the way of resources. If they start asking for authority, that's a signal they're headed towards some kind of power-based confrontation and that spells trouble. Nip it in the bud!
- Concentrate dispersed knowledge. Start and maintain an issues logbook. Let anyone go anywhere and talk to anyone about anything. Keep the communications barriers low, widely spaced, and easily hurdled. Initially, if things look chaotic, relax — they are.

Remember, the task of change management is to bring order to a messy situation, not pretend that it's already well organized and disciplined.

3

Leadership and Change Management: An Introduction

THE PHENOMENON OF CHANGE

Lewin produced the first viable model of change in his force field model. In this model, change was characterized as a state of imbalance between driving forces and restraining forces. If these forces were balanced or in equilibrium, no change could take place. Change is inherent in every context and is a relative concept. "Every phenomenon is subject to change, however apparently stable its nature". That change exists is a predictable notion. "In every industry and business, change ebbs and flows in recurring cycles that to at least some extent can be charted and therefore anticipated and managed". Change is disruptive, messy, and complicated.

Even with the best laid plans, events rarely occur exactly as they were predicted. "Real change in real organizations is intensely personal and enormously political". Change processes entail not only structures and ways of doing tasks, but also the performance, expectations and perceptions of all involved parties. Change has become widespread and unpredictable, but is still manageable.

An inherent characteristic of change is that it is risky, especially when it encompasses many different sectors within an organization or society. Change can also be planned or emergent. Wilson pointed out that a shift from emergent models of change to planned ones has steadily occurred over the past two decades. A total shift is not advised though, since the political and economic context of the surrounding environment can not be ignored, and must also be adapted to. Strategies to deal with unplanned change are just as necessary as planned ones.

EFFECTS OF CHANGE ON ORGANIZATIONS

To effectively adapt to change, most established organizations have a daunting task ahead of them in a variety of operational and procedural areas. Business processes must be redefined and redesigned and adapted to specific geographical and cultural settings. The workforce needs to be retrained to be ready for changes in how work is done, what skills and knowledge is needed, and how to relate to global collaborators and customers. The very culture of an organization needs to be reshaped to properly support the new processes introduced.

Structures, reward systems, appraisal measurements and roles need redefinition. Leadership styles and management procedures must shift and adapt, and ways of relating with customers, suppliers, and other stakeholders need refining. Technological advances and capabilities must be introduced, and preparation of the workforce to work with the new IT structures is needed.

Successful adaptation to change necessitates "an understanding about how to convert and rebuild from the complexities and legacies of the old, as well as generate designs about the new". Change necessitates that organizations realistically move beyond antiquated processes, empower and retrain employees, and incorporate advances in IT into the everyday work setting.

No longer are organizations reacting to sequential or occasional change. New changes now occur as organizations are in the throes of initiating the change process. Change has become perpetual. In order to cope, organizations need a design process with strategies and guidelines for thriving amongst a multitude of changes. "Real change is an integrated process that unfolds over time and touches every aspect of an organization,".

THE ROLE AND ISSUES OF LEADERS IN GUIDING CHANGE

The creation and design of change processes within an organization is most often a role of the leaders within it. Change processes which encompass human resources, IT adoption and upgrades, tools and techniques, as well as the basic rules and controls within the organization are the mandate of leaders engaged in the management of change.

It is up to the leaders to make these change initiatives tangible rather than abstract and to awaken enthusiasm and ownership of the proposed changes within the corporate milieu. Leaders are responsible for bridging the gap between strategy decisions and the reality of implementing the changes within the structure and workforce of the organization.

A myriad of details and effects must be acknowledged and addressed for successful adaptation to change in all sectors of a firm. "Underlying this principle is the fact that almost everything in an organization's infrastructure has an influence on some other part of it. Management style affects culture, technology affects the way staff interact with customers, internal communication methods affect how people work together,".

A holistic approach to change management encourages the redesign and adaptation to change at all organizational levels. In essence, process itself can become the platform for change to occur, as well as the protector of the existent daily operations. A clear picture of how the business operates currently is afforded, as well as a picture of how the business must plan, schedule, and undergo the change process.

Nadler and Nadler emphasized the importance of leaders in organizing and maintaining a climate for change within organizations. Although participation of all players is necessary, the role of the leader in the change process is crucial. Dubbed the "champions of change" it is the leaders, - the top management players who keep the change process moving while maintaining the operational integrity of the organization.

Adaptive leaders provide direction, protection, orientation, conflict control, and the shaping of norms while overseeing the change process within the corporate structure. Priorities need to be set which encourage disciplined attention, while keeping a keen eye focused for signs of distress within the company members.

Steps to transform an organization were identified by Conger et al.

The steps included:

- Establishing a sense of urgency;
- Forming a powerful guiding coalition;
- Creating a vision;
- Communicating the vision;
- Empowering others to act on the vision;
- Planning for and creating short-term wins;
- Consolidating improvements and producing still more change and
- Institutionalizing new approaches.

A new model of organizational learning is important for survival and adaptation in the new century. Learning is a key requirement for both leaders and followers for any effective and lasting change to occur. "Without learning, the attitudes, skills and behaviours needed to formulate and implement a new strategic task will not develop, nor will a new frame by which selection and promotion decisions are made". The authors proposed an action learning process, called Organizational Fitness Profiling to help leaders to learn how to skillfully transform the particular business they are managing.

Scheduled dialogues with followers provide information on how leadership style and behaviours impact on values, organizational design, strategies, and follower perceptions. Organizational success is a process of mutual adaptation between leader values and behaviours, existing people, culture, and organizational design amidst an environment of continual and prolific change.

This profiling process requires that leaders are courageous enough to learn about their own assumptions and values about change, leadership and management roles and tasks. In essence, "...a paradigm shift in management thinking about leadership and organization development is needed".

TYPES AND COMPLEXITIES OF CHANGE

According to Wilson technology has become the engine of change for many organizations. Nadler and Nadler credited increased competition and globalization as the most sweeping factors in the new global change environment. Eccles outlined six contexts of change common to the corporate world. Takeover change, injection change, succession change, renovation change, partnership change, and catalytic change were all identified as inherent and challenging for most modern organizations. Takeover change primarily entails a change in management players. Injection change purports a change in CEO or the top senior manager.

Succession change is felt when the top management layer is succeeded by current members who move up the ladder as the existent management retires or moves on. Renovation change entails the planned change process set by management, while partnership change occurs when the decisions for change is shared across the spectrum of organizational players. "Finally, and in a different style to the other five contexts, there is catalytic change in which an agency, typically a set of consultants or advisors, intervenes on behalf of one or more stakeholders, usually the management,".

Lasting change must occur on many levels within an organization. The people, the work, and the formal as well as the informal organization are all key factions to be considered and worked on. Nadler and Nadler identified four different types of organizational change. Incremental or continuous change is the orderly sequence of change that is expected as time and growth progress. Step by step continuous improvement is the most logical reaction to incremental change. Discontinuous or radical change is another matter.

"Complex, wide-ranging changes brought on by fundamental shifts in the external environment are radical, or discontinuous, changes". Discontinuous change requires radical departures in approach and strategy, often leading to a complete overhaul of the organization. Anticipatory change is done in the absence of threat, and in preparation for anticipated environmental changes. Reactive changes represent the opposite of anticipatory change, and are responses to threats and competition in the environment.

Nadler, Shaw and Walton warned that the present era is swiftly becoming one of discontinuous change. "The core competency for business leaders in the twenty-first century will be change management". Leaders will need both skill and the motivation to become constant visionary change agents. Discontinuous change profoundly affects three key areas of any organization: leadership capability, organizational architecture, and corporate identity. Improvisation, innovation and visionary awareness will be the name of the game for successful firms.

Planned spontaneity and deliberate opportunism will be the key to survival in a turbulent global environment. Changes may occur in several different sectors of an organization simultaneously. Strategic, structural, cultural, technological, merger and acquisition, breakup and spin-off, downsizing, and expansive changes are all common, complex, and challenging to incorporate into the organizational milieu.

LEADERSHIP CHANGE TOOLS AND STRATEGIES

Bainbridge outlined a five step process of redesign for organizations undergoing planned change.

The five steps included:

- The design stage to determine overall requirements;
- The definition stage where the design is specified and documentation of the design stage requirements occurs;
- The development stage, where new capabilities are cultivated through training, education and restructuring;
- The dismantling stage, where redundant parts of the organization are removed or converted into new capabilities; and
- The deployment stage, where new capabilities are introduced into the new organizational environment, both internally and externally.

This design process is accomplished within a carefully arranged change process architecture. "This includes the link to strategic objectives, the definition of measures and the production of the high-level design itself". The vision of change must be expressed as clearly as possible and used consistently to spearhead every step of the change design process, including the specification of design principles.

Design principles reflect the context and also the content of both internal and external desired change outcomes. Specification and communication of these principles by leaders are necessary to facilitate adoption and adaptation within the organizational culture. Pettigrew pointed out the wisdom of considering the content, the context (inner and outer) and the process of change within organizations. There is a need to "explore content, context and process linkages through time". Strategies of organizational change have become a viable vehicle for business success and the creation of competitive performance.

The ability to handle strategic change is now a defining characteristic of successful post-industrial organizations. "The leitmotiv of modern management theory is that of understanding, creating and coping with change. The essence of the managerial task thus becomes one of establishing some rationality, or some predictability, out of the seeming chaos that characterizes change processes". An open systems approach can facilitate emergent change processes within an organization. The linkages and interdependencies between the organization and the external environment can be used to create a pattern for emergent change adaptation. Galpin described a process for implementing planned change at a grassroots level, using the strengths and capabilities of the human resources within an organization as the central hub for change.

This process included stages of:

- Setting goals;
- Measuring performance;
- Providing feedback and coaching and
- Instigating generous rewards and recognition.

Galpin also outlined the strategic steps leaders needed to employ in order to initiate the change process.

These steps were:

- Defining the need to change;
- Developing a vision of the result of change;
- Leveraging teams to design, test, and implement changes;
- Addressing the cultural aspects of the organization that will help and sustain change; and
- Developing the essential attributes and skills needed to lead the change effort."

Cognitive mapping and computer assistance for group decision support are alternative change strategies that can help to cultivate group support for the planned initiatives. The cognitive maps or strategic belief systems of managers and employees can have a profound effect on how change is planned and implemented. Cognitive maps become a practical tool "by acting as a device for representing that part of a person's construct system they are able and willing to make explicit,". However, the cognitive map is "significantly biased by the necessary social interaction, or social gaze, that is the basis of elicitation through interview". Still, cognitive maps can be a strategic tool for negotiation and decision making in the change planning and implementation process.

Flamholtz and Randle identified strategic transformational planning as a key tool for change in an organization. This process describes the planning necessary to transform an organization into what it needs to become to maximize the fit and reduce the gaps between corporate size, environment, business concept and organizational design. Flamholtz and Randle labeled these transformations as First, Second, and Third kinds.

A First kind transformation related to professional management transformation. Planning revitalization or second kind transformation related to all layers of the corporate pyramid, while business vision transformations focused on changes needed to address new markets and the firm's role in the existing markets. All three of these transformations were addressed by using the transformational planning process:

- Assessing the environment;
- Reviewing the existing business;
- Resolving core transformational issues and
- Developing the written strategic transformational plan.

Organizational managers at the top must exhibit leadership, commitment, and conviction to the change and transformation process. Incremental change, often the result of a carefully thought out analysis and planning process, has been the most common form of planned change within organizations. A feeling of control is afforded, enough time and commitment are present, and each step of the process can be trialed and adapted to.

However, with the advent of technology and globalization, a deep change is necessary. "Deep change differs from incremental change in that it requires new ways of thinking and behaving. It is change that is major in scope, discontinuous with the past and generally irreversible. Deep change means surrendering control". Deep change on any level entails inherent risk. To adapt to the profound changes of our times, leaders must be willing to go out on a limb, to take some big risks by stepping outside of well-established boundaries.

EFFECTS AND CONSEQUENCES OF CHANGE

Noer cautioned leaders to not rely too heavily on external tools for change. "The futile quest for an external, objective tool is a dysfunctional heritage of the old paradigm; the outgrowth of the erroneous attempt to graft the objectivity of the scientific method onto the subjective phenomena of the human spirit. It is a fundamental mismatch". According to Noer, the leader, as a person, is the most important tool for change.

The leader's spirit, insight, wisdom, compassion, values, and learning skills are all important facets in the capabilities to lead others to embrace change and redesign. To be lasting, deep change must not only be made amidst organizational layers, but within each of the players themselves. Deep personal change can be uncomfortable, yet the need for each member of an organization to become empowered, and internally driven is essential for success in this era of change and evolvement.

Quinn cautions that if players are not willing or able to make these deep personal changes, then"slow death" is the alternative. Slow death, "a meaningless and frustrating experience enmeshed in fear, anger, and helplessness, while moving surely towards what is most feared" is the consequence of resistance to change. Burnout can occur if this resistance to change persists, resulting in loss of employment or even destruction of the organization as a whole. The leader who instigates change within a firm is often subject to speculative suspicion.

"Because resistance is so common, learning to overcome it is crucial to managing change at every level". The transition stage where the change process is instigated must be handled expertly and with enthusiasm. Leaders must own and align the proposed changes, setting expectations, and modeling and communicating the rationale to all members of the organization. The processes of engaging and rewarding help to motivate members, smoothing the transition period, and attempting to win the hearts and minds of all involved to the change process.

PREPARING FOR AND THRIVING IN THE CONTINUOUS CHANGE OF THE FUTURE

Quinn enthused that "We are all potential change agents. As we discipline our talents, we deepen our perceptions about what is possible. Having experienced deep change in ourselves, we are able to bring deep change to the systems around us". Leaders who have embraced deep change personally are able to design change processes that reflect a heroic yet enlightened leader stance, one that imparts enthusiasm and vitality into the other members and creates a new perspective of the logic and wisdom of moving with the flow of change. Nadler and Nadler described a four part matrix of responses to change: tuning, adapting, redirecting and overhauling. "Tuning" represents an anticipatory change process in response to incremental or continuous change, while "adapting" represents a reactive response.

"Redirecting" is an anticipatory response to discontinuous, radical change, while "overhauling" represents a reactive response to discontinuous change. To survive the effects of continuous change, leaders need to accomplish three major tasks: a) to shape the political dynamics of the change process; b) to motivate change; and c) to manage the transition period. Pasmore identified flexibility as a key trait for successful change implementation. "Another strategy must be employed, one that prepares the organization for continuous change in a world that provides no stability and accepts no excuses for being unprepared; a strategy based on flexibility.

Being flexible means being able to change everything, all at the same time". In today's world, this flexibility relates to people, technology, ways of thinking, ways of leading, and to the actual organizational design. The trick it seems, is to realize that once a change is achieved, change is not finished. It is ongoing and perpetual. "Norms, values, and common operating principles rather than rules and direct supervision will furnish the cohesion necessary to provide direction and coordination".

The effective leader will shape the vision and values of the organization, and spend considerable time in developing team leaders and members. A strongly developed and integrated culture and network of individuals who use their own sense of leadership will boost the organizational capabilities for successful adaptation to changes of all kinds and magnitudes. Conger, Spreitzer and Lawler warned that old ways of shaping behaviours in employees, namely rational persuasion and coercion are outmoded and will not work in the future. In the past these have rarely been successful in perpetuating lasting change.

In the future, they could be deadly to any organization. Instead, a change style reminiscent of the behaviours used by Martin Luther King, and M. Gandhi are suggested: an empowering self-modification strategy. This technique is based more on a moral-relational premise rather than a politicaltechnical paradigm, which "requires the change agent to employ a high level of cognitive, behavioral, and moral complexity". To shake people out of complacent stances, or from taking "the path of least resistance" true empowerment must be experienced. Members must feel both challenged and supported for feelings of empowerment to develop. In effect, this entails leaders who are willing to model the desired behaviours: the ability to walk at the edge of chaos by stepping outside the comfort zone and letting go of control.

The internal discipline, vision, expectation and sensitivity of the leader is enhanced, which is apparent to followers and peers alike. "In freeing self from external sanctions through personal modification, the change agent obtains increased understanding, enlightenment, or vision about direction and strategy".

CONCLUSION

Today's fast-paced environment requires people and organizations to develop the ability to adapt to pervasive change and upheaval. "Cutting-edge technology, the triumph of capitalism over communism, a burgeoning global economy, a billion new entrants to the global workforce, and a surplus of products all feed into an environment that is highly competitive and fastchanging". The key to successful organizational change, is heroic and learned change management by competent and visionary leaders. Change can be managed in a top-down style or as a highly participative exercise from all levels of personnel.

Change is context specific, meaning that no single change process is appropriate for every situation or corporate entity. Leaders are responsible for setting the context for change within an organization. A culture and vision must be cultivated that can support the planned changes, and deal with unplanned change. Envisioning, energizing, and enabling are all important strategies for rallying support for change initiatives. Leaders must be able to counsel, teach, coach, and reward employees as they adopt and move through the change process.

For lasting change to occur, habits, attitudes, and values at all levels of an organization must be congruent with the vision and goals inherent in the process. Transformative leaders share fundamental characteristics that allow them to enable organizational members in the change process. They are able to generate the energy needed to undertake the change process; use vision to lead; have a total system perspective; create a sustained process of organizational learning embedded in a systemic change implementation process. "They must create a transformative process architecture to orchestrate the passage from current to vision state". As success in the transitional context of change is experienced, comfort and preparedness is developed, equipping the organizational members with capabilities to deal with even greater change. Change has become the name of the game, and the wise leader embraces it with open arms. The success of the corporate entity and the people within it depends on it.

4

Coalitions and Consequences: Changes and Leadership in India

This stage attempts to explore a missing aspect of the large literature that has grown up around coalition governments in India and then to include that aspect in a discussion of the consequences of coalition governments. Are they good or bad for economic development, social change and honest, effective government? Do they work better at the state level rather than the national? The missing aspect is the 'educational process' by which Indian politicians have learned the benefits and requirements of coalition governments and then how to make them work.

I argue that such a process began in the state of Kerala, took nearly a generation to 'learn' and partly depended on the availability of individual leaders. The same educational process that fostered understanding of the rewards that coalitions can bring also sensitised politicians to the need to deliver goods to their constituents. This need to satisfy voters leads to consideration of questions about the 'goodness' or 'badness' of coalitions.

In arguing that the educational process has been overlooked in study of coalitions in India, I am not discounting other aspects. I would particularly acknowledge the fragmentation of Indian politics as sub-regions and previously marginal and illiterate groups have produced people who understand the political system and are able to work effectively within it. Potent local political parties emerge and it becomes difficult to create a powerful state-wide party, much less a powerful national party.

COALITIONS IN KERALA: LEARNERSHIP AND LEADERSHIP

Although the state of Kerala accounts for less than three per cent of India's population, it has acquired notoriety for its 'model' of economic development and for its election of a Communist government in 1957. Kerala also 'learned' coalitions before the rest of India. Kerala had to. The composition of the state and its social structure were in some ways a microcosm of India. To begin with, Kerala state of the Indian Union was created only in 1956 by the joining of two old princely states and the British-ruled district of Malabar in the north. In each of the old units, sentiments and interests made people conscious of 'their' particular place, however much the Malayalam language and an overarching Malayali culture may have made a united Kerala seem a good idea. Kerala was also socially segmented, highly literate and widely mobilised, even at independence.

The population was roughly 20 per cent Muslim, 20 per cent Christian, 20 per cent high-caste Hindu and 40 per cent lower-caste Hindu. But Muslims were concentrated in Malabar district; Christians of various sects in Cochin and central and north Travancore. Churches, education societies and social organisations tended to work most effectively within the administrative unit where they originated. The most notable exception to the latter statement was the Communist Party of India.

Often banned from the 1930s to the 1950s, the CPI used different jurisdictions to enable members to slip between the butter-fingers of different police forces and continue their agitations. Sympathisers of the *Indian National Congress* were present in all three units, but they had few of the links or reasons for cooperation that the Communists had. The three-dimensional patchwork of Kerala — jurisdictions, social groups and political and social organisations — looked in some ways like India in miniature.

But high levels of literacy and social upheaval accelerated participation in politics. First, the national movement against princely rule drew people into action and organisation. After 1947, the struggle between Communists and the Congress brought political activity to every village. Travancore held the first universal-suffrage elections in India in February 1948. The Travancore State Congress, loosely affiliated to the Indian National Congress, was inundated with members prior to the elections and scored a huge victory, taking 56 seats without a contest and winning 41 out of 61 contested seats with 48 per cent of the vote. It formed a government under the man who led the anti-princely movement; but the government collapsed in six months. Over the next 22 years, residents of the Travancore area experienced a dozen governments and three periods of President's Rule from New Delhi.

No government served a full term. Between 1970 and 2007, however, Kerala governments have completed their full five-year terms on six occasions. Why did Kerala produce such unstable government in the earlier when in the rest of India, the period from 1947–67 was controlled by the Congress Party, and political scientists characterised this as an era of a 'dominant-party system'? First, almost nowhere else in India had a political challenge to the Congress comparable to that of the Communist Party.

This competitive struggle mobilised groups for politics. People were exhorted to identify with 'their party' — or their religion or their caste. Because literacy was high and newspapers readily available, such exhortations went wide and deep in ways that other areas of India did not replicate until a generation later. Thus the ingredients existed for locally based political organisations, calling themselves 'parties' and claiming state-wide reach though having a genuine base only in a small area. Such 'parties' split off from both left and right of politics. They gave themselves names like 'the Kerala Congress' and often added bracketed initials or names to identify the leader who was running the group — for example, Kerala Congress. Second, political leaders had to discover what the consequences of particular behaviours were. Let me focus on Pattom A.

Thanu Pillai. Thanu Pillai had three occasions as Chief Minister — of Travancore for a few months in 1948, of Travancore–Cochin for a few more months in 1954–55, and nearly two years in 19460–62; each government ended in collapse. Other politicians looked on and perhaps some learned. Thanu Pillai came from a background typical of India's 'freedom struggle' elites. He came from a higher caste, and he was a lawyer, well-read in English.

His critics said he was inspired by the haughtiness of princelings of old and behaved more like a Dewan than a democratic politician. He had been a European-dressed lawyer, practising in the Travancore courts, until 1938 when he joined the Travancore State Congress to give it the social variety it desperately needed. He and his colleagues caused consternation in sleepy Trivandrum when they first appeared in the local legislature wearing *khadi* — 'cloth which till two days back they would have barked at', according to a critic. Thanu Pillai, though a distinctive product of south Travancore, brought to legislative politics after independence expectations that were characteristic of many state politicians of his generation and experience.

As lawyers, they were steeped in English legal precedent and British parliamentary history. They had, one might argue, swallowed the myth of 'the British party system', which suggested that political parties, once formed, behaved as disciplined units, piloted by their leaders as if they were ships. Added to such impressions was their own experience of the national movement.

The Congress had emerged as the unquestioned force in Indian politics and Gandhi as the 'father of the nation.' In spite of the dissensions and desertions of the 1937–39 Congress governments in the provinces, there was nevertheless a sense that leaders like Gandhi should be followed. By extension, if a person were the Gandhi of his or her region, shouldn't such person be followed too? Such aloofness and expectations appeared to characterise Thanu Pillai. Thanu Pillai's first short-lived Chief Ministership in 1948 ended quickly: an overwhelming Congress majority fragmented in a few months and the government fell.

He left the Congress Party to become a 'socialist' and in effect took over the local franchise of one of the Indian socialist parties. Leading the *Praja Socialist Party*, he became coalition Chief Minister in 1954–55 and again in 1960–62 at the head of a coalition that had defeated the Communists in mid-term elections in 1960. Thanu Pillai and those like him lacked the ideological glue to hold legislative alignments together and had not acquired the realisation of how much there was to lose by uncompromising positions.

Old elites, as embodied by Thanu Pillai, had experiences and beliefs that encouraged them to take such positions; they also had connections, resources and professions that gave them something to fall back on if governments fell apart. Increasingly, however, this was not true of scores of Members of Legislative Assemblies who were being elected in Kerala. They came from less affluent circumstances, they saw politics as a career in itself, not the outcome of a career. And they began to see the defects of the inability to sustain governments. Thanu Pillai's reputation saw him appointed to a Governor's post in 1962, and in the next eight years, Kerala politics experienced three elections and two periods of President's Rule. The Communist Party itself split in 1964 into a CPI and a CPI.

The ideological commitment that had been a Communist strength left the two new parties bitterly divided for years. The fruits of Kerala's unplanned 'learning experience' began to show in 1969 and owed a good deal to a changed political style and sense of expectations, again embodied, for my purposes, in a particular politician. C. Achutha Menon became Chief Minister briefly in 1969 after the collapse of multi-party coalition elected in 1967. After mid-term elections in 1970 again failed to produce a victory for any party, Achutha Menon assumed leadership of what appeared an unlikely and ramshackle coalition. It ruled, however, for seven years, and Achutha Menon became the longest serving Chief Minister of the state. Kerala's era of stable coalition government began. How had this happened? Experience and personality are part of an answer.

On the surface, Achutha Menon and Thanu Pillai were similar: both were Nairs; both were lawyers. But Achutha Menon was from the more cosmopolitan area of Cochin State. As a Communist he had been underground evading the police in the late 1940s. He had been Finance Minister in the 1957–59 Communist government and stayed with the Moscowline Communist Party of India when the Party split in 1964. Achutha Menon was also reputed to be cool-headed, erudite and honest — and, though he was only 57 in 1970, to have a bad heart. By 1970, Kerala politicians perceived that there were few advantages for them personally in unstable governments — or indeed, long periods of President's Rule under bureaucrats. The lesson was becoming clear that compromise on a basic common programme would allow the fruits of office to be tasted for a full five-year term.

Such fruits were, and are, worth having — salary, offices, expenses, travel, telephones, cars and great possibilities for patronage and influence. My argument is that in 1970 two conditions for stable coalitions were fulfilled in Kerala. First, an appreciation had emerged among many politicians that if power was to be hung onto for a beneficial period, compromises and adjustments were essential. Ideological purity, or unrestrained self-interest, were both counter-productive. The argument is not that hundreds of political aspirants suddenly came to this realisation, but, rather, that more than twenty years' experience of brief governments had taught such lessons.

Second, to make such adjustments possible, there needed to be an acceptable, experienced leading figure — much more than a figurehead but less than a potential allin- all dominator of the Indira Gandhi kind. Kerala's experience from 1948 had accelerated the education of politicians in some unwritten rules of coalition survival, and Achutha Menon's reputation and background made him the right sort of leader. The government he formed in 1970 remained in office for nearly seven years, its life extended by Indira Gandhi's 'emergency' of 1975–77. The 1970–77 government had its share of crises and confrontations. But they were resolved without threatening the government, largely as a result of a delicate equation. It was widely perceived that a figure comparable to Achutha Menon was not readily available, and this perception grew with his reputation.

The longer he was Chief Minister, and the longer the ministry worked moderately effectively, the greater the 'irreplaceable factor' became. Achutha Menon, too, cultivated the impression that his health was not good and his ambitions were few; he could leave the job if his colleagues did not want him. Such apparent detachment added to his authority, and such authority strengthened the glue that held the coalition together. From 1970, Kerala has had a virtual two-party system with alternating coalition governments, built around the pole of the either the Congress Party or Communist Party of India.

THE CONSEQUENCES OF COALITIONS: KERALA

What sort of government can such fragile entities provide? Kerala is frequently known for its 'Kerala model', a term which arises from remarkable social statistics: high literacy and life expectancy, a sex ratio favouring women, low infant mortality and a falling birthrate. One of the causes is often held to be Kerala's political environment, characterised by 'public action', to use the phrase of Amartya Sen. 'Public action' requires that citizens be capable of organising and exerting pressure on their governments. In celebrated examples, Maternal and Child Health centres, if closed for more than a day or so, would provoke demonstrations of angry locals, organised by political parties that were *out of* power.

Members of the Legislative Assembly, elected from territorial constituencies, acquired a strong interest in being able to show voters that they were delivering the goods in the form of health services, housing, schools, colleges, bridges, roads and transport. The delicately poised nature of politics meant that MLAs had leverage in the capital because the threat of loss of support of even a few could generate an annoying, even fatal, crisis for a government.

Thus the 1970 government pursued a well-publicised land reform that gave security of tenure to every landless labourer living on what had previously been landlord's land. And the 'one lakh housing' scheme aimed to build 100,000 houses for homeless, or poorly housed, families. If the social and political consequences of coalitions in Kerala could produce positive results, the economic results are usually considered less positive or fruitful. Kerala's economy, based on agricultural raw materials and the export of its skilled people, depends on remittances from Malayalis working elsewhere in India or overseas. In spite of its high levels of literacy, Kerala lags well behind Indian states like Karnataka, Tamil Nadu and Gujarat in economic development.

The computer industry grew up in Bangalore; call-centres, around Bangalore and Delhi; Kerala, if anything, has lost some of its traditional basic industries, like processing of cashew-nut, to neighbouring states with lower wages and laxer labour laws. The explanation often advanced is that Kerala's coalition governments have been unable to maintain order and implement far-sighted policies among a fractious, politically alert population.

If police intervene in a labour dispute on the side of capital, the argument runs, political forces will force a coalition government to back down. One of the striking examples, which helped to cement this reputation throughout India, was the great Idukki dam project of the 1960s and 1970s which ran years over schedule because of labour disputes prolonged by a multiplicity of political influences. Kerala's coalitions have been unable both to act decisively and to enforce labour law strictly and effectively. Capital therefore avoids Kerala, and is invested in other states with majority governments able to discipline their citizens. So, at least, does this popular argument run.

COALITIONS IN INDIA: LEARNERSHIP AND LEADERSHIP

My argument is that at the national level India has followed a pattern similar to that of Kerala. Politicians and people associated with them have needed to learn how coalitions work and why there was personal benefit in making them work — or at least, considerable personal loss in having them fail. Accompanying the learning there needed to be the discovery of suitable coalition leaders with particular characteristics.

At the national level, indications that the 'one-party dominant' story of Indian politics was in its final stages came with the 1967 general elections, the first after the death of Jawaharlal Nehru. His daughter, Indira Gandhi, installed by party bosses as a short-term expedient, led the Congress Party to a narrow victory with only 283 seats in a lower house of 516 members. This was a loss of 80 seats and a majority of 'only' about 20 seats. The Congress lost control of nearly half the Indian states at the same elections. It held 60 per cent of the total seats in state legislatures in 1962; the share fell to 48 per cent in 1967. In the states, the process of coalition-learning began in earnest. The next four years became the era of 'aya ram aur gaya ram' — the time of legislators coming and going from one party to another as state governments rose and fell throughout the country.

What are my reasons for asserting that this period of instability was part of a learning process? Ideologically, some politicians, both of the left and right, were convinced that the purity of their parties' principles had to be asserted once a role in government was achieved. At the most obvious, Communist parties would not support a government that included the right-wing Jana Sangh, which, in turn, would not support a ministry that included Communists.

Face-saving measures had yet to be devised that allowed governments to function, and benefits to flow, without sullying a party's ideological purity. Such examples developed in Kerala in 1969–70 when the Congress found it possible to support a CPI-led government 'from outside' the ministry until it became comfortable to join as full-scale coalition partners. Elsewhere, experience had to teach such practical devices and the benefits of ideological elasticity. Practically, newcomers to legislatures needed to experience both the fruits of office and the rapidity with which they could disappear. In the first flush of being elected, and being able for the first time to influence the making of a state government and the patronage available from it, these newcomers tended to move eagerly from one alignment to another.

But, over time, it became clear that constant movement usually led to dissolution of the legislature and new elections. An MLA then stood to lose the privileges of office and had the expense of fighting another campaign with no guarantee of winning. Indeed, in Kerala experience began to show that incumbency was more likely to be harmful to than helpful. These lessons, bitterly taught to Kerala's politicians from 1948 to 1970, were learned in other Indian states between 1967 and 1977. At the national level, however, that process began in 1977, and fructified only in 1999. There was a second element — leadership — that had to be understood. Again, instructive parallels emerge between Kerala and the national experience. Indira Gandhi had ruled with a minority government between 1969 and 1971 after the Congress Party split that she engineered.

The first coalition government in New Delhi formed only in 1977 and was, in theory, a government of the Janata Party, hastily cobbled together when Mrs Gandhi ended her 19-month 'emergency' and called elections. The Janata Party was in fact a patchwork of the Jana Sangh, ex-Congress politicians and socialists. It had a number of aspirant Prime Ministers but no obvious choice, and the mantle finally fell on Morarji Desai austere longtime Congress politician and Prime Ministerial aspirant since the time of Nehru. His pride and aloofness echoed characteristics of Pattom Thanu Pillai in Kerala.

This was the wrong leader for the job. In 1979, his short-lived successor, Charan Singh was a wily regional politician, but lacking in the breadth of experience, contacts and perspective that are characteristics of the successful coalition leader in India. The 1989–91 period provided a further, and perhaps seminal, lesson in this experience of 'learning coalitions'. Rajiv Gandhi's huge Congress majority of 1984 crashed to a minority of 200 seats in 1989, and opposition parties struggled to form a government.

This led to perhaps the most famous double-cross in modern Indian politics — and a lesson in the need for a basic level of probity if coalitions were to survive. V.P. Singh, the leading candidate, told his rival, Chandra Shekhar, that he, Singh, would withdraw from the contest for Prime Minister and support Devi Lal, a regional leader from north India. Singh did not tell Chandra Shekhar that Devi Lal would decline the office and nominate Singh — which was what happened, to Chandra Shekhar's surprise, in the crucial meeting. For coalitions to last, there need to be grounds for basic trust among the parties.

The V.P. Singh coalition wrote a key entry about the downside of duplicity in the annals of national politics. The new coalition government lasted less than a year, and between 1989 and 1999 India experienced eight governments and seven Prime Ministers. The similarity with Kerala's experience is apparent. This era of intense coalition-learning at the national level ended in 1999 with the formation of the coalition led by the Bharatiya Janata Party. Its longtime leader A.B. Vajpayee became Prime Minister and led the multi-party government through a full fiveyear term. The alliance consisted of 15 parties, four of which returned only one member to the Lok Sabha.

They controlled about 300 seats in a lower house of 543 members, and Vajpayee formed a 70-member ministry, which aimed to balance regional, party and individual interests. The government alliance went united, if somewhat realigned, into the 2004 elections, which it lost to the rival Congress-led alliance, again suggesting a pattern similar to that of Kerala. It was not the mechanics of the coalition — the various balancing acts — that was, in my view, the key ingredient of the survival of the Vajapayee government of 1999–2004. Stability resulted in part from the dearly won awareness of legislators that to be in office was better than being out of it — the lessons of the previous ten years. But what had to be added were the characteristics that Vajpayee brought to the prime ministership.

Though his ideological background was different, he had a number of similarities with Achutha Menon. Vajpayee was 72 in 1999, and though apparently in good health was usually able to make clear to coalition members that they needed him more than he, at his age, needed them. His years of grassroots politics gave him a network and aplomb that allowed him to meet people and resolve differences with ease. He was recognised as someone who had earned his spurs and paid his dues.

These have emerged as the qualities of a successful Indian coalition leader: urbanity, probity, reputation for achievement and an apparent willingness for renunciation — to be able to walk away from the job if colleagues do not measure up. Manmohan Singh, Vajpayee's successor after the Congress-led coalition's narrow victory in the 2004 general elections, may seem an unlikely comparison with Vajpayee.

An economist trained in Punjab and at Cambridge and Oxford, he spent part of his working life abroad working for the IMF. Until 1989, he was an official, a former Governor of the Reserve Bank of India.

It was a career in marked contrast to Vajpayee's devotion to the cause of Hindu-oriented politics. Manmohan Singh, however, has other characteristics in common with those of successful coalition leaders. First, in the timing of his coming to office, he has benefited from the lesson-learning that national politicians have undergone about the brevity of political life, the fruits of public office and the need for a certain stability if fruits are to be enjoyed. He has had to deal with less fractious colleagues than those who sought to build coalitions from the 1970s to the 1990s.

Second, he has standing and reputation, though different from those of an Achutha Menon or Vajpayee who earned theirs in the hard scrabble of longtime politicking. His international experience, and his experience at the top of the bureaucratic tree, command respect. As a Sikh, he is 'a minority', which implies an ability to mix with both the 83 per cent 'majority' of 'Hindu India' and the other 17 per cent, the so-called 'minorities.' He has the ease and openings with a wide variety of people that Achutha Menon acquired as jailbird Communist and Vajpayee as a relentlessly campaigning politician.

Finally, Manmohan Singh came to the Prime Ministership in an unusual way, the surprise nominee of Sonia Gandhi, president of the Congress Party. At one level, it can be said that he has no political base and could not hope to win an election in his own right. On the other hand, his qualities are rare. Just as Achutha Menon and Vajpayee were able to play a card that said, 'If not me, who?', so too can Manmohan Singh. He can also do as they did: give the impression of readiness to be a renouncer — to leave the post if political turmoil becomes unacceptably great. In summary, my argument is that people in politics need to learn through experience the conventions of successful coalition government.

That experience came first in the state of Kerala through the 1950s and 1960s. At the national level, the lesson began in 1977 and resumed in 1989. An aspect of this experience is the discovery that a particular kind of leader is necessary to make coalitions stick. Such leaders cannot be stiff, aloof, doctrinaire and narrow. Rather, they require an ease, broad experience and a hint of reluctance sufficient to make the fractious fear a resignation. These two sets of circumstance — learnership and leadership — are not the sole ingredients of coalition-building; but they are important aspects that have tended to be overlooked.

THE CONSEQUENCES OF COALITIONS: INDIA

Does my tentative conclusion that in Kerala, coalition government has been better for social development than economic development apply equally to the Indian experience? With great tentativeness, let me suggest that they do. At the most general level, the decade 1991–2001 saw some of the most notable improvements in social statistics in post-independence history in a number of states.

To choose two small but significant examples, in Rajasthan and Uttar Pradesh, neither state noted for its cutting-edge modernity, literacy rates grew from 39 per cent to 61 per cent and 41 per cent to 57 per cent, respectively, between 1991 and 2001. Superficial observation suggests that similar advances were seen in other states and in other areas of individual well-being such as infant mortality.

This is not to argue that the uncertainty of coalitions means that members of the national parliament rush round their constituencies to ensure that schools are attended, mothers and babies looked after and roads and bridges built and that their diligence results in notable change. Rather, it is to argue that coalitions at the national level do no harm to such processes and may indeed do them some good. The reasons are similar to those for Kerala in the 1960s and after. As politicians become increasingly aware of the tenuousness of their hold on office, they search for ways to improve their chances.

Pleasing their constituents is one such way. The uncertainty of coalitions brings attention and diligence. For economic development, coalition governments are generally perceived as a negative force. According to such a view, their multi-faceted fragility make them indecisive, unable to take big decisions and inclined to resile even on the decisions they make. This point is often made in contrasting India's economic development in the past 20 years with China's, where roads get built, rivers dammed and labour deals done with far greater speed and predictability. It needs to be noted, however, that it was a fragile minority government that pursued the economic liberalisation programme that began in 1991.

From 1996, India has known only coalition governments, yet the period is usually described as the most economically dynamic since independence. The short answer to the question, 'Are coalitions bad for economic development?', may be that for 21st century India there is no alternative. Two factors suggest this. First, India is socially segmented — by language, religion, region and caste. Second, growing literacy, mobility and media penetration mean that larger proportions of the population than ever before are able to compare their circumstances and needs with others and to seek ways of changing their lot. Such political mobilisation usually occurs where it seems most meaningful — at the locality or the region. Thus we see, even within states, localised political groups. Such patterns are repeated for national elections.

The current national government of the 'United Progressive Alliance' of 2007 had a dozen parties supporting it, plus 'outside' support from four Left parties and the Bahujan Samaj Party, the Dalit-based party of Uttar Pradesh. The previous BJP-led government similarly had more than a dozen constituents. It is not impossible that the BJP, the Congress or indeed, a new formation could galvanise the country and win an absolute majority in national elections.

Half of India now goes home each night to a place with a television set. All-India messages can be shared simultaneously as never before, and an exciting personality, perhaps from the media could conceivably create a wave of enthusiasm. But at a national level this will be exceedingly difficult. The nature of Indian society makes the coalition formula seem likely to last. This is not necessarily a bad thing, even for economic development. Now that many of the lessons of sustained coalition government have been learned, including identification of appropriate qualities in a coalition leader, coalition governments may be expected to survive their full terms and thus provide continuity of policy.

The Kerala example suggests — and Indian experience since 1991 tentatively confirms — that coalitions, and the attentive-to-their-electorate politicians they promote, may contribute positively to social development. Moreover, the uninspiring economic story of Kerala is unlikely to be repeated nationally. The business traditions, and hold of globalised capitalism, in other parts of India will continue to impel economic change. The disparate forces driving such change are more powerful than the disparate forces that would restrain it.

And national governments, intent for example on winding up unprofitable state-owned industries, will take advantage of the country's diversity. A closure in one corner of the country may incense local political parties, but they will find it difficult to win much support from regional parties elsewhere. Thus some economic change may go ahead piecemeal and almost by stealth. This is not Chinese-style 'decisive government'; but once learnership and leadership are in place coalition governments in India appear capable of both surviving and delivering sustained, though unspectacular, social and even economic change.

5

Leadership Theories and Change Management Functions

REVIEW OF LEADERSHIP THEORY

A review of the leadership literature reveals an evolving series of 'schools of thought' from "Great Man" and "Trait" theories to "Transformational" leadership. Whilst early theories tend to focus upon the characteristics and behaviours of successful leaders, later theories begin to consider the role of followers and the contextual nature of leadership.

- Great Man Theories: Based on the belief that leaders are exceptional people, born with innate qualities, destined to lead. The use of the term 'man' was intentional since until the latter part of the twentieth century leadership was thought of as a concept which is primarily male, military and Western. This led to the next school of Trait Theories
- Trait Theories: The lists of traits or qualities associated with leadership exist in abundance and continue to be produced. They draw on virtually all the adjectives in the dictionary which describe some positive or virtuous human attribute, from ambition to zest for life
- Behaviourist Theories: These concentrate on what leaders actually do rather than on their qualities. Different patterns of behaviour are observed and categorised as 'styles of leadership'. This area has probably attracted most attention from practising managers
- Situational Leadership: This approach sees leadership as specific to the situation in which it is being exercised. For example, whilst some situations may require an autocratic style, others may need a more participative approach. It also proposes that there may be differences in required leadership styles at different levels in the same organization
- Contingency Theory: This is a refinement of the situational viewpoint and focuses on identifying the situational variables which best predict the most appropriate or effective leadership style to fit the particular circumstances

- Transactional Theory: This approach emphasises the importance of the relationship between leader and followers, focusing on the mutual benefits derived from a form of 'contract' through which the leader delivers such things as rewards or recognition in return for the commitment or loyalty of the followers
- Transformational Theory: The central concept here is change and the role of leadership in envisioning and implementing the transformation of organisational performance

Each of these theories takes a rather individualistic perspective of the leader, although a school of thought gaining increasing recognition is that of "dispersed" leadership. This approach, with its foundations in sociology, psychology and politics rather than management science, views leadership as a process that is diffuse throughout an organisation rather than lying solely with the formally designated 'leader'.

The emphasis thus shifts from developing 'leaders' to developing 'leaderful' organisations with a collective responsibility for leadership. We will focus primarily on the more traditional, individualistic views of the leader as we feel these have greatest relevance to the development of management and leadership standards.

THE TRAIT APPROACH TO LEADERSHIP

The Trait Approach arose from the "Great Man" theory as a way of identifying the key characteristics of successful leaders. It was believed that through this approach critical leadership traits could be isolated and that people with such traits could then be recruited, selected, and installed into leadership positions. This approach was common in the military and is still used as a set of criteria to select candidates for commissions. The problem with the trait approach lies in the fact that almost as many traits as studies undertaken were identified.

After several years of such research, it became apparent that no consistent traits could be identified. Although some traits were found in a considerable number of studies, the results were generally inconclusive. Some leaders might have possessed certain traits but the absence of them did not necessarily mean that the person was not a leader. Although there was little consistency in the results of the various trait studies, however, some traits did appear more frequently than others, including: technical skill, friendliness, task motivation, application to task, group task supportiveness, social skill, emotional control, administrative skill, general charisma, and intelligence. Of these, the most widely explored has tended to be "charisma".

THE BEHAVIOURAL SCHOOL

The results of the trait studies were inconclusive. Traits, amongst other things, were hard to measure. How, for example, do we measure traits such as honesty, integrity, loyalty, or diligence? Another approach in the study of leadership had to be found. After the publication of the late Douglas McGregor's classic book The Human Side of Enterprise in 1960, attention shifted to 'behavioural theories'. McGregor was a teacher, researcher, and consultant whose work was considered to be "on the cutting edge" of managing people. He influenced all the behavioural theories, which emphasize focusing on human relationships, along with output and performance.

McGregor's Theory X & Theory Y Managers

Although not strictly speaking a theory of leadership, the leadership strategy of effectively-used participative management proposed in Douglas McGregor's book has had a tremendous impact on managers. The most publicized concept is McGregor's thesis that leadership strategies are influenced by a leader's assumptions about human nature. As a result of his experience as a consultant, McGregor summarised two contrasting sets of assumptions made by managers in industry.

Theory X and Y Managers:

- Theory X managers believe that:
  - The average human being has an inherent dislike of work and will avoid it if possible.
  - Because of this human characteristic, most people must be coerced, controlled, directed, or threatened with punishment to get them to put forth adequate effort to achieve organizational objectives.
  - The average human being prefers to be directed, wishes to avoid responsibility, has relatively little ambition, and wants security above all else.
- Theory Y managers believe that:
  - The expenditure of physical and mental effort in work is as natural as play or rest, and the average human being, under proper conditions, learns not only to accept but to seek responsibility.
  - People will exercise self-direction and self-control to achieve objectives to which they are committed.
  - The capacity to exercise a relatively high level of imagination, ingenuity, and creativity in the solution of organizational problems is widely, not narrowly, distributed in the population, and the intellectual potentialities of the average human being are only partially utilized under the conditions of modern industrial life.

It can therefore be seen that a leader holding Theory X assumptions would prefer an autocratic style, whereas one holding Theory Y assumptions would prefer a more participative style.

BLAKE AND MOUTON'S MANAGERIAL GRID

The Managerial Grid developed by Robert Blake and Jane Mouton focuses on task and employee orientations of managers, as well as combinations of concerns between the two extremes. A grid with concern for production on the horizontal axis and concern for people on the vertical axis and plots five basic leadership styles. The first number refers to a leader's production or task orientation; the second, to people or employee orientation. Blake and Mouton propose that "Team Management" - a high concern for both employees and production - is the most effective type of leadership behaviour.

THE CONTINGENCY OR SITUATIONAL SCHOOL

Whilst behavioural theories may help managers develop particular leadership behaviours they give little guidance as to what constitutes effective leadership in different situations. Indeed, most researchers today conclude that no one leadership style is right for every manager under all circumstances.

Instead, contingency-situational theories were developed to indicate that the style to be used is contingent upon such factors as the situation, the people, the task, the organisation, and other environmental variables.

Fiedler's Contingency Model

Fiedler's contingency theory postulates that there is no single best way for managers to lead. Situations will create different leadership style requirements for a manager. The solution to a managerial situation is contingent on the factors that impinge on the situation. For example, in a highly routine environment where repetitive tasks are the norm, a relatively directive leadership style may result in the best performance, however, in a dynamic environment a more flexible, participative style may be required. Fiedler looked at three situations that could define the condition of a managerial task:

- Leader member relations: How well do the manager and the employees get along?
- Task structure: Is the job highly structured, fairly unstructured, or somewhere in between?
- Position power: How much authority does the manager possess?

Managers were rated as to whether they were relationship oriented or task oriented. Task oriented managers tend to do better in situations that have good leader-member relationships, structured tasks, and either weak or strong position power. They do well when the task is unstructured but position power is strong. Also, they did well at the other end of the spectrum when the leader member relations were moderate to poor and the task was unstructured. Relationship oriented managers do better in all other situations.

Thus, a given situation might call for a manager with a different style or a manager who could take on a different style for a different situation. These environmental variables are combined in a weighted sum that is termed "favourable" at one end and "unfavourable" at the other. Task oriented style is preferable at the clearly defined extremes of "favourable" and "unfavourable" environments, but relationship orientation excels in the middle ground. Managers could attempt to reshape the environment variables to match their style.

Another aspect of the contingency model theory is that the leader-member relations, task structure, and position power dictate a leader's situational control. Leader-member relations are the amount of loyalty, dependability, and support that the leader receives from employees. It is a measure of how the manager perceives he or she and the group of employees is getting along together. In a favourable relationship the manager has a high task structure and is able to reward and or punish employees without any problems.

In an unfavourable relationship the task is usually unstructured and the leader possesses limited authority. The spelling out in detail of what is required of subordinates affects task structure. Positioning power measures the amount of power or authority the manager perceives the organization has given him or her for the purpose of directing, rewarding, and punishing subordinates. Positioning power of managers depends on the taking away or increasing the decision-making power of employees.

The task-motivated style leader experiences pride and satisfaction in the task accomplishment for the organization, while the relationship-motivated style seeks to build interpersonal relations and extend extra help for the team development in the organization. There is no good or bad leadership style. Each person has his or her own preferences for leadership. Task-motivated leaders are at their best when the group performs successfully such as achieving a new sales record or outperforming the major competitor. Relationship-oriented leaders are at their best when greater customer satisfaction is gained and a positive company image is established.

The Hersey-Blanchard Model of Leadership

The Hersey-Blanchard Leadership Model also takes a situational perspective of leadership. This model posits that the developmental levels of a leader's subordinates play the greatest role in determining which leadership styles are most appropriate. Their theory is based on the amount of direction and socio-emotional support a leader must provide given the situation and the "level of maturity" of the followers.

- Task behaviour is the extent to which the leader engages in spelling out the duties and responsibilities to an individual or group. This behaviour includes telling people what to do, how to do it, when to do it, where to do it, and who's to do it. In task behaviour the leader engages in oneway communication.

- Relationship behaviour is the extent to which the leader engages in two-way or multi-way communications. This includes listening, facilitating, and supportive behaviours. In relationship behaviour the leader engages in two-way communication by providing socio-emotional support.
- Maturity is the willingness and ability of a person to take responsibility for directing his or her own behaviour. People tend to have varying degrees of maturity, depending on the specific task, function, or objective that a leader is attempting to accomplish through their efforts.

In summary therefore leader behaviours fall along two continua:

- Directive Behaviour
  - One-Way Communication
  - Followers' Roles Clearly Communicated
  - Close Supervision of Performance
- Supportive Behaviour
  - Two-Way Communication
  - Listening, providing support and encoura-gement
  - Facilitate interaction Involve follower in decision-making

For Blanchard the key situational variable, when determining the appropriate leadership style, is the readiness or developmental level of the subordinate.

As a result, four leadership styles result:

- *Directing*: The leader provides clear instructions and specific direction. This style is best matched with a low follower readiness level.
- *Coaching*: The leader encourages two-way communication and helps build confidence and motivation on the part of the employee, although the leader still has responsibility and controls decision making. Selling style is best matched with a moderate follower readiness level.
- *Supporting*: With this style, the leader and followers share decision making and no longer need or expect the relationship to be directive. Participating style is best matched with a moderate follower readiness level.
- *Delegating*: This style is appropriate for leaders whose followers are ready to accomplish a particular task and are both competent and motivated to take full responsibility. Delegating style is best matched with a high follower readiness level.

To determine the appropriate leadership style to use in a given situation, the leader must first determine the maturity level of the followers in relation to the specific task that the leader is attempting to accomplish through the effort of the followers. As the level of followers' maturity increases, the leader should begin to reduce his or her task behaviour and increase relationship behaviour until the followers reach a moderate level of maturity. As the followers begin to move into an above average level of maturity, the leader should decrease not only task behaviour but also relationship behaviour. Once the maturity level is identified, the appropriate leadership style can be determined.

Tannenbaum & Schmidt's Leadership Continuum

One criticism of early work on leadership styles is that they looked at styles too much in black and white terms. The autocratic and democratic styles or task-oriented and relationship-oriented styles which they described are extremes, whereas in practice the behaviour of many, perhaps most, leaders in business will be somewhere between the two. Contingency theorists Tannenbaum and Schmidt suggested the idea that leadership behaviour varies along a continuum and that as one moves away from the autocratic extreme the amount of subordinate participation and involvement in decision taking increases.

They also suggested that the kind of leadership represented by the democratic extreme of the continuum will be rarely encountered in formal organisations. Four main leadership styles can be located at points along such a continuum:

- Autocratic: The leader takes the decisions and announces them, expecting subordinates to carry them out without question.
- Persuasive: At this point on the scale the leader also takes all the decisions for the group without discussion or consultation but believes that people will be better motivated if they are persuaded that the decisions are good ones. He or she does a lot of explaining and 'selling' in order to overcome any possible resistance to what he or she wants to do. The leader also puts a lot of energy into creating enthusiasm for the goals he or she has set for the group.
- Consultative: In this style the leader confers with the group members before taking decisions and, in fact, considers their advice and their feelings when framing decisions. He or she may, of course, not always accept the subordinates' advice but they are likely to feel that they can have some influence. Under this leadership style the decision and the full responsibility for it remain with the leader but the degree of involvement by subordinates in decision taking is very much greater than telling or selling styles.
- Democratic: Using this style the leader would characteristically lay the problem before his or her subordinates and invite discussion. The leader's role is that of conference leader, or chair, rather than that of decision taker. He or she will allow the decision to emerge out of the process of group discussion, instead of imposing it on the group as its boss.

What distinguishes this approach from previous discussions of leadership style is that there will be some situations in which each of the above styles is likely to be more appropriate than the others.

- Telling: In an emergency, a telling style may be most appropriate and would normally be considered justified by the group.
- Selling: The selling style would tend to fit situations in which the group leader, and he or she alone, possesses all the information on which the decision must be based and which at the same time calls for a very high level of commitment and enthusiasm on the part of group members if the task is to be carried through successfully.
- Consulting: The consulting style is likely to be most appropriate when there is time in which to reach a considered decision and when the information on which the decision needs to be based lies among the members of the group.
- Joining: The joining style is appropriate under similar conditions, with the important exception that this is likely to be appropriate only in those instances where the nature of the responsibility associated with the decision is such that group members are willing to share it with their leader, or alternatively the leader is willing to accept responsibility for decisions which he or she has not made personally.

Adair's Action-Centred Leadership Model

John Adair has a long pedigree in the world of leadership. The Adair model is that the action-centred leader gets the job done through the work team and relationships with fellow managers and staff. According to Adair's explanation an action-centred leader must:

- Direct the job to be done
- Support and review the individual people doing it
- Co-ordinate and foster the work team as a whole

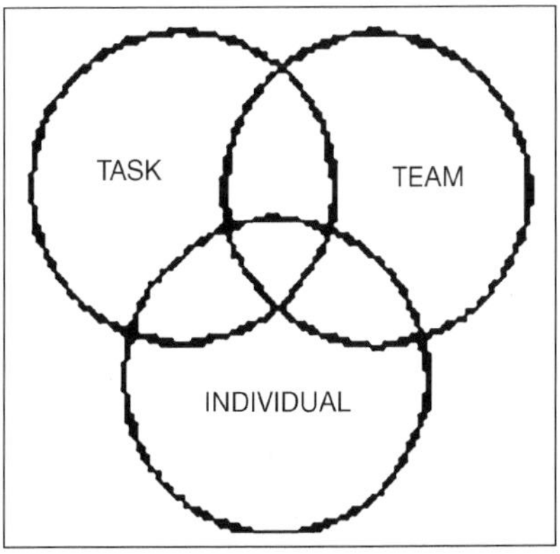

Fig. Action-Centred Leadership Model

His famous three circle diagram is a simplification of the variability of human interaction, but is a useful tool for thinking about what constitutes an effective leader/manager in relation to the job he/she has to do. The effective leader/manager carries out the functions and exhibits the behaviours depicted by the three circles. Situational and contingent elements call for different responses by the leader. Hence imagine that the various circles may be bigger or smaller as the situation varies *i.e.* the leader will give more or less emphasis to the functionally-oriented behaviours according to what the actual situation involves. The challenge for the leader is to manage all sectors of the diagram:

- Task:
  - Define the task
  - Make the plan
  - Allocate work and resources
  - Control quality and rate of work
  - Check performance against plan
  - Adjust the plan
- Team:
  - Maintain discipline
  - Build team spirit
  - Encourage, motivate, give a sense of purpose
  - Appoint sub-leaders
  - Ensure communication within group
  - Develop the group
- Individual:
  - Attend to personal problems
  - Praise individuals
  - Give status
  - Recognise and use individual abilities
- Develop the individual

LEADERS AND FOLLOWERS

The models discussed so far have dwelt on the leader as some frontal figure who stands out from the rest as being somehow different and "leading" the rest of the people. The discussion now moves to recognition of the importance of the leaders' relationship with his/her followers and an interdependency of roles. No longer the hero or solo leader but the team leader. Not the leader always out in front but the leader who has the capacity to follow. Not the master, but the servant.

Servant Leadership

The notion of "Servant Leadership" emphasises the leaders' duty to serve his/her followers - leadership thus arises out of a desire to serve rather than a desire to lead Robert Greenleaf, founder of the Center for Servant Leadership describes it as follows:

- "The servant-leader is servant first... It begins with the natural feeling that one wants to serve, to serve first. Then conscious choice brings one to aspire to lead. He or she is sharply different from the person who is leader first, perhaps because of the need to assuage an unusual power drive or to acquire material possessions. For such it will be a later choice to serve – after leadership is established. The leader-first and the servant-first are two extreme types. Between them there are shadings and blends that are part of the infinite variety of human nature.
- The difference manifest itself in the care taken by the servant-first to make sure that other people's highest priority needs are being served. The best test, and difficult to administer, is: do those served grow as persons; do they, while being served, become healthier, wiser, freer, more autonomous, more likely themselves to become servants? And, what is the effect on the least privileged in society; will they benefit, or, at least, will they not be further deprived?"

Characteristics of Servant Leaders are as follows:

- "Servant-Leadership is a practical philosophy which supports people who choose to serve first, and then lead as a way of expanding service to individuals and institutions. Servantleaders may or may not hold formal leadership positions. Servant-leadership encourages collaboration, trust, foresight, listening, and the ethical use of power and empowerment."

The emphasis on serving a higher purpose has made this model popular within the Church and other religious institutions.

The Following Part of Leading

Katzenbach and Smith, authors of 'The Wisdom of Teams' talk of the "following part of leading", saying that the critical behaviours of leaders are:

- Key Behaviours of Leaders:
  - *Asking questions instead of giving answers*: By asking such questions such as "What do you think we should do?" or "How do you suggest we proceed?" you take a step behind another person. Whether you stay behind, of course, depends on your intention to actually follow the suggestion or answer of that other person.
  - *Providing opportunities for others to lead you*: This goes beyond the traditional notion of looking for growth opportunities for other people. Unless the opportunity in question bears a real risk for your personal performance outcome, you are not actually positioning yourself as a follower.
  - *Doing real work in support of others instead of only the reverse*: Rolling up your sleeves and contributing "sweat equity" to the efforts and outcomes of other people earns you their

appreciation as someone upon whom they can depend, regardless of the relative hierarchical or functional position each of you holds.

  - *Becoming a matchmaker instead of a "central switch"*: In addition to following other people yourself, you must learn to help them follow each other. This requires you to get beyond considering yourself the "central switch" through which all decisions flow. Instead, you need to look for every possible chance to help people find their best collaborators. "Have you asked Sally or Rasheed what they think?" is often the only input required to facilitate the effort at hand, although you then must submit your effort and support to whatever the people in question suggest.
  - *Seeking common understanding instead of consensus*: The pejorative meaning associated with consensus management has nothing to do with either effective leading or effective following. Leaders who know when and how to follow build deep common understanding, not superficial consensus, around the purpose, goals, and approach at hand. They submit themselves and others to the discipline of ensuring that all sides to any disagreement are fully understood by everyone, recognizing that mutual understanding is far more powerful than any particular decision to choose path A over path B. All people will follow strong, commonly understood purposes and goals more easily than the "put-up jobs" associated with consensus.

They go on to say that the indicators of when a leader must follow are:

- When a leader must follow Leaders:
  - Individual performance: As a leader, you must follow another individual, regardless of hierarchy, if:
    i. That individual, through experience, skill, and judgement, knows best.
    ii. That individual's growth demands that you invest more in his or her skill and self-confidence than in your own.
    iii. Only that individual, not you, has the capacity to "get it done"
  - Team performance: As a leader, you must follow the team if:
    i. The team's purpose and performance goals demand it
    ii. The team, not you, must develop skills and self-confidence
    iii. The team's agreed-upon working approach requires you, like all the others, to do real work
  - Organizational performance: As a leader, you must follow others, regardless of hierarchy, if:
    i. The organization's purpose and performance goals demand it
    ii. The need for expanding the leadership capacity of others in the organization requires it
    iii. "Living" the vision and values enjoins you to do so

Team Leadership

In the late 1970's Meredith Belbin conducted a study of teams focusing on the factors separating successful and unsuccessful teams via a college business game at Henley a feature of which was shared leadership. Through the game Belbin found that the composition of the team was important and that individual differences in style, role and contribution far from underlining personal weaknesses, were a source of potential team strength.

Balanced teams comprised of such individuals who engaged in complementary role behaviour performed better than unbalanced teams. Nine distinctive roles were identified in the study, with most people being found to embrace a mix of two or three roles whilst also avoiding others with which they were uncomfortable. Where there was an individual with clear, useful and appreciated attributes they would fit into a team on the basis of the strengths they brought.

These people would also have weaknesses that belonged to the same cluster of characteristics as the strength itself. These potential deficiencies were considered the price that has to be paid for a particular strength, a price that is worth paying, and were referred to as 'allowable weaknesses. Belbin found no 'ideal' team member, individual who could perform all of the roles. From this work, Belbin drew the distinction between the "Solo" and the "Team" leader. He suggests that "leaders are not notable for admitting their weaknesses, whether allowable or not. They act as though they have no weaknesses".

To many people the image of the leader - a person heading up a team of followers, ever ready to take on any role and assuming any responsibility - is very familiar to us for it is the one based upon our past experiences and beliefs. Belbin classified such leaders as 'Solo leaders' and in the workplace this type of behaviour may have great advantages, for internal barriers can be overcome and decisions, especially those of an urgent nature, can be made and put into effect with little or no delay.

The increasing complexity and the discontinuous nature of modern work however, poses greater problems where Solo leadership is less appropriate and 'Team leadership' more suited. The key difference between the 'Solo leader' and 'Team leadership' revolves around the behaviour and participation of the two.

Solo and Team Leader:

- Solo Leader:
  - Plays unlimited role – the Solo Leader interferes in everything
  - Strives for conformity – the Solo Leader tries to mould people to particular standards
  - Collects acolytes – The Solo Leader collects admirers and sycophants
  - Directs Subordinates – subordinates take their leads and cues from the Solo Leader

- Projects objectives – the Solo Leader makes it plain what everyone is expected to do 1. Chooses to limit role to preferred team roles – delegates roles to others
- Team Leader:
  - Chooses to limit role to preferred team roles – delegates roles to others
  - Builds on diversity – the Team Leader values differences between people
  - Seeks talent – The Team Leader is not threatened by people with special abilities
  - Develops colleagues – the Team Leader encourages the growth of personal strengths
  - Creates mission – the Team Leader projects the vision which others can act on as they see fit

Using Team Role theory the word 'shape' indicates to us 'shaper', whilst the word 'vision' implies 'plant'. Looking at leadership using Handy's definition is interesting for vision is certainly important to leadership, but does it have to be unique to an individual? Where it is unique to an individual with a drive to enact it such as a 'Shaper', strong Solo leadership is likely to prevail. Vision alternatively may be 'borrowed' by a 'Shaper' who treats it as a product of the self and similarly will adopt a Solo leadership style.

Many organisations have rewarded Solo leadership behaviour by promoting individuals to management and leadership positions, for such individuals have met past organisational needs In today's organisation the alternative approach, the Team Leader, is more appropriate. Whilst Team leadership may not be as natural as Solo leadership, Belbin suggests it can be learned through understanding the nature of leadership and the qualities required. In the rapidly changing and uncertain work environment of today no one person has all the answers to leadership. A Team leadership style based upon the development of the strengths and the allowable weaknesses of all of the roles will permit a more holistic, or participative, style of leadership where teamwork, problem solving, decision making and innovation can flourish with heightened teamwork and work performance.

Transactional and Transformational Leadership

James MacGregor Burns writing in his book 'Leadership' was the first to put forward the concept of "transforming leadership". To Burns transforming leadership *"is a relationship of mutual stimulation and elevation that converts followers into leaders and may convert leaders into moral agents"*. Burns went on to also further define it by suggesting that:

- "[Transforming leadership] occurs when one or more persons engage with others in such a way that leaders and followers raise one another to higher levels of motivation and morality..."

Burns draws upon the humanistic psychology movement in his writing upon 'transforming leadership' by proposing that the transforming leader shapes, alters, and elevates the motives, values and goals of followers achieving significant change in the process. He proposed that there is a special power entailed in transforming leadership with leaders *"armed with principles [that] may ultimately transform both leaders and followers into persons who jointly adhere to modal values and end-values"*. Burns sees the power of transforming leadership as more noble and different from charismatic leadership, which he terms 'heroic' leadership, and executive or business leadership. Despite this it is surprising that most of the application of Burns' work has been in these two types of leadership. Bernard Bass developed Burns' concept of transforming leadership in 'Leadership and Performance Beyond Expectations' into 'transformational leadership' where the leader transforms followers – the direction of influence to Bass is thus one-way, unlike Burns' who sees it as potentially a two-way process. Bass, however, deals with the transformational style of executive leadership that incorporates social change, a facet missing from Burns' work. For Bass 'transformational leaders' may:

- Expand a follower's portfolio of needs
- Transform a follower's self-interest
- Increase the confidence of followers
- Elevate followers' expectations
- Heighten the value of the leader's intended outcomes for the follower
- Encourage behavioural change
- Motivate others to higher levels of personal achievement.

Tichy and Devanna in their book 'Transformational Leadership' built further on the work of Burns and Bass in organisational and work contexts. They described the hybrid nature of transformational as *"... not due to charisma. It is a behavioural process capable of being learned"*.

Bass writing with a research colleague Avolio suggested that *"Transformational leadership is closer to the prototype of leadership that people have in mind when they describe their ideal leader, and it is more likely to provide a role model with which subordinates want to identify"*. Transactional leadership has been the traditional model of leadership with its roots from an organisational or business perspective in the 'bottom line'. Stephen Covey writing in 'Principle-Centred Leadership' suggests that transformational leadership "... focuses on the 'top line'" and offers contrast between the two.

Comparison of Transactional and Transformational Leadership:

- Transactional Leadership:
  - Builds on man's need to get a job done and make a living
  - Is preoccupied with power and position, politics and perks
  - Is mired in daily affairs
  - Is short-term and hard data orientated
  - Focuses on tactical issues

  - Relies on human relations to lubricate human interactions
  - Follows and fulfils role expectations by striving to work effectively within current systems
  - Supports structures and systems that reinforce the bottom line, maximise efficiency, and guarantee short-term profits
- Transformational Leadership ddd. Builds on a man's need for meaning
  - Is preoccupied with purposes and values, morals, and ethics
  - Transcends daily affairs
  - Is orientated towards long-term goals without compromising human values and principles
  - Focuses more on missions and strategies
  - Releases human potential – identifying and developing new talent
  - Designs and redesigns jobs to make them meaningful and challenging
  - Aligns internal structures and systems to reinforce overarching values and goals

Both kinds of leadership are necessary. Transactional leadership has remained the organisational model for many people and organisations who have not moved into or encouraged the transformational role needed to meet the challenges of our changing times.

- "The goal of transformational leadership is to 'transform' people and organisations in a literal sense – to change them in mind and heart; enlarge vision, insight, and understanding; clarify purposes; make behaviour congruent with beliefs, principles, or values; and bring about changes that are permanent, self-perpetuating, and momentum building"

According to Bass and Avolio, transformational leaders display behaviours associated with five transformational styles. Transformational leadership is a process in which the leaders take actions to try to increase their associates' awareness of what is right and important, to raise their associates' motivational maturity and to move their associates to go beyond the associates' own self-interests for the good of the group, the organization, or society.

Such leaders provide their associates with a sense of purpose that goes beyond a simple exchange of rewards for effort provided. The transformational leaders are proactive in many different and unique ways. These leaders attempt to optimize development, not just performance. Development encompasses the maturation of ability, motivation, attitudes, and values. Such leaders want to elevate the maturity level of the needs of their associates. They convince their associates to strive for a higher level of achievement as well as higher levels of moral and ethical standards.

Through the development of their associates, they optimize the development of their organization as well. High performing associates build high performing organizations. Hooper and Potter extend the notion of transformational leadership to identify seven key competences of "transcendent leaders": those able to engage the emotional support of their followers and thus effectively transcend change.

- Setting direction
- Setting an example
- Communication
- Alignment
- Bringing out the best in people
- The leader as a change agent
- Providing decision in a crisis and on the ambiguous

DISPERSED LEADERSHIP

The importance of social relations in the leadership contract, the need for a leader to be accepted by their followers and a realisation that no one individual is the ideal leader in all circumstances have given rise to a new school of leadership thought. Referred to as 'informal', 'emergent' or 'dispersed' leadership, this approach argues a less formalised model of leadership where the leaders' role is dissociated from the organisational hierarchy. It is proposed that individuals at all levels in the organisation and in all roles can exert leadership influence over their colleagues and thus influence the overall leadership of the organisation. Heifetz distinguishes between the exercise of "leadership" and the exercise of "authority" – thus dissociating leadership from formal organisational power roles whilst Raelin talks of developing "leaderful" organisations through concurrent, collective and compassionate leadership.

The key to this is a distinction between the notions of "leader" and "leadership". "Leadership" is regarded as a process of sense-making and direction-giving within a group and the "leader" can only be identified on the basis of his/her relationship with others in the social group who are behaving as followers. In this manner, it is quite possible to conceive of the leader as emergent rather than predefined and that their role can only be understood through examining the relationships within the group.

The origins of such an approach have their foundations more in the fields of sociology and politics than the more traditional management literature and draw on concepts such as organisational culture and climate to highlight the contextual nature of leadership. It is a more collective concept, and would argue for a move from an analysis and development of individual leader qualities to an identification of what constitutes an effective leadership process within an organisation. A move in focus from the individuals to the relationships themselves.

LEADERSHIP MODELS AND COMPETENCY FRAMEWORKS

This part of the report will look at some different leadership models and frameworks used in practice across the public and private sector organisations. The chosen models were selected as the organisations were known to researchers at the Centre for Leadership Studies and/or details of the framework were publicly available. They are not intended to represent a comprehensive, or even representative, sample of available frameworks but rather a preliminary examination of readily available materials. The inclusion of a particular framework does not necessarily indicate that it is in any way assumed "better" or more "typical" than those that were not included and, indeed, there may well be many excellent models which have not been discussed.

To many participating organisations the material reviewed represents an element of their "competitive advantage" and is thus confidential. We have therefore chosen in this report, not to include the full framework but simply to refer to the key elements. Where further information is available on the Internet we have included the web address. For ease of presentation, they have been divided into private-sector, public-sector and generic frameworks.

PRIVATE SECTOR FRAMEWORKS

AstraZeneca Leadership Capabilities

The AstraZeneca Leadership Capabilities were defined shortly after merger in 1999 and have been used in performance management, development planning and management planning across the global company. They are a central part of leadership development programmes and a 360 degree feedback tool has been developed to support their application.

The leadership behaviours provide a link between business priorities and the AZ values of: respect for the individual and for diversity; openness, honest, trust and support for each other; integrity and high ethical standards; and leadership by example at all levels. There are seven key capabilities, each with associated indicators/behaviours:

- Provides clarity about strategic direction
- Ensures commitment
- Focuses on delivery
- Builds relationships
- Develops people
- Demonstrates personal conviction
- Builds self-awareness

BAE Performance Centred Leadership

Performance Centred Leadership competencies provide a set of related behaviours used to improve business performance. They have been developed from 360 degree feedback information, benchmarked against the competencies of high performing organisations, changed to reflect input from the Senior leader focus groups and statistically evaluated by London University. The competencies and related behaviours are used to evaluate performance in Peer Recognition and Employee opinion survey, identifying development opportunities through 360 degree feedback and are used as part of the appointment process. There are five core competences, each with a set of related behaviours:

- Achieving High Performance
- Focusing on the Customer
- Developing Others
- Continuously Improving
- Working Together

The framework forms a basis for leadership development in BAE which is fully integrated with all other strategic processes in the organisation through the Performance Centred Leadership Development Framework.

Federal Express Leadership Qualities

FedEx has a system for rating aspiring leaders according to 9 attributes:

- Charisma
- Individual consideration
- Intellectual stimulation
- Courage
- Dependability
- Flexibility
- Integrity
- Judgement
- Respect for others

Lufthansa Leadership Compass

The Lufthansa Leadership Compass sets out a framework for effective leadership that is used by the Lufthansa School of Business in its leadership development education. It includes the following six key categories, which set out a range of skills and behaviours including: vision, decisiveness, concern for people, self-reflection and professional know-how:

- Entrepreneurial leadership
- Breakthrough problem solving
- Winning others
- Leading people
- Attitude and drive
- International business competencies

Development Centres based on this framework are used to help "high potential" employees define their current position and determine the next steps for their professional career. This involves a self-assessment exercise, development centre and a post DC process whereby the participant develops an individual development plan with the support and coaching of their superior. It is intended that this process should occur about 1 year before moving into a C grade post.

Philips Leadership Competencies

Six Leadership Competencies define the behaviour that is required to achieve business success in Phillips. They provide a balanced approach, stating the importance of task aspects while recognising that results are obtained through people. These competencies are as follows:

- Shows determination to achieve excellent results
- Focuses on the market
- Finds better ways
- Demands top performance
- Inspires commitment
- Develops self and others

Shell Leadership Framework

The Leadership Framework used by Shell includes nine key elements as indicated below:

- Builds Shared Vision
- Champions Customer Focus
- Maximises Business Opportunities
- Demonstrates Professional Mastery
- Displays Personal Effectiveness
- Demonstrates Courage
- Motivates, Coaches & Develops
- Values Differences
- Delivers Results

Vodafone Global Leadership Competencies

The Vodafone leadership competencies underlying their Global Leadership Programme are divided into five categories:

- Values communication
- International team development
- Strategic vision
- Building organisational capability
- Commercial drive

PUBLIC SECTOR FRAMEWORKS

Senior Civil Service Competency Framework

This framework sets out key attributes that have been identified by Civil Service Corporate Management as required for the *Senior Civil Service* (SCS). There are six main sets of competences, each with a series of related behaviours.

The competencies are as follows:

- Giving purpose and direction
- Making a personal impact
- Thinking strategically
- Getting the best from people
- Learning and improving
- Focusing on delivery

DfES - Management and Leadership Attributes

This framework sets out what is expected of managers and leaders in the Department for Education and Skills as the organisation moves forward to deliver the Department's Strategic Framework. It is based on the SCS Competency Framework and was developed following a period of internal consultation in the DfES. It distinguishes between "effective" and "ineffective" behaviours in relation to three clusters of attributes each of which comprises a set of behaviours, skills and knowledge.

- Interpersonal Attributes: Making a personal impact, Giving purpose and direction
- Delivery Attributes: Focussing on delivery, Thinking strategically
- Improvement Attributes: Getting the best from people, Learning and improving

The framework takes a situational/contingency view of leadership in that it states that:

- Competent DfES managers and leaders at all levels will demonstrate varying combinations of these attributes in different circumstances and at different times. The effective behaviours and skills within each attribute are examples of what competent managers and leaders do when they are modelling good management and leadership – they may not do all of them all of the time!"

Northern Ireland Senior Civil Service Core Criteria

This is the Northern Ireland equivalent of the SCS Competency Framework, covering 8 key competencies including leadership:

- Leadership: Envisioning, Team building, Standards and integrity
- Conceptual and strategic thinking and planning: Conceptual thinking, Strategic thinking, Planning
- Focus on outcomes: Customer orientation, Outcomes focus, Meeting and improving performance standards
- Managing and developing staff: Managing staff effectively, Promoting and facilitating development
- Managing relationships and partners
- Communication: Oral/written, Influencing, Presentation
- Managing resources innovatively: Cost awareness, Improvement orientation

- Personal effectiveness: Change orientation, Develop orientation, Self confidence and resilience, Commitment, Intellect in action

Scottish Executive Framework

This framework, devised for the Scottish parliament, identifies seven sets of criteria and, for each, what everyone should do and what managers and leaders should also do. Indicators are also given as to when development needs may be identified.

The specific leadership dimensions of the framework are as follows:

- Achieving
- Self management
- Analysis and investigation
- Outward focus
- Communication
- Managing others
- Working with others

Ministry of Defence

The MoD uses a number of competency frameworks related to leadership for annual appraisal, including a revised SCS Competency Framework and *Officers Joint Appraisal Report* (OJAR).

MoD Senior Civil Service Competency Framework

This is based on the SCS Competency Framework and redefines it as indicated below:

- Leading and working together: Working together, Providing the lead, Enabling others to give of their best
- Being personally effective: Striving to achieve results, Promoting change and continuous improvement, Communicating and influencing, Solving problems and taking decisions, Taking a wider perspective
- Delivering results: Focussing on customers and service delivery, Developing and delivering effective policies and programmes, Managing work and resources to achieve results, Exploiting information and knowledge

Officers Joint Appraisal Report

The OJAR, introduced in March 2001, covers 10 performance attributes explored during annual appraisals for officers across the forces.

These are as follows:

- Leadership
- Professional effectiveness
- Effective intelligence
- Judgement

- Management
- Initiative
- Reliability
- Powers of communication
- Subordinate development
- Courage and values.

EO for Local Government – Compendium of Competencies

The *Employers' Organisation* for local government's (EO) role is to help councils achieve the high standards of people management needed to ensure the continuous improvement of services. Their web site includes a compendium of leadership competencies developed by and/or used by local authorities across the UK.

These have been classified into 20 different categories as indicated below:

- Change: includes Challenge, Leadership for Change, Managing Change/Strategic Thinking.
- Communication: includes Communicating, Communication and Customer Care, Listening and Organising
- Corporate Focus: includes Collective Responsibility, Corporate Focus, Developing a Learning Organisation, Evaluating and Improving Organisational Performance, Organisational Awareness, Organisational Effectiveness
- Customer Focus: includes Commitment to Quality Customer Service, Customer Focused Service Delivery, Sharpening Customer and Service Focus
- Decision Making: includes Analysing and Solving Problems, Decision Making, Identifying and Solving Problems, Judgement.
- Equality and Diversity: includes Achieving Equal Opportunities, Demonstrating Leadership in Implementing Equalities, Managing Equitably, Valuing Diversity
- Focus on Results: includes Achievement Focused, Focusing on Results, Managing for Results
- Impact and Influence: includes Acting Assertively, Impact and Influence, Interpersonal Skills, Networking and Influencing, Partnership Working, Persuasiveness
- Information Management: includes Gathering and Using Information, Getting Unbiased Information, Giving Clear Information, Information and Communication Management, Searching for Information
- Integrity: includes Behaving Ethically, Integrity
- Leading People: includes Appraising People and Performance, Developing Others, Disciplining and Counselling, Enabling, Leadership, Managing People, Managing, Developing and Understanding Others, Personal and Staff Development, Training, Coaching and Delegating, Valuing People

- Partnerships: includes Community Leadership, Co-operating with Others, Leading Integrated Working, Networking and Influencing, Working in Partnership
- Personal Management and Drive: includes Determination, Managing Self, Motivation and Drive, Personal Effectiveness, Personal Management, Planning and Scheduling Work, Setting Goals and Standards, Time Management and Prioritising
- Political Awareness: includes Democratic Support, Political and Organisational Awareness, Working Competently within the Political Environment
- Project and Process Management: includes Managing Projects, Organisational and Project Management
- Resource Management: includes Managing Resources
- Safety
- Service Improvement: includes Continuous Improvement to Service Delivery, Delivering Excellence, Leading the Challenge on Continuous Service Improvement, Managing the Executive Programme and Performance, Service Co-ordination and Management, Sharpening Customer and Service Focus
- Strategic Focus: includes: Acting Strategically, Developing Strategy, Managing Change/Strategic Thinking, Strategic Behaviour, Vision
- Team Building: includes Building Teams, Working in and Developing Teams

NHS Leadership Qualities Framework

The NHS Leadership Qualities Framework, developed by the NHS Leadership Centre, identifies 15 key qualities across three broad clusters: Personal qualities, Setting direction and Delivering the service.

- Personal qualities: Self belief, Self awareness, Self management, Drive for improvement, Personal integrity
- Setting Direction: Seizing the future, Intellectual flexibility, Broad scanning, Political astuteness, Drive for results
- Delivering the service: Leading change through people, Holding to account, Empowering others, Effective and strategic influencing, Collaborative working

As with the DfES model, there is an emphasis on the situational nature of leadership and an attempt to indicate the circumstances under which different leadership qualities will take precedence.

National College for School Leadership – Hay McBer Model

In 1999 the NCSL commissioned Hay McBer to research leadership in schools. This research led to the development of a model of school leadership which formed the basis of further discussion. The NCSL now seems to be moving away from this approach towards an integrated leadership development framework.

The 17 school leadership qualities in the Hay McBer Model are as follows:
- Analytical Thinking
- Challenge and Support
- Confidence
- Developing Potential
- Drive for Improvement
- Holding People Accountable
- Impact and Influence
- Information Seeking
- Initiative
- Integrity
- Personal Convictions
- Respect for Others
- Strategic Thinking
- Teamworking
- Transformational Leadership
- Understanding the Environment
- Understanding Others

Senior Executive Service

This framework sets out leadership competencies for the *Senior Executive Service* (SES) in the US.

It identifies 26 competencies across five categories:
- Leading Change: Continual Learning, Creativity and Innovation, Resilience, Service Motivation, Strategic Thinking, Vision.
- Leading People: Conflict Management, Leveraging Diversity, Integrity/Honesty, Team Building
- Results Driven: Accountability, Customer Service, Decisiveness, Entrepreneurship, Problem Solving, Technical Credibility
- Business Acumen: Financial Management, Human Resources Management, Technology Management
- Building Coalitions/Communication: Influencing/Negotiating, Interpersonal Skills, Oral Communication, Partnering, Political Savvy, Written Communication

GENERIC FRAMEWORKS

CEML Framework of Management and Leadership Abilities

The Council for Excellence in Management and Leadership conducted an extensive piece of research using primary and secondary data sources to identify a key set of management and leadership abilities.

The resultant framework identified 83 distinct management and leadership abilities which were grouped into 8 meta-groups and three generic categories.

The categories and meta-groups are as follows:

- Thinking Abilities: Think Strategically
- People Abilities: Manage self, Manage and lead people, Lead direction and culture, Manage relationships
- Task Abilities: Manage information, Manage resources, Manage activities and quality

METO Management Standards

These are the previous management standards developed by METO, the Management Education Training Organisation.

The seven key roles are as follows:

- Manage Activities
- Manage Resources
- Manage People
- Manage Information
- Manage Energy
- Manage Quality
- Manage projects

Investors in People Leadership and Management Model

The IIP Leadership and Management Model sets out a framework for the assessment of leadership and management capabilities in relation to the new "leadership and management" dimension of the Investors in People Award. There are four main principles each with associated indicators.

EFQM Business Excellence Model

The European Foundation for Quality Management Award is an internationally recognised quality award based around business processes. The leadership dimension covers the following four areas:

- 1a Leaders develop the mission, vision and values and are role models of a culture of Excellence;
- 1b Leaders are personally involved in ensuring the organisation's management system is developed, implemented and continuously improved;
- 1c Leaders are involved with customers, partners and representatives of society;
- 1d Leaders motivate, support and recognise the organisation's people.

Institute of Chartered Management – Chartered Management Skills

Chartered Manager candidates need to demonstrate learning, development and impact in the workplace against two of these six categories.

- Leading People

- Meeting Customer Needs
- Managing Change
- Managing Information and Knowledge
- Managing Activities and Resources
- Managing yourself

IMF Management Competencies

As a first step in fostering effective managerial practices, the International Monetary Fund has defined a set of effective managerial behaviours, encapsulated in management competencies. Management competencies comprise a set of critical knowledge, skills, and behaviours that lead to effective management practices.

These management competencies are tools you, as a manager, can use to perform your supervisory functions. Effective performance of each competency is described by a series of behavioural benchmarks. Below are the 15 different management competencies, grouped in 6 broad categories.

- Intellectual Leadership Factor: Sound Judgment/Analytical Skills, Strategic Vision
- Work Management Factor: Planning and Organizing, Drive for Results, Adaptability
- Communication Factor: Oral Presentation Skills, Creating Open Communication, Written Communication Skills
- Interpersonal Factor: Building Relationships, Negotiating and Influencing, Country/Client Relations
- People Management Factor: Motivating Performance, Delegating, Fostering Teamwork, Appraising and Developing Staff

IMF Management competencies are used in a number of ways:

- They are the starting point for developing managerial performance expectations. Competencies can help senior managers articulate the skills needed to be an effective manager—as distinct from those needed to be an effective economist or technical contributor.
- Competencies are the basis for assessing potential managers in the Management Development Center.
- Competencies are the basis for identifying training and development areas.
- They form a common basis on which to assess managers within and across departments.

Hamlin's Generic Model of Managerial and Leadership Effectiveness

This model is based upon a meta analysis of leadership and management behaviours in four UK public-sector organisations. It distinguishes between positive and negative indications of management and leadership.

- Positive indicators:
  - Effective organisation and planning/proactive management

   - Participative and supportive leadership/Proactive team leadership
   - Empowerment and delegation
   - Genuine concern for people/Looks after the interests and development needs of staff
   - Open and personal management approach/Inclusive decision making
   - Communicates and consults widely/Keeps people informed
- Negative indicators:
   - Shows lack of consideration or concern for staff/ineffective autocratic or dictatorial style of management
   - Uncaring, self serving management/undermining, depriving and intimidating behaviour
   - Tolerance of poor performance and low standards/ignoring and avoidance
   - Abdicating roles and responsibilities
   - Resistant to new ideas and change/negative approach

The results have been compared to the Zenger Miller Grass-Roots Leadership Model and used to argue for a universalistic model of leadership/ management.

The Zenger Miller Grass-Roots Leadership Model

This model was developed from empirical research in which collected 1,871 "critical incidents" from 450 US and Canadian organisations. The model has been refined from the original Zenger Miller CLIMB strategies model.

- Create a compelling future: Create and describe a vision, Manager changes required to realize a vision
- Let the customer drive the organization: Respond to identified customer needs
- Involve every mind: Support individual effort, Support team effort, Share information, Make decisions that solve problems, Manage work horizontally, Build personal credibility
- Manage work horizontally: Manage cross-functional processes, Display technical skills, Manage projects, Manage time and resources
- Build personal credibility: Take initiative beyond job requirements, Take responsibility for your own actions and the actions of your group, Handle emotions in yourself and others, Display professional ethics, Show compassion, Make credible presentations

A SELECTION OF LEADERSHIP DEVELOPMENT INITIATIVES

In most cases, used as a basis for the development of leadership and management development provision within organisations as well as appraisal and performance review.

It is beyond the scope of this report to offer a detailed review of the associated programmes and the range of leadership and management development initiatives available, however, we would like to introduce a number of approaches that we feel are particularly interesting in the manner in which they seek to develop the behaviours, skills and attitudes of leaders.

NHS CHIEF EXECUTIVES PROGRAMMES

The NHS manage a wide range of programmes through their Leadership Centre, including a suite of programmes for Chief Executives. These comprise a number of initiatives based upon the NHS Leadership Qualities Framework, including: National and International Learning Experiences:

- Development Assignments
- Transformational Thinking
- Study Tour to Canada
- Duality Leadership Programme
- Action Learning Sets

Modular Programmes:

- Experienced Chief Executives Development Programme
- Drive for Results

Of interest here, is the range of learning opportunities being offered, from action learning sets, study tours and exchanges to modular programmes. The participants are free to choose their preferred modes of learning yet the thinking behind the programme implies that each will contribute towards developing qualities from the Leadership Qualities Framework.

NCSL LEADERSHIP DEVELOPMENT FRAMEWORK

The National College for School Leadership is one of the leading organisations in relation to their awareness of the importance of distributed leadership. Recent years have seen an increasing move from the competency-based approach of the Hay McBer Model to the development of a Leadership Development Framework. The outcomes of a Think Tank report lead to 10 propositions about school leadership. School leadership must:

- Be purposeful, inclusive and values driven
- Embrace the distinctive and inclusive context of the school
- Promote an active view of learning
- Be instructionally focused
- Be a function that is distributed throughout the school community
- Build capacity by developing the school as a learning community
- Be futures oriented and strategically driven
- Be developed through experiential and innovative methodologies
- Be served by a support and policy context that is coherent and implementation driven
- Be supported by a National College that leads the discourse around leadership for learning

These propositions have been actualised through a series of programmes aimed at five different stages in a school leader's career:

- Emergent leadership, when a teacher is beginning to take on management and leadership responsibilities and perhaps forms an aspiration to become a headteacher
- Established leadership, comprising assistant and deputy heads who are experienced leaders but who do not intend to pursue headship
- Entry to headship, including a teacher's preparation for and induction into the senior post in a school
- Advanced leadership, the stage at which school leaders mature in their role, look to widen their experience, to refresh themselves and to update their skills
- Consultant leadership, when an able and experienced leader is ready to put something back into the profession by taking on training, mentoring, inspection or other responsibilities

The focus on, and research into, leadership at different organisational levels and career stages is refreshing when contrasted to the majority of competency/quality frameworks which tend to be based on research with senior managers only. The model therefore, reflects a contingency approach, but without being prescriptive, and seeks to develop a "leadership culture" rather than just a finite number of "leaders".

ACEVO - LEADERSHIP JOURNEY

The "leadership journey" currently being delivered to members of the *Association of Chief Executives of Voluntary Organisations* (ACEVO) uses a somewhat emergent group learning process to develop and explore leadership capabilities, whereby a group of 12 or so Chief Executives from different voluntary-sector organisations embark on a one-year learning experience together. The programme, run by a consultancy organisation is based around a series of two-day residential modules and associated action learning sets and individual and group challenges. Whilst the basic structure of the programme is outlined in advance, the emphasis is very much on getting the group to agree on future topics, activities and speakers and thus input and develop the programme as it proceeds.

A further central element of the programme is the "make a difference challenge" which is an active development challenge for participants to complete within their organisation and share with other members of the group. The programme is, therefore, very experiential and depends to a large extent on peer-group interaction, support and development.

LEAD2LEAD

The Lead2Lead programme, managed by Lancaster University, uses the process of leadership exchange and reflection to help improve leadership awareness. It involves a process of careful paring of participants, often from different organisations, sectors, and even countries. Once matched, participants are given training in observation and reflection techniques, followed by a three-day exchange to each others work place, and a facilitated debriefing session.

The process of observing and being observed can generate significant insights and awareness that could not be delivered through more formalised training. It gives first-hand experience, stories, and personal insights that can be very important to leadership. Furthermore, the "time-out" and reflection elements give the leader space to think and consider their leadership practises.

INTERNATIONAL MASTERS IN PRACTISING MANAGEMENT (IMPM)

The International Masters Programme in Practicing Management is designed to be the "Next Generation" Masters Programme, combining management development with management education. It is a degree programme that focuses directly on the development of managers in their own contexts - their jobs and their organizations.

The IMPM is therefore deeper than conventional programmes of management development and more applied than traditional degree programmes. It was launched in March of 1996 to acclaim from participants and their companies alike, as well as from the international business press.

The IMPM seeks to break the mold of the functional "silos" so common in management education - marketing, finance, organization behaviour, and so on. Instead, the Programme is structured around managerial "mindsets", one for each module. It opens in Lancaster with Managing in general and the *reflective* mindset in particular.

Then it moves to McGill, where attention turns to Managing Organizations and the *analytic* mindset. Bangalore follows with Managing Context, the *worldly* mindset. In Japan, it takes up Managing Relationships, the *collaborative* mindset. The Programme closes at INSEAD with Managing Change, the *action* mindset. More detail is given about each of these mindsets by Mintzberg and Gosling:

- The reflective mindset refers to "managing self" – developing the ability to reflect and make meaning – a form of emotional intelligence.
- The analytic mindset refers to "managing organisations" – developing the ability to analyse and synthesise not only the hard data, but also the soft – "to appreciate scores and crowds while never losing sight of the ball".
- The worldly mindset refers to "managing contexts" – to appreciate cultural and local differences and similarities and respond accordingly.

- The collaborative mindset refers to "managing relationships" – developing partnerships and networks; working with people – managing "relationships" not "people".
- The action mindset refers to "managing movement"– managing change without losing track of continuity.

It is argued that the good manager/leader must master and integrate each of these mindsets and so offers a more cognitive and reflective approach to management development than more traditional behaviour and skills-based programmes.

THE LEADERSHIP GAME

The Leadership Game is a dynamic action-learning event for senior to middle managers designed to maximise learning through experiential techniques supported by expert analysis, feedback and coaching. It is a two-day programme that creates a temporary learning zone to explore issues such as:

- Leadership and decision-making under pressure
- Leaders within hierarchies, virtual teams and self-managed teams
- Team effectiveness under different leadership styles/structures
- How teams work together across functional boundaries
- Understanding the big picture: strategic vision and organisational dynamics.

Day 1 – "The leadership Game" uses a mixture of plenary, work team and cross-team groups and a real-life work related challenge. The process is observed by expert consultants who give team and individual analysis and feedback as required. Day 2 – "Learning Assessment and Implementation" unleashes the learning from Day 1 to address the personal and organisational challenges that arise from the Leadership Game. The programme is run in conjunction with the Tavistock Consultancy Service and represents a current manifestation of the "Human Relations" school started by Kurt Lewin and applied through the National Training Labs of the 1950s. This approach encourages a contextualisation of emotional intelligence and a coming to terms with authority. It offers an alternative to the trait theories of leadership and provides a forum for exploring the emotional aspects of leadership in context and through activities.

TOWARDS AN ALTERNATIVE FRAMEWORK OF LEADERSHIP

REVIEW OF COMPETENCIES

From the review of leadership theory, current models and competency frameworks in use throughout the public and private sectors it would appear that a somewhat limited version of "transformational" leadership is being promoted. Most frameworks go beyond simple definitions of behaviours, to also consider some of the cognitive, affective and inter-personal qualities of leaders, however, although the role of followers may be recognised it is usually in a rather simplistic, unidirectional manner. Leadership, therefore, is conceived as a set of values, qualities and behaviours exhibited by the leader that encourage the participation, development, and commitment of followers. It is remarkable how few of the frameworks refer to the leader's ability to "listen" and none refer to the word to "follow".

The "leader" is thus promoted as the sole source of "leadership". He/she is seen to act as an energiser, catalyst and visionary equipped with a set of tools that can be applied across a diverse range of situations and contexts. Whilst contingency and situational leadership factors may be considered, they are not generally viewed as barriers to an individuals' ability to lead under different circumstances. Fewer than half of the frameworks cited refers directly to the leaders' ability to respond and adapt their style to different circumstances. In addition to the "soft" skills, the leader is also expected to display excellent information processing, project management, customer service and delivery skills, along with proven business and political acumen. They build partnerships, walk the talk, show incredible drive and enthusiasm, and get things done. Furthermore, the leader demonstrates innovation, creativity and thinks "outside the box".

They are entrepreneurs who identify opportunities - they like to be challenged and they're prepared to take risks. Of interest, too, is the emphasis on the importance of values such as honesty, integrity, empathy, trust, ethics and valuing diversity. The leader is expected to show a true concern for people that is drawn from a deep level of self-awareness and personal reflection.

This almost evangelistic notion of the leader as a multi-talented individual with diverse skills, personal qualities and a large social conscience, however, posses a number of difficulties. Firstly it represents almost a return to the trait theory of leadership, just with a wider range of attributes. Secondly when you attempt to combine attributes from across a range of frameworks the result is an unwieldy, almost over-powering list of qualities such as that identified in the CEML research. And thirdly there is little evidence in practice that the "transformational" leader is any more effective than his/her alternatives.

Personal qualities of the leader are undoubtedly important but are unlikely to be sufficient in themselves for the emergence and exercise of leadership. Furthermore, the manner in which these qualities translate into behaviour and group interaction is likely to be culturally specific and thus depend on a whole host of factors, such as the nature of the leader, followers, task, organisational structure, national and corporate cultures, etc.

EXPERIENCE OF USING COMPETENCY FRAMEWORKS

The very fact that organisations will go to great effort and expense to develop their own leadership framework is perhaps evidence in itself that there is no "one size fits all" even though there does seem to be a remarkably great degree of similarity between them. Perhaps, in this case, it is not so much the framework in itself that is important, but the process by which it is developed. The identification of what is required of leaders and the manner in which this integrates with other activities is an important voyage of discovery for the organisation and one for which it is vital that key players take ownership.

To achieve this takes time, reflection and discussion - simply printing off or copying a pre-defined set of standards wouldn't achieve the same results. In the organisations with whom we've spoken the leadership competency framework is an integral element of the leadership development process – whereby it is used to define the content and mechanism of delivery and to help individuals measure and explore their own level of development. It frequently forms the basis of the 360-degree feedback process, by which they can monitor their progress and identify personal learning and development needs, and also underlies assessment and appraisals. Astrazeneca expressed the importance of keeping the framework to a manageable number of dimensions so that it remains easier to operationalise.

Experience of larger frameworks confirms that longer lists may result in a box-ticking mentality which does little, if anything, to enhance leadership and management capability. A further challenge also remains: what is the realistic life-span of a framework? Once formalised and implemented it is becomes easy to stop challenging and developing the framework - the search for leadership competencies within an organisation could thus become self-fulfilling and stagnate. Like any continuous improvement process, the development and identification of leadership talent needs to remain dynamic and current. It needs to move with the times and encourage creativity and diversification.

EVIDENCE-BASED LEADERSHIP DEVELOPMENT

Whilst it has been argued that the leadership and management frameworks may suffer from an over-emphasis on the individual leader, they may also suffer from a lack of research basis. For many of the frameworks little, if no information, was available on how they were developed and it seems likely that no detailed research was conducted. Alan Hooper reported that following his research with companies to develop the "transcendent leadership" competencies he found the majority of corporate leadership frameworks to be loosely based on notions of the company culture, guidance of the CEO and "what seems to be acceptable around here".

Even for those frameworks where research has been performed, there are some concerning methodological omissions. For example, the NHS Leadership Framework was developed following interviews with 150 Chief Executives yet is being used to direct leadership development at all levels within the organisation. Such a lack of empirical grounding is concerning for a number of reasons. Firstly, there is a danger that the qualities identified have little bearing on the effectiveness of leadership in the organisation. Secondly, there is a danger of forming a clique, whereby people are selected into leadership positions because of their similarity to existing leaders, thus neglecting those individuals who don't fit this mould and forming leadership "blind spots".

And thirdly, a lack of concern over research at this stage is frequently translated into a lack of concern for the evaluation of leadership development activities. Research is increasingly stressing the necessity of building evaluation structures into leadership and management development. Huge spending is made on this type of activity yet to most organisations this remains a leap of faith. It may be a difficult task to evaluate beyond immediate post-course reactions but the ability to identify whether such activities are leading to behavioural, attitudinal and organisational changes is a major source of competitive advantage.

It not only enables the improvement of existing provision and identification of future provision but also an appreciation of the wider-scale impact of the intervention. Multi-stakeholder evaluation, for example, explores the aspirations and experiences of diverse stakeholder group and may well reveal that activities beneficial for one may have a negative effect on others.

James and Burgoyne argue that "evaluation, like breathing, is not optional" whether done formally or informally it will always influence subsequent decisions about investments and budgets. It would be best, therefore, that this is based on some proof rather than vague aspirations – few businesses would survive if they based business decisions on such weak logic.

EMERGENT AND COLLECTIVE LEADERSHIP DEVELOPMENT

The findings of our review are very similar to those of another recent review of leadership and leadership development literature for the Learning and Skills Research Centre. The authors developed a useful model for the consideration of both leadership and leadership development along two dimensions.

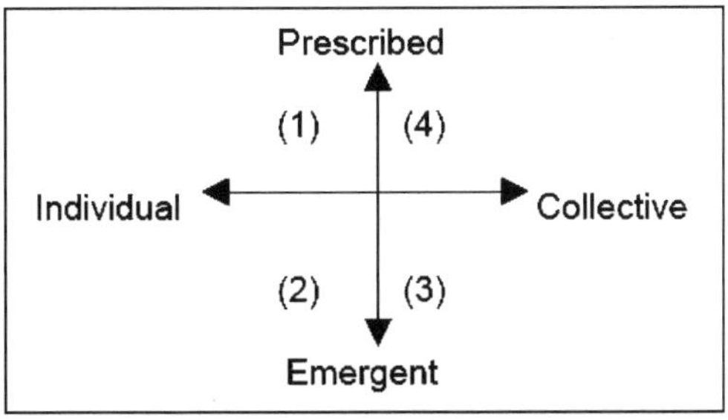

The model proposes that leadership development initiatives differ in the degree to which they focus on individual or collective processes and prescriptive or emergent models and approaches. It is proposed that the vast majority of leadership initiatives lie within cell of the grid, with about 15 per cent in cell and the remaining 5 per cent on the collective side. The authors also argue that there is an almost exclusive emphasis on the leadership inputs and outputs with little attention being paid to the processes in between and they challenge us to consider a more "relational" notion of leadership. Such an emergent and collective view of leadership is reflected. In the Lead2Lead and Leadership Game approaches, for example, far greater attention is paid to the processes than the specific inputs or outputs.

To this extent, the process is conceived as one which is likely to generate leadership insights, understanding and awareness but the exact inputs will be different in every case and the outputs will emerge from the process rather than being predefined. Indeed, there is also an extent to which emergent and collective methodologies are used within programmes closely associated with a competencies/qualities framework. For example, the study tours and exchanges on the NHS Chief Executives programme assume that relevant knowledge and understanding will somehow arise from these experiences.

Furthermore, in a review of the Experienced Chief Executives Development Programme, the programme designers report how they used Activity Theory as a basis for programme conception. The programme was "designed to help participants step back from day-today pressures, reflect on the activities in which they were engaged and their inherent dilemmas, and explore new options". The National College for School Leadership is likewise looking for means to develop a more collective form of leadership within schools. It is moving away from the relatively individualistic approach of the Hay McBer framework to a more fluid Leadership Development Framework that specifies a strategy for developing school leaders at all levels.

AN ALTERNATIVE TO LEADERSHIP AND MANAGEMENT FRAMEWORKS?

In our research and discussion related to the current review, we have begun to hear voices of dissent. The Scottish Leadership Foundation, for example, is currently working with public-sector organisations in Scotland to move them away from competency and standards frameworks.

The National College for School Leadership seems to be reconsidering its position; and the Institute for Leadership and Management is launching a process to develop its own leadership standards in reaction to the current project under way by the Management Standards Centre.

It seems much has already been done to define what "qualities", "competencies", "standards" should be sought from our leaders but, as the current debate would imply, this has done little to improve the quality of our leaders and leadership other than, perhaps, for specific organisations. Take, for example, the work of CEML on identifying management and leadership abilities. They produced a list of 83 attributes based on a meta analysis of previous research, however, this has not been adopted as the norm as the current exercise contests. What is to ensure that the new National Occupational Standards in Management and Leadership will be any more successful?

Perhaps, therefore, it is time to conceive of alternative ways to view management and leadership standards:

- Should we be recommending ethically and socially acceptable forms of behaviour? – almost a "Leadership Charter" that leaders can sign up to?
- Should we be promoting "mindsets" that leaders need to master rather than the behaviours they exhibit?
- Should we be questioning leadership styles, approaches, behaviours and methods to reveal their weaknesses rather than searching for some Holy Grail of leadership?
- Should we focus instead on leadership development to explore what does and doesn't help improve organisational performance rather than providing a post-hoc description of leadership qualities?

In many ways a leadership competencies or standards framework is like a psychometric profile – useful for illuminating current practice in comparison to a norm but dangerous and potentially damaging if misused. To work as a psychometric assessor you must be qualified in the tools' application and interpretation – perhaps the same should be true of leadership and management frameworks to prevent their abuse.

6

Managing Change

INTRODUCTION

A sales manager has some control over how he/she manages their time but far less over the degree of change that can take place in their own company. Often, uncertainty and the speed of change can bring real challenges to a sales environment.

We will now discuss:

- How sales people react to a changing situation
- Why companies want to change
- Why people can be fearful of trying to do something new or different
- The best ways of gaining commitment to the change process.

Not everyone interprets change in the same way. However, by adapting to change, sales managers are better preparing their sales people for the future.

FACTORS AFFECTING CHANGE

It is natural for people to feel uncomfortable if they believe their job role will become more difficult after new measures are brought in. As today's companies try to find ways to sell more of their products and services, changes will occur frequently. This might apply to factors affecting your company, or your industry. It could be due to government legislation, a company merger or site closure. Change is, therefore, about adjusting to a set of new and different circumstances.

It could be within your control or outside of it. It might be with your approval or without it. People understand and react to change differently. Your sales team will get used to a certain way of working and grow to feel comfortable in that environment.

INTERNAL AND EXTERNAL FACTORS

Change in a sales environment can be internally or externally driven. How the sales manager proposes to manage this will depend on what is being introduced. Some of the most common factors affecting change can be shown in the following way.

Internal factors affecting change:

- New sales personnel
- New products coming out
- Change in company structure
- Change in work procedures
- New sales targets
- Change of Directors in the company
- Your relationship with your colleagues

External factors affecting change:

- Demand for your product/service
- Change in the number of suppliers in your industry
- Suppliers to your company
- Company take over
- A recession or economic boom
- New technology
- Your own domestic situation

Some factors affecting change in an organization will be out of your control. However, part of the sales manager's role is to anticipate change and to prepare for the task of managing its impact on the sales operation.

Adapting to this both internally and externally is also about education. You can help by finding ways of sharing information with the team about current trends.

This can be done in various ways:

- A presentation at a team meeting
- Distributing copies of a relevant newspaper article
- Showing selected video/Compact Disc (CD) material
- Inviting a guest speaker to address the sales team.

INTRODUCING CHANGE INTERNALLY

Introducing change internally can come from the desire to:

- Increase sales/productivity.
- Improve the quality of your product or service, staff motivation and the relationship with existing customers, prospects and suspects.
- Reduce costs.

These initiatives may be driven by different levels of management in a company, depending on where the desire to change originated and why it is being sought. Whatever the reason for change and whoever is driving it, there is normally a pressure to consistently over achieve! This is the nature of selling and it can bring with it, a degree of stress. If this is well managed, then sales people will remain committed to the company. If it is not, it can create a loss of confidence and some of the team may even decide to leave.

A strong motivation to change something is often related to a company's growth ambitions/market share and how to increase it. Senior management may alter their strategy if they find it is not working. If an initiative is handled properly a team of sales people should remain motivated. There are a number of other factors that determine the success of any change process.

These will be based on:

- How effectively it is introduced
- Whether the sales team have been properly involved in the process
- What feedback the sales team receive throughout the process
- Whether they receive incentives and rewards for meeting new targets and implementing the changes properly.

All these factors demand a high degree of communication skills. The sales manager's task is to remove as much uncertainty as possible and to show clear leadership and direction.

POLITICS

The culture of your company is also a significant factor in managing change. A sales manager will need to assess how this is viewed by his/her team.

Their reaction can be understood by studying:

- The history of your company
- The industry you are in and your traditional markets
- The current influence of different departments and managers
- The average length of time sales people have been in their job
- Whether change is a common occurrence.

Every company has its own culture and way of managing it's staff. It is important for every sales manager to be aware of this. You should also make the sales team aware of the positive elements of any proposed change. By understanding the type of company you are working for, managing change becomes easier. No company is exactly the same, even if they sell the same type of product or service.

A sales manager can learn from the internal structure and the interaction between different managerial levels and different departments. Change is now part of a sales manager's everyday life. It can offer opportunities as well as cause uncertainty for the team. There are many factors affecting it. These have to be understood so that you can prepare yourself and the sales team properly.

ANALYSING A NEED FOR CHANGE

There has to be a good reason to do something differently and this must be communicated clearly by a sales manager. Constant change that is not understood and appears to offer no benefits can lead to confusion. This may affect each person's sales performance. Before you change something (whether you are the instigator or not), think about the consequences of it and how it is best managed. Some decisions will be forced upon you. This can mean that you have little or no control over them. But even if this is the case you can still try to manage this effectively.

ASSESSING THE SITUATION

Perhaps the first priority of a sales manager introducing new practices is to assess the current situation correctly. This means understanding the context – comparing the past to the present. It also looks at future possibilities.

The three phases affecting change are:

By considering these three factors you maximize your chances of successfully applying any new business practices.

UNDERSTANDING THE OBJECTIVE

If you are looking to make changes internally there are four main areas to consider that will affect you and your sales team? Any one of these areas might also affect another.

The four areas are:

- The work people do
- The existing structure of the company
- The culture of the company you work for
- The individuals who report to you.

In many ways analysing a new challenge is about preparation and planning. The degree of success you will have could depend on your interpretation and delivery of the proposed change. By sharing selected information with your sales team (providing this is possible) and getting their approval, you will increase your chances of success. It will be a test of your leadership skills and will require a degree of diplomacy and sensitivity.

A sales manager had to announce at the beginning of a New Year that targets had increased. At the same time, the team was also trying to cope with the introduction of an important new product. The manager decided to ask an experienced (and high performing) sales person to contribute towards the presentation and to focus on the positive aspects of the pay plan. The emphasis was on the potential for increasing income. Therefore, by discussing the issues with the team, the sales manager found it easier to gain their acceptance. His willingness to involve, listen and respond in this way enabled the changes to be more effective. That year, the district exceeded their new target.

LEVELS OF CHANGE

Part of the preparation and planning for any change will involve two factors:

- The degree of difficulty
- How long it will take to achieve specified goals.

This will largely be determined by the impact on different managerial levels and departments. It can take time for change to properly filter through to certain parts of a company. The diagram below illustrates the likely relationship between these two factors.

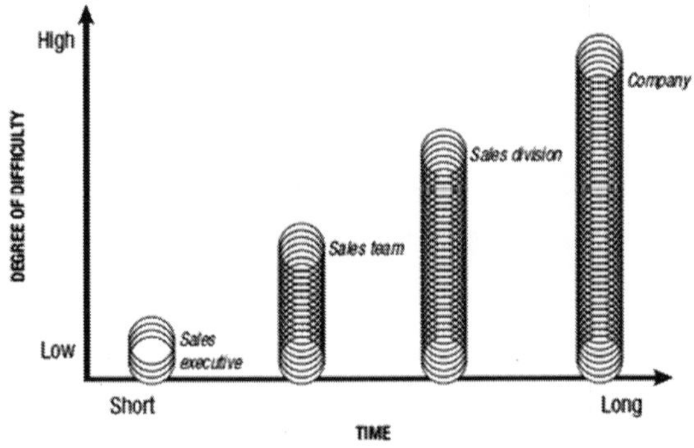

If a company introduces a high degree of change, it will take much longer to implement than something for one individual. A change to one part of a company or division can have an effect on other people in another part. A sales manager may not have all the necessary information to predict how long it will take for a change to work. But if they are to manage the situation successfully, they will need to find this out and assess the likely impact on their sales people. If two companies were to merge, the degree of time it would take to bring them together may be measured in months, perhaps years.

Introducing a change to an individual's working practice could take only a number of days or weeks. Sales managers increase their chances of achieving their objective if enough thought is given to the level of change required and its effect on people. Another factor to consider is how well something new is implemented. You should ensure that any changes affecting the sales team become part of each person's everyday behaviour. If this is not done, they have less chance of wanting to revert back to previous work routines. For sales managers, the success of managing a change may depend on three factors:

- The strength of their relationship with the sales team
- The relationship they have at different managerial levels
- How well they communicate with other internal departments.

In order to analyze a need for change it is important to look at the different roles of the people the change is designed for. You should also look at who is most affected by it and how you can make a person feel part of the process. People need managing in different ways and this must be taken into consideration. A correct analysis of the situation will help you manage changes more effectively.

RESISTANCE TO CHANGE

Many people are actually fearful of change. A new set of circumstances can make us feel uncomfortable and wary. There are normally three main responses to this.

These are to:

- Embrace it
- Accept it
- Resist it.

It is the third aspect that we will now deal with – resistance to change.

FORCING CHANGE THROUGH

You may be able to influence whether/how something should change. If this happens, you will have a certain amount of control over the outcome. However, many decisions involving change are made at a senior management level and involve a directive being given to the whole company. This can cause friction and negativity if people see the change as an imposition. They may feel that they have not been consulted or that there is little concern for their job role.

If any changes you make are met with resistance, the chances of success will depend on:

- The strength of character of the individuals concerned
- Your determination to see it through.

If the driving force of the change is stronger than the resisting force, it is more likely to be effective. It is unlikely that a corporate decision will be reversed. A sales manager will, therefore, be faced with the task of trying to achieve the right level of acceptance and commitment from the sales team. You might face resistance to a company directive and find it difficult to re-focus certain members of the team. Therefore, before taking any action, assess the degree of support within the sales operation and the strength of any opposition. For example, influence may be brought to bear through other people rather than direct action. The following table is one method of assessing the forces you are dealing with in this area. Change will be interpreted differently. Some people will see the change as offering them positive opportunities – they are the 'winners'. Others will see themselves as the 'losers'.

Relative power and influence

	Low	High
WINNERS	1. Tele-sales team *New income opportunities*	2. Senior account managers *See opportunity to increase income on other products*
LOSERS	3. Support team *Will have more sales support work to do*	4. Junior account managers *Commission affected*

By looking at change in this way, a sales manager is able to assess the impact of a new initiative. The telesales team: (1) will now be able to sell a number of products previously sold by account managers. They see this as an advantage. The senior account managers (2) have perceived greater income opportunities and will also support the change. The task will be to convince the support team (3) and junior account managers (4). If you can determine why people see themselves as losers or winners you can then develop a plan to help them.

For example, you may wish to get support from experienced members of the sales and support teams. With their co-operation the initiative will be more likely to succeed. The strength of someone's resistance will affect how you manage that person. Many people will have no clear opinion and may not see new work practices as a win or lose situation. These might include junior or new sales people who have no previous experience in the company. Their expectations could be lower because of this and you should find that they accept changes more easily.

REASONS FOR RESISTANCE

In order to manage change better, a sales manager needs to understand the reasons why someone is resisting. People resist for many reasons.

These include:

- They do not believe they will benefit: Sales people are trained to assess a situation independently. This can cause a degree of resistance if their perception of a situation differs from the management view. Suspicion and misunderstanding can set in when a sales person believes they will be worse off after a change has taken place.
- They do not understand the change: Sometimes company directive will not be communicated very well. If this is the case, sales people may not have fully understood it. They may not want to confront their fear of change and therefore choose to resist it.
- They do not like the change: If someone dislikes the change, it gives that person a reason to resist it – or ignore it!

- Resentment: Some might feel that the change has been forced upon them. People rarely like something that is imposed on them without consultation or agreement. Alienation arises from lack of involvement in the decision-making process. This can lead to disruption.
- They are tired of constant changes: Many companies are constantly altering day-to-day working procedures. This can cause frustration and a hardening of attitudes towards new initiatives. This can cause a reluctance to appreciate the benefits of a change.
- They may have had a previous bad experience: A bad experience resulting from a previous company directive may cause resistance to it. Someone may have disagreed with a previous change and witnessed a negative outcome. This will affect their attitude when interpreting the effect of future initiatives.
- Fear that a change may expose them: Many people resist change because they fear new skills will be introduced which will expose them. They fear that they may not be able to adapt to meet the new company expectations.

All of these reasons require opportunities for discussion and a sensitive response. This can be discussed individually or with the team.

The degree of resistance will be determined by:

- The strength of someone's personality
- The number of people involved (in resisting) their attitude
- The influence of individual team members.

If a sales manager can see that a majority of the team support the change, he/she can use this to influence those who still resist it. With the number of changes sales people are expected to make every year, many may be wary of new measures. You need to manage the change process carefully and you should not be surprised to meet some resistance. A skilled manager will analyze a situation before they attempt to implement a change. We can now look at ways in which to prepare for this.

INVOLVING PEOPLE IN THE CHANGE PROCESS

In order to introduce changes successfully, try and involve your line manager and your sales team in the process. This should make people feel part of it. You might not be able to control the change itself. However, you can use this to your advantage, as you are in the same position as your staff. A sales manager needs to be sympathetic yet firm. Involvement shows respect and concern. It will help you receive the support of your team. They will find it easier to understand if they feel that you are considering their interests as well as your own.

WAYS TO GAIN COMMITMENT

The main ways to gain people's support in the change process include:

- *Communication:* By talking to people as a group and on an individual level you will find out about any fears they might have. With this information you can gauge the reaction to a change and assess how it will affect your team's sales performance.

- *Education:* People often feel threatened by change if it means that they have to learn new skills. You may need to find out if training measures are going to be introduced or education provided. This can lessen the resistance and reassure people that they will cope in the future.
- *Group discussion:* Whatever measures are being introduced, they will still have to be implemented properly. Discussion with those who will be most affected can lead to them giving their approval.
- *Support:* People who worry about change may have concerns that can be overcome if they know that they have your support. Some people are too proud to ask for help at a time when they most need it. It can also be reassuring to know that your sales manager will support you during this time.
- *Negotiation:* For those people who are strong willed and who resist new measures, a degree of negotiation may be needed to gain their support. By reaching an agreement you increase the chances of the change being effective. You also reduce the chances of someone becoming uncooperative and a potentially destructive force. A degree of manipulation might be necessary. It could involve altering a person's role or offering them some incentive to influence them. You may be able to use persuasion as a way of trying to bring people round to your point of view.
- *Dominance:* This should be a sales manager's last resort. It requires a more forceful approach and could be a test of the respect and loyalty the team has for their manager. There are two key elements to this approach:
  - Describe their behaviorist effect, your feelings and your future expectation
  - To explain the reasons and benefits for the change and to reinforce the fact that it will go ahead with or without their co-operation.

This approach has advantages because it prompts an instant response and you have the opportunity of dealing with issues immediately. However, it can cause resentment and actually create further resistance. Your leadership skills will be called upon to manage this type of situation effectively. Ideally this approach will not be necessary and you will be able to try one (or a combination) of the methods we have described.

STEPS INVOLVED IN THE CHANGE PROCESS

No amount of planning and preparation can prepare a sales manager for every changing situation. However, if you are involved in making changes there are a number of steps to consider.

These are to:

- Analyze
- Prepare
- Involve
- Communicate
- Implement
- Monitor.

There are times when the steps will not come in this order. For example, you may decide to involve your sales team earlier in the change process. The key to involving any group of people is to be adaptable. If you can give them the opportunity to contribute, this might be enough to achieve their full co-operation. A sales manager's approach will have a large influence on how any new changes will be perceived. If you see this as an opportunity it will be reflected by many of your staff. It will set the tone for future behaviour and shorten the time taken for people to adjust.

SUMMARY

We have looked at 'Managing change'.

This included:

- Factors affecting change
- Analysing a need for change
- Resistance to change
- Involving people in the change process.

Change management' has become a common occurrence in business. The success of any company can depend on what to change, when and how often. Introducing new measures will often put a company in a stronger position to compete in the future. Sales managers need to be flexible, sensitive and adaptable when deciding how to manage change.

7

Change Management Process in the Era of Web

CHANGE MANAGEMENT STANDARDS

- All substantive changes to the IT Environment must adhere to the XX change Management process. A substantive change has the potential to affect the ability of users and systems to interact with each other.
- All changes must conform to the published guidelines that dictate the "look and feel" of the XX web environment.
- All web page content changes must have the approval of the web page owner prior to change implementation.
- All changes to the production systems within IT will have a corresponding set of documentation that describes the change, the business reason for the change and the disposition of the change. This includes emergency and exception changes.
- The risk and/or impact ratings of the requested change will determine which of the four phases of the change workflow will be required to promote the change into production. For "minor" changes only Analysis and Implementation will be required.
- Anyone with a valid XX Notes access will be able to enter a change into the Change Request process. Only authorized approvers will be able to accept a change request into the Change Management process.

STATUS OF CHANGES

The following status codes are used to reflect the status of a change request:

- *Open*: The change has been received and accepted but has not been assigned
- *In-Progress*: The change has been received, acknowledged and assigned. Work is in progress to fulfill the change request.
- *Approved*: The business and technical assessments have been completed and the change has been approved and committed to the change scheduler.

- *Rejected*: The change has been rejected and will be routed back to the Request for Service process and sent back to the customer with an explanation and a recommended course of action.
- *Closed*: The change request has been closed.
- *Canceled*: The change request has been canceled.

TYPES OF CHANGES

The Change Management Procedure applies to all types of changes related to the XX IT environment. The following is a description of each of the types of changes that can take place and the rules that apply to each.

- *Application Changes*: Changes to any application code that is running on or linked to by any hardware or software in the XX IT environment. These changes are typically made to enhance the function or performance of or to fix a known error in the IT application environment. These changes cannot be implemented without approval of the owner of the application and cannot be requested by any programmer other than the one assigned to the programme. Assignment of Risk Category Level of the change is to be a joint effort of both the owner and the Change Implementer.
- *Hardware Changes*: All XX IT and IT support equipment installations, discontinuances and relocations are controlled by the Change Management Procedure. This activity can be requested by anyone but must have the approval of the Operations Manager.
- *Visual Image Changes*: Changes to the "artistic" presentation of web pages are not required to make entries into the Change Management system. Changes to "Active" areas of the web page are required to use the XX Change Management procedure.
- *Software Changes*: The criteria for entering a software change into the Change process are based upon the effect that the changes may have on the IT support resources. If the changes affect the system, users or the support staff there is a requirement to enter it into the Change process. If the change is made for the exclusive benefit of the requester and if failure could not affect anyone else, that change would be exempt from the Change Process. For example, a change made by a programmer affecting a procedure or a programme under development on a test application requires no entry. However, when stand-alone test time is required on a production system, a change request form is required.
- Typically, software changes would include changes to the Operating System, Vendor supplied Programme Products, *e.g.*, Visual Studio, Java, etc. or common application support modules. However, during the last two and first five workdays of each month changes are restricted to emergency and critical necessities as determined by the Director of Information Technology.

- *Network Changes*: All installations, discontinuances and all relocations of equipment used for IT teleprocessing communications are entered into the change process. This includes all routers, switches and telephone lines as well as Personal Computers if they are connected to the network.
- *Environmental Changes*: Environmental changes normally involve the facilities associated with the IT Installation. These facility changes include items such as air conditioning, chilled water, raised flooring, security, motor generators, electricity, plumbing and the telephony system for voice and data. For example, when there is a planned weekend power outage initiated by the local power company this information is submitted to the Change Management Process a minimum of two weeks prior to the scheduled outage and communicated to management, staff and the user community.
- *Documentation Changes*: All procedural changes to the standard operating procedures will be implemented through the Change process. Also, all permanent deviations from the published schedule time for running of production applications will be communicated through the Change Management system.

CHANGE LEVELS

The following guidelines for definition of Change risk levels are provided for consideration during the planning cycle. It must be clearly understood that these requirements are the minimum for each of the defined levels. The Requester may wish to plan additional lead times, documentation or reviews to insure that targets can be met and planned implementation schedules can be achieved. All changes are tracked, correlated and used for management reporting, statistiXX, trending, etc., to identify when and where additional resources should be provided.

For any change that fails, the Change Requester must enter an explanation in the comments section of the Change Record for that change and notify the Change Coordinator. The Change Coordinator will then close the change with the appropriate close status. If the change is to be attempted at a later time, the Change Requester should reenter the change with the new date. Changes that cause a Platform outage will be reviewed at a Quality Measurement Meeting.

LEVEL E CHANGES

Emergency changes are those changes that are vital in order to ensure that IT's committed service levels are maintained. An Emergency change should not be used in order to bypass the appropriate lead-time for a change that has been entered into the system. Exception changes are those changes that are a result of a business need and must be installed prior to the required lead-time.

These types of changes proceed to the implementation phase when the requester's manager and the Director of Information Technology acknowledge that an Emergency or an Exception situation exists and authorize the modification planned.

These changes will be post-reviewed to assure successful implementation, along with identification of any external impacts or new requirements. Post-review will also evaluate the reason for the Level E change request and try to determine a way of eliminating this requirement in the future. The post-review will also evaluate if, in fact, the change addressed a real or a perceived emergency condition.

In all cases, the review must determine if additional action is required, what that action should be and who will be responsible for the action. Documentation requirements for Emergency changes are the same as any change. The Requester is responsible for meeting all requirements for the change documentation within one week of the implementation.

For non-application changes:

- Is the change needed to restore immediate service to the end user?
- Is the change necessary to fix an existing problem immediately?
- Is this a change that must be installed immediately but the need for it was not recognized early enough to be approved through the regular process?

For application changes:

- Must this change be done immediately to fix problems for jobs that ABENDed during the previous night or are required to run in order to bring up on-line systems?

What Types of Management Approval is Required for Level E Changes

Approval required by:

- Director of Information Technology or her designee
- Change Management Process Owner or his designee
- Manager of the user department requesting the change

Depending on the scope and impact of the proposed change, approval by one or more of the following individuals may be required.

- Operations Manager
- Application Development Manager
- Network & Technical Services Manager.

LEVEL 4 CHANGES

A Level 4 Change would have a major impact on IT services if a problem occurs during install. The install time is lengthy and the backout is very difficult or impossible. Level 4 Change Requests are to be entered into the Change Management Data Base at least thirty business days prior to the planned implementation date. The Requester or representative for a Level 1 change is required to attend the Change Communication meeting immediately prior to implementation so that any questions or concerns may be addressed. Whenever a Level 4 change must be expedited to address a critical timing situation, a special meeting must be held. To expedite a Level 4 change, all parties that may be affected by this change must be present or represented at the special meeting. It is the responsibility of the change requester to arrange the meeting and assure attendance by the required groups or individuals. If the required groups or individuals cannot be assembled, the change cannot be expedited and an escalation will be required.

How do you know that the change falls under Level 4

For non-application changes:

- From the end user's eyes, is it possible for the change to have a major impact on services if problems occur?
- Is the change visible to all end users?
- Is this a high-risk change?
- Is this the first time this change has been done?
- Is the change difficult or impossible to backout?
- Is it extremely difficult to install the change?
- Does the change involve a lengthy install time?

For application changes:

- Would failure of the job being changed stop the flow of all jobs for critical files or an application system?

What types of management approval is required for Level 4 changes

Approval required by:

- Change Review Board
- Manager of user department requesting change

Depending on the scope and impact of the proposed change, approval by one or more of the following individuals may be required.

- Operations Manager
- Application Development Manager
- Network & Technical Services Manager.

LEVEL 3 CHANGES

A Level 3 Change may impact a large number of end users. It is a high-risk change that requires a significant effort to backout. Level 3 Change Requests must be entered into the Change Management database fifteen business days prior to implementation. All Level 3 changes will be communicated via the Change Management reporting system. The requester or representative for a Level 3 change is required to attend the Change Communication Meeting immediately prior to implementation so that any questions or concerns may be addressed.

How do you know that the change falls under Level 3?

For non-application changes:

- Will the change be visible to a large number of end users?
- Is this a high-risk change?
- Has the change been done only infrequently?
- Will a significant effort be required to backout the change?
- Is it difficult to install the change?

For application changes:

- Would failure of the job being changed stop the flow of jobs for non-critical files or applications?

What types of management approval is required for Level 3 changes

Approval required by:

- Manager of user department requesting change
- Network & Technical Services Manager
- Change Review Board

LEVEL 2 CHANGES

A Level 2 Change is not transparent, but is minimal in risk and impact. It is the responsibility of the Requester to notify any areas of a potential impact. The change is a Level 2 if it requires an IPL of a system, subsystem or the restart of a critical component on a production system. Level 2 Change Requests must be entered into the Change Management database prior to the Scheduled Change Window being requested. The Requester or representative for a Level 2 change is required to attend the Change Communication meeting immediately prior to planned implementation so that any questions or concerns may be addressed. All Level 2 changes will be communicated via the Change Management reporting system and will be tracked and reported by the Change/Problem Coordinator.

Examples of Level 2 changes:

- Single fixes - APAR, PTF, etc.
- Low usage programme product upgrades, installations
- PARMLIB updates which require an IPL to implement
- Regular maintenance updates to system or application libraries
- Hardware Preventative Maintenance
- Data management to critical volumes

How do you know that the change falls under Level 2

For non-application changes:

- Will the change have only minor impact on services provided to the end users if problems occur?
- Will the change be visible only to a small group of end users?

- Is this a moderate risk change?
- Is the change relatively simple to install?
- Has the change been implemented successfully a number of times before?
- Does it require only a moderate effort to backout the change quickly?
- Will it require only an IPL, recycle of major application or reloading of an NCP to implement or backout?

For application changes:

- Is this the first time the job has been installed?
- Must this job be fixed to run tonight?

What types of management approval is required for Level 2 changes

Approval required by:

- Manager of user department requesting change
- Change Review Board

LEVEL 1 CHANGES

A Level 1 Change has little or no external visibility, no external dependencies or no operator intervention. There is no associated risk or impact with the change, either to the system if the change is incompatible or to the Requester if the change implementation is delayed. The change does not require an IPL or recycle of an application to implement or backout. Level 1 changes are entered into the Change data base and will be communicated daily to any affected areas where impact or interest can be identified outside of the Requester's own area.

How do you know that the change falls under Level 1

For non-application changes:

- Will the change have only minimal or no impact on services provided to the end users if a problem occurs?
- Is the change familiar or common to those who will implement it?
- Is the change reliable and low risk?
- Is the change easy to backout if a problem occurs?
- Can it be backed out without an IPL, recycle of a major application, or reloading of an NCP?

For application changes:

- Would failure of the job stop just this job?
- Is this a low priority job?

What types of management approval is required for Level 1 changes?

Approval required by:

- Manager of user department requesting change
- Change Review Board

CHANGE REQUEST FLOWS

ENTER CHANGE REQUEST FLOW

- *Description:* The Enter Change Request flow begins when a change request is submitted. In this activity, all required information about the change and supporting documentation is entered into the Change Management system. The change request should be submitted in accordance with the time frame required by the initial impact assessment.
- *Scope Inclusion:* All changes, including software, hardware, control mechanisms, configurations, environments, facilities, databases, business applications, processes, and procedures.
- Scope Exclusion:
  - Development activities that produce the actual change content.
  - The coordination of sets of changes.
  - Testing of the change package.
- Goal:
  - To introduce changes into the environment with minimal disruption to information technology and its users.
  - To communicate such that all affected users are aware of changes.
  - To log all changes into the change management system.
  - To ensure all pertinent change information is collected.
  - To ensure all changes meet lead time criteria.
- Start Trigger:
  - Change Request
- Stop Trigger:
  - Fully documented and approved change request.

Workflow Details for Enter Change Request:

- *Document and Submit Change Request* Collect system change request and begin preliminary review of the change.
- *Valid Request:* Determine whether or not to submit change request into change management system based on whether the request form has a managers signature, it is within IT responsibility, and filled in correctly.
- *Notify Requester Change Request rejected – phone call or e-mail:* If change request is rejected, provide a form of notification.
- *Notify Requester Change Request received – e-mail:* If change request is approved for the change management system, a change record is opened and a change number is assigned. A notification is auto-sent to the change requester by Peregrine.
- *Assign request to IT analyst:* Assign the change request to an initial analyst to review the change record.

- *Establish Initial Impact:* Determine impact of the change to the customer community. This will include times when service is not available, testing time, new procedures, new support requirements, and any other impact that may occur as a result of the change.
- *Conduct Technical Assessment:* Determine the feasibility of the change from a technical perspective. This assessment will include the amount of resources, level of knowledge, and skills necessary for the change.
- *Complete Change Record to Request Level:* Based on initial impact and technical assessment, determine the type and category level of change, and complete all descriptive fields. Additionally, the completeness of the change success criteria is validated.
- *Valid Request:* Based on the initial assessments, determine whether to perform this change. This decision is based on the change conforming to the strategy, resources being available, and whether or not it is already being worked on.
- *Close Change:* Mark change record as closed when it doesn't pass validation requirements.

ASSIGN CHANGE IMPLEMENTER FLOW

Description:

- The Assign Change Implementer flow begins once a change request has been documented and selected for the change management process. During this workflow, a change record is assigned to an appropriate owner, the change record is updated with this assignee information, and the change is sent to the assignee.

Scope Inclusion:

- All changes reviewed by the Change Review Board.

Scope Exclusion:

- Changes not accepted by the Change Management process or Changes not reviewed by the Change Review Board.

Goal:

- To ensure that change requests are assigned to appropriate implementers.
- To ensure that the change management workload is allocated by area of expertise.
- To balance workload within an area of expertise.

Start Trigger:

- Initial change record.

Stop Trigger:

- Initial change record is assigned to an owner.

Workflow Details for Assign Change Implementer:

- *Update Change Record w/ Assignee:* Assign the change an owner based on the classification of the change.

- *Send Change to Assignee:* Place the assignee information into the change record and send an e-mail notification to the assignee.

MONITOR CHANGE CALENDAR FLOW

Description:

- The Monitor Change Calendar flow determines the scheduling for changes to be deployed. During this workflow, changes are penciled into a calendar, and the schedule is monitored for changes that are completed or have run out of time in their scheduled change deployment window. If time has expired for a change then it can be escalated and rescheduled based on escalation standards.

Scope Inclusion:

- Changes that are formally put into the change calendar.

Scope Exclusion:

- Changes that are not formally put into the change calendar.

Goal:

- Monitor the change calendar for changes that have not been completed and have run out of time for the purpose of change escalation.
- Allow for changes to be rescheduled.
- Allow for changes to be removed from the change calendar upon completion.

Start Trigger:

- A change request has been assigned an owner and has been sent to that assignee.

Stop Trigger:

- A change is complete and removed from the calendar.

Workflow Details for Monitor Change Calendar:

- *Change Complete?:* Monitor the change calendar for change work that has been completed.
- *Time Expired?:* Determine whether a change record that is incomplete has run out of time.
- *Escalate Change:* Reclassify the change to a higher change category level if time has expired.
- *Reschedule Change:* Update the calendar with a schedule for the change after it has been escalated or if the change package is incomplete.

PERFORM ASSESSMENTS FLOW

Description:

- The Perform Assessments flow involves conducting both a business and technical review of the change package. The assessments determine if the change package is complete and can therefore continue through the change management process.

- Specifically, the perform business assessment flow involves validating the impact of the proposed change on XX from a business perspective, evaluating the completeness of the success criteria and communication plan and reviewing the backup/ backout/ recovery plans. The assessment looks at the proposed timing of the change and ensures that the customer's management has given the agreement necessary for the change to be approved and scheduled. Standards, business requirements, and SLAs are reviewed and a recommendation is made to approve, reject, or reschedule the change.
- The perform technical assessment flow reviews the completeness of the change plan, test plan, backup/ backout/ recovery plans, platform impact assessment, estimated install time, etc. from a technical perspective. The change success criteria are validated and the impact of the change to the environment is reviewed to ensure it has been accurately evaluated. Technical standards are enforced and a decision is made to approve, reject, or reschedule the change.

Scope Inclusion:

- All documented changes with a change category that requires a formal business or technical assessment.

Scope Exclusion:

- Changes with change categories that specifically do not require formal business or technical assessments.

Goal:

- To ensure that all factors have been taken into consideration in terms of the business aspects of the change.
- To ensure that all factors have been taken into consideration in terms of the technical aspects of the change.
- To ensure that everything required to deploy the change and to maintain service is included in the change request.

Start Trigger:

- Fully documented change record.

Stop Trigger:

- Assessed change

Workflow Details for Perform Assessments:

- *Business Review of Change Package:* Review the change package for the following points:
  - Ensure that the business requirements will be met.
  - Verify existence and completeness of backup/ backout recovery plans.
  - Verify existence of test plans, including the testers names and expected results.
  - Ensure that the change conforms to business standards and policies.

  - Determine whether the change conforms to service level agreements.
  - Review communication plan for change.
- *Technical Review of Change Package:* Review the change package for the following points:
  - Determine the impact on the technical environment.
  - Ensure that the change conforms to technical standards.
  - Verify the completeness of the change plan.
- *Package Complete?:* Make a decision on whether the package is complete based on the results of the business and technical reviews.
- *Return to Assignee:* If the package is determined not complete than the change is returned to the assignee and can be rescheduled.

APPROVE CHANGE FLOW

Description:

- The Approve Change flow is initiated as soon as both the business and technical assessments have been completed. If the change is approved, it is passed on to the next sub-process to finalize scheduling. If the change is rejected or determined to be rescheduled, it may be sent back to the business or technical assessment subprocesses once the necessary actions are taken. All parties that have been involved to this point in the process should be notified of the approval, rejection or rescheduling.

Scope Inclusion:

- All changes that have been forwarded for approval from a business and technical perspective and whose change categories indicate the requirement for formal approval.

Scope Exclusion:

- Changes with change categories that specifically so not require formal approval.

Goal:

- To ensure that appropriate approval is obtained for change requests.
- To ensure that the change record is properly updated.
- To minimize service interruption.

Start Trigger:

- Completed change record with business and technical review including recommendation.

Stop Trigger:

- Approval for change deployment.

Workflow Details for Approve Change:

- *Final Change Review:* Final review of change prior to acceptance and scheduling.

- *Accept Change?:* Based on the result of the final change review, determine whether to go ahead with or close the change.
- *Close Change:* If it is decided not to continue with change, then change record is closed by change coordinator.
- *Notify Requester Change Request rejected – phone call or e-mail*

IMPACT OF INFORMATION AND COMMUNICATIONS TECHNOLOGY CHANGE ON THE MANAGEMENT AND OPERATIONS OF ACADEMIC LIBRARIES

Information and Communications Technology (ICT) have transformed Library and Information services globally. The Internet has provided universal access to information. Technological innovation has dramatically increased the rate of conversion of knowledge, information and data into electronic format. Developments in the software arena has generated powerful knowledge management software which has transformed the way knowledge is organized, stored, accessed and retrieved.

The digital revolution driven by ICT innovation has transformed academic libraries fundamentally. It has impacted on every sphere of academic library activity *e.g.* the form of the library, collection development strategies, library buildings and consortia. Information and communications technology have changed the academic library in a profound way. Computers and networked electronic resources had become an integral part of the academic library the past decade. This has been underscored by the phenomenon of knowledge or information commons in academic libraries, which refer to a specific environment in the library where a designated number of PC workstations, networked to databases and other e-resources, are made available to students.

Every sphere of the academic library is being affected by ICT quite radically. No longer is the library the untouchable custodian of information. It is being shaken to its very foundation, in fact its existence is being threatened. The academic libraries' traditional role of information custodian had been reduced to that of being one of many information providers. Of all the information and communication technologies the Internet and particularly the World Wide Web with its graphical user interface, has had the greatest impact on the information revolution.

The number of electronic resources available on the Internet is growing at a phenomenal rate. One of the major search engines Alta Vista has reported in 1996 that it has indexed 30 million Web pages. By 1998 the number of Web pages indexed by this search engine has leaped to 90 million. According to Farrow wide spread publicity has lead to assumptions that the Internet will meet all user information needs and that there will be no need for professional librarian intervention in future between user and information resources. Moyo states that student expectations that all their research needs will be met online are on the increase. Not only do students expect to find the information they need online, they also expect it to be available in full text. According to Tam & Robertson these assumptions have lead to a reluctance to use the physical library materials and to a decrease of visits to the library. This phenomenon has fuelled fears of potential future job losses amongst librarians. Cheng explores the impact of information technology from an information ecological perspective. In information ecology the focus is not on information technology but on the human activities that are served.

Cheng cites Nardi and O'day who draw a parallel between the explosive growth of information technology and the consequential Information explosion and a volcanic eruption. This eruption is impacting on everyone existing with the information ecosystem. Cheng emphasize the importance that we as academic librarians are clear about the challenges posed by this situation and also the opportunities offered.

Cheng highlights some of the changes that took place within the information ecology:

- The way we gather information, organize it, disseminate and use information has changed.
- The evolution of the Web has lead to availability of masses of information, electronic journals and databases.
- The way information is being published is evolving rapidly *e.g.* it is threatening current practices.
- New problems have come to the fore *e.g.* the issue of intellectual property rights of e-resources.
- User expectations have changed. Users expect full text delivery to the desktop.

Pugh is of the opinion that the changes that library and information services face are of an unknown and unpredictable nature. He states that it is impossible for library managers to predict future trends accurately. He feels traditional change management techniques are inadequate to deal with the changing environment that libraries are facing. For him it is a scenario where one has to brace oneself for whatever occurs. Under these conditions it is crucial that libraries make optimal use of the entire workforce. It is of fundamental importance that customer service be given top priority. It is also essential that flexible organizational structures be created where workloads and responsibilities are shared and trust and responsibility are the norm rather than control. For library and information services in academic libraries to prevail under these conditions real leadership and real changes in management styles and organizational structures are necessary.

CONCEPTS DEFINED

Change

Robbins & Coulter defines change as any alterations in people, structure or technology. Change involves moving from the current state of things, the status quo, to a new state of things. It is therefore a process of moving from what is known to the unknown.

Information and Communications Technology (ICT)

Adeyoyin cites Bayode who defines ICT as "the acquisition, processing, storage, and dissemination of information by means of computers and other telecommunication equipment." The Wikipedia free Internet encyclopaedia defines "information technology (IT) or information and communication(s) technology (ICT)" as the "technology required for information processing. In particular the use of electronic computers and computer software to convert, store, protect, process, transmit, and retrieve information".

From the definitions it is clear that the terms IT and ICT are used interchangeably and has the same meaning. According to Jimba information technology is rooted in three sectors namely information technology, telecommunications and the media and these sectors are converging on one another.

TYPES OF CHANGE

Del Val and Fuentes define change along a continuum ranging from low-scope to high-scope change.

Evolutionary change

Evolutionary change is incremental by nature. Incremental change is smooth and happens gradually in an organized and predictable way. Incremental change tends to be small changes that lead to improvement but does not alter the operational structure of the academic library.

Strategic change

Strategic, revolutionary or transformational change leads to radical transformation and often changes the general organizational structure. Transformational change tends to be very traumatic by nature. It can be generated as a response to a major crisis or a complete change in organizational strategy or purpose. The outcome of this type of change can lead to organizational transformation to the effect that the organization might look completely different from what it used to be.

Discontinuous change

The academic library is confronted with change that is unlike anything it has been exposed to before. Management theorists use the term discontinuous change. Pugh notes that discontinuous change is different from revolutionary change that is change undertaken to generate rapid results. Discontinuous change is unique in the sense that established management practices are inadequate to deal with it, in fact there is no model, paradigm or pool of experience that managers can fall back onto. Graetz describes discontinuous change as turbulent, complex, traumatic, uncertain and of a revolutionary nature which requires different management skills to survive, supported by highly trained, motivated, flexible and multi-skilled staff that can be redeployed quickly and effectively if necessary.

There is a stark contrast between the clearly defined boundaries of businesses in the 1960's and 1970's and the postindustrial era that is characterized by volatility, complexity and uncertainty. "This type of random, discontinuous change - which, by definition, is fast, traumatic, and revolutionary – requires very different management and leadership skills if the challenges it presents are to be handled innovatively and opportunistically." What organizations need in order to survive is highly committed, skilled, informed and trained staff which is willing to give their all. Until 15 years ago change was incremental.

One could build on lessons learned before. Since then change had become discontinuous. In this climate old management behaviours are inadequate. New ways of doing things are imperative which questions the practices that worked in the past. Information services in the academic library are driven by ICT with all its uncertainties and instability. Change is occurring at a greater dimension than ever before. The volume, pace and complexity of change is increasing at an unprecedented rate. A comparison between 1970 and to-day reveals that in 1970 only 5 per cent of change within organizations was of a continuous nature. Currently 75 per cent of all organizational change is of a continuous nature.

IMPACT OF ICT DEVELOPMENTS ON STAFF

Managers often introduce drastic change without considering its impact on people. People respond to change in a myriad of ways. Any significant change will impact on people's self-esteem, their motivation to do well, their status or the stress they experience be it positive or negative. It is of vital importance that managers do not overlook people when dealing with an ever-changing environment. According to Morgan research suggests that 90 per cent of change initiatives fail because people are not taken into consideration. Change is good for academic libraries but its adoption requires tremendous input of physical, mental and emotional energy. After having to make intense inputs to accomplish change people expect to reach a plateau, a period for review and restoration of energy. The problem is that in the academic library this plateau had become non-existent because one peak follows after the other.

Phases people go through when exposed to radical change

Elizabeth Kubler-Ross has identified 5 stages that patients experience when confronted with personal loss or death. These stages are denial, anger, bargaining, depression and acceptance.

Conner has used Kubler-Ross's 5 stages as a basis and extended it to 8 stages.

- *Stability*: This is the phase just prior to change where everything is still normal.
- *Immobilized*: When confronted with radical change people initially experience shock, confusion and become disoriented. During this phase people are out of touch with reality.
- *Denial*: Conner defines denial as a refusal to accept reality. According to Fossum denial is a psychological defence mechanism that kicks in when individuals are confronted with radical change. It is a refusal to accept reality while the person's internal resources are being mobilized to eventually face a situation. To help staff to deal with this phase managers should use techniques designed to promote awareness that change has occurred or is in the process of occurring. The denial phase is a critical stage in the change process and people experience it differently. While some people are still dazed and out of touch with reality others may be ready to move on. Spending time on an individual bases with people struggling with this phase can be very useful.
- *Anger*: During this phase people experience anger and outrage. They become emotional, irritated, frustrated and hurt and may often lash out at those supporting them.
- *Bargaining*: This is a negotiation phase with a view to avoid the negative aspects of change. A typical example would be negotiating an extension of a deadline one is facing. This phase indicates the person is reaching a position where he or she can no longer avoid reality. This phase also demarcates the beginning of acceptance.
- *Depression*: It is normal for people to become depressed when confronted with major change that affects them negatively. This is a very unpleasant phase but is an indication that the individual has come to complete realization of the negative change being faced. It is an unpleasant phase but indicates another step towards acceptance.
- *Testing*: At this point a sense of control is regained. A person might explore how to set new goals.
- *Acceptance*: At this point people accept change. To go with an employee through the negative response model can be a costly exercise because people need support at every step of the way. However the cost of an employee failing to go through the process can be more costly to an organization.

Resistance

Managing change within the academic library is essentially about managing people since it is people that effect change. People who are such a critical factor in change implementation can also be a stumbling block to the change process by resisting change. Change initiatives are often shipwrecked because of resistance. Resistance leading to escalation in costs often delays change processes. Resistance is such a central element in change management that it deserves serious attention in the change implementation process.

Pugh states that one must neither fear resistance nor make efforts to avoid it. He states " the inertia of systems which have relied on doing things as they have always been done and achieving objectives through well-tried methods is not to be underestimated. It is part of the organizational instinct for survival and as well as comfort and complacency and it breeds resistance." The successful implementation of change in the academic library is by and large dependent on the attitudes of people to the change process. People respond in different ways to change. Whereas some people will experience change as an exiting and stimulating event others may find it frightening and intimidating and consequently resist change.

Causes of resistance

Pendlebury identified the following causes of resistance:

- Lack of realization of a problem.
- Not grasping the implementation of a solution.
- Outright rejection of a solution as it is seen as the incorrect option.
- Fear of the outcome of change.
- Lack of interest.

This kind of behaviour is often the result of a vision not clearly communicated or staff's unwillingness to face up to the demands of change. Kirkpatrick identifies the following additional reasons why people resist change:

- *Security*: Fear of potential job losses.
- *Financial*: Fear of loss of income.
- *Pride and satisfaction*: Technological innovation might make jobs and skills redundant.
- *Freedom*: Structural changes might impact on freedom of decision-making.
- *Authority, responsibility and status*: Restructuring might lead to a loss of authority and responsibilities.

Resistance tends to manifest itself in many different ways. Conner distinguishes between overt and covert resistance. Overt resistance is open and can be constructive. Covert resistance is submerged and can gain momentum unobtrusively and ruin a project. Fossum describes covert resistance as a passive-aggressive form of resistance. It is difficult to manage because on the surface a person appears to do nothing but is often busy sabotaging a project through negative statements. In major change there will always be resistance. Creating an environment where people can openly express their fears will go a long way to minimize resistance. Managers need to be aware that resistance often manifests itself in an increase in absenteeism, reductions in quality, decreased productivity, strikes or slowdowns and increase in grievances.

STRATEGIES TO FACILITATE CHANGE WITHIN THE ACADEMIC LIBRARY

The prevailing organizational culture will determine how easy or complex it will be to communicate the need for change, share the vision and get people's opinions and participation. In an open culture communication is easiest. The leadership style, the trust people have in top management and the extent to which people are able to openly express themselves is of cardinal importance. Managers who have successfully implemented change understand that resistance is a natural reaction and would encourage it rather than suppress it. They would even reward people for open resistance in a constructive manner.

Fossum states that clear and open communication about pending change is crucial. Managers must not allow people to hear via rumours or the grapevine or the media about pending change. They should be open and upfront about pending change. Hearing from a third party will undermine trust and credibility. When communicating change it is important to send out positive and optimistic messages. Conner is of the opinion that effective leaders can change people's mindsets to a realization that meaningful change is not only essential but also possible. Morgan argues that buy-in is crucial in change management. If staff can take ownership of change, it will bolster commitment and assist in overcoming any obstacles.

It is also crucial to involve staff in the decision making process. Participation will break the management versus staff syndrome. Instead of letting management do the problem solving it is useful to involve staff at all levels in this process. Managers must be careful not to make assumptions about the acceptance of change. It is better to get accurate feedback through interviews or surveys.

Techniques to make change positive

Change creates conflict but the negative energy generated can be turned in constructive energy. Managers should realize that conflict in itself is not necessarily negative. It creates an opportunity to do creative problem solving with the staff. Conflict must never be taken personally. If people disagree managers should see it as an opportunity to find a more elegant solution that more staff members will find acceptable. People should be encouraged to be honest about how they feel and support one another. Managers should maintain their sense of humor. It is essential to cultivate an atmosphere that will transform negative issues of conflict into positive constructive energy.

Celebrate success

It is important to sign-off change to ensure closure and enable people to move on. It need not be a celebration in the real sense. It could be a scenario where the team is thanked for their contribution. It helps to let people see the big picture. In that way they will see smaller change events as temporary unpleasant things to deal with and move on. If change events are seen as individual unrelated events it can lead to resistance.

ACADEMIC LIBRARY STRUCTURES

Organizational structure can be defined as "one of the interrelated components that define any organization referring to the definition of individual jobs and their relationship to each other as depicted in organizational charts and job descriptions." It clarifies how information is distributed, and jobs are organized.

For decades the hierarchical structure of management was regarded as the most efficient way of managing an organization. This system worked well in and environment where the future was predictable and librarians were in the driving seat. Hierarchies were not designed to foster creativity and lead workers to self-fulfillment. It is therefore very difficult to introduce fundamental change within hierarchical structures which are naturally resistant to change.

In an effort to bring about reorganization within organizations institutions try to either modify the existing hierarchical structure or replace it with something else. Deming as cited by Mullins states that management systems still prevalent today have had a destructive impact on people. According to Deming "people are born with intrinsic motivation, self-esteem, dignity, curiosity to learn...

" Qualities such as these are undermined by a management style that reward top achievers and punish those that do worse. Managers that exhibit such management styles use disapproval as a negative control measure. This approach leads to a climate where staff performance is primarily directed at pleasing their superiors and that inevitably lead to average performance. According to Pugh managers have a natural tendency to maintain the status quo.

They would instinctively fall back on models and practices that worked in the past. The volatile nature and unpredictability of information services is forcing managers to adopt new management styles.

It is beginning to dawn on people that the bureaucratic way of management is becoming outdated and that change will be more effectively achieved through education, sharing, motivation, teamwork and coaching. Moran states that unprecedented change has forced managers to re-evaluate structures. Customary practices designed to maintain organizational stability are being questioned.

To cope with change, organizations have started flattening structures to induce more flexibility within those organizations. These new structures being adopted have decreased levels of hierarchy, increased flexibility and resulted in diminishing boundaries between departments.

Issues to consider when introducing new structures

Management theorists are very reluctant to prescribe to a particular structural model but advise that structure should rather be designed to meet organizational needs and goals. Organizations should try and learn as much as possible from others who have implemented organizational change. They should never introduce a structure simply because it is being used elsewhere but always to meet specific organizational needs.

Of cardinal importance is to determine how people within the organization will adopt the new structure. Al-Ansari share the following points learnt from a process of restructuring at Kuwait University library. Before implementing a process of restructuring it is important to have clear vision, goals and objectives with the focus on service delivery.

It is useful to establish a core team to lead the restructuring process. It is vitally important that senior management support the process *e.g.* a deputy vice-chancellor. It is important to involve the entire staff component, listen to their inputs and concerns since ownership by the staff is vital for successful change implementation. Staff development programmes should be part of the process to prepare staff for new functions or roles they may be involved in.

After implementation it is important to critically analise the performance of the academic library within the new structure. Managers often do not adapt easily to the flatter less bureaucratic structures that are generally being adopted. Even staff members at lower levels experience this problem. Generally it is very difficult to introduce change that goes against prevailing organizational culture. Proper planning is needed to take the organization from the existing structure to the new one.

Employee input in developing such a strategy is crucial. Research indicates that organizational transformation had been most successful in scenarios where employees had maximum input. Finally evaluation is necessary after change implementation to determine its success. In reorganized libraries structures are always flatter resulting in manager's roles reverting from directing to coordinating. The prime purpose of reorganization is to create a more effective organization.

Reorganization results in academic libraries becoming learning organizations. The learning organization is characterized by staff empowerment, is team based, decentralized, practices participative management and information sharing. In the learning organization the person closest to a problem has the responsibility and authority to deal with it. Tom Wilson as cited by Moran states that the academic library is in bad need of reconstruction. To Wilson academic libraries were essentially designed to manage physical artifacts. The rise of the Internet has completely transformed the way information is created, distributed and accessed.

The e-journal is a typical example. Johansen and Swigart as cited by Moran states "we had outlived the usefulness of models from the Industrial era but don't yet have robust organizational models for the information era". It is therefore of paramount importance that academic librarians continuously re-evaluate current structures and through an experimental process adopt new models. Moran states that for people who advocate restructuring there is good and bad news. The good news is that people understand that technological change will compel fundamental organizational change. The bad news is that there is a lack of urgency. Generally organizational change appears to be incremental rather than radical.

IMPACT OF ICT CHANGE ON ACADEMIC LIBRARIES

Anita Lowring as cited by Herrington is of the opinion that the Internet has made information access and retrieval both simplistic and complex. Information retrieval systems are being designed to suit the needs of end users and therefore try to simplify the process. Simultaneously however the user is overwhelmed with so much information resources and choices that the process becomes complex.

This creates a situation where the users need skills and knowledge in terms of search strategies and conceptualisation. Herrington is of the opinion that information literacy instruction at the point of need can be very effective. Wood & Walther is of the opinion that unlike popular believe the Internet will not completely replace the skills of professional librarians but rather make them indispensable.

Changes in the job description of academic librarians

An overview of the core competencies required by academic library and information workers gives one an idea of how dramatically information and communications technology has changed the library profession.

Cheng identifies the following core competencies needed by the future librarian:

- Good communication skills.
- Should be more than just computer literate and should have a good understanding of ICT and its relation to information resources.
- Should have an in-depth understanding of organizational and user needs that is research based and should organize library resources to satisfy those needs.
- Competent in Web publishing techniques.
- Skilled in manipulating metadata to organize digital information.
- Skilled in training users in the use of e-resources.
- Skilled in filtering, evaluating and appraising Internet information.

Wood & Walther identifies another quality required, an in-depth understanding of what information resources are available on the Internet, as well as insight in terms of its reliability and scope.

The changing nature of the academic library

ICT is busy transforming the nature of academic libraries. A variety of terms such as hybrid, digital and virtual library are used to refer to the academic library. A digital library can be defined as "a managed collection of information, with associated services, where the information is stored in digital formats and accessible over a network".

The virtual library has been defined as "remote access to the contents and services of libraries and other information resources, combining an on-site collection of current and heavily used materials in both print and electronic form, with an electronic network which provides access to, and delivery from, external worldwide library and commercial information and knowledge sources". Hybrid libraries are libraries that provide access to both electronic resources and paper-based resources. From the definitions it is clear that most of today's academic libraries fall in either the hybrid or virtual category.

The library of the future is unlikely to be a physical entity as we know it but would probably be a Web portal providing access to information. The emphasis will be on access to information rather than physical ownership. Akeroyd supports this view and states that as a physical space entity the library, as we know it is unlikely to prevail in a digital environment. One reason for this is that because of Web access the digital library is accessible from anywhere.

Changes in the information seeking behaviour of users

Academic librarians have a good understanding of the tremendous value of printed and electronic resources available to students at academic libraries. Academic library users do not necessarily share this insight. New generation academic library users have a preference for Web resources rather than visiting the library.

Hiller as cited by Callinan observed in 2002 that University of Washington students would visit the library to study rather than using books and periodicals. Seiden et al. as cited by Callinan reported that students from Skidmore College in New York had a definite preference for digital resources. Research done on undergraduate engineering students in 2004 revealed that they would turn to the Internet as the primary resource for information for their projects. Moyo refers to a scenario where users were asked what they expect from an academic library service.

They responded as follows:

- All resources should be available in full text and be printable.
- The library service should be fast and easily accessible.

- 24/7 availability of a virtual reference service.
- Wish to do all library transactions online.
- Web resources that is easy to use and Web search engines that meet information needs.

What is clear is that new generation academic library users prefer the convenience of digital access above reliance on assistance from librarians. This preference for the Internet poses a serious challenge to the academic library which has to move from a paradigm of the library as a physical entity to a library where the users do not have to come to physically to make use of it's services. Electronic access to information resources does have many advantages *e.g.*

- Multiple access which implies more that one user can access a resource simultaneously.
- Lots of resources are available in full text.
- 24/7 access which means users can access resources remotely *e.g.* from off campus or from dormitories.

One of the disadvantages of remote access from an academic library point of view is that users are not always aware of the fact that they are using library resources. One user stated: "No, I don't need to use the library, I use Internet resources". Despite the apparent preference for digital content the need for access to high quality digital content remains constant. Greater cooperation between library and faculty is necessary to develop ways to connect users and high quality digital materials.

IMPACT OF ICT ON COLLECTION MANAGEMENT

Collection development can be defined as the selection and acquisition of library materials based on current and potential user needs. Collection management goes beyond this. It is concerned with managing the utilization, storage and accessibility of a collection. Collection development can thus be seen as a subdivision of collection management.

Academic librarians find themselves in an era of unparalleled access to information. The latest edition of Uhlrich's has indicated the availability of more than 172 000 journal titles. Although this appears to be a most ideal situation it is not because the financial resources available in acquisitions departments have not necessarily increased. The sheer volume of information available also makes selection of the most suitable information a complex task.

The impact of electronic resources has made collection management a very complex and challenging task. There are budgetary constraints, numerous formats, ever changing user needs. Collection management implies involvement in tasks such as analysis of needs, negotiation of contracts and evaluation of resources. There was a time when the size of an academic library collection determined its stature. At that time the library's resources were generally adequate to meet most of its users needs. Since then the academic library has exchanged the ownership model for an access model where physical location becomes completely irrelevant.

Access versus ownership

Information and communications technology has had a fundamental impact on library collection development policies. Academic libraries had traditionally applied an ownership or just-in-case approach to collection development. The premise was that users would need the material and make use of it. Having the material available in the library would also provide immediate access to it than having to borrow it from a third party.

The cost of maintaining collections and increased demands for more information had forced academic libraries to reconsider the ownership model and adopt another model. Unparalleled price increases and shrinking budgets had ushered in a new model called access or just in time where the focus is to give the user the information that they need when they want it.

Cost

Technically it is more cost effective to produce an e-resource, for example an electronic journal, because the first copy costs are reduced. There is also savings in terms of packaging, delivery and storage. In practice these savings have not lead to reductions in the cost of e-journals. It has been suggested that the academic library adopts a pay-as-you-use approach. This make sense according to research done in 1997 that indicated that 22 per cent of science articles published in 1984 were never cited for the next 10 years. In the social sciences this figure goes up to 48 per cent.

Storage space

With the access model there is no need for storage space *e.g.* back copies. Moahi cites Cooper who states that the storage cost per single copy is between $25 and $40. Calculations to determine JStor pricing lead to the conclusion that the cost per single volume was between $24 and $41. When costs for re-shelving and maintenance were included, the estimated cost rose to $45 per title per year for a core journal and $180 per title per year for a large research library.

Enhanced access to information

One of the benefits of ICT is enhanced access to library services and resources. The academic library can expose its users to a much larger collection than it can house physically because users can access information remotely. With online access it is possible to accurately measure utilization of e-resources and that is invaluable in determining which resources to purchase.

It is easier to search e-resources and access speed is greatly enhanced. Other advantages are that users can simultaneously access the same resource, and there are no incidences of lost copies or mutilated issues. Singh is of the opinion that a paradigm shift is taking place within the academic library as more academic librarians are doing collection management rather that collection development. The focus is rather on interpretation of information rather than selection. Librarians are becoming knowledge managers rather than collection managers.

Digital preservation of data

One of the major costs facing the academic library is the cost related to the conversion and preservation of information in digital format. The cost of this process amounts to $1 per page. This does not include the cost relating to the annotation for indexing purposes and the cost of conversion of audio-visual material. One of the problems with converting records into digital image is the fact that the technology used to store these pages as a digital photograph results in large files which have storage implications and place demands on band-with. Funding allocated to preservation of digital material is generally inadequate.

This has to do with expectations that the costs of digital preservation over length of time might be very high. It is also difficult to forecast cost in terms of how long to retain digital material in an archive and computer architectures needed to access material. Preservation of digital materials poses many challenges. It is further complicated by the fact that computer technology changes at an unprecedented rate. There are concerns that changing interfaces, standards, formats and operating systems will render it impossible to read today's computer discs at some point in future. The implication of this is that one needs migration strategies to move data to new operating systems and structures or have scenarios where computers can simulate data structures and operating systems of previous eras.

This scenario will make digital preservation prohibitively expensive. A great deal of current research into digital preservation is based on overcoming the technical issues to ensure long-term preservation of digital content. The issue of digital preservation initially came to the fore as an impending crisis. Fears were expressed that large portions of our cultural heritage were in danger of disappearing forever. Examples were cited of Web sites available today that might be gone to-morrow. Although digital materials are more fragile by nature than analog materials the risk varies within different categories of digital materials. Although it is true that a Web site currently available may disappear overnight, the same does not apply to electronic journals.

This realization has transferred the focus from the immediate rescue notion to an approach that sees digital preservation as part of a carefully planned digital access management process. One way academic libraries can deal with digital preservation is through cooperation. Through cooperation various institutions can share costs. Another advantage would be that it would reduce redundancy. Because of the fragile nature of digital materials libraries cannot put off decisions to preserve digital information *ad infinitum*. Time is of the essence.

Unlike a book that can be repaired or rebound, once a digital file becomes corrupt it may be impossible or prohibitively expensive to restore the data. Another problem facing the academic library is the long-term preservation of digital information. There are questions concerning the long-term stability of digital information stored on disks and tapes. There is the potential of these media deteriorating over a period of time. Another way digital preservation is approached is by letting the vendors do the preservation. These days there are also escrow repositories *e.g.* Elsevier has agreed to provide the National Library of Netherlands with a copy of Science Direct which the National Library will maintain and make available should Elsevier be unable to do so.

ELECTRONIC RESOURCES

ICT has fundamentally changed academic library collections. Forever gone is the era when an academic library's physical collection determined its stature. In the modern networked technological era the emphasis has shifted from ownership of physical resources to access to electronic resources that are globally accessible.

Internet information

There are huge amounts of unedited information on the Internet. There are countless Web sites and no single listing of them all. There is also the phenomenon of Web sites disappearing overnight that create problems in terms of access.

The invisible Web

Academic library users make use of search engines such as Google and Altavista to find information on the Web. As a result they are only exposed to a small portion of the Web called the "Publicly Indexable Web" These students are only exposed to Web pages accessible via hyperlinks. Search engines do not index Web pages that requires authentication or Web pages behind search forms.

The Web consists of two components namely the "Publicly Indexable Web" also referred to as the visible Web and the invisible Web. The invisible Web refers to all those information resources available yet not indexed by conventional search engines yet accessible via the Web. Masses of information available via the invisible Web are found in subject databases. Most of the databases that academic libraries make available to their users resort under the invisible Web *e.g.* EbscoHost and Eric. Conventional search engines can find databases such as EbscoHost but cannot access them. Search engines can only find content that was indexed by their software called spiders or crawlers. The problem is that they only index Web content available in formats such as HTML and PDF. Michael K. Bergman in year 2000 in a paper on the invisible Web for an Internet Search Company called Bright Planet suggests that the invisible Web is 500 times larger that the visible Web with approximately 550 billion documents.

The issue of quality of resources available on the visible Web

The Internet had become a very important research tool for academic endeauvour. Slaouti as cited by Stapleton notes that the relevance and importance of the Web as a research tool should not be underestimated. There is a stark contrast in the way resources are published on the Web versus traditional publishing. In the traditional print environment publishing generally was done by a publisher hence a controlled environment that impacted on quality as well as the scope of the audience being reached.

The open nature of the Web, the development of sophisticated search engines, browsers, Web creation and publishing software and easy access to networks via low cost connectivity has developed the Web into a tool that can be easily utilized by the masses for publishing purposes, people who were formally shut out of the publishing process. This has lead to a flood of Web publications of variable quality. During the 1990's library scholars recognized this dilemma and suggested criteria to evaluate Internet resources *e.g.* authority, purpose, coverage and objectivity and accessibility. These days a single search can yield hundreds of thousands of items.

The unfiltered nature of Web resources has made evaluation of these resources essential. One often finds that unlike in traditional printed media, e-resources found on the Web often lack important criteria such as author or date. Web pages because of its non-linear textual nature has added new effects to the search process such as sound, videos and access to thousands of items by clicking a mouse. These new elements imply that new sets of skills are required on the part of the researcher.

Reference works

According to Moyo reference statistics in academic libraries are plunging. At the same time electronic access of these resources are increasing. This tendency can be ascribed to the fact that users can access these resources remotely via the Internet. Internet connectivity and e-resources had become absolutely essential for the new reference service paradigm. One of the key elements of e-reference service success is that the service is available at the point of need. The tremendous growth in the use of online reference works has created a need within the academic library to develop services to support this type of service. Academic libraries are turning to on-line real time reference tools also referred to as ORR to support students remotely.

The Pen State University library has more than 300 databases that students may access. On-line real time reference support is used to assist students at the point of need. E-reference works share all the benefits of e-resources *e.g.* 24/7 remote accessibility, concurrent access for multiple users and the potential for online updating to keep content up to date. Electronic communication had become the primary mode of communication in e-reference services. Online chat had become the method of choice. Some e-reference application providers have added *Voice over IP* (VOIP) to their products which enable voice dialogue with the library user. E-reference services have many advantages *e.g.*:

- Availability via the Internet
- Service at the point of need.
- Easy for people who are unable to come to the academic library *e.g.* the physically disabled.
- 24/7 availability.

Moyo cites Stormont who states that online real time reference support is very labour intensive. In order to cope academic libraries have adopted a distributed staffing model where the load of the service is shared among various libraries.

E-Journals

The e-journal can be defined as "a version of the traditional print or paper-based journal which is disseminated electronically in some form or other directly to the end user." Although e-journals had been in existence since 1976 it became prominent during the 1990's. Since it's inception in 1665 the printed journal remained the primary vehicle for communication among academics and researchers. The advent of the Internet transformed publishing radically as it made it possible to publish cheaply. Internet also made access universally available. Because of the Internet academics and researchers became more creative and productive.

Cost factors

There had been major increases in the cost of journal subscriptions during the last two decades. According to Rao between 1986 and 1996 the average increase per journal subscription had been a whopping 147 per cent. This state of affairs had been laid at the door of the commercial publishers. Moahi states that simultaneously there had been a significant increase in the number of science and engineering journals published. Because of ever decreasing budgets academic libraries are unable to purchase the titles they deem necessary.

Falk cites McCabe of Georgia Institute of Technology stating that publishers offer libraries bundled packages of e-journals under the pretense that it is cheaper but these deals actually inflate prices. Moahi is of the opinion that a consequence of these bundled deals is that academic libraries end up with titles they do not want or need.

Despite the fact that publishers have substantial cost savings on first copy production of e-journals and also save on distribution costs, these savings are not passed onto their customers. Cost of e-journals tend to be similar or higher that their printed counterparts. What further complicate matters are the fact that provision has to be made for connectivity and desktops, which means additional costs. Aggregate publishers also tend to drop titles without prior consultation with academic librarians.

Academic library's response to publishers

Despite general expectations that e-journals should be cheaper than printed versions publishers maintain the status quo by maximizing profits. Publisher's attitudes have forced academic institutions to take a tougher stance against them.

Recently the Senate of the University of California instructed the library to sever all ties with Elsevier, *e.g.* cancel subscriptions and cease submission of research papers if negotiations with them fail to obtain a reduction in the price of subscriptions.

Harvard University has cancelled their Elsevier subscriptions of bundled journals. The Senate of North Carolina State University urged that excessive prices from publishers be resisted. Four North Carolina universities had signed a deal for a bundle of 1300 journals in 2003 with the proviso that no titles are dropped. When these institutions wanted to renew subscription for 2004 the price was so exorbitant that they all cancelled the deal. Cornell University and the University of Missouri also cancelled subscription with Elsevier for the same reasons.

Three North Carolina universities have drafted policies to only forward research to publishers whose journals are reasonably priced and widely accessible. In the event of this not being possible they will include an "authorization to publish' clause in contracts that empower the author to retain copyright to reproduce research for academic and research purposes. Kansas University includes a clause in their contracts that give them permission to use their research for teaching and research purposes and retain the right to make it available on public accessible Web sites.

Open access journals

The open access initiative is aimed at making scholarly research freely available via the Internet. Open access journals are journals available on the Internet for academics, researchers and the general public. The open access journal philosophy received a tremendous stimulus with the birth of the *Public Library of Science* (PLoS). At its conception 30 000 scientists promised their support in terms of submitting research. The first open access journal to emerge was PLoS Biology in the year 2003 which was received with great enthusiasm. In the publishing arena the Biomed Central publishing house embarked on free access to peer-reviewed journals. Recently the *Directory of Open Access Journals* (DOAJ) made open access journals available covering different languages and subjects.

Open access archives

Many leading universities are setting up electronic archives as depositories for their research output and are granting access to it. There are plans in progress to use theses archives as a platform to provide open access journals. The *Massachusetts Institute of Technology* (MIT) has made software freely available for managing electronic archives. Currently there are approximately 140 universities that have established open access archives.

The number of journals held in these archives have increased from 20 000 in 2001 to 1.3 million in 2003. Although this is still fairly insignificant compared to the 2 million peer reviewed journals printed annually it nevertheless sends out a clear warning signal to commercial publishers of what is to come. In Europe the Open Archives Forum was established. The goal of this forum is to establish electronic archives and make it globally available.

E-Books

There are various definitions for e-books but e-books are essentially published books and reference materials that were digitized and are distributed electronically. In the year 2000 e-books were heralded as the new publishing revolution. One market research company predicted that by 2005 there would be 1.9 million users. Forrester Research predicted that income generated from e-book sales would increase from $9 million in 2000 to $414 million in 2004. Unfortunately e-book popularity never rose to expected heights. Despite the negativity surrounding e-books it had not demised completely.

There are still some companies dealing with e-books that are profitable and experiencing growth. One of the first commercial e-book services, NetLibrary, was established by OCLC in 1998. The NetLibrary collection has since grown to over 400 000 titles. The shortcoming in the NetLibrary system is the fact that an e-book can only be used by one user at a time. Questia, another commercial e-book service went live in 2001. Their target market was students and they employed librarians to manage collection development. By 2003 Questia had more than 400 000 titles from more than 200 publishers.

Advantages of e-books

E-books have numerous advantages. There are no printing, storage, warehousing and shipping costs. Consequently e-books can be published at costs much lower than conventional books. Additional advantages are online availability, keyword-searching capability, cross-referencing, adjustable fonts, electronic bookmarks and imbedded audio. Updating e-books will be easier than re-editing conventional books. From an academic library point of view benefits would include cost savings in terms of shelving, binding, circulation, overdue notices and management of fines.

All needed would be a person to maintain the collection and a person to manage user accounts. Print collections in academic libraries are very expensive to acquire and maintain. E-books are also environmentally friendly in the sense that no tree pulping is necessary to for its production. The flaws in current e-book technology will be overcome. When that day dawns e-books being much cheaper to produce and publish than printed books as well as economies of scale will tip the balance in favour of e-books.

Disadvantages

The devices needed to read e-books are relatively expensive *e.g.* hand held devices, PC's and laptops. In order to minimize piracy publishers use proprietary hardware devices and software platforms. This lack of universal standards is a problem. The question many ask is whether e-books pose a threat to libraries. Can it eventually put libraries out of business. Although e-books did not take off as well as expected within the public domain, the use of e-books at schools, colleges and universities are rapidly increasing.

Use of e-books

Falk refers to research done by Forrester that indicated that 4 million e-books were sold at campus stores in year 2000. Forrester forecasted that by year 2005 e-book sales should have increased to 140 million. Research indicates that students are developing a preference for e-books. At the University of Rochester Rush Rhees Library course reserve section students were exposed to printed books and their e-book equivalents. Statistics compiled on a weekly base indicated a three to one preference in favour of the e-books.

SOME OF THE PROBLEMS RELATING TO ELECTRONIC RESOURCES

Online full text implies availability of articles rather that the entire content of a particular journal. The complete contents of a publication are seldom put into a full text database. This implies that an author one might have seen in a physical publication may not be traceable in electronic format. This predicament also applies to archiving where there is uncertainty about the percentage of a journals content that is archived in digital format. Another concern is that the academic library in a sense has lost control over the resources it make available to its users.

When academic libraries subscribe to aggregator databases *e.g.* EbscoHost or ProQuest they subscribe to a service, a list of titles bundled together of which many are useful and many not so useful. One of the problems is that aggregators sometimes drop titles. Typically this would happen when publishers withdraw all their titles. In such cases those publishers' titles get dropped as was the case with Sage Publications. The Chronicle of Higher Education has reported in 2003 that Elsevier has been removing articles from aggregator files because of various reasons *e.g.* scientific misconduct, plagiarism and errors. On the Web there are masses of information available. With search engines *e.g.* Google or Yahoo one may find useful information and record the URL or title. There is however no guarantee when one wants to revisit the site that it may still be available.

Sites on the Web sometimes disappear overnight. An organization may have merged with another one or the host server might have become dysfunctional. The quality of information available on the Web is also sometimes questionable. Any individual with access to the Web and basic hardware and software can publish on the Web regardless of whether the person's views are factually correct.

On the Web are more than an estimated billion Web pages and this create problems for users of the academic library to distinguish between what is useful or not. Another problem is that search engines cover only a small portion of what is what is available on the Web. There are lots of information behind firewalls and thus inaccessible. Many crawlers of search engines only focus on html and ignore graphics. Generally ASCII files will not be found. To assist users academic library services should try and inform users when sites have relocated or are no longer available.

CHANGES IN THE EDUCATIONAL ENVIRONMENT

ICT have changed every fibre of society including education. Lifelong learning has become essential. A very competitive working environment has influenced this. Even educational methodologies have changed. Greater interaction between learner, educator and material is becoming the norm. Learners have greater choices in terms of curricula.

The 24 hour networked classroom became reality leading to the birth of the virtual library. Network technologies and new educational methodologies have empowered learners, given them a greater measure of control and participation in the learning process and enabled network interaction with both fellow students and lecturers.

Change in institutions of higher education will compel academic libraries to change accordingly. The most dramatic change according to visionaries will take place in distance education. This was a direct influence of the Internet. When the day dawns when distance education becomes the norm, universities the way we know them may vanish and virtual libraries may become a reality.

Recently an author warned that the railroad managers overlooked the fact that they were in the transport business. He noted that universities must remember they are in the education business and not the campus business. If campuses disappear libraries will disappear. There are already examples of cyberspace universities *e.g.* Phoenix. If academics should fail to restructure their institutions' external forces will do it. Of cardinal importance is to focus on what education wants to achieve and how one can fulfill it. Survival of the academic library will depend on its ability to continuously reshape and reorganize.

Distance education

New technologies driven by ICT innovation have enhanced the virtual delivery of academic programmes and stimulated unparalleled growth of distance education at institutions of higher learning. The phenomenal growth in distance education technologies has lead to an escalation in the availability of online academic programmes and a tremendous increase in remote users. In order to support these programmes academic librarians have developed excellent portfolios and programmes for remote students.

One aspect that is neglected is evaluation of these programmes. What is of critical importance is to establish how these programmes are used, which ones are used more frequently than others and why. Monash University library in Australia provides online curriculum content to their students all over the world. The university library provides online access to more than 440 online databases, 140 000 e-books and 20 000 e-journal subscriptions. Apart from full text databases and e-books the university library also provides digital audio recordings of lectures that become available minutes after conclusion of lectures.

According to Ho Monash University library has made a paradigm shift to a complete new service module that utilizes e-commerce technologies. Moyo is of the opinion that the transformation in distance education has created a need for distance librarianship.

Changes in scholarly communication

The rising of the Internet and subsequent Web during the 1990's has resulted in the decline of the printed journal as the principal medium of scholarly publication. The costs of journals have increased dramatically driven by commercial publishers trying to control research content. This resulted in depriving many researchers of access to needed resources. The Web has also made fast and easy electronic publication possible and has increased direct communication between researchers.

Publishers immediately started making electronic versions of printed journals available on the Web. This was however seen as perpetuating the status quo in a new medium. Scholars started seeing in the new technology the potential to develop a new model for publishing research and an opportunity to return ownership of scholarly output to the rightful owners of the research.

These sentiments were driven by shortcomings in existing scholarly journal publishing which were:

- The time to publish an article was to too long.
- The existing model demanded transfer of copyright to the publishers.
- A too rigid peer review system that tends to favour publication of authors from the more prestigious institutions.
- Journal prices had become unaffordable.

One of the outcomes of this dissatisfaction was the birth of the e-print which is essentially an electronic version of a research paper.

E-prints lead to the development of e-print repositories that are an archive of e-prints accessible to the public. Some of the advantages of e-print repositories are the reduction of publishing barriers, increased visibility of research and rapid dissemination of research results to a wide audience.

Consortia collaboration

Initially libraries got involved in consortia in order to reduce costs particularly with regard to the acquisition of e-resources. Consortia development is thus an attempt to maximize limited resources through co-operation and resource sharing. In the consortia scenario the emphasis is on access to information rather than ownership. Consortia collaboration provides more power when it comes to negotiating contracts. It also provides a platform for libraries to co-operate in terms of services. Nowadays libraries also turn to consortia to provide advice and guidance in complex decision-making. The input of consortia is also valuable in terms of evaluating e-resources in terms of quality, different options *e.g.* whether to subscribe to journals or pay article-by-article.

The South African scenario

In terms of network infrastructure South Africa is not on par with first world countries where consortia cooperation is very effective. For the establishment of an information society in South Africa proper connectivity infrastructure is an absolute prerequisite. There is an uneven distribution of telecommunications infrastructure across South Africa stemming from the political ideologies of the apartheid government.

This inequity is also prevalent in South African academic libraries. Institutions for the privileged white people were well financed and resourced under the apartheid regime. Institutions for blacks were under funded and thus under resourced; hence the distinction between advantaged and historically disadvantaged institutions. Because of this there are great differences in wealth and the collections of academic libraries. In South Africa there are 5 academic library consortia.

- CALICO (Cape Library Cooperative) based in Cape Town
- ESAL (Eastern Seaboard Association of Libraries based in Kwazulu-Natal.

- FRELICO (Free State Libraries and Information Consortium) based in Free State
- Gaelic (Gauteng and Environs Library Consortium) based in Gauteng.
- SEALS (South Eastern Academic Libraries System in the Eastern Cape.

Essential for the development of successful consortia is low cost tariffs coupled with high bandwith connectivity. Academic institutions constantly engaged with government agencies to achieve this ideal. Library consortia can also be invaluable in assisting member libraries with change management because "An organization needs external coaches to catalyze, guide and facilitate a change process", the reason being that people within the academic library are sometimes to closely involved with daily activities to see things objectively. An outside view often helps to see things in the right perspective.

ICT MANAGEMENT ISSUES

Libraries are caught midstream between print versus a digital setup. To navigate the transition from print to digital remains enormously challenging. Rapid ICT development had resulted in lots of incompatible systems being used within libraries. To manage ICT is a complex and daunting task. To select the right ICT technologies is a major management issue. It is very difficult in a world where hardware and software changes at a phenomenal rate.

The shift in the academic library from printed resources to electronic resources that are accessible via campus networks or remotely and the fact that users can even request services via the network has lead to a decline in users visiting the library. The growing electronic nature of the academic library is resulting in it becoming less visible as a physical entity to its users. What is also disturbing is the fact that users are often oblivious to the fact that they are using library resources because of the seamlessness of access.

Users are not aware of the fact that to make those resources available are costly in terms of subscriptions, infrastructure and staff. Academic libraries need to find a way to reverse this scenario of the library loosing its visibility. Hooper suggests that the academic library should use ICT to stimulate interaction between user and the library. It should be done in such a way that the user could identify with the academic library providing the service and experience a sense of ownership. As a starting point the academic library can interact with the user relating to loans, database searches and other services available. It is also important to create an environment where the user can provide feedback relating to service shortcomings and suggestions that could lead to improvement.

Stakeholder relationships are also very important. It is of vital importance for the academic library to ensure that their operations dovetail with the strategic goals of the university it supports. In these days where accountability is becoming the norm it is essential to run operations in such a way that the academic library at any point is in a position to provide proof of the value of its services as a return on investment made by the university authority.

MANAGERIAL CHANGE FOR THE SURVIVAL OF LIBRARY AND INFORMATION CENTRES IN INFORMATION AND COMMUNICATION TECHNOLOGY ERA

DIGITAL LIBRARY AND ITS IMPACT

The origin of ICT has changed the performance and service pattern of every institution and organization, library is not excluded from it. Impact of ICT has transformed the 'traditional library' into 'automated library'. 'Digital library' and 'virtual library' are also the gift of ICT. Many libraries have been serving as hybrid libraries. A library digital is an organized collection of electronic resources.

Digital library is a very complex and dynamic entity. It has brought phenomenal change in the information collection, preservation and dissemination scene of the world. It is a complex entity because it is completely based on ICT systems and the concept is of recent origin. Its main aim is to provide ready access to the required information at a right time to the right user with right information.

The collection of digital library are not limited to document surrogates they extend to digital artifacts which cannot be represented or distributed in printed formats. Therefore, digital library is not a single unit, but a complex of multiple units that provide instant access to all information, for all sectors of society, from anywhere in the world. Therefore, in this context, the digital library must cope up with the changing technology, information seeking behaviour of its user, user needs etc. The day has come to adopt change management at par with information management in the library.

CHANGES IN LIBRARY AND INFORMATION CENTRE MANAGEMENT

Due to fast-paced technological change and new skill requirements, information professionals are increasingly required to renew their skills and practice in order to gain an awareness of technological advances. As a result, the profession itself exists in a state of flux alongside these emerging technologies, with traditional roles being increasingly subsumed by new skills and working environments, and, therefore, job descriptions.

Thus, information professionals are now expected to be aware of and capable of using and demonstrating emerging ICTs. There is a need for additional training to augment the traditional skill and knowledge base with a competency in ICT use. Information professionals must be flexible, and adopt traditional skills to incorporate the requirements of technological advances.

Given the current situation, wherein ICTs are being continuously updated or introduced and traditional formats are being replaced or supplemented by digital formats, it seems likely that there will continue to be a need for regular training for information professionals.

There is also an increased focus on communication skills, with more people involved in the electronic information environment. Information professionals are being called upon to work closely with ICT users and providers – including IT staff – and to work in collaboration with others in the profession. Some groups of users lack the necessary IT skills to obtain quality information and information professionals will therefore be called upon to act as both educators and intermediaries. Given these circumstances, information professionals are required to have additional teaching and communication skills. Thus, it is vital for those in management positions to recognize the imperative of *continuing professional development* (CPD) and ensure that the staff is proactive in maintaining up-to-date levels of expertise. The significance of CPD in this milieu has been acknowledged by both the United Kingdom's *Chartered Institute of Library and Information Professionals* (CILIP) and the United States' *American Library Association* (ALA).

Certain active roles are necessary for change management to:

- Establish the quality goals of the library: Library and Information Centres (LICs) should aim to establish the quality goals for qualitative service to its user community.
- Provide the resources to their library: LICs should provide all necessary resources suitable in the ICT era to manage the LICs in a better way.
- Provide the quality-oriented training to the library staff: New generation library staff are almost trained with ICT applications to LICs but old staff and others who are novices in such applications need quality training because without quality training library staff are unable to provide automated services.
- Stimulate quality improvement in the day to day activities of library: This is the age of competition. Like other organizations, to survive the LICs, top management should stimulate the staff for quality improvement in the day to day activities of LICs.
- Review progress of the library activities: Higher management should review the progress of library activities to maintain the quality and quantity of assigned job to the staff.
- Give recognition to library staff: Top level management should recognize the operational level library staff for quality performance, without which they will be demoralized to perform the job in a better way.

With the change in environment the objectives need to be revised to face the challenges of future. Over a period of time, due to the impact of technological advances, research and development, economic, social and political factors, the objectives also tend to change. To adopt these changes, it is essential to state objectives and functions of information system in changing context. For this purpose the following steps should be followed.

Structure Related Changes

The structure related changes in libraries and information centres may include:

- *Change in the work design*: The work design of a traditional library is not similar to modern automated library, so a change in the work design is compulsory for the success of automated library.
- *Change in the basis of departmentalization*: There are various departments in university and research libraries. In case of automated library, book acquisition, classification and cataloguing, circulation, serial control assignments are being done through computer with specific software instead of doing manually. Besides these departments, modern library has other departments like barcoding, RFID tagging, OPAC/web-OPAC, e-journals, e-books, CD-ROM, digital library, touch screen kiosk, server maintenance etc.
- *Change in the number of operation levels to perform various activities, routine work of library staff*: As there is a major change in the processing and service departments a change in the number of staff in the lower level or operational level management has become essential.
- Change in the plans, programmes, policies and procedures to and improving integration among various sections: Due to changse in the pattern of service; plans, programmes, policies and procedures and integration within various departments it is very essential to cater to the service in a better way.
- *Change in the span of management and levels of management for effective co-ordination mechanism and flow of task*: Since the nature of job of modern automated library is more complex than traditional library, it is very difficult to manage large number of operational level staff under one middle level manager. In view of this span of management should be narrow and levels of management should be changed because top and middle level management have to be directly linked with every department to perform each department's functions in a better way as well as for effective co-ordination mechanism with every department.
- *Change in line-staff and functional authority, work group relations between people and functions to improve their ability*: Line positions are responsible for accomplishing the organization's primary objectives; they have final authority to make decisions. Staff positions, on the other hand, provide suggestions and advice for the line positions

but cannot, theoretically make decisions for the line positions. An organization seeks to keep authority for decision making in the positions accountable for results and to preserve a clear chain of command from the top to the bottom of the organization. But in the automated library system there should be no hurdle between line and staff position because anyone who is aware about a particular system can give his advice. It helps to improve the work group relation as well as the ability of the all levels of management.

Structural changes affect relationships among the organizational positions and in the interactions among internal departments, the reporting mechanism, interactions of all sections in the library and the functional relationships.

Changes for Technological Advancement

The technology refers to the sum total of human knowledge providing ways to do the things in a better way with the help of techniques. It may include inventions and techniques affecting the ways of doing things.

Thus, technology related changes may include:

- Use of new machines and equipments for developing new services or modifying existing services: Many new machines and equipments, *e.g.* computer, server, barcoding equipments, RFID tools are necessary for developing new services or modifying existing manual services. So the awareness about the use of new machines, equipments and tools is very essential.
- The procedure of doing things which may result in change of work process: The methods and procedures of doing new tasks should be changed in context of old library system. So that the work process is not disrupted.
- Introduction of technological devices like computers and computer related technologies: Introduction of technological devices like computers and computer related technologies is necessary for automated library. Without computers and related technologies, we are unable to cater to services in automated library system.
- Change in the existing techniques for making or doing the things in effective way or adoption of new techniques for creative work: Automated library is ICT oriented and some technique is involved in every work. So existing techniques of traditional library management should be changed and adoption of new techniques is very essential to carry out every task and service in automated library environment.
- Change in the methods of using new tools equipments and products: In the traditional library system, there are only a few equipments like fumigation chamber, catalogue cabinet, book rack, cardex, journal display rack etc. But now computer terminals, server, barcoding

equipments, RFID tools etc. equipments and products are being used, so it is very natural to change the methods of using new tools, equipments and products.

The change in the technology affects the nature of work and activities, organizational structure, the processes and the people's behaviour.

Task Related Changes

Technology related changes determine the ways to complete the task effectively and efficiently. Task related changes helps to achieve major gains in terms of cost, service and time.

Task related changes may include:

- Identifying the steps involved in performing tasks: It is very necessary to organize meeting with library staff at all levels to identify the steps to perform the tasks effectively.
- Task identification: Every task should be identified to depute the staff who is efficient in that work. So, proper task identification is the key factor to perform the task properly and to serve the user community in a better way.
- Significance of task related changes in attaining the organizational and institutional objectives: As the nature of library has been changed so it is very significant to change the task which is relevant in changed atmosphere to attain the organizational and institutional objectives.
- Identifying the skills and abilities required for the changed task: It is very natural to identify the skills and abilities required for the changed task and to assign the specific job to the specific staff that is suitable for that particular job.
- Improving both quality and quantity of work/ service: For the satisfaction of our customer we should improve our quality as well as quantum of day to day work/service.
- Bringing cost-effective solutions through maximum use of available resources: Cost-effectiveness is concerned with the value. It asks, "This is what the service costs. Is it worth it?" So effectiveness of the resources is the key to maximum use of available resources.
- Improving the work performance: Quality training of staff is very essential to aware the task of each and every personnel effectively which improves the work performance.

People Related Changes

Change in any factor has an impact on human resources and human behaviour. In the context of Library and Information Science, the people related categories include:

- *The library staff*: In case of library staff, it requires the corresponding changes to be made in the skills, abilities and the performance of the employees.

According to Jones, Gareth R. 'Typical kinds of change efforts directed as human resources include...

- New investment in training and development activities so that employees acquire new skills and activities: New skills and activities are required in automated library system so new investment in training and development is essential. Library can get the fund from UGC for this purpose by making a systematic and comprehensive proposal
- Socializing employees into the organizational structure so that they learn the new routines on which organizational performance depends....': Top management should meet with middle and operational level management to become aware about the every bit of work with theory and practical and to assign the job to every personnel as well as time required for this purpose. Through socializing the employees organizational efficiency can also be increased.

Accordingly the change may include:

- Change in skill levels of the workforce: Skill levels of each and every employee should be changed to cope up with new task.
- Change in the training programmes to improve performance levels: Training programme should be organized in a scientific way to sensitize the employee about every practical aspect of work and service. So change in training programmes is essential to improve performance levels of the staff.
- Change in attitude and values: Change in attitude and values is a must for better performance in work and service in the changed library environment.
- Change in behaviour and interaction pattern: As the library scenario has changed from traditional to automated one, behavioural and interaction pattern regarding work and service should also be changed.
- Change in technology requires different skills of the operator: Presently, library is technology controlled. To cope up with this change, the library personnel requires different skills to carry out their own task because it is very difficult to work properly for a unskilled staff.
- Change in the structure requires change in their position, their authority, responsibility etc.: Due to shift from traditional to automated library, structural change is required. For this purpose positional, authoritative and responsibility change is necessary for better performance.
- The readers: Readers/users/customers are our prime focus. To serve the right user to the right information at the right time, we have to

organize our resources systematically through which they can collect their information himself/herself. Such a systematic arrangement helps us to work and serve the users with less human resources.

Any change in the processes demands that it should be communicated to the readers to enable them to adjust to these changes. Readers are ultimately getting the benefits of all the technological advances, procedures, services, activities as well as other resources for their satisfaction in the libraries and information centres.

Changes in Library Policies

Change in the objectives and functions of the library and information system by the planning body would directly impact the existing plans and policies of the library. Accordingly, change in plans and policies become essential. The developmental plans and policies should be in conformity with the objectives and functions of library and information system as well as the institution it serves.

Changes in Objectives and Functions of Information System

The information system in the changed environment shall aim at:

- Ensuring maximum use of all available resources: Top management should ensure maximum use of all available resources through cost-effective solutions.
- Promotion and development of all units in the library: In the automated library, to cater the service to the users in a right way, it is very essential to develop all units in a proper way.
- Better communication of ideas to achieve the objectives in an ever changing environment: To communicate every new ideas to all levels of management is essential to achieve the objectives in constantly changing environment of library work and service.
- Minimizing the time, cost and efforts involved in all the activities, processes and functions: Top level management should plan with with staff at middle and operational level for proper coordination of every function with minimum time, cost and efforts because duplicity of activities, processes and functions increases the time, cost and efforts.

In order to achieve the newly stated objectives as per the requirement of changing circumstances, certain functions are to be carried out. These functions may relate to adoption of latest technologies, use of modern tools and techniques, updating professional skill, ability and knowledge through education and training, future prospects of change in goals, objectives and functions etc.

"Librarians will need to be ready for competition and prepared to find new ways to make their skills and services distinct from those offered by the competition from media companies, publishers, internet companies, intermediary service providers and also from technologists parking on traditional library territory with technical names for old fashioned library ideas".

PROCESS OF MANAGERIAL CHANGE IN LIBRARIES AND INFORMATION CENTRES

The various steps involved in a planned change are:

- Identifying need for change: In the changing scenario of library, it is very essential to identify every need of users for effective planning and execution.
- Elements to be changed: It is very natural that the elements in traditional library and automated library are different. So top level management should foster awareness about every element of change and communicate the relevant elements to every unit.
- Planning for change: Every organization/institution plans the total work procedures for proper execution. So, for the sake of efficiency all the steps for success in the changing scenario.
- Assessing change forces: It is very essential to assess the change forces for success of the new project/assignment.
- Change actions: Each and every action should be changed for proper functioning of every unit for better work and service.
- Feedback: This is very important aspect of every organization/ institution. Without feedback system, an organization/institution cannot assess their customer needs and information seeking behaviour as well as their satisfaction level.

Above steps in a planned change can be applied for managing the changes in libraries and information centres.

Identifying Need for Change

Various external and internal factors necessitate change in libraries and information centres. This change may be made in staff, library building or internal layouts with infrastructural facilities, the hardware and software requirements, activities and services etc. While identifying the need for change, the following should be considered:

- How the change will have an effect on the system, space, staff, services, activities etc.?
- What will be the frequency and nature of change?
- How it will impact use of information sources for study, research and development?
- How it will impact users information requirements?
- How it will have an effect on the procedures, policies and programmes?

Identification of need for change depends on:

- Readers' expectations;
- Changing objectives of libraries and information centres according to changing environment;
- Policies and programmes to be implemented to achieve these objectives; and
- New challenges created by change in technology.

These steps will determine the rationale why change is essential and if change will be made, whether it will create problems or not?

Elements to be Changed

What elements of the libraries and information centres should be changed is to be decided for managing the change. It will be decided on the basis of the need for the change as well as the objectives of the change. The identification of need for change will determine the base for why change is essential whereas this step will specify what elements in the system are to be changed. Generally change is required in the structure, technology, hardware and software requirements, database design, IT infrastructure, skills of the staff, and nature of library services etc. The nature and extent of change in the elements will further depend upon the nature of problems being faced by the libraries. Sometimes a change in one element may require change in another element *e.g.* a change in any activity from manual to machine may require change in staff and their skills but at the same time change in the structure of the libraries may also be required.

Planning for Change

Planning for change includes deciding in advance about:

- When to bring change?
- Who will bring change? and
- How to bring change?, Etc.

In the libraries and information centres change is usually required in the structure, technology, staff and services. Careful planning for bringing change in these elements is essential because 'Planning looks at how the librarians and information scientists can develop the means to locate the resources which are most relevant to the need of users community, integrate these resources into their infrastructure, adopt the necessary technology and finally to anticipate the future trends in changing circumstances".

Accessing Change Forces

Various internal and external forces enable us to bring change. To manage the change effectively, it becomes necessary to ensure the co-operation of the people to create an environment in which change will be accepted by all. Change force, both internal and external, is an important consideration to anticipate and respond properly for the problems in the existing system. Success in managing the change is possible only when we assess change forces and their impact on the efficiency and effectiveness of the existing system. If the effect of these change forces can be accessed, it becomes possible to take necessary actions for change.

Actions for Change

A distinguished social psychologist, Kurt Lewin, developed what he called 'Action Research' which happens to be a more motivational approach and a more evolutionary one. According to him 'since most change efforts flounder because carefully expected plans are ignored or sabotaged', this first step is critical:

- Seek change when the people who are going to have to effect the changing are distressed and feel they have a problem.

The next step involves getting them to accept some procedure for exploring how the problem can be solved. The manager...gets the department to establish a study or mini research project on the problem:

- What kind of information is needed?
- Who will collect it?
- Who should analyse it and how; what is secret and what can be openly discussed?

The manager may have to help to get the project underway. It may require some outside technical aid, a survey, a review of old records, interviews with people in the departments This step means the manager must:

- Get consensus on what kinds of data and what method of collection and assessment the group will accept as valid for evolving a solution to its problem.
- Make feedback then, the critical element; it becomes a catalyst to the people who will have to change, emphasizing the discrepancy between what they believed and the reality of the situation.
- Aid people in coping, skill transfer, experimenting with new methods.
- Then the cycle is repeated.

Usually, the initial efforts won't be roaring successes; there will still be unresolved problems, and some innovations won't work as planned or hoped. So the group which is the focus of change is encouraged to continue:

- Research/study the work flow problems – by collecting data
- Evaluate and feedback
- Consider further innovations
- Get help in implementing these
- Then check how these are working.

The manager's role is one of felicitato, so that the individuals will be motivated to change, in contrast to being told to change; Further, the process is, or ought to be, a continuing one'. The Lewin model has suggested that every change requires three steps – "the first step is unfreezing – individuals who will be affected by the impending change must be laid to recognize why the change is necessary. Next, the change itself is implemented. Finally, refreezing involves reinforcing and supporting the change so that it becomes a part of the system. These steps can also be effectively applied in library and information centres to manage the change. At first step, the library staff as well as the reader community have to be informed about why change is essential to improve efficiency of services.

At second step, they have to be made aware about new methods of working, new procedures adopted, their expected roles in changed environment etc. We have to conceive them to recognize the basic purpose of change and ensure that they fit into the new organizational change for the benefit of all. At third step, integrating change into actual practice, the staff as well as readers has to adapt to the new environment with improved performance. They have to be protected from reverting back to the old and traditional behaviour.

Feedback

Feedback is essential to ensure that changed pattern is going to achieve the objectives with minimum time, money and energy and determine whether follow-up action is essential to ensure success of change in management. The impact of change is to be measured in terms of attainment of objectives, improvement of services, readers' increased satisfaction, employee motivation and increased level of efficiency and effectiveness of each activity, product and service.

8

Role of Motivation in Leadership and Change Management

INTRODUCTION

Motivation is the activation or energization of goal-orientated behaviour. Motivation is said to be intrinsic or extrinsic. The term is generally used for humans but, theoretically, it can also be used to describe the causes for animal behaviour as well.

This stage refers to human motivation. According to various theories, motivation may be rooted in the basic need to minimize physical pain and maximize pleasure, or it may include specific needs such as eating and resting, or a desired object, hobby, goal, state of being, ideal, or it may be attributed to less-apparent reasons such as altruism, selfishness, morality, or avoiding mortality. Conceptually, motivation should not be confused with either volition or optimism. Motivation is related to, but distinct from, emotion.

INTRINSIC AND EXTRINSIC MOTIVATION

Intrinsic motivation refers to motivation that comes from within the individual instead of from outside. Intrinsic motivation has been studied by social and educational psychologists since the early 1970s.

Research has found that it is usually associated with high educational achievement and enjoyment by students. Intrinsic motivation has been explained by Fritz Heider's attribution theory, Bandura's work on self-efficacy, and Ryan and Deci's cognitive evaluation theory. Students are likely to be intrinsically motivated if they:

- Attribute their educational results to internal factors that they can control,
- Believe they can be effective agents in reaching desired goals,
- Are interested in mastering a topic, rather than just rote-learning to achieve good grades.

Extrinsic motivation comes from outside of the individual. Common extrinsic motivations are rewards like money and grades, coercion and threat of punishment. Competition is in general extrinsic because it encourages the performer to win and beat others, not to enjoy the intrinsic rewards of the activity. A crowd cheering on the individual and trophies are also extrinsic incentives.

Social psychological research has indicated that extrinsic rewards can lead to overjustification and a subsequent reduction in intrinsic motivation. In one study demonstrating this effect, children who expected to be rewarded with a ribbon and a gold star for drawing pictures spent less time playing with the drawing materials in subsequent observations than children who were assigned to an unexpected reward condition and to children who received no extrinsic reward.

SELF-CONTROL

The self-control of motivation is increasingly understood as a subset of emotional intelligence; a person may be highly intelligent according to a more conservative definition, yet unmotivated to dedicate this intelligence to certain tasks. Yale School of Management professor Victor Vroom's "expectancy theory" provides an account of when people will decide whether to exert self control to pursue a particular goal.

Drives and desires can be described as a deficiency or need that activates behaviour that is aimed at a goal or an incentive. These are thought to originate within the individual and may not require external stimuli to encourage the behaviour. Basic drives could be sparked by deficiencies such as hunger, which motivates a person to seek food; whereas more subtle drives might be the desire for praise and approval, which motivates a person to behave in a manner pleasing to others.

By contrast, the role of extrinsic rewards and stimuli can be seen in the example of training animals by giving them treats when they perform a trick correctly. The treat motivates the animals to perform the trick consistently, even later when the treat is removed from the process.

MOTIVATIONAL THEORIES

The incentive theory of motivation

A reward, tangible or intangible, is presented after the occurrence of an action with the intent to cause the behaviour to occur again. This is done by associating positive meaning to the behaviour. Studies show that if the person receives the reward immediately, the effect would be greater, and decreases as duration lengthens. Repetitive action-reward combination can cause the action to become habit. Motivation comes from two sources: oneself, and other people. These two sources are called intrinsic motivation and extrinsic motivation, respectively. Applying proper motivational techniques can be much harder than it seems. Steven Kerr notes that when creating a reward system, it can be easy to reward A, while hoping for B, and in the process, reap harmful effects that can jeopardize your goals. A reinforcer is different from reward, in that reinforcement is intended to create a measured increase in the rate of a desirable behaviour following the addition of something to the environment.

Drive-reduction theories

There are a number of drive theories. The Drive Reduction Theory grows out of the concept that we have certain biological drives, such as hunger. As time passes the strength of the drive increases if it is not satisfied. Upon satisfying a drive the drive's strength is reduced. The theory is based on diverse ideas from the theories of Freud to the ideas of feedback control systems, such as a thermostat. Drive theory has some intuitive or folk validity. For instance when preparing food, the drive model appears to be compatible with sensations of rising hunger as the food is prepared, and, after the food has been consumed, a decrease in subjective hunger. There are several problems, however, that leave the validity of drive reduction open for debate. The first problem is that it does not explain how secondary reinforcers reduce drive.

For example, money satisfies no biological or psychological needs, but a pay check appears to reduce drive through second-order conditioning. Secondly, a drive, such as hunger, is viewed as having a "desire" to eat, making the drive a homuncular being—a feature criticized as simply moving the fundamental problem behind this "small man" and his desires. In addition, it is clear that drive reduction theory cannot be a complete theory of behaviour, or a hungry human could not prepare a meal without eating the food before he finished cooking it. The ability of drive theory to cope with all kinds of behaviour, from not satisfying a drive, or adding additional drives for "tasty" food, which combine with drives for "food" in order to explain cooking render it hard to test.

Cognitive dissonance theory

Suggested by Leon Festinger, this occurs when an individual experiences some degree of discomfort resulting from an incompatibility between two cognitions. For example, a consumer may seek to reassure himself regarding a purchase, feeling, in retrospect, that another decision may have been preferable. Another example of cognitive dissonance is when a belief and a behaviour are in conflict. A person may wish to be healthy, believes smoking is bad for one's health, and yet continues to smoke.

Need theories

Need hierarchy theory

Abraham Maslow's theory is one of the most widely discussed theories of motivation.

The theory can be summarized as follows:

- Human beings have wants and desires which influence their behaviour. Only unsatisfied needs influence behaviour, satisfied needs do not.
- Since needs are many, they are arranged in order of importance, from the basic to the complex.
- The person advances to the next level of needs only after the lower level need is at least minimally satisfied.
- The further the progress up the hierarchy, the more individuality, humanness and psychological health a person will show.

The needs, listed from basic to most complex are as follows:

- Physiology
- Safety/Security/Shelter/Health
- Belongingness/Love/Friendship
- Self-esteem/Recognition/Achievement
- Self actualization

Herzberg's two-factor theory

Frederick Herzberg's two-factor theory, a.k.a. intrinsic/extrinsic motivation, concludes that certain factors in the workplace result in job satisfaction, but if absent, they don't lead to dissatisfaction but no satisfaction.

The factors that motivate people can change over their lifetime, but "respect for me as a person" is one of the top motivating factors at any stage of life.

He distinguished between:

- Motivators; which give positive satisfaction, and
- Hygiene factors; that do not motivate if present, but, if absent, result in demotivation.

The name Hygiene factors is used because, like hygiene, the presence will not make you healthier, but absence can cause health deterioration.

The theory is sometimes called the "Motivator-Hygiene Theory" and/or "The Dual Structure Theory." Herzberg's theory has found application in such occupational fields as information systems and in studies of user satisfaction.

Alderfer's ERG theory

Alderfer, expanding on Maslow's hierarchy of needs, created the ERG theory. Physiological and safety, the lower order needs, are placed in the existence category, while love and self esteem needs are placed in the relatedness category. The growth category contains our self-actualization and self-esteem needs. Alderfer argues that there are three groups of core needs — existence, relatedness, and growth hence the label: ERG theory. The existence group is concerned with providing our basic material existence requirements.

They include the items that Maslow considered to be physiological and safety needs. The second group of needs are those of relatedness- the desire we have for maintaining important interpersonal relationships. These social and status desires require interaction with others if they are to be satisfied, and they align with Maslow's social need and the external component of Maslow's esteem classification. Finally, Alderfer isolates growth needs' an intrinsic desire for personal development. These include the intrinsic component from Maslow's esteem category and the characteristics included under self-actualization.

Self-determination theory

Self-determination theory, developed by Edward Deci and Richard Ryan, focuses on the importance of intrinsic motivation in driving human behaviour. Like Maslow's hierarchical theory and others that built on it, SDT posits a natural tendency towards growth and development. Unlike these other theories, however, SDT does not include any sort of "autopilot" for achievement, but instead requires active encouragement from the environment. The primary factors that encourage motivation and development are autonomy, competence feedback, and relatedness.

Broad theories

The latest approach in Achievement Motivation is an integrative perspective as lined out in the "Onion-Ring-Model of Achievement Motivation" by Heinz Schuler, George C. Thornton III, Andreas Frintrup and Rose Mueller-Hanson. It is based on the premise that performance motivation results from the way broad components of personality are directed towards performance. As a result, it includes a range of dimensions that are relevant to success at work but which are not conventionally regarded as being part of performance motivation.

Especially it integrates formerly separated approaches as Need for Achievement with *e.g.* social motives like dominance. The Achievement Motivation Inventory is based on this theory and assesses three factors relevant to vocational and professional success.

Cognitive theories

Goal-setting theory

Goal-setting theory is based on the notion that individuals sometimes have a drive to reach a clearly defined end state. Often, this end state is a reward in itself. A goal's efficiency is affected by three features: proximity, difficulty and specificity. An ideal goal should present a situation where the time between the initiation of behaviour and the end state is close. This explains why some children are more motivated to learn how to ride a bike than mastering algebra. A goal should be moderate, not too hard or too easy to complete. In both cases, most people are not optimally motivated, as many want a challenge.

At the same time people want to feel that there is a substantial probability that they will succeed. Specificity concerns the description of the goal in their class. The goal should be objectively defined and intelligible for the individual. A classic example of a poorly specified goal is to get the highest possible grade. Most children have no idea how much effort they need to reach that goal.

Models of behaviour change

Social-cognitive models of behaviour change include the constructs of motivation and volition. Motivation is seen as a process that leads to the forming of behavioral intentions. Volition is seen as a process that leads from intention to actual behaviour. In other words, motivation and volition refer to goal setting and goal pursuit, respectively. Both processes require self-regulatory efforts. Several self-regulatory constructs are needed to operate in orchestration to attain goals. An example of such a motivational and volitional construct is perceived self-efficacy. Self-efficacy is supposed to facilitate the forming of behavioral intentions, the development of action plans, and the initiation of action. It can support the translation of intentions into action.

Unconscious motivation

Some psychologists believe that a significant portion of human behaviour is energized and directed by unconscious motives. According to Maslow, "Psychoanalysis has often demonstrated that the relationship between a conscious desire and the ultimate unconscious aim that underlies it need not be at all direct." In other words, stated motives do not always match those inferred by skilled observers.

For example, it is possible that a person can be accident-prone because he has an unconscious desire to hurt himself and not because he is careless or ignorant of the safety rules. Similarly, some overweight people are not hungry at all for food but for fighting and kissing. Eating is merely a defensive reaction to lack of attention. Some workers damage more equipment than others do because they harbour unconscious feelings of aggression towards authority figures. Psychotherapists point out that some behaviour is so automatic that the reasons for it are not available in the individual's conscious mind. Compulsive cigarette smoking is an example.

Sometimes maintaining self-esteem is so important and the motive for an activity is so threatening that it is simply not recognized and, in fact, may be disguised or repressed. Rationalization, or "explaining away", is one such disguise, or defence mechanism, as it is called. Another is projecting or attributing one's own faults to others. "I feel I am to blame", becomes "It is her fault; she is selfish". Repression of powerful but socially unacceptable motives may result in outward behaviour that is the opposite of the repressed tendencies. An example of this would be the employee who hates his boss but overworks himself on the job to show that he holds him in high regard.

Unconscious motives add to the hazards of interpreting human behaviour and, to the extent that they are present, complicate the life of the administrator. On the other hand, knowledge that unconscious motives exist can lead to a more careful assessment of behavioral problems. Although few contemporary psychologists deny the existence of unconscious factors, many do believe that these are activated only in times of anxiety and stress, and that in the ordinary course of events, human behaviour—from the subject's point of view—is rationally purposeful.

Intrinsic motivation and the 16 basic desires theory

Starting from studies involving more than 6,000 people, Professor Steven Reiss has proposed a theory that find 16 basic desires that guide nearly all human behaviour. The desires are:

- Acceptance, the need for approval
- Curiosity, the need to learn
- Eating, the need for food
- Family, the need to raise children
- Honour, the need to be loyal to the traditional values of one's clan/ ethnic group
- Idealism, the need for social justice
- Independence, the need for individuality
- Order, the need for organized, stable, predictable environments Physical activity, the need for exercise
- Power, the need for influence of will
- Romance, the need for sex
- Saving, the need to collect
- Social contact, the need for friends
- Status, the need for social standing/importance
- Tranquility, the need to be safe
- Vengeance, the need to strike back/to win

In this model, people differ in these basic desires. These basic desires represent intrinsic desires that directly motivate a person's behaviour, and not aimed at indirectly satisfying other desires. People may also be motivated by non-basic desires, but in this case this does not relate to deep motivation, or only as a means to achieve other basic desires. Other theories:

- Reversal theory
- Motivating operation

CONTROLLING MOTIVATION

The control of motivation is only understood to a limited extent. There are many different approaches of motivation training, but many of these are considered pseudoscientific by critics. To understand how to control motivation it is first necessary to understand why many people lack motivation.

Employee motivation

Workers in any organization need something to keep them working. Most times the salary of the employee is enough to keep him or her working for an organization. However, sometimes just working for salary is not enough for employees to stay at an organization. An employee must be motivated to work for a company or organization. If no motivation is present in an employee, then that employee's quality of work or all work in general will deteriorate.

Keeping an employee working at full potential is the ultimate goal of employee motivation. There are many methods to help keep employees motivated. Some traditional ways of motivating workers are placing them in competition with each other.

When motivating an audience, you can use general motivational strategies or specific motivational appeals. General motivational strategies include soft sell versus hard sell and personality type. Soft sell strategies have logical appeals, emotional appeals, advice and praise. Hard sell strategies have barter, outnumbering, pressure and rank. Also, you can consider basing your strategy on your audience personality. Specific motivational appeals focus on provable facts, feelings, right and wrong, audience rewards and audience threats.

Drugs

Some authors, especially in the transhumanist movement, have suggested the use of "smart drugs", also known as nootropics, as "motivation-enhancers". The effects of many of these drugs on the brain are emphatically not well understood, and their legal status often makes open experimentation difficult.

APPLICATIONS

Education

Motivation is of particular interest to educational psychologists because of the crucial role it plays in student learning. However, the specific kind of motivation that is studied in the specialized setting of education differs qualitatively from the more general forms of motivation studied by psychologists in other fields. Motivation in education can have several effects on how students learn and how they behave towards subject matter. It can:

1. Direct behaviour towards particular goals
2. Lead to increased effort and energy
3. Increase initiation of, and persistence in, activities

4. Enhance cognitive processing
5. Determine what consequences are reinforcing
6. Lead to improved performance.

Because students are not always internally motivated, they sometimes need situated motivation, which is found in environmental conditions that the teacher creates.

There are two kinds of motivation:

- Intrinsic motivation occurs when people are internally motivated to do something because it either brings them pleasure, they think it is important, or they feel that what they are learning is significant.
- Extrinsic motivation comes into play when a student is compelled to do something or act a certain way because of factors external to him or her.

Note also that there is already questioning and expansion about this dichotomy on motivation, *e.g.*, Self-Determination Theory. Motivation has been found to be a pivotal area in treating Autism Spectrum Disorders, as in Pivotal Response Therapy. Motivation is also an important element in the concept of Andragogy.

Sudbury Model schools' approach to motivation

Sudbury Model schools adduce that the cure to the problem of procrastination, of learning in general, and particularly of scientific illiteracy is to remove once and for all what they call the underlying disease: compulsion in schools. They contend that human nature in a free society recoils from every attempt to force it into a mold; that the more requirements we pile onto children at school, the surer we are to drive them away from the material we are trying to force down their throats; that after all the drive and motivation of infants to master the world around them is legendary. They assert that schools must keep that drive alive by doing what some of them do: nurturing it on the freedom it needs to thrive.

Sudbury Model schools do not perform and do not offer evaluations, assessments, transcripts, or recommendations, asserting that they do not rate people, and that school is not a judge; comparing students to each other, or to some standard that has been set is for them a violation of the student's right to privacy and to self-determination. Students decide for themselves how to measure their progress as self-starting learners as a process of self-evaluation: real life-long learning and the proper educational evaluation for the 21st century, they adduce.

According to Sudbury Model schools, this policy does not cause harm to their students as they move on to life outside the school. However, they admit it makes the process more difficult, but that such hardship is part of the students learning to make their own way, set their own standards and meet their own goals.

The no-grading and no-rating policy helps to create an atmosphere free of competition among students or battles for adult approval, and encourages a positive cooperative environment amongst the student body.

Business

At lower levels of Maslow's hierarchy of needs, such as physiological needs, money is a motivator, however it tends to have a motivating effect on staff that lasts only for a short period. At higher levels of the hierarchy, praise, respect, recognition, empowerment and a sense of belonging are far more powerful motivators than money, as both Abraham Maslow's theory of motivation and Douglas McGregor's theory X and theory Y demonstrate.

Maslow has money at the lowest level of the hierarchy and shows other needs are better motivators to staff. McGregor places money in his Theory X category and feels it is a poor motivator. Praise and recognition are placed in the Theory Y category and are considered stronger motivators than money.

- Motivated employees always look for better ways to do a job.
- Motivated employees are more quality oriented.
- Motivated workers are more productive.

The average workplace is about midway between the extremes of high threat and high opportunity. Motivation by threat is a dead-end strategy, and naturally staff are more attracted to the opportunity side of the motivation curve than the threat side. Motivation is a powerful tool in the work environment that can lead to employees working at their most efficient levels of production.

Nonetheless, Steinmertz also discusses three common character types of subordinates: ascendant, indifferent, and ambivalent whom all react and interact uniquely, and must be treated, managed, and motivated accordingly. An effective leader must understand how to manage all characters, and more importantly the manager must utilize avenues that allow room for employees to work, grow, and find answers independently. The assumptions of Maslow and Herzberg were challenged by a classic study at Vauxhall Motors' UK manufacturing plant. This introduced the concept of orientation to work and distinguished three main orientations: instrumental, bureaucratic and solidaristic.

Other theories which expanded and extended those of Maslow and Herzberg included Kurt Lewin's Force Field Theory, Edwin Locke's Goal Theory and Victor Vroom's Expectancy theory. These tend to stress cultural differences and the fact that individuals tend to be motivated by different factors at different times. According to the system of scientific management developed by Frederick Winslow Taylor, a worker's motivation is solely determined by pay, and therefore management need not consider psychological or social aspects of work. In essence, scientific management bases human motivation wholly on extrinsic rewards and discards the idea of intrinsic rewards.

In contrast, David McClelland believed that workers could not be motivated by the mere need for money—in fact, extrinsic motivation could extinguish intrinsic motivation such as achievement motivation, though money could be used as an indicator of success for various motives, *e.g.*, keeping score. In keeping with this view, his consulting firm, McBer & Company, had as its first motto "To make everyone productive, happy, and free."

For McClelland, satisfaction lay in aligning a person's life with their fundamental motivations. Elton Mayo found out that the social contacts a worker has at the workplace are very important and that boredom and repetitiveness of tasks lead to reduced motivation. Mayo believed that workers could be motivated by acknowledging their social needs and making them feel important. As a result, employees were given freedom to make decisions on the job and greater attention was paid to informal work groups. Mayo named the model the Hawthorne effect. His model has been judged as placing undue reliance on social contacts at work situations for motivating employees.

In Essentials of Organizational Behaviour, Robbins and Judge examine recognition programmes as motivators, and identify five principles that contribute to the success of an employee incentive programme:

- Recognition of employees' individual differences, and clear identification of behaviour deemed worthy of recognition
- Allowing employees to participate
- Linking rewards to performance
- Rewarding of nominators
- Visibility of the recognition process

CHARACTERISTICS OF HIGH ACHIEVEMENT MOTIVATION

Characteristics of individuals with high achievement motivation include an orientation towards problem-solving and moderate challenges, according to theorists like John Murray, David C. McClelland and John Atkinson. These individuals also place a high emphasis on accomplishment and success.

MODERATE CHALLENGE

Individuals with high achievement motivation prefer tasks and problems that involve moderate levels of difficulty. Usually, these individuals gravitate towards challenging but achievable goals where their abilities and efforts can affect the outcome.

PERSONAL REWARDS

Instead of deriving motivation from the potential for rewards, individuals with high achievement motivation use rewards, such as professional recognition and financial gain, as a way to measure their accomplishments. These individuals place a higher value on a personal sense of achievement.

RELEVANT FEEDBACK

Another characteristic of individuals with high achievement motivation is the desire for feedback. These individuals do not seek feedback about their own personal qualities but instead about the success of their efforts. Feedback serves as way to measure the effectiveness of their work.

PROBLEM-SOLVING

Individuals with high achievement motivation also have a strong orientation towards problem-solving. They spend extensive time thinking about potential solutions to current problems, as well as actively considering and analyzing additional possibilities for improvement.

INTERPERSONAL SKILLS

Due to their focus on achievement and accomplishment, individuals with high achievement motivation are often characterized by poor interpersonal skills as well. These individuals have a tendency to overemphasize results and have difficulty managing people effectively.

CLASSIFICATION OF MOTIVES

They are the motive. According to Maslow, motives are of the following types:

1. Physiological
2. Security
3. Affiliation/ Belongingness
4. Esteem
5. Self- Actualisation

TYPES OF MOTIVATION

Motivation involves the basic psychological reasons for a person's actions and behaviour. These are the forces or factors that cause a person to act a certain way or to behave in the manner that they do. There are various types of motivations that can influence a person. These include the following:

PRIMARY OR BASIC MOTIVATION

This mainly pertains to motives involved with our need for self-preservation. This includes needs such as hunger and thirst, warmth, sex, avoidance of pain and other primary motives which influence a person's behaviour at a very basic level.

SECONDARY MOTIVATION

More known in psychology as "learned" motivation, this type of "drives" differ from one person to another. In many ways they involve a person's own sense of values and priorities in life. Many of the behaviour derived from secondary motivation are conscious ones. That is, a person consciously desires a particular goal or result, and behaves in a way that brings them closer to that particular goal. What drives them to do something or to act in a particular way is the longing for something which they currently do not have or possess. This kind of motivation generally falls into two basic types: intrinsic and extrinsic motivation.

EXTRINSIC MOTIVATION

Extrinsic motivation is likely to involve the concept of rewarded behaviour. Thus, by engaging in a particular type of activity or behaving in a particular manner, you are "rewarded" by a desired end result.

For instance, you are motivated to save money for a vacation. Hence, you resist the urge to make impulsive purchases and in general become more discriminating in how you spend your money.

After a time you find that you have a steadily growing amount of savings which you set aside. When you find that you have saved enough for that trip, you utilize your savings for the intended purpose and go on vacation. The external motivation is the vacation, which is also the reward for your act of saving for it.

INTERNAL MOTIVATION

On the other hand, there are other less-visible types of motivation. It would be a mistake to say that such behaviour does not come without its own rewards. To be more precise, the end goal is not a visible or external thing, but more internal and psychological. The achievement of these goals - by itself also correctly seen as a reward - is in general not visible to other persons.

Thus, for instance, a student is motivated to get good grades or simply, he desires to know more about a particular subject. Getting good grades is the reward visible to others. For the student, the fact that he has become an expert in a particular subject or lesson is also a psychological reward for his intrinsic desire to learn.

SUCCESSFUL MOTIVATED BEHAVIOUR

Good and effective actions or behaviour usually involves the harmonizing of these two types of motivation. If one is driven by both intrinsic and extrinsic motivations, then inner conflict is reduced and a person is more likely to devote uninterrupted and harmonious actions towards a particular task.

The inner and external rewards too, are good reinforcing mechanisms. For many people, this is really the means towards success. By choosing goals that you desire - both in its intrinsic and extrinsic rewards - you can harmonize your own actions and devote your energies to your goals. In such instances, the chances of achievement increases greatly.

MORALE

Motivation is defined as an urge in an individual to perform goal directed behaviour. Therefore, motivation cannot be inflicted from outside but it is an intrinsic desire in a man to achieve the target goal through performance or activity.

Motives are expression of person's need. Hence, they are personal and internal. Incentives on the other hand are external to the person. They are made part of work environment by management in order to encourage workers to accomplish task. The motivational model indicates that a sense of felt deprivation generates needs and such needs create tension in an individual. The individual perceive and makes cost benefit analysis on the ways and means of releasing such tension. Once such perception is cleared, individual pounces upon the activities and achieves some results. If it is success he feels rewarded and falls in the cycle of motivation again. If it is failure he feels punished and once again after due modification of ways and means pounces back on the cycle or feels frustrated. Therefore, motivation leads to a goal directed behaviour.

When people join an organization, they bring with them certain needs that affect on-the-job performance. Some of these needs are physiological; others are related to psychological and social values. The later are much more difficult to determine and satisfy, and they vary greatly from one to another. Maslow has developed a hierarchy of needs as follows: physiological, security, social, esteem, and self-actualization needs. They interact with the environment to shape on-the-job wants that are the basis of motivation. In addition, motivation is affected by people's perceptions, including their feelings of equity or fairness in a situation. According to a model developed by Herzberg, motivation is influenced by maintenance and motivational factors. Important motivational factors are the work itself, achievement, growth, responsibility, advancement and recognition. These are primarily intrinsic motivators rather than extrinsic ones. The Maslow and Herzberg models have many similarities because they both focus on needs, but they do so from somewhat different points of view.

Two different models of motivation are the expectancy model and behaviour modification. The expectancy model states that motivation is a product of how much one wants something and the probability that a certain action will lead to it. The formula is valence X expectancy = motivation. Valence is the strength of a person's performance for one outcome in relation to others. Expectancy is the strength of belief that a given act will be followed by particular outcomes.

Behaviour modification states that behaviour depends on its consequences. It is achieved through operant condition. Its various approaches include positive and negative reinforcement, shaping, and extinction. Punishment normally is not used. Reinforcement can be continuous or partial.

Criticism of behaviour modification are that it manipulates people and does not apply very well in complex work environments. Cognitive models dominate thinking about motivation, but behaviour modification is finding increasing use. Most attention has been given to type A motivation; but in order to build a complete motivational environment, more emphasis must be given to type B motivation.

Motivation therefore, though is a dominant intrinsic urge in an individual yet the leader of the team can guide the ways and means by which the followers can satisfy their needs. It is obviously difficult to motivate an individual since he is guided by expressed motivation or unconscious motivation and multiplicity of motivational sequences. It is easy to introduce a team motivation or group motivation where the individual idiosyncrasy looses importance and the group goal becomes the target. It is then not motivation per se but a group morale - an "espirit de corps" *i.e.* a sense of group activity with desire for high achievement of the group goal where an individual can comfortably ignore his personal goals or needs. Such morale is mostly psychological in nature and not physiological.

A leader's job is, therefore, to inculcate the extirpation of the group morale if he proposes to achieve the target through his follows where equal weight is given to performance of task and welfare of the followers, a stage of suspended pendulum or middle of the road method.

MOTIVATION AND PRODUCTIVITY

Raising productivity in UK firms to match levels in other European countries and the US is a key objective of this government's economic policy agenda. This is, of course, a major and long-standing issue.There is a range of factors involved, each of which require action on a number of fronts.There are no simple solutions. Closing the productivity gap will require increased investment in research and development, capital and people, improved education and training, and a modernised, productive infrastructure including transport. The problem of short-termism in British industry needs to be resolved; and within companies continuous improvements are needed in management practice, corporate governance and organisational design. But as productivity is fundamentally about how productive people are at work, their skills, motivation and commitment are key.1 This is the context in which the government has introduced a number of new arrangements, including tax incentives in the 2000 and 2001 budgets, to encourage employee commitment through employee shareholding, with the aim of improving Britain's productivity:

'Share ownership offers employees a real stake in their company... I want, through targeted reform, to reward long-term commitment by employees. I want to encourage the new enterprise culture of teamwork in which everyone contributes and everyone benefits from success.' Gordon Brown, Chancellor of the Exchequer, 1999 budget speech Will this work? What is the theory behind it, and is there any evidence in support? These are the questions that the current report seeks to address.The results suggest that in economic terms there is certainly a rich seam to be tapped here, and indeed that by further developing government policy in this area, still more could be achieved.

THE THEORY

The theory is that owning shares will provide employees with financial incentives that will make them more committed to the organisation and more motivated at work. If the company is more profitable, employees will gain financially through dividend payments and an increased share price. Greater motivation will have a direct effect in improving productivity through greater effort and possibly innovation. There may be a further benefit, alluded to in the Chancellor's comments, if greater commitment to the firm results in reduced labour turnover. This will make it more worthwhile for firms to invest in training for their workforce.

Less commented on – in either academic literature or public policy discussions – is the fact that the payback from investment in product and process innovation depends crucially on the tacit knowledge accumulated by the workforce, so reduced labour turnover can increase the long-term payback from such investments.This effect may not only increase productivity and profitability, it may make the difference between the firm deciding whether or not to proceed with the proposed investment. There is a large amount of literature on both the theory and practice of these processes which will be touched on only briefly in this report,2 but what we need to try to test can be illustrated in simple terms along the lines depicted in Figure.

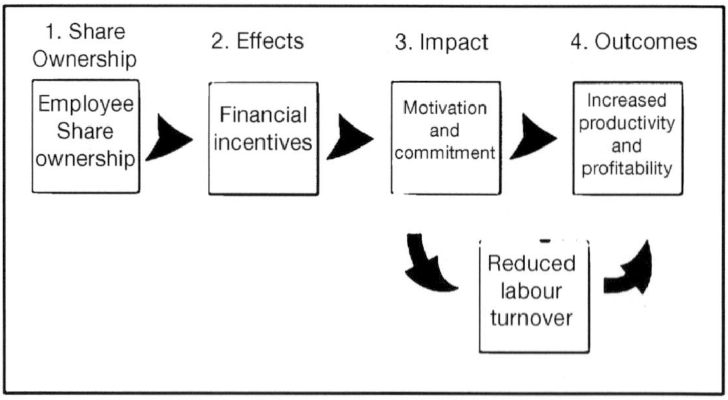

We need to ascertain whether any of these causal arrows actually exist in the real world and if so, how significant they are.

THE EVIDENCE

Capital Strategies produces an Employee Ownership Index of the share prices of firms that have a 'significant degree' of employee share ownership.Over the period 1992–2000 this index outperformed the FTSE All-Share Index by 173 per cent. What, though, are the causal mechanisms at work? McNabb and Whitfield, using the 1990 Workplace Industrial Relations Survey data, found financial participation positively related to financial performance. But they also show that strong interaction effects mean that the influence of financial participation schemes cannot be analysed independently of other types of employee participation schemes, and that the effects of problem-solving schemes, for example, are dependent on the linkage with a financial participation scheme, while downward communication tends to have a positive effect regardless.

However, using the 1998 Workplace Employee Relations Survey data, Addison and Belfield find different results, for example discerning no significant association between downward communication and firm performance.McNabb and Whitfield confirm that the two datasets generate different results, concluding that while there are enduring links between employee participation and financial performance, the precise nature of these requires more careful investigation than has thus far been possible.

Also using thc 1998 WERS data, Conyon and Freeman found that firms and establishments with shared compensation arrangements perform better than other firms in productivity and financial performance. The stock price of firms with shared compensation practices also outperformed those of other firms. Conyon and Freeman then surveyed 1,518 UK listed companies and found that, of their 299 returns, those with approved profit sharing or all-employee share schemes outperformed the FTSE All Share index by 40 per cent.They also found that firms and establishments with some form of shared compensation, particularly those with deferred profit sharing and employee share ownership are more likely to establish formal communication and consultation channels with workers than other establishments.

This raises the question of what is actually causing the improved performance; it may be through increased commitment and motivation, but what is causing this? Is it just the financial incentive, or is it the improved communication and consultation which appears to be associated with employee share ownership?

Certainly there is a large body of literature suggesting that employee commitment and motivation can be enhanced through a range of progressive human resource management practices, including but not restricted to employee share ownership. It may be that the key effect of employee share ownership on performance is through making it more likely that firms introduce these other HRM practices – of communication, involvement and participation. In addition, where such practices are pursued, the existence of employee share ownership may underpin and enhance the positive effect that these have on commitment and motivation, by increasing employees' faith that such involvement and participation is genuine and long term.

Surveying employee share ownership across the EU, Pendleton et al concluded that: 'There is a relationship between financial participation arrangements and other forms of employee participation —enterprises that have financial participation are more likely to also have other participation and communications arrangements in place. This supports research findings that financial participation works best when it is integrated with other participative, information and consultation arrangements, for example, in supporting 'high performance'work organisations'.

The 'collective voice' aspect of participation at work has been found to have a significantly positive effect on motivation and commitment. Where this collective voice takes the form of an employee shareholding trust, this may again make the introduction of progressive HRM policies both more likely and more effective. These considerations introduce a number of additional causal links that need to be explored, as illustrated in Figure:

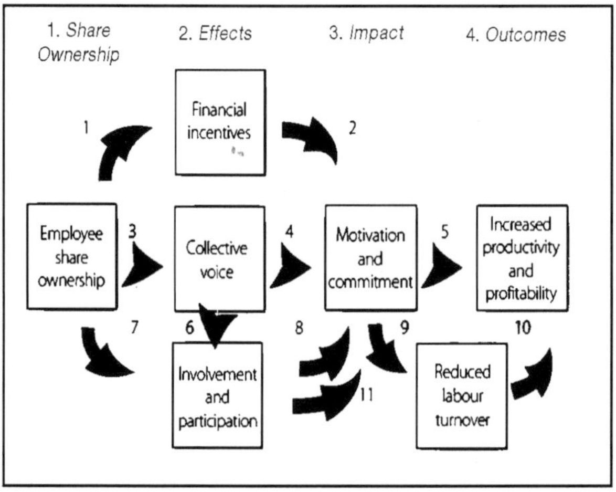

The causal links can be grouped within three categories, the first two of which are being assumed by the Chancellor, and upon which his policy depends for its efficacy. The third category are the additional effects just described, which if found to have substance would suggest that the Chancellor's policy agenda in this area may have the potential for delivering more than he had hoped. However, to benefit from these additional effects the policies themselves may need to be further developed.

First, the Chancellor is assuming that employee share ownership will be seen by employees as representing a positive financial incentive and that this will lead them to be more committed and motivated. The existing academic literature, as well as our own research, provides supporting evidence for both assumptions, with one caveat – namely, that employees are aware that an increase in their own individual effort at work will not have a significant enough impact on productivity and profitability to alter the dividend they receive on their shares, nor on the share price. Any such effect requires increased commitment and effort from the workforce collectively—the sort of teamwork that the Chancellor refers to. Second, the Chancellor is assuming that increased commitment and motivation will lead to increased productivity and profitability, both directly through increased 'effort' and also indirectly through reducing labour turnover and hence increasing the payback that firms enjoy from investment, both in training and in new products and processes with a concomitant tendency for firms to increase such investments accordingly.

These links have been tested for in what might be termed the 'High Commitment Work Systems' literature. As with any such statistical work on large datasets, measuring what are inevitably very different firms in changing circumstances, with managements and workforces that are not homogenous either within or between firms, the results from different studies differ, but most do find such a causal link from motivation to outcomes. That literature also tends to find a positive link from progressive HRM practices that encourage involvement and participation, through to increased motivation and commitment.

The third group of arrows are additional effects to those assumed by the Chancellor:

- Employee share ownership may lead to employees feeling that they have a collective voice in the company.
- This feeling of having a collective voice may have a direct, positive effect on commitment and motivation.
- That collective voice may encourage the adoption of progressive HRM policies involving involvement and participation.
- Employee share ownership itself may also make the adoption of such practices more likely.
- Finally, and perhaps most important of all, the positive effect that involvement and participation policies have on motivation and commitment may be enhanced and made more effective and significant if they are underpinned by and combined with employee share ownership. The interviews, surveys and focus groups reported on seek to shed light on how important managers and employees believe any of these effects to have been.

THE EXISTING LITERATURE

Before turning to these interviews and focus groups,we will put them in context by reporting on the academic research addressing these questions. Grouping the effects into their three categories, there is evidence to support the Chancellor's view that financial participation is positively related to financial performance. That work does suggest that these factors are inextricably linked to other types of employee participation schemes.

This supports the broader view we have sketched, whereby different progressive HRM policies may reinforce each other and indeed be linked causally.This is related to another finding from the 'High Commitment Work Systems' literature, that the effect of introducing progressive HRM policies may depend on how these are combined. There are both theoretical reasons and empirical evidence for believing that such practices may be more than the sum of their parts if implemented appropriately. Conversely, pursuing one or more policies may be a waste of effort if other symbiotic policies are not also being implemented.

It may be a waste of resources to train an employee if they don't have the motivation to contribute, or if there is not the appropriate work organisation to allow them to make a greater contribution. Likewise, motivation itself may be insufficient if other factors are not in Place.

As regards the second grouping of effects, of participation and involvement on motivation and commitment, and from there to increased productivity and profitability, the bulk of the research to date has been in the US, and on manufacturing.That work generally finds significantly positive linkages.4 The work in the UK, using the 1990 Workplace Industrial Relations Survey and 1998 Workplace Employee Relations Survey datasets has found similarly positive linkages to outcomes,5 including on increased innovation.6 However, there are limits to how much those datasets can reveal. Drawing upon data from a ten-year study of over a hundred small and medium-sized manufacturing enterprises in the UK, Patterson et al found that HRM practices were the most powerful predictors of company performance. Conducting our own surveys,we also found significantly positive linkages, particularly with innovation as an outcome, and with the causal links sketched above seeming to correctly describe the underlying processes at work.7 However, our latest survey finds rather mixed results when looking at productivity and profitability.

The 'third group' of effects might lead to a greater boost to productivity as a result of government policy than would be forthcoming from the simple 'financial incentive' mechanism alone, at least if those policies were developed to capture these additional benefits. Here the existing literature is weakest.Whether the existence of employee share ownership will lead to employees feeling that they have a collective voice will depend on whether the shares are held collectively in a trust or some other such arrangement.

The literature does suggest that a collective holding may encourage a teamwork culture and a co-operative company spirit that would deliver productivity benefits which would not follow from individual employee share holding because of the 'free rider' problem.

In 1987, the US General Accounting Office study found that Employee Stock Ownership Plans had an inconclusive impact on outcomes, except when employee ownership was coupled with employee participation in management decision making —ie, the link depicted by Arrow 11. Since then research findings have suggested a more positive link. Kruse and Blasi review 'the accumulated evidence concerning the prevalence, causes, and effects of employee ownership, covering 25 studies of employee attitudes and behaviours, and 27 studies of productivity and profitability.

They find that:'Perceived participation in decisions is not in itself automatically increased through employee ownership, but may interact positively with employee ownership in affecting attitudes... The dispersed results among attitudinal and performance studies indicate the importance of firm-level employee relations, human resource policies, and other circumstances.' Kruse and Blasi report that there has been little study of the salient organisational mechanisms that might help explain the actual connection between employee ownership and performance. They call for further research on complementary HRM policies and practices, and ESOPs, which might jointly produce positive effects on corporate performance. Logue and Yates discuss much of the existing literature, and also analyse survey data. They argue that there are, potentially, strong positive links from collective employee shareholding to corporate outcomes, but only where these are combined with policies of participation and involvement.

For the UK, Conyon and Freeman analysed the 1998 WERS data, linking the financial performance and labour productivity of each establishment to the percentage of non-managerial workers covered by the Inland Revenue-approved employee ownership schemes.Their analysis took account of differences in number of employees, age of establishment, industry, distribution of workforce by skill and gender, and the degree of competition in the sector. The relationship between employee share ownership and economic performance was found to be positive.

QUANTITATIVE AND QUALITATIVE RESEARCH

These quantitative studies, analysing large datasets, are inevitably limited to the questions asked in the surveys and the quality of the responses given. The WIRS and WERS datasets are impressive in scope, but are of limited use in attempting to go beyond testing for the sorts of statistical correlations reported above. To discover the causal mechanisms, in order to design policies that can take advantage of these, requires an exploration of people's motivations and behaviour.This requires an interactive process whereby responses can be questioned and explored – ie, interviews and discussion. The existing quantitative work reported above was therefore built on in the current project by asking both managers and employees about motivations, attitudes and behaviour in the workplace. This was done first by visiting a number of workplaces. We also conducted our own surveys, primarily among companies already committed to the idea of employee ownership, to test whether the preconceptions of the individuals concerned had been borne out in practice.

9

Effects and Impacts of Group Dynamics and Terms in Leadership and Change Management

GROUP FORMATION

Well functioning groups do not just form out of the blue. It takes time for a group to develop to a point where it can be effective and where all members feel connected to it. Bruce Tuckman has identified four stages that characterize the development of groups. Understanding these stages can help determine what is happening with a group and how to manage what is occurring.

FORMING

This is the initial stage when the group comes together and members begin to develop their relationship with one another and learn what is expected of them. This is the stage when team building begins and trust starts to develop. Group members will start establishing limits on acceptable behaviour through experimentation. Other members' reactions will determine if a behaviour will be repeated. This is also the time when the tasks of the group and the members will be decided.

STORMING

During this stage of group development, interpersonal conflicts arise and differences of opinion about the group and its goals will surface. If the group is unable to clearly state its purposes and goals or if it cannot agree on shared goals, the group may collapse at this point. It is important to work through the conflict at this time and to establish clear goals. It is necessary for there to be discussion so everyone feels heard and can come to an agreement on the direction the group is to move in.

NORMING

Once the group resolves its conflicts, it can now establish patterns of how to get its work done. Expectations of one another are clearly articulated and accepted by members of the group. Formal and informal procedures are established in delegating tasks, responding to questions, and in the process by which the group functions. Members of the group come to understand how the group as a whole operates.

PERFORMING

During this final stage of development, issues related to roles, expectations, and norms are no longer of major importance. The group is now focused on its task, working intentionally and effectively to accomplish its goals. The group will find that it can celebrate its accomplishments and that members will be learning new skills and sharing roles. After a group enters the performing stage, it is unrealistic to expect it to remain there permanently. When new members join or some people leave, there will be a new process of forming, storming, and norming engaged as everyone learns about one another. External events may lead to conflicts within the group.

To remain healthy, groups will go through all of these processes in a continuous loop. When conflict arises in a group, do not try to silence the conflict or to run from it. Let the conflict come out into the open so people can discuss it. If the conflict is kept under the surface, members will not be able to build trusting relationships and this could harm the group's effectiveness. If handled properly, the group will come out of the conflict with a stronger sense of cohesiveness then before.

SKILLS TO MANAGE GROUP DEVELOPMENT

You may know the name of the different stages of development but there are different skills and techniques needed to guide a group through the stages. Here are some suggestions.

Forming

Be inclusive and empowering. Make sure that everyone connected to the group is involved. Seek out diverse members and talents and model inclusive leadership. Identify common purposes and targets of change. Create an environment that fosters trust and builds commitment to the group.

Storming

Be ethical and open to other people's ideas. Allow differences of opinion to be discussed. Handle conflict directly and civilly. Keep everyone focused on the purpose of the group and the topic of conflict. Avoid personal attacks. Examine biases that may be blocking progress or preventing another member to be treated fairly.

Norming

Be fair with processes. New members should feel welcomed, informed, and involved. Continue to clarify expectations of individuals and of the group. Engage in collaboration and teamwork.

Performing

Celebrate accomplishments and find renewal in relationships. Encourage and empower members to learn new skills and to share roles that keep things fresh and exciting. Revisit purpose and rebuild commitment.

FORMAL AND INFORMAL ORGANIZATIONS AND THEIR INTERACTION

FORMAL ORGANIZATION

Formal organization is a fixed set of rules of intra-organization procedures and structures. As such, it is usually set out in writing, with a language of rules that ostensibly leave little discretion for interpretation. In some societies and in some organization, such rules may be strictly followed; in others, they may be little more than an empty formalism.

- To facilitate the accomplishment of the goals of the organization: In a formal organization the work is delegated to each individual of the organization. He/She works towards the attainment of definite goals, which are in compliance with the goals of the organisation.
- To facilitate the co-ordination of various activities: The authority, responsibility and accountability of individuals in the organization is very well defined. Hence, facilitating the co-ordination of various activities of the organisation very effectively.
- To aid the establishment of logical authority relationship: The responsibilities of the individuals in the organisation are well defined. They have a definite place in the organisation due to a well defined hierarchical structure which is inherent in any formal organisation.
- Permit the application of the concept of specialization and division of Labour, division of work amongst individuals according to their capabilities helps in greater specializations and division of work.
- Create more group cohesiveness

Characteristics of a formal organization

- Well defined rules and regulation
- Arbitrary structure
- Determined objectives and policies
- Status symbol
- Limitation on the activities of the individual
- Strict observance of the principle of co-ordination
- Messages are communicated through scalar chain

Distinction from informal organization

Formal rules are often adapted to subjective interests — social structures within an enterprise and the personal goals, desires, sympathies and behaviours of the individual workers — so that the practical everyday life of an organization becomes informal. Practical experience shows no organization is ever completely rule-bound: instead, all real organizations represent some mix of formal and informal. Consequently, when attempting to legislate for an organization and to create a formal structure, it is necessary to recognize informal organization in order to create workable structures. However, informal organization can fail, or, if already set in order, can work against mismanagement.

Formal organizations are typically understood to be systems of coordinated and controlled activities that arise when work is embedded in complex networks of technical relations and boundary-spanning exchanges. But in modern societies, formal organizational structures arise in highly institutional contexts. Organizations are driven to incorporate the practices and procedures defined by prevailing rationalized concepts of organizational work and institutionalized in society. Organizations that do so increase their legitimacy and their survival prospects, independent of the immediate efficacy of the acquired practices and procedures.

There can develop a tension between on the one hand, the institutionalized products, services, techniques, policies, and programmes that function as myths, and efficiency criteria on the other hand. To maintain ceremonial conformity, organizations that reflect institutional rules tend to buffer their formal structures from the uncertainties of the technical activities by developing a loose coupling between their formal structures and actual work activities.

The Hawthorne Experiments

The deviation from rulemaking on a higher level was documented for the first time in the Hawthorne studies and called informal organization. At first this discovery was ignored and dismissed as the product of avoidable errors, until it finally had to be recognized that these unwritten laws of work of everyday life often had more influence on the fate of the enterprise than those conceived on organizational charts of the executive level. Numerous empirical studies in sociological organization research followed, ever more clearly proving this, particularly during the Human Relations Movement. It is important to analyze informal structures within an enterprise to make use of positive innovations, but also to be able to do away with bad habits that have developed over time.

Reasons for informal organization

There are many different reasons for informal organization:

- Informal standards: personal goals and interests of workers differ from official organizational goals.
- Informal communication: changes of communication routes within an enterprise due to personal relations between coworkers.

- Informal group: certain groups of coworkers have the same interests, or the same origin.
- Informal leaders: due to charisma and general popularity, certain members of the organization win more influence than originally intended.
- Different interests and preferences of coworkers.
- Different status of coworkers.
- Difficult work requirements.
- Unpleasant conditions of work.

Managerial organization theory often still regards informal organization as rather disturbing, but sometimes helpful. In the opinion of systems theory and cybernetics, however, formal organization fades into the background and only serves, if necessary, to supplement or to correct. Changes in structure always redevelop because of the conduct and differences among coworkers, and the ability of self-organization is recognized as a natural characteristic of a social system.

INFORMAL ORGANIZATION

The informal organization is the interlocking social structure that governs how people work together in practice. It is the aggregate of behaviours, interactions, norms, personal and professional connections through which work gets done and relationships are built among people who share a common organizational affiliation or cluster of affiliations. It consists of a dynamic set of personal relationships, social networks, communities of common interest, and emotional sources of motivation. The informal organization evolves organically and spontaneously in response to changes in the work environment, the flux of people through its porous boundaries, and the complex social dynamics of its members.

Tended effectively, the informal organization complements the more explicit structures, plans, and processes of the formal organization: it can accelerate and enhance responses to unanticipated events, foster innovation, enable people to solve problems that require collaboration across boundaries, and create footpaths showing where the formal organization may someday need to pave a way.

The informal organization and the formal organization

The nature of the informal organization becomes more distinct when its key characteristics are juxtaposed with those of the formal organization.

Key characteristics of the informal organization:

- Evolving constantly
- Grass roots
- Dynamic and responsive
- Excellent at motivation

- Requires insider knowledge to be seen
- Treats people as individuals
- Flat and fluid
- Cohered by trust and reciprocity
- Difficult to pin down
- Essential for situations that change quickly or are not yet fully understood

Key characteristics of the formal organization:

- Enduring, unless deliberately altered
- Top-down
- Missionary
- Static
- Excellent at alignment
- Plain to see
- Equates "person" with "role"
- Hierarchical
- Bound together by codified rules and order
- Easily understood and explained
- Critical for dealing with situations that are known and consistent

Historically, some have regarded the informal organization as the byproduct of insufficient formal organization—arguing, for example, that "it can hardly be questioned that the ideal situation in the business organization would be one where no informal organization existed." However, the contemporary approach—one suggested as early as 1925 by Mary Parker Follett, the pioneer of community centers and author of influential works on management philosophy—is to integrate the informal organization and the formal organization, recognizing the strengths and limitations of each. Integration, as Follett defined it, means breaking down apparent sources of conflict into their basic elements and then building new solutions that neither allow domination nor require compromise. In other words, integrating the informal organization with the formal organization replaces competition with coherence.

At a societal level, the importance of the relationship between formal and informal structures can be seen in the relationship between civil society and state authority. The power of integrating the formal organization and the informal organization can also be seen in many successful businesses.

Functions of informal organizations

Keith Davis suggests that informal groups serve at least four major functions within the formal organizational structure:

1. They perpetuate the cultural and social values that the group holds dear. Certain values are usually already held in common among informal group members. Day-to-day interaction reinforces these values that perpetuate a particular lifestyle and preserve group unity

and integrity. For example, a college management class of 50 students may contain several informal groups that constitute the informal organization within the formal structure of the class. These groups may develop out of fraternity or sorority relationships, dorm residency, project work teams, or seating arrangements. Dress codes, hairstyles, and political party involvement are reinforced among the group members.

2. They provide social status and satisfaction that may not be obtained from the formal organization. In a large organization, a worker may feel like an anonymous number rather than a unique individual. Members of informal groups, however, share jokes and gripes, eat together, play and work together, and are friends-which contributes to personal esteem, satisfaction, and a feeling of worth.
3. They promote communication among members. The informal group develops a communication channel or system to keep its members informed about what management actions will affect them in various ways. Many astute managers use the grape- vine to "informally" convey certain information about company actions and rumors.
4. They provide social control by influencing and regulating behaviour inside and outside the group. Internal control persuades members of the group to conform to its lifestyle. For example, if a student starts to wear a coat and tie to class, informal group members may razz and convince the student that such attire is not acceptable and therefore to return to sandals, jeans, and T-shirts. External control is directed to such groups as management, union leadership, and other informal groups.

10

Leadership, Management and Command

INTRODUCTION

There is a plethora of fiction on leadership, management and command. In the civilian (business) market, there are – literally – thousands of books on leadership; management; and leadership and management as a 'dual' concept. However, there are no books in the business market on what the military call 'command'.

In contrast, in the military domain, there are an equal amount of books on leadership; command; and leadership and command together. However, very little has been written – to date – about military management; this represents a very serious limitation. New business practices and performance management systems now require capable senior managers and leaders and private sector organizations have found clear strategic benefit in providing a structured approach to the developmental needs of senior executives.

Although it is recognized that leadership, management and command are closely related (especially in the military environment), comparatively little has been written on the nature and practice on the 3 subjects as 'a state of being three'. This view has also been recognised in the recent Defence Training Review Report where it states: "The pressures of limited resources and increased accountability have placed new demands on Ministry of Defence leaders, as has the challenge of leading a more diverse workforce...in parallel, our studies showed that we must do more to prepare our people effectively, in the post-Strategic Defence Review environment, and, especially to improve management and leadership development, both civilian and military".

LEADERSHIP, MANAGEMENT, COMMAND, AND CONTROL

The four pillars of an organization are Leadership, Management, Command, and Control. They are important for every leader and manager to understand because they directly drive the organization. Used properly, the business will grow; used improperly, the business will sink.

These are not distinct processes, but rather concepts that all leaders perform in order to build and strengthen their organizations.

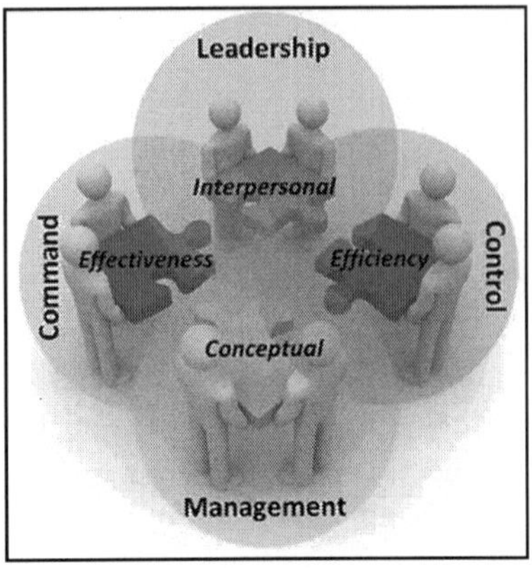

As the above diagram shows, the four pillars overlap, thus they are not separate processes. This blending gives the organization the ability to focus on opportunities and deal with threats:

- Leadership drives the interpersonal aspects of the organization, such as moral and team spirit.
- Management deals with the conceptual issues of the organization, such as planning and organizing.
- Command guides the organization with well thought-out visions that makes it effective.
- Control provides structure to the organization in order to make it more efficient.

Benefits of the Four Processes

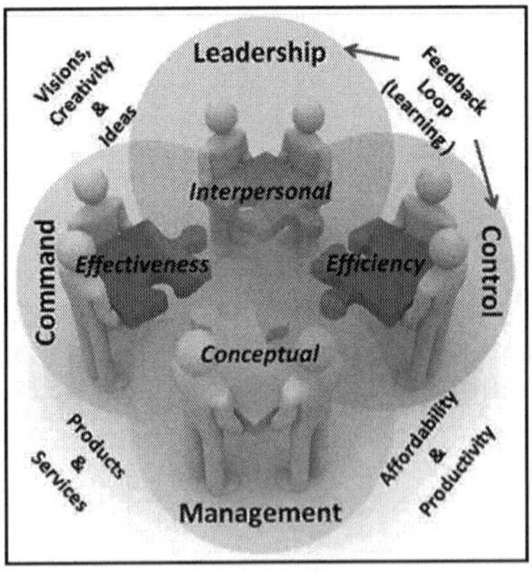

Command and Control

Command is the imparting of a vision to the organization in order to achieve and end-goal. It does this by formulating a well-thought out vision and then clearly communicating it. It emphasizes success and reward. That is, the organization has to be successful to survive and in turn reward its members (both intrinsically and extrinsically).

An example would be visioning a process that helps to increase informal learning and make it more effective. A bad vision would be implementing a social media tool, such as a wiki or Twitter. This is because social media tools are the means rather than an end-goal. That is, they are more like specific objectives that enable you to achieve your end-goal (vision).

Now you might implement a social media tool as explained below, but the real goal is to increase interactions that lead to informal learning, while a supporting process is the tool itself. Visions do not have to come from the top, but rather anywhere in the organization. Informal leaders are often good sources of visions, however if the vision requires resources, then it normally needs the support of a formal leader.

In contrast, Control is the process used to establish and provide structure in order to deal with uncertainties. Visions normally produce change, which in turn produce tension. These tensions or uncertainties must be dealt with so they do not impede the organization. For example, the organization might implement a new social media tool to enable its worker to interact with others and aid the process of informal learning more effectively. After implementing the tool the leader might ask, "Is the tool we provided to increase the effectiveness of informal learning really working?" Thus control is also used to measure and evaluate.

Inherent in evaluation is efficiency—the act of examining the new tool often leads to processes that make it more efficient. This can be good because it can save money and often improves a tool or process. The danger is if the command process is weak and the control process is strong then it can make efficiency the end-goal. That is, it replaces effectiveness with efficiency.

A good example of this is our present economy that caused many organizations to perform massive layoffs. Now the same organizations are complaining that they can't find qualified workers. Efficiency overrode effectiveness—they failed to realize that they would need a trained workforce in the future.

Leadership and Management

Management's primary focus is on the conceptual side of the business, such as planning, organizing, and budgeting. It does the leg work to make visions reality. Do Not equate the term "management" with "controlling people." Management is more about ensuring that the organization's resources are allocated wisely, rather than trying to control people. In fact, good managers know that trying to control others is extremely difficult if not impossible. Thus management helps to acquire, integrate, and allocate resources in order to accomplish goals and task. Going back to the above example of increasing informal learning by implementing a new social media tool, the managers must look at the real goal, rather than the tool. The real goal is to increase informal learning and human interactions in order to make them more effective, not to put into place a media tool.

If the tool becomes the primary goal, then the wrong polices could be put into place that decrease its value as an informal learning tool, for example, implementing a policy that no one in the company can ask a question on Twitter as it might make us look stupid or our competitors will know what we are trying to do. This policy removes the real purpose of the tool—enabling the employees to learn informally from others. Secondly, if the focus is only on the tool, then other options are omitted, such as tearing down cubicles and creating spaces where people can meet. In contrast, Leadership deals with the interpersonal relations such as being a teacher and coach, instilling organizational spirit to win, and serving the organization and worker.

THE EXISTING SITUATION OF LEADERSHIP, MANAGEMENT AND COMMAND

Therefore, most Officers hold a basic definition of each component of this trinity and indeed, how they are related to each other.

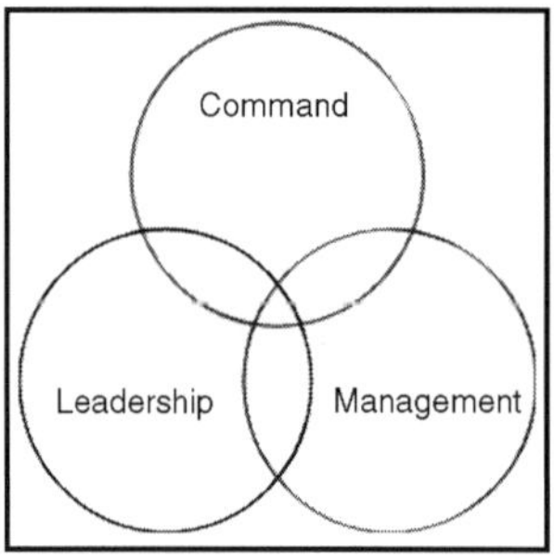

Fig. A Simple Interrelationship Between Command, Leadership and Management

AN ALTERNATIVE MODEL FOR LEADERSHIP, MANAGEMENT AND COMMAND DOCTRINE

A New Approach

The world of work is changing at a rapid pace, greatly influenced by shifting societal trends, technology and globalization. These trends cannot be treated as separate issues; their interdependent effects will continue to exert powerful influences on the RAF, its culture and how leadership, management and command is viewed and practiced. Therefore, proactively adapting leadership, management and command philosophies to meet these challenges of this millennium will enhance the overall effectiveness of the RAF.

To date, however, the military style of leadership, management and command training (and doctrine) has often focused on 'hard' skills such as planning, organizing and directing, all within an impersonal hierarchical structure. However, current thinking (from both the corporate world and academia) is now shifting towards an increase in the importance of 'soft' skills such as communication and motivation. In addition, the supply of human capital is undergoing a pervasive and powerful shift: the workforce – in the UK today – is a mosaic of individuals with varied ages, backgrounds, skills, aspirations and styles. Therefore, the definition of diversity will continue to evolve from merely race and gender to include age, disability, family structure, sexual orientation, ethnic culture, language and religious affiliation. Thus, organizations that can lead, manage and command this diversity will have a greater opportunity to thrive in the years ahead.

Indeed, research now shows that 'respect for the differences in people' is now one of the most important qualities in a leader. Further, the Industrial Society has now published research on the 5 weakest areas of the less successful leader:

- Failure to be sensitive to peoples feelings.
- Failure to recognize other peoples' stress.
- Failure to develop and guide staff.
- Failure to encourage feedback on their own (the leader's) performance.
- Failure to consult those affected before making decisions.

Although the above list was generated from Industrial leaders, it has equal applicability to the RAF and serves to reinforce previous arguments about the personal or human side to leadership, management and command: the above failures are all 'soft-skill' orientated.

Therefore, to undergo the necessary transformation in leadership, management and command philosophies and, therefore, to provide the relevant training, Officers will now have to accept the feasibility of working alliances with subordinates who question old practices and propose new solutions and to think of the link between them, as essential as the link between strategy and operations.

Furthermore, it will be vital that too much emphasis is not put on leadership traits or leadership doctrine from the past: even successful organizations may undo themselves in the future if they continue to act today in the way they have acted in the past.

Organizational Leadership

Leadership exists at every level of the organization and it is not a function of rank. From the airmen in the RAF today, to the Air Marshals at the corporate level, everybody has an individual leadership responsibility to those who serve under them.

Indeed, given their generational characteristics, the recruits of tomorrow (both Officers and airmen) will likely have little organizational loyalty: they will view themselves as 'free agents' who will only work for a leader who provides the most developmental challenges and opportunities, that focus on promoting commitment, involvement, intellectual stimulation and individual consideration. Therefore, leaders will need to routinely ask for inputs from subordinates and share information freely while focusing on trust, respect and empowerment that will help to strike a balance between the leaders and those that they lead.

Leadership and Strategy

The necessity to make the right decision and then carry it out in the 'right way,' is reflected currently by the Services formal decision-making tool, the Formal Estimate. In essence, this estimate consists of 4 parts:

- Mission Analysis.
- Evaluation of factors.
- Consideration of courses of action.
- Selection of the best course of action.

Whilst the format of the process and the language has a unique military favour, the concept of working out what to do, analysing the relevant factors, and selecting a choice, is the basis for strategy in the civilian world. In this context, it is here that leadership is closely related to strategy. Strategy is the job of projecting into the future: surveying an organizational situation or problem and deciding between alternative courses of action that have many possible consequences. Again, strategic leadership exists at every level in the RAF.

LEADERSHIP

Good leaders are made not born. If you have the desire and willpower, you can become an effective leader. Good leaders develop through a never ending process of self-study, education, training, and experience (Jago, 1982). This guide will help you through that process.

To inspire your workers into higher levels of teamwork, there are certain things you must **be,** know, and, do. These do not come naturally, but are acquired through continual work and study. Good leaders are continually working and studying to improve their leadership skills; they are NOT resting on their laurels.

Before we get started, lets define leadership. Leadership is a process by which a person influences others to accomplish an objective and directs the organization in a way that makes it more cohesive and coherent. This definition is similar to Northouse's (2007, p3) definition — Leadership is a process whereby an individual influences a group of individuals to achieve a common goal.

Leaders carry out this process by applying their leadership knowledge and skills. This is called Process Leadership (Jago, 1982). However, we know that we have traits that can influence our actions. This is called Trait Leadership (Jago, 1982), in that it was once common to believe that leaders were born rather than made.

Roles and Relationships

Roles are the positions that are defined by a set of expectations about behaviour of any job incumbent. Each role has a set of tasks and responsibilities that may or may not be spelled out. Roles have a powerful effect on behaviour for several reasons, to include money being paid for the performance of the role, there is prestige attached to a role, and a sense of accomplishment or challenge.

Relationships are determined by a role's tasks. While some tasks are performed alone, most are carried out in relationship with others. The tasks will determine who the role-holder is required to interact with, how often, and towards what end. Also, normally the greater the interaction, the greater the liking. This in turn leads to more frequent interaction. In human behaviour, its hard to like someone whom we have no contact with, and we tend to seek out those we like. People tend to do what they are rewarded for, and friendship is a powerful reward. Many tasks and behaviours that are associated with a role are brought about by these relationships. That is, new task and behaviours are expected of the present role-holder because a strong relationship was developed in the past, either by that role-holder or a prior role-holder.

Culture and Climate

There are two distinct forces that dictate how to act within an organization: culture and climate. Each organization has its own distinctive culture. It is a combination of the founders, past leadership, current leadership, crises, events, history, and size. This results in rites: the routines, rituals, and the "way we do things." These rites impact individual behaviour on what it takes to be in good standing (the norm) and directs the appropriate behaviour for each circumstance.

The climate is the feel of the organization, the individual and shared perceptions and attitudes of the organization's members. While the culture is the deeply rooted nature of the organization that is a result of long-held formal and informal systems, rules, traditions, and customs; climate is a short-term phenomenon created by the current leadership. Climate represents the beliefs about the "feel of the organization" by its members. This individual perception of the "feel of the organization" comes from what the people believe about the activities that occur in the organization. These activities influence both individual and team motivation and satisfaction, such as:

- How well does the leader clarify the priorities and goals of the organization? What is expected of us?
- What is the system of recognition, rewards, and punishments in the organization?
- How competent are the leaders?
- Are leaders free to make decisions?
- What will happen if I make a mistake?

Organizational climate is directly related to the leadership and management style of the leader, based on the values, attributes, skills, and actions, as well as the priorities of the leader. Compare this to "ethical climate" — the feel of the organization about the activities that have ethical content or those aspects of the work environment that constitute ethical behaviour. The ethical climate is the feel about whether we do things right; or the feel of whether we behave the way we ought to behave. The behaviour (character) of the leader is the most important factor that impacts the climate.

On the other hand, culture is a long-term, complex phenomenon. Culture represents the shared expectations and self-image of the organization. The mature values that create tradition or the "way we do things here." Things are done differently in every organization. The collective vision and common folklore that define the institution are a reflection of culture. Individual leaders, cannot easily create or change culture because culture is a part of the organization. Culture influences the characteristics of the climate by its effect on the actions and thought processes of the leader. But, everything you do as a leader will affect the climate of the organization.

LEADERSHIP STYLES

A leadership style is a leader's style of providing direction, implementing plans, and motivating people. There are many different leadership styles that can be exhibited by leaders in the political, business or other fields.

Authoritarian

The authoritarian leadership style or autocratic leader keeps strict, close control over followers by keeping close regulation of policy's and procedures given to followers. To keep main emphasis on the distinction of the authoritarian leader and their followers, these types of leaders make sure to only create a distinct professional relationship. Direct supervision is what they believe to be key in maintaining a successful environment and follower ship. In fear of followers being unproductive, authoritarian leaders keep close supervision and feel this is necessary in order for anything to be done.

Examples of authoritarian communicative behaviour: a police officer directing traffic, a teacher ordering a student to do his or her assignment, and a supervisor instructing a subordinate to clean a workstation. All of these positions require a distinct set of characteristics that give the leader the position to get things in order or get a point across. Authoritarian Traits: sets goals individually, engages primarily in one-way and downward communication, controls discussion with followers,and donates interaction.

Paternalistic Leadership

The way a Paternalistic leader works is by acting as a father figure by taking care of their subordinates as a parent would. In this style of leadership the leader supplies complete concern for his followers or workers. In return he receives the complete trust and loyalty of his people. Workers under this style of leader are expected to become totally committed to what the leader believes and will not strive of and work independently. The relationship between these co-workers and leader are extremely solid. The workers are expected to stay with a company for a longer period of time because of the loyalty and trust. Not only do they treat each other like family inside the workforce, but outside too. These workers are able to go to each other with any problems they have regarding something because they believe in what they say is going to truly help them. "

One of the downsides to a paternalistic leader is that the leader could start to play favourites in decisions. This leader would include the workers more apt to follow and start to exclude the ones who were less loyal. In today's market paternalism is more difficult to come by according to Padavic and Earnest who wrote "business dimensional and Organizational Counseling." They believe this because there have become more lay-offs and stronger unionization. This affects paternalistic leaders because the co-workers may not believe that their jobs are 100 per cent ensured. When this happens, workers begin to look for bigger and better job opportunities instead of staying at one company for a longer period of time. Because of this, The leader may be thinking that you could be leaving and not fully believe you when you tell them something about a job opportunity. This could put the workers and leader at risk for a bad situation. "

According to B. M. Bass who wrote Leadership and Performance Beyond Expectations, workers who follow paternalistic leadership also have better organization skills. The leader encourages organization because they allow the workers to complete tasks so that they can stay on top of their work. The workers complete tasks this boosts self-confidence and it makes them work harder to reach a goal and exceed the goal to prove to their boss they are working hard. Having this style of leadership can also help implement a reward system. This system will allow their workers to work even better because there is something for them at the end of the tunnel. While doing this they will also be able to accomplish more work in a set time frame.

Democratic

The democratic leadership style consists of the leader sharing the decision-making abilities with group members by promoting the interests of the group members and by practicing social equality.

This style of leadership encompasses discussion, debate and sharing of ideas and encouragement of people to feel good about their involvement. The boundaries of democratic participation tend to be circumscribed by the organization or the group needs and the instrumental value of people's attributes (skills, attitudes, etc.). The democratic style encompasses the notion that everyone, by virtue of their human status, should play a part in the group's decisions. However, the democratic style of leadership still requires guidance and control by a specific leader. The democratic style demands the leader to make decisions on who should be called upon within the group and who is given the right to participate in, make and vote on decisions. Traits of a Good Leader compiled by the Santa Clara University and the Tom Peters Group:

- *Honest*: Display sincerity, integrity, and candor in all your actions. Deceptive behaviour will not inspire trust.
- *Competent*: Base your actions on reason and moral principles. Do not make decisions based on childlike emotional desires or feelings.
- *Forward-looking*: Set goals and have a vision of the future. The vision must be owned throughout the organization. Effective leaders envision what they want and how to get it. They habitually pick priorities stemming from their basic values.
- *Inspiring*: Display confidence in all that you do. By showing endurance in mental, physical, and spiritual stamina, you will inspire others to reach for new heights. Take charge when necessary.
- *Intelligent*: Read, study, and seek challenging assignments.
- *Fair-minded*: Show fair treatment to all people. Prejudice is the enemy of justice. Display empathy by being sensitive to the feelings, values, interests, and well-being of others.
- *Broad-minded*: Seek out diversity.
- *Courageous*: Have the perseverance to accomplish a goal, regardless of the seemingly insurmountable obstacles. Display a confident calmness when under stress.
- *Straightforward*: Use sound judgement to make a good decisions at the right time.
- *Imaginative*: Make timely and appropriate changes in your thinking, plans, and methods. Show creativity by thinking of new and better goals, ideas, and solutions to problems. Be innovative!

Research has found that this leadership style is one of the most effective and creates higher productivity, better contributions from group members and increased group morale. Democratic leadership can lead to better ideas and more creative solutions to problems because group members are encouraged to share their thoughts and ideas. While democratic leadership is one of the most effective leadership styles, it does have some potential downsides. In situations where roles are unclear or time is of the essence, democratic leadership can lead to communication failures and uncompleted projects. Democratic leadership works best in situations where group members are skilled and eager to share their knowledge. It is also important to have plenty of time to allow people to contribute, develop a plan and then vote on the best course of action.

Laissez-Faire

The laissez-faire leadership style was first described by Lewin, Lippitt, and White in 1938, along with the autocratic leadership and the democratic leadership styles. The laissez-faire style is sometimes described as a "hands off" leadership style because the leader delegates the tasks to their followers while providing little or no direction to the followers.

If the leader withdraws too much from their followers it can sometimes result in a lack of productivity, cohesiveness, and satisfaction. Laissez-faire leaders allow followers to have complete freedom to make decisions concerning the completion of their work. It allows followers a high degree of autonomy andself-rule, while at the same time offering guidance and support when requested. The laissez-faire leader using guided freedom provides the followers with all materials necessary to accomplish their goals, but does not directly participate in decision making unless the followers request their assistance.

This is an effective style to use when:

- Followers are highly skilled, experienced, and educated.
- Followers have pride in their work and the drive to do it successfully on their own.
- Outside experts, such as staff specialists or consultants are being used.
- Followers are trustworthy and experienced.

LEADERSHIP ORGANIZATIONS

Leadership has been closely studied over the years, both as a matter of academic interest and with an eye to making leadership easier and more effective in organizations. There is no formal and agreed definition of leadership (or even of its functions), although there are common features to many of the definitions available.

In 1988, Warren G Bennis completed writing his classic book On Becoming A Leader. This richly praised book details: how people become leaders; how they lead; and how organizations encourage or indeed, stifle leaders. Underlying the 'how's,' he goes onto claim that leaders must understand the context in which they are working in and notes: "The changes in the last generation have been so radical that it seems...not just that the rules have changed (but that) it is a different game".

Indeed, for the RAF, the pace of change in the last 30 years alone has been extraordinary, with simultaneous changes in both international security and domestic society. Therefore, in this dynamic and fast-changing environment, strong leadership is required at every level of the organization; there is nothing more important to an organization than the quality of its leadership and indeed, of its leadership philosophy. However, one criticism of today's organizations is that they are over managed and under led: they (organizations) are overly concerned with policies, practices, procedures and rule books and not concerned enough with the important issues like trust, mission and an overarching and compelling vision.

Indeed, Warren Bennis has detailed 4 things that people want from their leaders:

- Purpose, direction and meaning (a strong determination to achieve a goal).
- Trust.
- A sense of we-can-do-it (optimism).
- Results.

Everyone knows that excellent leadership can be felt throughout an organization; leadership gives pace and energy to the work and empowers the workforce, which is most evident in 4 themes: people feel significant (everyone feels that he or she makes a difference to the success of the organization); learning and competence matter (leaders value learning and mastery and so do the people who work for leaders); people are part of the community (where there is leadership, there is a team – a family a unit); and work is exciting (where there are leaders, work is stimulating, challenging, fascinating and fun).

Therefore, in simple terms, leaders create vision, trust, meaning, success and healthy environments – if they survive the bureaucracy. A better definition of leadership, therefore, is how to achieve worthwhile goals through other people via a vision. Critically, to survive in the 21st Century, the RAF will require a new generation of leaders – leaders, not managers. This distinction is an important one: leaders conquer the context, the volatile, turbulent, ambiguous surroundings that sometimes seem to conspire against the organization, whilst managers surrender to the bureaucracy! Effective leadership, therefore, is very important to unlocking the immense talent in any organization, including the RAF. Moreover, organizational vision can also challenge people to stretch beyond their current capabilities and often beyond their limitations. As Nanus comments: "There is no more powerful engine driving an organization towards excellence and long range success, than an attractive, worthwhile and achievable vision of the future, that is widely shared".

This vision must be alive in every command level of the RAF and a corporate vision must operate at 3 levels:

- Strategic – The RAF's overriding philosophy.
- Operational – That philosophy in action.
- Tactical – That philosophy manifested in the behaviour of each airman/woman.

Thus, the leaders responsibilities include disseminating vision to all 3 levels and this vision needs to permeate throughout the organization. Finally, leaders must evaluate vision, before the vision fails or is inadequate to handle new challenges. Vision needs constant attention in light of the dynamic environment in which we live and work in and leaders who are not strategists are simply caretakers and gatekeepers. Though they may run efficient and effective organizations (*i.e.* they are managers), they do not really serve the long-term interests of their institutions unless they plan, set goals and provide strategic vision. Leaders who care about their missions and about their people normally want to leave their organization in better shape and with a clearer strategic direction, than when they took over.

In summary, the difference between a good unit and a bad unit is leadership: sound leadership within a dynamic environment, is at the heart of the RAF's institutional character. It is the most important bond among airmen and is the foundation for successful Air Force achievements in peace and war; of the many skills and abilities used in the profession of arms, none is prized more highly. Enhancing leadership as we transform to meet the challenges of this millennium can strengthen the foundation of mutual trust and respect among ranks and across the organization as a whole.

DEFINITION OF LEADERSHIP

The word "leadership' has been used in at least three different ways. Occasion-ally it refers to a position within an organization, *e.g.*, "We are inviting all of the leadership to attend the seminar. 'Leadership" has also been used to describe a personality characteristic, *e.g.*. 'Our new supervisor doesn't have as much leadership as our previous one."

Neither of these definitions is very useful in studying organizational behavi-or, and a better definition is needed to understand why some individuals are at he more effective leaders than others. The most useful definition of leadership, well, and the one we will use in this chapter, is a form of behaviour by which one person influences others. 'Our team won the championship because of the leadership of the quarterback." In other words, leadership is the incremental influence one individual exerts over another, above and beyond mechanical compliance with routine directives. Leadership occurs when one individual MBO-influences others to do something voluntarily rather than because they were the required to do it or because they feared the consequences of non-compliance. It strong is this voluntary aspect of leadership that distinguishes it from other influence processes, such as power and authority.

Although leaders may use force or coercion to influence the behaviour of followers, leaders by our definition use their ability to induce voluntary com-mittee. By this definition, anyone in the organization can be a leader, whether or not that individual is formally identified as such. Indeed, informal leaders are extremely important to the effectiveness of most organizations.

An important distinction is made by some between leadership and manage-ment. To manage means to direct, to bring about to accomplish, and to have responsibility for. The functions of management, are planning, organizing, directing, and controlling. The successful manager is viewed as someone who achieves results by following the prescribed activities and by maintaining behaviours and products within prescribed limits. To lead, however, is to inspire, to influence, and to motivate. Effective leaders inspire others to pursue excellence, to extend themselves and to go beyond their perform job requirements by generating creative ideas. It has been said that managers are people who do things right and leaders are people who do the right thing."

This distinction is somewhat overstated, since effective leaders do a lot of managing and effective managers need to lead. But it serves to emphasize an Important organizational outcome: the creation of an energetic and highly committed workforce that is successfully adapting to the demands of a changing environment and competently producing a viable product or service

NEED FOR LEADERSHIP

Why is leadership necessary? Most organizations are highly structured and have relatively clear lines of authority, stated objectives, and momentum to carry them forward. Why, then, is there a need for incremental influence beyond the routine directives and formal job requirements? Four reasons have been proposed to explain the need for ongoing leadership.

Incomplete Organizational Structure

The first reason why leadership is necessary is because there is a degree of incompleteness in every organization design. Social organizations cannot be designed to be like machines, which are simply turned on and allowed to run untouched. Leaders are needed to structuring the tasks, decide who should do what, and delegate work assignments, level. Leaders help the people they lead to accomplish their collective goals.

External Change

The second reason why leadership is necessary is because the organization exists in a changing environment. As the external environment changes, leaders are needed to identify the strategic mission of the organization and help it adapt to its changing environment.

Internal Change

The third reason for leadership stems from the dynamics of internal change in the organization. Leadership is needed to coordinate the efforts of diverse organizational units, particularly during periods of rapid growth or decline. Leadership is necessary to solve internal conflicts and settle differences of opinion.

Motivate and Inspire

The fourth reason why organizations require leader-ship stems from the need to motivate people and maintain their involvement in the organization.

Individuals are not permanent fixtures within the organiza-tion. Instead, they come and go, and when they are present, their needs and Intel interests change. Effective leadership provides meaning and purpose by creating a vision of where the organization is going. This ability to inspire and motivate others and transform them into committed contributors to the organi-zation is the function of leadership that has captured the interest of philoso-phers and scholars and propelled the study of leadership.

IN SEARCH OF LEADERSHIP

Although early writers attempted to describe the characteristics of effective leaders, systematic investigations of leadership traits first began after the turn of the century. World War I highlighted the need for selecting and training effective leaders, and for the quarter century between World War land World War II, numerous studies investigated the personal traits of good leaders.

These studies are generally referred to as trait studies, since their primary goal was to identi6' the traits and personal characteristics of effective leaders. A variety of methods was used to study leadership traits, and this variety is probably one reason why the results were so inconsistent. Most studies com-pared effective leaders with ineffective leaders or leaders with non-leaders.

The—studies were inconsistent in the methods used to identify leaders Some were identified by outside observers, some were selected by the group via nominations or voting, others were named by qualified observers such as teachers, and$_1$ some were selected because they occupied a position of leadership such as student-body president or team captain. The studies were also inconsistent -the way they measured traits. In some studies the traits were measured b psychological tests; other studies relied on observers to identify the traits they saw; and some studies relied on the individuals to report their own character traits.

In general, the trait studies were quite disappointing, especially to researchers who had hoped to develop a measure of leadership that predicted leader effectiveness as accurately as intelligence tests predicted problem solving ability. Because of weak results, the focus of leadership research shifted from trait studies to contingency studies, which examined more than just the traits of the leader.

Research on leadership traits should not be dismissed too quickly, however. Although the traits studies were disappointing, they were not worthless. Several traits produced a significant difference in leadership effectiveness, but they did not act alone. Instead, they interacted with other situational variables to influence leader effectiveness, Four major reviews have surveyed the trait studies, and the results can be summarized according to physical traits, intelligence, and personality traits).

PHYSICAL TRAITS

Trait studies examined such physical factors as height, weight, physique, energy, health, and appearance. To the extent that anything can be concluded regarding the relationship between these factors and leadership, it appears that the leaders tend to be slightly taller and heavier, have better health, a superior physique, a higher rate of energy output, and a more attractive appearance. To illustrate, one of the early studies on the effects of height found that executives in insurance companies were taller than policyholders, that bishops were taller than clergymen, that university presidents were taller than college presidents, that sales managers were taller than sales representatives, and that railway presidents were taller than station agents." Results of this sort, how-ever, have not always been consistent.

While one literature review found nine studies showing that leaders tend to be taller, it reported two studies showing that leaders tended to be shorter. Attractiveness and a pleasant appearance found to be highly correlated with leaders among Boy Scouts: but among groups of delinquent youth, leaders were rated as more slovenly and unkempt.' In summary, studies of personal characteristics are not particularly inter-esting or useful. The results are generally too weak and inconsistent to be useful in selecting leaders, nor are they useful for training purposes, since very little can be done to change most of these physical traits.

INTELLIGENCE

Numerous studies have investigated the relationship between leadership and general intelligence, and they generally agree that leaders are more intelligent than non-leaders. The relationship between intelligence and leadership probably stems from the fact that so many leadership functions depend upon careful problem solving. All three leadership roles—origination, interpolation, and administration require significant mental ability.

One review of leadership studies reported twenty-tree experiments showing that leaders were brighter and had greater levels of intelligence." Only five studies reported that intelligence made no difference. In general, it appears safe to conclude that leaders are more intelligent than non-leaders, but again the correlations are small. Obviously, many other variables besides intelligence influence leadership effectiveness.

An interesting conclusion coming from these studies is the suggestion that leaders should be more intelligent than the group but not by too wide a margin. Members who are significantly brighter than other group members are seldom selected as leaders. Because of their superior intellect, other group members tend to reject them; they are too different from and out of touch with the rest of the group. Individuals with high IQ's tend to have different vocabularies, interacts, and goals, which create communication and interpersonal relations prob-lems.

Leadership effectiveness also appears to be related to two other variables closely associated with intelligence: scholarship and knowledge. Leaders generally excel scholastically and receive better than average grades. General information, practical knowledge, and simply knowing how to get things done appears to be important for effective leadership, and several studies have shown a positive relationship between general knowledge and leadership ability.

PERSONALITY TRAITS

Studies of the relationship between leadership and personality traits have ex-amined a lengthy list of factors. Unfortunately, most of the results have been inconsistent and even contradictory. Only a limited number of personality traits appear to be related to leadership, and most of these relationships are not especially strong.

A list of the personality traits most frequently associated with leadership are lead shown in Exhibit 16.2. This list is based upon the 1948 review by Ralph Stogdill were of 124 studies of leadership traits)This list suggests that the average leader is use a more social, displays greater initiative, is more persistent, knows how to get things done, is more self-confident, displays greater cooperativeness and adapt-ability, and possesses greater verbal skills to facilitate communication. Studies examining personality integration or emotional adjustment consistently found that leaders were more emotionally mature than non-leaders.

Rather consistent. The support was also found for the relationship between leadership and self-confidence or self-esteem. Indeed, the relationship between self-confidence and leadership generally produced some of the highest correlations of any of the personality traits tested Consequently, it is not correct to conclude that personal characteristics are unrelated to leadership; there are indeed some relationships, but they are more complex than they first appear to be.

After four major reviews of the trait studies, researchers concluded that the effective leadership does not depend solely upon a combination of personality the traits. Situational variables were also important: they frequently determined of whether a personality characteristic was positively or negatively associated with effective leadership. Each review concluded that leadership must be examined as an interaction of three variables: characteristics of the leader, characteristics of the subordinate, and the nature of the task.

Table. Personality Factors Most Frequently Associated with Effective Leadership

Capacity	Achievements	Responsibility	Participation	Status
Intelligence	Scholarship	Dependability	Activity	Socioeconomic position
Alertness	Knowledge Initiative	Sociability	Popularity	

Verbal facility	Athletic accomplishment	Persistence	Cooperation
Originality	Personality adjustment	Aggressiveness	Adaptability
Judgement		Self-Confidence	Humor
		Desire to Excel	

While the trait studies focused on individual leaders, another line of research examined leader behaviours within the context of a group and attempted to describe what leaders actually do. These studies essentially asked whether certain ways of behaving were more effective than others: How do effective readers behave differently from other group members?

Most of these studies occurred during the 1940s and 50s. Various styles of leadership were defined as a result of these studies of leader behaviours. One of the earlier studies compared three leadership styles: authoritarian democratic and laissez-faire. Perhaps the best research on styles of leadership, however, occurred simultaneously at The Ohio State University and the University of Michigan.

At each university, researchers identified two leader behaviours that were essentially similar, even though both investigations were conducted independently. These two dimensions of leadership have been to form an instrument, called the Managerial Grid®, that has been used for research and training.

Authoritarian, Democratic, and Laissez-Faire Leadership

The contrasting political systems in the United States and Germany preceding World War II inspired one of the early classic studies of leadership that com-pared the effects of three leadership styles: authoritarian, democratic, and laissez.faire.i5 This study involved groups of ten-year-old boys who were orga-nized in groups of five. Each group met regularly after school to engage in hobbies and other activities under the direction of a leader who adopted one of the three styles of leadership.

Every six weeks the leaders were rotated among the groups so that each group experienced each type of leadership. The leaders of these groups, who were graduate students in social psychology, were trained to lead the boys using one of three leadership styles.

Under the democratic style of leadership, group decisions were made by majority vote in which equal participation was encouraged and criticism and punishment were minimal. Under the autocratic leader, all decisions were made by the leader and the boys were required to follow prescribed procedures under strict discipline. Under the laissez-faire leader, the actual leadership was minimized and the boys were allowed to work and play essentially without supervision.

During the eighteen weeks of this study, the performance of the boys was observed in order to assess the effects of the three leadership styles. Under democratic leadership, the groups were more satisfied and functioned in the most orderly and positive manner. Aggressive acts were observed most frequently under the autocratic leadership. The effects of the leadership styles on productivity were somewhat mixed, although actual objective measures of productivity were not obtained. Under autocratic leadership the groups spent more time in productive work activity and had more work-related conversations.

However, the autocratic groups appeared to be more productive Only when the leader was present. When the leader left the room, the amount of work-related activity dropped drastically.

The results of this study were somewhat surprising to the researchers who had expected the highest satisfaction and productivity under democratic leadership.

This study was conducted under the direction of Kurt Lewin, a behavioural scientist who came to America from Germany just prior to World War Lewin believed that the repressive autocratic political climate he had left in Germany was not as satisfying, productive, or desirable as a democratic society. He expected the results of the experiment to confirm his hypothesis. Although the boys preferred a democratic leader, they appeared to be more productive under autocratic leadership.

Other studies have also shown that democratic leadership styles are not always the most productive. In fact, some studies have found that both the satisfaction and the productivity of group members is higher under directive leaders than democratic leaders.

For example a study of 488 managers in a consumer loan company found that employees who had high authoritarianism scores (high acceptance of strong authority relationships) were more satisfied and productive when they worked for supervisors who had little tolerance for freedom.

'Greater satisfaction with an authoritarian leader was also found in another study of over 1,000 workers. This study found that employees who worked independently but were required to have frequent interaction with their superior preferred and were more satisfied with an autocratic leader. Some examples of such employees are fire fighters, police officers, and administrative aides.

LEADERSHIP, MANAGEMENT AND COMMAND RELATED TO EACH OTHER

Leadership, management and command are 3 distinctive and complementary systems of action and the precise activities—and the characteristics required—of each system are intensely human matters.

Critically, leadership, management and command (as individual components, and as a trinity) are necessary for success in an increasingly complex and volatile military environment. The simple model of leadership, management and command. The main difference between leadership is now the dominant component of the trinity.

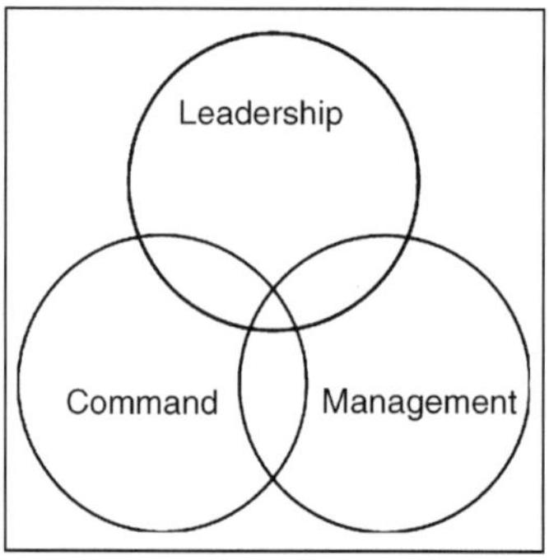

Fig. A Revised Model of Leadership, Management and Command

Part of the reason leadership has become so important (and therefore, the dominant component of the trinity) in recent years, is that the macro-environment (consisting of political, economic, socio-cultural and technological dimensions) has become more competitive and more volatile. The net result is that doing what was done yesterday – or even doing it 5 per cent better – is no longer a formula for success. For example, consider a simple military analogy: a peacetime Air Force can usually survive with good command and management procedures up and down the hierarchy, coupled with good leadership at the very top. A wartime Air Force, however, needs competent leadership at all levels. No one yet has figured out how to manage people effectively into battle; they must be led! Indeed, in times of rapid change, there is no substitute for leadership.

Unfortunately, most organizations are still based on the old-fashioned form of bureaucracy: the mind-set of control, order and predict. Those are the things of command and management. If we existed in an environment where we could control order and 'predict', a manager and commander would be a terrific thing and bureaucracy in a stable environment – as in the Victorian era – would be a great social invention. But today, organizations have become 'unhinged': they are confusing, rapidly changing, unpredictable and full of surprises. This is why leadership is now critical: it (leadership) moves people into the arena of creative solutions, by first breaking barriers that inhibit fresh and new 'unthinked' thinking. Indeed, preparing airmen for future (rather than past wars) involves constant encouragement of open-minded thinking to ensure intellectual growth. Thus the art of leadership involves moving people forward towards a goal and inspiring them to perform and succeed for the greater goal.

In this sense, leadership cannot be bestowed upon a person by higher authority. Therefore, it is misleading to think that leadership is only a characteristic of senior ranks or specific positions. Leadership is needed and must be practiced at every level of an organization: great leaders understand that to achieve their vision and gain respect and authority, they must be willing to give power (command authority) to others; they delegate responsibility to other individuals and give those individuals the knowledge and resources to succeed.

LEADERSHIP AND MANAGEMENT

Management develops the capacity to achieve its plan by organizing and staffing – creating an organizational structure and a set of jobs for accomplishing the plan. The equivalent leadership activity, however, is aligning people: this means communicating a new direction to those who can create coalitions and who both understand the vision and are committed to its achievement.

In addition, management ensures plan accomplishment by controlling and problem solving (monitoring the results versus the plan in some detail (both formally and informally) by means of reports, meetings and other tools; identifying deviations; and then planning and organizing to solve the problems). But for leadership, achieving a vision requires motivating and inspiring – despite major obstacles to change – by appealing to the basic, but often untapped, human needs, values and emotions. More than anything else, however, the difference between the leader and the manger rests with the status quo: managers are willing to live with it and leaders are not. In summary, then, perhaps the best way to explain the difference between leadership and management.

The Manager	The Leader
The manager administers	The leader innovates.
The manager is a copy	The leader is an original.
The manager maintains	The leader develops.
The manager controls	The leader inspires trust.
The manager has a short-range view perspective.	The leader has a long-range
The manager asks how and when	The leader asks what and why.
The manager has his or her eye on	The leader has his or her eye on the
	the bottom line horizon.
The manager is the classic good soldier	The leader is his or her own person.
The manager does things right	The leader does the right thing.

LEADERSHIP AND COMMAND

Leadership and 'headship' are uniquely different and it is always important to focus on the leader as a person, and not those who merely serve as heads ('commanders') in positions of leadership. While many people regard 'command' and 'leadership' as much the same thing, it is more helpful to treat them as 2 separate but related functions. Successful leaders persuade people willingly to endure hardships (usually prolonged) and incur dangers (usually acute) that if left to themselves, they would do their utmost to avoid. Leadership is, therefore, concerned with inspiration and motivation. Command, by contrast, is the direction, coordination and effective use of military force."

MANAGEMENT

Management is defined as the allocation and control of resources (human, material and financial) to achieve the goals and objectives of the organization and the measure of good management is the ability to achieve the right balance: neither an over-abundance nor a shortage of resources, either of which would undermine the concentration of effort on the main objective, whatever that may be.

UNDERSTANDING THE ROLES OF THE MANAGER

Mintzberg analysed a managers' job in terms of roles and identified 10 managerial roles clustered around 3 main categories (interpersonal, informational and decisional).

Table. The Roles of the Manager The Manager's Role

Interpersonal	Informational	Decisional
Figurehead	Monitor: scans for information.	Entrepreneur: seeks change.
Leader	Disseminator: shares information with other people.	Disturbance handler: responds to pressures and crisis.
Liaison	Spokesperson: shares	Resource allocator: gives information with outsiders. resources to others. Negotiator: reaches agreement.

Management practices and procedures are largely a response to one of the most significant developments of the 20th Century: the emergence of large organizations.

Without good management, complex enterprises in a fast-moving and dynamic environment tend to become chaotic in ways that threaten their very existence and effective management, therefore, brings a degree of order and consistency to the key decisions made by managers.

WHAT ACCURATELY IS COMMAND

So what exactly is command then? In the military literature, there are a vast amount of definitions of command. Indeed, one-third of the United Kingdom Doctrine for Joint and Multinational Operations is dedicated to Command.

Furthermore, in the Queen's Regulations for the RAF, the concept and act of commanding is explained at length; however, no formal definition for command exists. Moreover, command is also different at each level of war and this task becomes all the more difficult in joint and multi-national operations, where senior commanders may have to impose their will, in an atmosphere of political, legal and even moral confusion.

Lawful and Process

Firstly, command has a legal and constitutional status, as codified in the Queen's Regulations. In the Queen's Regulations for the RAF, it states that at the highest level: "The government and command of each of the Services is vested in Her Majesty the Queen, who has charged the Secretary of State with general responsibility for the defence of the Realm and established a Defence Council having command and administration over Her Armed Forces;" and, in turn, Commanders in Chiefs who: "in conjunction with other duties are operationally responsible to the Defence Council for command of personnel in their area". Therefore, command is vested in a commander by higher authority and gives him direction (often encapsulated in a mission) that assigns forces to him, to accomplish that mission.

The concept of authority requires further definition: traditionalists define authority as 'the right to command and to induce compliance.' They regard authority as a central feature of the structure of formal organizations that 'prescribe expectations that certain individuals should exert control and direction over others within defined areas of competence.' In this context, authority involves the right and freedom to use the 'power of command' and ultimately to enforce obedience; whilst a commander can devolve specific authority to subordinates to decide and to act within their own areas of delegated responsibility, a commander retains overall responsibility for his command.

PERSONALITY COMMAND

Secondly, 'the exercise of command' includes the process by which a commander makes decisions, impresses his will upon, and transmits (*i.e.* tells) his intention to his subordinates. It, therefore, encompasses the authority, responsibility and duty to act. Therefore, individual command – at all levels – is defined as the art of decision-making, motivating and directing all ranks into actions to accomplish missions, whilst at the same time maintaining accountability and control.

The accountability and control require further analysis. Accountability is a corollary to both responsibility and authority; it involves a liability and obligation to answer to a superior for the proper user of delegated responsibility, authority and resources. Thus, he who delegates responsibility should grant sufficient authority to a subordinate for him to carry out his task; the subordinate, meanwhile, remains accountable to his superior for its execution.

In addition, Armed Forces often use the acronym C3I (command, control, communication and intelligence) and the addition of 'computers' to the list of Cs to produce C4. These definitions apply to command at every level: grand strategic, military strategic, operational and tactical. The German sociologist Max Weber (1864-1920) was one of the most prolific and influential sociologists of the 20th Century and he was the first person to coin the phrase 'command and control'. Three words describe his bureaucratic model: control, order and predict. Therefore, control is the process through which the commander—assisted by his staff—organizes, directs and co-ordinates his activities of the forces allocated to him. To achieve this, he and his staff employ a common doctrine for command and use standardized procedures for control in conjunction with the equipment, communication and information systems available. Command and control are thus inextricably linked with commanders requiring an understanding of both and the roles of each other if they are to perform their duties effectively. Command and control, however, are not 'equal partners' as control is merely one aspect of command.

In essence, command requires a vision of the desired result; an understanding of the concepts, missions, priorities and the allocation of resources; an ability to assess people and risks; and a continual process of re-evaluating the situation. A commander requires – above all – to decide on a course of action and to lead his command. Broadly speaking then, there are 2 styles of individual command: Befehlstaktik is an inflexible, authoritarian form of 'top-down' command in which subordinates receive rigid orders, that leave little or no scope to exercise low-level initiative. By contrast, Auftragstaktik emphasizes mission-type orders; the superior commander sets broad objectives, but then allows subordinates to use their initiative to achieve their part of the plan in the way that they think best. The BAFs version of Auftragstaktik is known as 'Mission Command.' Befehlstaktik dictates not just what is to be done, but how it is to be done and can be represented by the extreme left-end of the command circle in Figure 2.0 (*i.e.* 'tells'). Auftragstaktik can be represented by the right end of the command circle (*i.e.* shares the information).

Although BDD currently adopt Mission Command (the commander defines the limits of the operation and then lets the subordinates take the appropriate action at the coal-face), Befehlstaktik is wholly appropriate in certain circumstances; in times of crisis/emergency, a one-way, directional and autocratic approach to command must always be used. In this context, 'command-by-direction' is a description of the method used by commanders who directly command subordinates before and during battle; the commander feels he has positive control over each element. Van Creveld describes this as a method, which prioritises uncertainty; the commander, accepting that he will never have perfect information, nevertheless brings all uncertainty to himself and deals with whichever uncertainty assails him most at each moment.

Managerial Command

Thirdly, organizational command is related to organizational design: human beings profit from living in structured groups and irrespective of the organizational design (for example hierarchical, network/cellular or indeed a combination of the both – the matrix), organizations require a structure so that work can be divided to achieve coordination among its various work activities.

Organizational command, therefore, centres on the issues of:

- Division of labour.
- Allocation of authority.
- Departmentalisation.
- Span of control.

In addition, Burns and Stalker, 2 British Social Scientists, labelled organizations as either mechanistic or organic. The RAF employs (at present) a mechanistic organizational structure, which could be argued consists of tight rules and policies; limited individual job discretion; and coordination, which is both formal and written.

In addition, mechanistic organizations also posses:

- High divisions of labour.
- Low delegation of authority.
- Departments with great uniformity of work activities.
- Narrow spans of control.

At the organizational level then, senior commanders make countless decision about the division of labour, delegation of authority, departmentalisation and span of control. Over time, these decisions result in the elaboration of the organizations structure. Therefore, organizational command is defined as the arrangement of roles and reporting relationships, which govern employee behaviour with two primary components of organizational structure, namely centralization and co-ordination.

11

Power and Leadership

INTRODUCTION

Leadership is a form of social dominance, and leaders can exert powerful influences on the behaviours, ideals and feelings of the led. This chapter is concerned with rank and how, in humans, dominance expresses itself through the use of various forms of power. We will note that leaders can use their power in many different ways. They can use it to gain recognition, status and superiority for themselves and in so doing can act to suppress, intimidate, subordinate and structuralise the hierarchy and make sharper the boundaries between insider and outsider (the good and the bad). On the other hand leaders can act to relax, encourage and nurture subordinates, helping them to reduce their dependence on leaders, to de-structuralise the hierarchy and soften boundaries. To obtain a leadership position, obviously requires some type of power.

THE POWER MOTIVE AND PERSONALITY

Westerners often feel uncomfortable acknowledging power motives – gaining power seems associated with controlling others, dictatorial styles, and similar issues, it is an important motive for many people. The topic is regarded more positively and more openly discussed in certain Asian cultures. The power motive involves direct and legitimate control over other people's behaviour – that is, interpersonal power.

The power theme can be recognized when people evaluate and heighten their influence, impact, and control over others. For example, on TAT stories, a high-power person might tell stories in which characters directly express their power (*e.g.*, "They plan to attack the enemy"), or provide unsolicited protection (*e.g.*, "The mother protected her daughter against the others"), or try to influence, impress, or control other people (*e.g.*, "She told him she went to Harvard.") An example of a story with a power motive is the following response to a picture of an older man and a younger man together:

These two men are planning a break from the political party to which they both belong. The elder man is the instigator. Noticing the disapproval the young man has shown with the party policy, he is convincing him to join with him. The elder man was pushed into the party. At first, he thought it was a good idea. As he saw the workings of it he became more against it...The two will start a new opposition party.

Power-motivated people tend to enter professions in which they direct the behaviour of other individuals and in which they can reward or punish others within the legitimate policies and procedures of organizations (Winter, 1992b). Such occupations include business executives and managers, psychologists and mental health workers, teachers, journalists, and members of the clergy. Occupations in which the use of power is arguably more indirect, such as in law or science, or where the power is over someone's body as in medicine, rather than over someone's behaviour, are less likely to attract those high in n Power. Although you might guess that all politicians are high in n Power, many politicians run for office because of their need to achieve or to be loved instead. Politicians high in n Power, however, are more likely to initiate their own candidacies for office.

How do these power-seeking individuals attain power? They seek visibility, sometimes by taking extreme positions or gambles. Student leaders high in n power may write letters with extreme opinions to campus newspapers. Other high n power students may acquire possessions that others may not be able to afford (such as stereos, cars, nice apartments). In addition, high n power students in general build alliances with others, particularly with those of lower status, and encourage them to participate in the organizations in which they are trying to attain power. People high in power are not necessarily well liked, nor are they perceived as working hard or creating the best solutions for problems. In addition, such individuals may seek power to compensate for a fear of being controlled by others.

TYPES OF POWER

Hollander and Offerman, suggest three types of power: Power over others, the power to make or entice others to do things a leader wants; Power to, involving the degree of freedom to do as one wishes, also called empowerment; and Power from; involving the ability/power to resist the wishes/demands of others. As they point out high status involves all three forms of power, whilst subordinates have at best one or two and sometimes practically no such powers at all. When it comes to considering the forms of power psychologists have suggested five main forms are suggested.

Reward power is the ability to provide something that others want and will work for (e.g controlling access to wages, food, love, approval etc.). Coercive/punishment power is the ability to control others through actual or threatened aversive outcomes (*e.g.*, to injury the other or remove/withhold something of value to others). Both these are fairly direct, used by animals, and require little psychological capacity. The other three however require more complex psychologies. Legitimate power is linked to rights and obligations which require understanding and recognition of rights and obligations. It is used as a basis of law and socially defined roles (*e.g.*, the power of the captain, teacher, president, etc.). Expert power relates to an awareness of the superiority of another's knowledge or skill and it linked with respect and at times admiration (*e.g.*, doctors, priests, scientists). Referent power refers more to attractiveness, liking and person's charm or charisma. Many forms of power and indeed leadership requires that the dominant has access to and can control and the attention of subordinates.

Exercising Power

People often seek out leadership positions from which to use power and once there, their personality will influence how that power and position is exercised. So even though a social group may legitimise the use of power, and select an individual(s) for leadership roles, the way power is exercised depends on complex interactions between the person exercising it and those on whom it is exercised. Some may become leaders even against their wishes, via their popularity or the personal values they express. John Lennon, for example, along with other pop groups of the time, had an enormous effect on the values of the young. However, he consistently denied that he wished to be seen as any kind of leader. He wanted fame for his music.

Psychotherapists note that the acts of being attended and looked to, or treated as a leader (saviour, guru etc.) can ignite leadership desires. Indeed, without caution one can be intoxicated by it, becoming grandiose and carried away by it. There is an inflation of the up-rank archetype. For example, therapists have to be very careful of the idealisations, admirations and needs projected onto them, so as to avoid getting inflated ideas about themselves. Whether one is a doctor, lawyer or psychotherapist, it is very easy to fall victim to inflations of one's own rank and power; one's own importance.

One may never know how a person is going to behave until they are given or find themselves in positions of power; when they put on the uniform. Some years ago Zimbardo and his colleagues took a group of students and arbitrarily divided them into guards and prisoners. Before the week was out the experiment had to be stopped because about a third of the guards had become vindictive and authoritarian, devising various punishments for disobedient prisoners. The simmerings of a gestapo mentality were not hard to see. This was a shock to the researchers. So positions of power can inflate and excite underlying tendencies in a person.

LEADERSHIP

Lindholm notes, in his study of charisma, that we do not always behave in our own genetic self-interest when it comes to following leaders. There has been more than one leader who has taken us on a trip into mass destruction. In 1978 the world was shocked by the Jones Town suicide of men, women and children. Some, who were not present at the time, killed themselves later. And this was not the first, nor will it be the last, time that followers have killed others and themselves in devotion to a cause, manipulated by a leader. It is our rank psychology that courts so much craziness. So in this chapter we explore some facets of leadership.

Leaders vary in style and basic psychology (*e.g.*, in terms of their charisma, skills/knowledge, tendency to punish or reward). But they are also shaped and given access to leadership positions/roles via their cultures and social relationships. Some leaders are elected by those they will lead, others are imposed (as in the military) by superiors. Some leaders are encouraged to adopt certain styles and do certain things because of what is expected of (and projected onto) them.

We noted how George Orwell had to shoot the elephant, not from any personal desire to do so, but because of the expectations of the crowd and his concern to maintain his image of himself and of his "white-man" group. In his book, `On the Psychology of Military Incompetence', Norman Dixon notes that preferred leadership style varies according to the context. For example, in low stress times soldiers prefer democratic leaders, but in stressful situations, like war, they prefer autocratic, strong leadership on whom they can depend. Thus, subordinate preferences for styles of leaders are effected by personal and social stresses and the potentially saving, protective qualities the leader seems to provide.

Given this, some individuals are able to manipulate group values for their own ends and farm support. Authoritarian leaders can, for example, exaggerate threats, especially from outsiders and thus increase their appeal by offering themselves as strong, protective and decisive leaders. In low stress times leaders may rely more on their intelligence and less on experience but the reverse is the case in stressful times.Thus, there is a complex interaction between leadership behaviour, the psychology of followers, and social context which allows, encourages or even demands certain actions.

Leadership behaviours can be expressed in many contexts and at many different social positions. It involves various combinations of power such as directing the attention of others, and the ability/power to control, guide, influence, encourage or coerce the behaviour and values of others. Nearly all humans have the ability to adopt leadership behaviours. Even in simple two-some's one may be more the leader than the other, although they may swap roles from time to time.

Thus, leadership behaviours can emerge in just about any social relationship; *e.g.*, playground, street gang, terrorist group, church fete society, local cricket team, the hospital ward, business organisation, and government. Leadership research also makes the distinction between task orientated leadership and person orientated leadership. The person orientated leader will attempt to manipulate the values and emotions of subordinates, getting them 'devoted to the cause' that they will lead. Although leader-follower relationships are to some degree archetypal potentials (and this is what can give them their passion and emotion distorting qualities) we should note that our first experiences of 'leaders' are our parents.

The Family

Family structures are also authority, hierarchical structures. Human family relationships, however, are highly contextualised within their cultures. Cultures legitimise the use of power within the family. They may not only amplify gender differences in the power exercised within families (men as head of the household) but bestow rights. In many societies men are (more or less) bestowed the right of sexual access to their wives and even today there are issues around whether rape can occur inside marriage.

In the middle ages, wife beating was allowed, provided the stick was no thicker than a thumb. In modern societies, noted for their highly segregated and privatised families, power is exercised by the limitation of freedom of choice and rights. Thus, for example, women and children who are locked into abusive relationships may lack the resources or opportunities to move away. Male dominance of the family is thus encased in socially bestowed privileges and values.

For all animals, parents are automatically positioned to control the behaviour of their offspring. Thus, the parent-child relationship is also a dominant-subordinate one. In childhood, the experience of being subordinate to one's parents is also associated with enormous needs for care and acceptance from them. This combination of care eliciting and care giving with subordination, has the effect of blending different archetypal potentials together. It is not surprising, therefore, that humans can learn and develop their attitudes and emotional sensitivity 'to authority' from the experiences they have with, and of, their parents. So parenting is, in many ways, a leadership role because it involves differences in power and demands for obedience. And our attitudes to leadership and authority (seeking it, subordinating ourselves to it, or hating it) can be shaped during our formative years.

Society bestows and accepts the rights of parents to behave in certain ways to their children. Children are automatically assumed to come under the power and control of their parents. The use of physical punishment (and types of punishment in general), religious indoctrination, diet, indeed the right to impose various forms of life style are seen as parental rights. The state may intervene at times, as with laws on education, and there can be conflicts over the exact limits of power that can be exercised with families, *e.g.*, the state intervenes in cases of sexual abuse or if parents refuse blood transfusions on religious grounds. Generally though, children are indoctrinated to adopt the prevailing attitudes and values of their group be these religious, political, or gender. Young children can be taken on political marches, made to read the Bible or Koran, to view history through a particular lens and so forth. If any of these practices are crazy then we can easily pass them on.

Leadership Roles

Once out of the family there are other groups and social relationships in which we must find our place. Leadership roles can be ascribed and defined by social groups and one passes some entrance test or exam to enter them (*e.g.*, lawyer, doctor) which legitimises the use of power. In some societies obtaining the recognition of manhood legitimises the use of certain types of power and authority (*e.g.*, over women).

Historically, leaders could be given their roles 'as of right' (e.g. by an institutionalised class or caste system). In fact many leadership positions (Kings, Emperors, and so forth) were family determined. Even today the family of origin and the social rank of the family can significantly influence a person's chances and aspirations to leadership positions. Top leaders of social institutions are rarely those who have risen through the ranks, but usually begin their claims from class-bestowed privileged positions. But the importance of the rank of one's family is also noted in many non-human primates. Females especially, usually obtain their rank from their mother's and aunt's rank. As it has been for millions of years, we leave the family and emerge into the social world where rank is everywhere.

Secure and Insecure Dominance

Styles of leadership have been studied in animals as styles of dominance. In most non-human primate studies to date, subordinates show greater activation of stress hormones than dominant animals, especially higher levels of circulating cortisol.

However, in unstable groups dominant animals can show almost as high levels as subordinates. The work of Sapolsky, who has studied free ranging baboon's in Africa, suggests that secure, dominant baboons in stable groups have: Low stress cortisol levels, they differentiate well between a threatening rival and other animals; when threatened they escalate fights and usually win; if they lose they displace aggression on to a third party; they have high levels of non-sexual interactions with infants and females and are generally relaxed and affiliative.

High ranking but insecure baboons (especially if the group is unstable) have: High levels of stress hormones, tend to be more aggressive (generally and sexually), are more likely to pick fights (rather than just respond to threats), appear more suspicious, and are generally less relaxed and less affiliative. While these differences in leadership/dominance style reflect the stability of the group they also reflect individual differences. Thus, we see that security of the position may be important for the kinds of behaviour that dominant's express. This leads us to the idea of differences between secure and insecure dominance. Some human leaders certainly seem to show forms of insecure dominance.

This insecurity is mediated through both the social context and personality. It is possible that in humans insecurity may be, in part, a general personality trait (as it seems to be for baboons and chimpanzees). The combination of strong needs for power in humans (to control others) compensates, perhaps, for basic personal insecurities, quite possibly of an insecure, avoidant attachment style. In fact many researchers have argued that aggressive leaders have had disturbed backgrounds with low parental warmth. There is a basic view in psychotherapy that 'where love was not there shall be a power and fear.'

We noted many researchers draw distinctions between threat/aggression based dominance and affiliation based dominance styles. Insecure dominance, we can suggest, shows itself in the readiness to adopt threat based leadership styles; that is leadership is primarily organised via the defence system. In humans the interaction between threat and affiliation is complex because humans can be far more manipulative of their social-presentation and image, *i.e.*, presenting themselves as affiliative when in fact they are not. As we shall now see, insecure patterns of dominance show up quite commonly in leadership styles.

Personality

Although this book has tried to veer away from being overly focused on traits within individuals (and research on leadership suggests that personality is only one facet of leadership for it is always the interaction that is important), our exploration of leadership does require some consideration of personality. It seems to be the case that some leaders are more likely to have particular traits and personality styles which reflect quite serious insecurities. These may include: Narcissistic, obsessional, autocratic, authoritarian, psychopathic and hypomanic (or manic-depressive). The definition of narcissistic, which underpins many of them, is captured by Adler (1986).

These patients tend to be extremely self-centred, often needing praise and constant recognition in order to feel momentarily good about themselves. Rather than feeling a sense of their own worth or value, they require repeated bolstering from the outside. In their relationships with people, they tend to be exploitative and insensitive to the feelings and needs of others.

Their behaviour can be superficially charming on the one hand and arrogant on the other. They expect special privileges from those around them without giving anything in return, yet they can feel easily humiliated or shamed and respond with rage at what they perceive to be criticisms or failure of people to react in the way they wish Many can elaborate active fantasies about magnificent success in love, sex, beauty, wealth or power. They often devalue people they have previously idolised and tend to split, *i.e.* see people as either all good or all bad, or alternate between these extremes.

Adler's description highlights status evaluative and powerhostility components, the use of others for selfvaluing purposes, exploitativeness and sense of entitlement, and a comparative lack of the more prosocial aspects of human nature such as empathy, moral thinking, and care giving. They can have the motto 'if you're not with us you're against us'. They can be strident in emphasising the importance of their own vision and truck little disagreement. They can be envious, grandiose and expect allegiance. They can maintain this allegiance by a mixture of threats, shaming and offering favours and prestige to allies and followers. Yet for all this at times their style may inspire devotion.

The psychopathic person has many narcissistic traits but in addition is generally more callous, sadistic, distrustful, amoral, exploitative, ruthless and easily activated into violent fights. Their compassion for others is notable by its absence.

Autocratic and authoritarian personalities are similar to the narcissist but they are extremely ranked focused. Norman Dixonused psychoanalytic theory to argue that these personality styles are a defence against uncertainty and anxiety; *i.e.*, insecurity. They must know their place and can be incredibly deferential and submissive to those ranking above them and controlling of those ranking below. They have strong beliefs in the value of the ranked authority system, the importance of obeying orders and are not so keen on democracy.

The manic-depressive traits, from which some leaders suffer, are believed to relate more to a mood disorder. Winston Churchill was a classic example. This leads them to swing between grandiose ideas about their self-importance, have marked needs for power, low frustration tolerance but they have high energy, are charismatic, take risks and are creative.

However, when depressed they are riddled with self-doubt and feelings of worthlessness, with a tendency to hide away and feel suicidal. They usually lack the sadistic and callousness of the psychopath but can be paranoid to some degree and are very sensitive to threats and challenges to their own (and their group's) status. People with narcissistic traits (and these can be present in any of the above types) may not have full blown manic-depressive illnesses, but nonetheless they can show marked swings of mood and confidence.

Although these are usually regarded as personality or mood disorders, it is quite wrong to think that having a disorder consigns one to the backstreets of history. Indeed, some are not satisfied with simply being psychopathic and narcissistic in their own limited social domains. Their drive for leadership and greatness marks them out from other less leadership focused personalities. In such a pursuit these traits can be a positive advantage in making it big.

Unfortunately, in the past and to some degree still, these individuals can take hold of whole cultures, societies, groups and organisations with a terrible cost. More worryingly, once in power their poor emotional and/or physical health can have very serious consequences.

ANTI-SOCIAL AND PROSOCIAL LEADERSHIP STYLE

Running along side explorations of personality have been many efforts to distinguish leadership styles using different constructs. For example, Maslow distinguished democratic from authoritarian leaders; McClelland distinguishes the affiliative from the power orientated; Eisler distinguishes dominator (masculine) from partnership (feminine) styles; Kalma *et al.*, distinguish between sociable and aggressive leaders. And elsewhere I have distinguished the prosocial from the anti-social leader.

So there is no single system of understanding and all have their insights and limitations. Much may depend on where you look of course, *i.e.*, whether you focus on the tasks, results or on interpersonal style. The types of leaders we will note shortly may well get results, but they tend towards the authoritarian, dominator, aggressive, anti-social leadership style. I will refer to these collectively as anti-social because their style can have very negative effects on and for others.

Anti-social leaders tend to come from insecure backgrounds with a history of abusive, emotionally cold, rigid/authoritarian or neglectful parenting which leads them to develop various mixtures of the above mentioned traits. Judged through the lens of the last two chapters we could see these individuals as being highly shame prone, sensitive to humiliation, extraordinarily status conscious, and in need of defending against humiliation at all costs.

The way this is done, as in the Hitler complex, is not just via defence of self but an active promotion of one's superiority - in other words heightened activity of a primitive up-rank, archetypal mentality. To be superior promises the power to defeat any who would make claims on one's status or position. Although one can certainly link such psychologies to reproductive strategies - and genes - these distal explanations do not always help us understand the complex of forces which bring these archetypes to such prominence within any one person at a point in history.

Thus we should always consider family background and social context. Anti-social leaders have particular philosophies, motives and tendencies which include: A perception of the world as competitive and the strongest wins; a belief in the superiority of one's social group, often with a fear, dislike or even contempt for outsiders; a belief in the importance of strength and pride; a belief in the importance of close ingroup loyalties as a protection against external badness (us against them); a need for control and power over others; a fear of losing status; a belief that their own way (vision) is superior; a simple right versus wrong moral system or no moral system at all; a tendency to use people to met their own ends; and often a lack of care for others. Prosocial leaders tend to have very different backgrounds, coming from a secure and warm family life and have developed the archetypal abilities to empathise and care for others.

This there are far more altruistic strategies in their styles. Compared to anti-social leaders they have different philosophies, motives and tendencies which include: A preference for cooperative over competitive behaviour; a preference for partnership and peaceful solutions to conflicts rather than winning; a belief in the importance of valuing and nurturing others as people rather than as means to an end; a complex moral system; an opening up of groups and dissolving boundaries (we are all the same under the skin); and a sardonic sense of the heroic.

These are dimensions rather than absolute categories. One could compare (say) Nelson Mandala with Hitler to get a feel of the differences. But, in general, it is probably preferable to think of style rather than 'the individual' because at times a person may show one face of leadership but at other times another. They may have mild tendencies towards either prosocial or anti-social styles or these styles may be marked and rigid. They may appear highly prosocial to ingroup members who show allegiance but anti-social to outsiders and defectors.

They may be intuitively inclined towards (say) prosocial leadership but the social group (electorate) which supports them demands another style, and invalidates their prosocial efforts - telling them they need to be tough-minded. The ease (and degree) by which a leader will compromise their own values in order to get elected or chosen suggests that for some, gaining leadership roles is more important that pursuing personal principles. Personal principles can be too costly. On the other hand, the group might encourage an amplification of a preferred personal style. Some who are mildly aggressive become more so with being encouraged to go further and be more ruthless. As we noted above insecurity can effect style, but this insecurity may come from stresses in the environment.

People who are groomed for leadership by virtue of their families' social position, ie., they are placed in leadership positions, need not be socially skilled. However, some anti-social leaders are highly socially skilled, good orators and good at manipulating the values and (usually) needs for superiority, certainty, and strength in their followers.

Trepidation Based Patterns

Sometimes those with anti-social leadership styles can inspire devotion. At other times, as in China and the old USSR, they bring to life social patterns of fear and suspicion. Such regimes usually only survive with the support of a hidden class of 'secret police' who are ruthless and vicious and can create the fear of 'the knock on the door in the middle of the night'. Societies never seem to have had much problem in finding such folk and such 'police forces' can include a fair number of both narcissistic and sadistic personalities, who colour the whole police force. Anti-social leaders, protected by the young men of the secret police and other arms of enforcement, may slowly age and can in fact be quite old before they are deposed or simply die in post. China and the USSR were classic examples of this.

For some supporters, appeasement and compliance is used to reduce the potential aggression of the leader(s) and/or his/her supporters. That is, the primary internal psychological organisation in both leaders and subordinates is defensive rather than relaxed and open. The fear based anti-social leadership style and its effects are the most easily detected. Even if the leader appears friendly, fear and apprehension can be common experiences. The psychology of subordinate, is to make sure they know where the threat might be (and for what), and avoiding it, or at least taking necessary steps to reduce it. Behaviourists would call this 'punishment' based control. The ethologist Michael Chance called this pattern of social behaviour agonic - meaning that the defensive aspects of fight/threaten (in the dominant) and appeasement/ submit or flight/escape (in the subordinate) are primed. This leads to constrictions on the patterns of attention, reduces open exploration and may reduce the development of compassionate values.

If you watch members of a group interact when the leader is out of the room and compare this to when he/she is present you can sometimes have a feel for whether an anti-social style is operating. When an anti-social leader enters, the previous fun and jokey exchanges may cease, as does the free exploration of ideas. There is a switch in attention. Everyone watches their backs to ensure they are not the next to be attacked and they are preoccupied with the mood the leader is in. Bad moods signal hard times and times to watch yourself. Every thing is done to avoid putting the leader in a bad mood - even withholding important information about 'bad news' or mistakes. The poor folk who do put the leader in a bad mood can be blamed by other subordinates for causing them a hard time. At one meeting a subordinate said to another "why did you say that. You know what he's like. Now we are all going to suffer. Why couldn't just keep your mouth shut." My housemaster at school was very much like this and it was well known that the other masters (we called them master then not teachers) were wary, if not frightened, of him. He was a cane happy sod.

Of course, at times anti-social styles are unintended and reflect poor social skills, or stress, but at other times anti-social leaders enjoy the idea that others are apprehensive of them and believe this ensures them respect. Indeed, a belief in, and even admiration of, fear based respect probably marks the anti-social leader. Industry is just beginning to recognise that some leadership styles are disastrous; that there is a dark side to charisma. Perhaps in our modern age there is a gradual fading in the valuing of tough leadership (but it is gradual and at times I doubt it). Those who do well at interview and present themselves with confidence, keenness and are socially skilled (often being male helps too) have often appeared the preferable people to place in positions of power and leadership. However, unless you observe them working with their team you have little idea how they will perform as leaders. Some turn out to be narcissistic, who value themselves but not others, are competitive with subordinates and shaming. They create such poor morale and inhibit other's creativity that they can cost an organisation dearly. Nearly all of us will have had some experience of having to work with these characters. So management training is all the vogue right now, teaching how to be socially rewarding and supportive, able to appreciate subordinate feedback and build a cooperative-friendly team spirit.

The thing to watch out for is those who can mimic such behaviours in 'training workshops' but do not really (privately) value these behaviours. So there can be slippage in their non-verbal behaviour and style. They may say 'the right things' but not feel or act friendly. At the slightest conflict they become aggressive/shaming, threatening to escalate conflict unless the other backs-down. Non-verbal behaviour is so important, I believe, because it taps right into the reptilian brain, and this, in interpersonal interactions, is what can set the emotional tone of the relationship(s). Indeed, we know that people monitor non-verbal communication at least as much as verbal. The way leaders deal with conflicts (of interest) both verbally and non-verbally is crucial to the skill of a leader. Good prosocial leaders have the ability to keep conflicts serious but also playful. People don't feel personally attacked; they play the ball not the player. Leaders like the Dalai Lama, Nelson Mandela and Gandhi are well known for such abilities.

Prosocial leaders are rarely feared. They encourage free exploration and affiliative styles. They are easy to approach and open to the opinions of others. Subordinates do not fear them because as leaders they do not use shame and humilation as a means of control. Generally, subordinates enjoy working with and for them and do not feel patronised or looked down on. Prosocials are concerned to see others mature, grow and pass on. They are not envious of others success. Their dark side is that they may not perform well in conflict situations - or at least can be very stressed by it and indecisive. Their needs for affiliation can interfere with tough decision making.

Leadership and Deception

A prosocial style can be superficial - it is a con and deception devised to be attractive to others. It is seen most commonly in cults, but not uncommonly in politics where self-presentation to win votes may hide a dark, scheming and manipulative style. That the prosocial style is a deception is revealed at times of conflicts of view, doubt, or if a member of the group desires to leave the group and defect. Everything changes for the potential defector. Where before they were wanted and esteemed now they are degraded (*e.g.*, called scab, traitor, heretic, weak, or made fun of etc.). They can be threatened with fear of permanent expulsion, loss of status and prestige, loss of support, or outright persecution from the previously supportive group and its leader. To put this another way when a subordinate looks for the exit they find they are trapped - it is hard to leave, or if they do, impossible to return. Many religions use this threat of course. No-one can love you like God can love you - if you leave the clan, the religion, you will put yourself beyond God and his love. Don't defect.

So the superficial prosocial leader knows how to play the game. They can stay prosocial as long as they receive sufficient subordinate, compliant, loving, or devotional signals. As we shall see later, Jim Jones was almost certainly one of these types. They are among the most dangerous because of their skilful manipulation of needs for love, acceptance and conformity in subordinates, and their ability to create a sense of protection and belonging for ingroup members, with subtle (and sometimes not so subtle) undercurrents of fear.

Most of our history has not been shaped by leaders who have been on management training courses. It is alarming how much human history, not to mention our value systems, have been shaped by people who, at least from our position, seem rather crazy and certainly anti-social. Our civilization, culture and even our self-identities have been significantly shaped by our leaders and the mimicry of their values. Even now we don't take nearly enough care in choosing our leaders. But through most of our history we have not had that much choice.

Recent Leaders

Although we now live in a democracy, it is in the very nature of the manipulation of power that democracy often fails to provide prosocial leaders. Hugh Freeman, who was president of the Royal College of Psychiatrists, has given a powerful and frightening review of how psychological and physical health problems have plagued many of our recent leaders in Europe and America. His review highlights many concerns, some of which are noted here. Woodrow Wilson suffered a number of mini-strokes that led to a personality change. In 1945, at the time of the Yalta conference Roosevelt was so terminally ill he may not have really understood what was going on. J.F. Kennedy used amphetamine and steroids, both of which could have affected his judgement. Lyndon Johnson has been described as highly narcissistic with feelings of insecurity and grandiosity.

In 1966-67, when the Vietnam war was becoming preoccupied with carpet bombing and defoliation, Johnson viewed his critics as 'enemies and traitors'. Nixon was known to have many narcissistic traits, to be exploitative and untrustworthy. At the time of the Watergate scandal he was drinking to such an extent, "that his aids thought him incapable of dealing with any business - however urgent- at these times."(p. 24) Ronald Reagan, towards the end, was known to be suffering from dementia, now sadly well advanced. Yet it was believed that if he could have stood again he would have won. It is true of course that the personalities of leaders do not exclude them from bringing social advances. Johnson did introduce important polices of social reform and a "new deal." But the pressures of modern leadership can still play havoc with a person and while they may be helpful to insiders they can be highly destructive to outsiders.

In Britain, Anthony Eden, at the time of the Suez crisis, was abusing drugs and alcohol and was described by some to be, "quite simply mad". As the history books are written on Margaret Thatcher and the up-surgence of the right in the 1980's, we get clear evidence of the autocratic leadership style. Ian Gilmour's book `Dancing with Dogma' leaves little doubt that at least some of the elements that go to making an autocrat were present in Thatcher's style. For example, Gilmour (who was one of her ministers in the early years) writes:

Mrs Thatcher regarded her first cabinet not as an aid to good government but as an obstacle to be surmounted. Her belief that dialogue was a waste of time rather than a means of arriving at an agreed course of action was a part of her rejection of consensus politics. Consensus, the Prime Minster later proclaimed, was achieved only by 'abandoning all beliefs, principles and values. Whoever won a battle,' she asked, 'under the banner of, "I stand for consensus"?' In her mind, of course, 'conviction' was diametrically opposed to consensus."

As the years passed and more and more cabinet colleagues defected, speaking of her autocratic treatment of them, we began to get more insight into the psychology that controlled her. Rank and dominance and the need for greatness were written everywhere. And for whom was this greatness desired? Not for the poor who became poorer still, but for an elite; for an ideal of being British. Her obsession with enemies was revealed clearly when she said at the time of the miners strike in 1984, "We had to fight the enemy without in the Falklands. We always have to be aware of the enemy within, which is more difficult to fight and more dangerous to liberty." (Quoted by Gilmour). So the miners were not just ordinary people fighting, often violently, for their jobs (manipulated by their own leader to a degree) but were potential enemies of the cause. This was a time when a Prime Minister openly talked about ninnies and wimps, and efforts at shaming. It was a time that ideology and causes matter more than people. It was a time when there was no such thing as society only a collection of individuals, until that is, Brussels threatened British interests, then the idea of Britishness made a come back.

When her end came it was shabby, marred by back-stabbing and retribution for the failures in the courage and loyalty of her subordinates (colleagues). Such an old story and somewhat typical of a person who has little ability to reflect on the self and see the sources of her difficulties as coming from within. To be fair to Thatcher though, it is less clear how much she was motivated by a personal ambition to be great, or more to rescue an identity for family and country. Certainly, her stated intent was to free people from government control, although in this quango-ised state of ours even this is doubtful. It is now estimated there are 7,700 quangos of various sorts, often staffed by conservative appointees and costly the state £54 billion. She was certainly a strong leader and enjoyed the title the 'Iron Lady'. We must leave it to the historians to decide. She changed Britain significantly. Who knows what we may now be like without her. But it is her style that marks her as being the autocratic type.

So we can see that anti-social leaders have a number of qualities. A need for power; a belief in their own way, a focus on the importance of strength, a tendency to talk in terms of fighting, conquering, pride and becoming great, a need to stress the importance of being more powerful than competitors, paranoid or contemptuous attitudes to those who are not ingroup members, a preparedness to subdue subordinates not with argument but with fear or shame - the language of wimps and ninnies.

In whatever context leadership arises, the lack of compassion for followers and subordinates can lead to appalling abuses of power; the first world war being a most tragic example. As Dixon makes clear, at times military leaders have seen their subordinates as no more than cannon-fodder. But even democratically elected leaders can show a complete lack of interest in certain sections of the groups they lead, except to keep them in check. Many leaders in the West appear to have a view of the "workers" as manoeuvrable production units whose value depends on whether they can be fitted in with wealth creating—*i.e.*, production fodder. Rebellion can be ruthlessly put down.

If we are becoming increasing cynical about our leaders, religious and political, and even democracy, we might remember our history and what has gone before. There is no way to avoid leadership. Sure, some will try to manipulate us to get our vote and sure they will have the various human failings, like sexual ones, but we can still insist on compassionate values once we sort out in our own minds the issue of how we want the world to look for our grandchildren. Do we want them to live in a polluted, highly competitive, 'dump the losers', world?

We don't have to go with the message of a need to be special or great or if we do we can be great for other reasons apart from beating opponents or competitors. We may need strong leaders but they need to be chosen by us to tell the truth and advise us of the reality - a reality that in our hearts we all know.

As Freeman makes clear some of our problems with leadership arise because our jerry built brains were never designed to cope with the leadership of the mega-groups we now live within, nor the mass of information leaders have to cope with, nor the uncertainties of positions that can change rapidly, nor the complexity of the competing interests of all the subgroups that exist within the modern state, nor indeed with the grandiosity and scale of power that is so much part of a modern nation state. To say that political leadership, with its hands on nuclear buttons and the arms trade, is in crisis, is an understatement.

THE STYLE APPROACH TO LEADERSHIP

The basic premise of the style approach to leadership is that a leader's "style" determines his or her success. A style is the method of leading that a person uses.

Kurt Lewin was the theorist most responsible for this approach. We have discussed Lewin's theoretical contributions to small-group research throughout this book. It is now time to discuss the man himself. His life affected how he viewed leadership. Lewin was a German Jew who gained an international reputation for his research on perception during the 1920s. During the 1930s, Lewin was able to escape the fate that the Nazis planned for the Jewish citizenry of Germany by immigrating to the United States. As a new American, Lewin was enamored with our democratic traditions and decided to research leadership. He wished to show that democratic leadership is better than the authoritarianism that Hitler was using in Germany at the time.

As we explained, he conceived of a life-space for every person and group. There are regions within this life-space. Forces attract people to or repel them from the various regions. As we have described, we can represent the group itself as an entity that moves around its own life-space.

Lewin believed that a leader has the ability to manipulate the group's life-space and direct its movement towards various goals. Thus, the leader has power over the group. Lewin decided that there are three styles of leadership. The styles are based on the relationship that the leader has with his or her group. A leader has a "democratic" style if he or she manipulates the life-space to help the group reach its own goals. A leader with an "authoritarian" style manipulates the group's life-space to force the group to reach the leader's goals. A leader with a "laissez faire" style does not manipulate the group's life-space at all.

Findings

Lewin *et al.* performed a detailed analysis of the behaviour of the boys during their meetings. They also interviewed the boys concerning their feelings about the sessions. This work resulted in a mass of information from the study.

Maintenance output. First, the researchers found that the democratic leadership style led to greater satisfaction with the group experience than either the authoritarian or the laissez faire styles. The experimenters asked the 20 boys if they preferred the democratic or the authoritarian leaders.

Nineteen of them said that they favoured the democratic leaders. The scientists then asked 10 of the boys to compare the democratic and the laissez faire-style leaders. Out of these 10, 7 said that they preferred the democratic leadership method.

Second, the groups that had the democratic-style leaders appeared to be the most cohesive. During the study, one of the methods that scientists used to measure levels of cohesiveness was to determine the ratio between how often the members used group-oriented pronouns, such as "we" and "us," and how often they used individual-oriented pronouns, such as "I" and "me." In addition, the researchers looked at other indicators of cohesiveness, including the levels of friendly statements, mutual praise, sharing of work materials, and playfulness. The democratic groups had the highest levels of these factors. The laissez faire groups were also fairly cohesive, perhaps in response to their "nonleading" leaders.

In contrast, the groups with leaders who used an authoritarian style were far less cohesive than the other groups. Observers compared the behaviour of the boys in the authoritarian-led groups with the behaviour of those in the democratic-led groups. They noted 30 times as many acts of hostility and 8 times as many acts of aggression in the authoritarian groups. In addition, authoritarian-led sessions had the highest levels of statements of discontent and the largest levels of absenteeism.

Task output. As for their work output, both the authoritarian and the democratic groups outpaced the laissez faire groups. The boys in the authoritarian groups worked 74 per cent of the time when their leaders were present. This compared with a work level of 50 per cent for boys in democratic groups and 33 per cent in the laissez faire groups.

However, when the leaders left the room, these percentages changed. Groups following a democratic leader continued to work at a 46 per cent level. In contrast, the work time for authoritarian groups fell drastically to only 29 per cent, implying that the members of the authoritarian groups had little desire to work. On the other hand, groups with leaders using a laissez faire style actually worked more when their leaders left the room. Their work time increased to 52 per cent. This result implies that these members remained motivated.

Finally, the researchers judged the work of democratic groups highly. They considered this work to be of higher quality and originality than the performance of authoritarian and laissez faire groups.

CONTINGENCY THEORY OF LEADERSHIP

The most popular and extensively researched situational theory of leadership was first proposed by Fred Piedler during the 1960s. Fiedler's model claims that group performance depends on the interaction of the leader style and the favourableness of the situation. Fiedlers major contributions consist of(1) iden-tifying the leadership orientation of the leader and developing a way to measure it, and (2) identifying three situational factors influencing leadership and developing a method of measuring them

Leader orientation. Fiedler's definition of the leader's orientation emerged largely from earlier studies in which leaders were classified as either relationship-oriented or task-oriented. Relationship-oriented leaders look at others as coworkers and see close interpersonal relations as a requirement for accomplishing the task. Task-oriented leaders show a strong emotional reaction against people with whom they have difficulty working. If they are forced to make a choice between getting the job done or worrying about interpersonal relations, they choose the task first and worry about interpersonal relations later. Following earlier research, Fiedler suggested that individuals could be placed along one continuum characterized by two basic leader orientations: relationship-oriented versus task-oriented.

LPC scale. Leadership orientation is measured by the least preferred co-worker (LPC) scale, as illustrated in Exhibit 16.5. Individuals are asked to think of a person with whom they have worked who they least preferred as a co-worker, and describe this person using sixteen scales. When the responses arc summed, an individual with a favourable description of the least preferred co-worker would have a high LPC score, suggesting a relationship-oriented leader. An unfavourable description of the least preferred coworker would result in a low score, suggesting a task-oriented leader.

Difficulty in interpreting the LPC scores has been a problem for Fiedler's contingency theory. The LPC scale is not related to any of the well-known personality measures. In spite of uncertainty about what exactly it measures, however, the evidence indicates that it is a reliable measure of something, and Fiedler concludes that "there can be little doubt that we are dealing with a very important aspect of personality." A review of 25 years of research using th~3 LPC scale concluded that high LPC leaders are primarily relationship-oriented while low LPC leaders are primarily task-oriented consistent with Fiedler's claims.' In general, a low LPC leader is more directive, more structuring, more goal-oriented, and more concerned with efficiency. A high LPC leader is more considerate, more human relations oriented, more participative, and more sensitive to the feelings of others.

Situational favourableness. Fiedler's model claims that whether a high LPC leader or low LPC leader will be more effective depends upon the favourableness of the situation. In some situations, a high LPC leader is most effective, while a unenthusiastic low LPC leader is more effective in other situations. Fiedler claimed that the favourableness of the situation is determined by three variables: (1) whether the relationships between the leader and the members are good or poor. (2) whether the task is relatively structured or unstructured, and (3) whether the power position of the leader is relatively strong or weak.

In studies testing the model, Fiedler and his colleagues developed instruments to measure each of these three situational variables." Of the three situational variables, the leader-member relations variable was considered to be the most important for determining the favourableness of the situation. Leader-member relations were measured using a simple questionnaire with ten scales on which the leader was asked to describe the group. This instrument was called a "group atmosphere scale" and two sample items are shown here.

The second most important situational variable was the task structure which was evaluated by judges who examined four aspects of the task structure.

- *Coal clarity:* the degree to which the requirements of the job are clearly stated and known by the people performing then,
- *Coal-path multiplicity:* the degree to which the problems encounter in the job can be solved by a variety of procedures.
- *Decision verifiability:* the degree to which the correctness of the solutions or decisions can be demonstrated and ascertained.
- *Decision specificity:* the degree to which there is generally more than one correct solution involved in performing the task.

In a highly structured task, goals are very clear, there is on! y one correct procedure for performing the task, the correctness of the decisions can be immediately verified, and there is only one correct solution. Obviously, a highly structured task does not require leaders to provide additional structure.

The third situational variable was the power position of the leader. This factor was measured by a series of questions asking whether the leaders could recommend rewards or promotions, whether they could assign tasks and evalu-ate performance, and whether they had been given official titles by the organization to differentiate them from subordinates.

By determining whether a group is high or low on each of the three situational factors, Fiedler classified each group into one of eight categories, which ranged along a scale from extremely favourable situations to extremely unfavourable situations for the leader. A highly favourable situation consisted of good leader-member relations, a highly structured task, and a strong power position, as illustrated in Exhibit 16.6. On the other hand, an extremely unfavourable situation existed when the leader-member relations were poor, the task was unstructured, and the leader possessed a weak power position.

Group effectiveness. Fiedler examined the relationship between the leaders' LPC score and the effectiveness of the group in a variety of situations. The results indicated that a high LPC leader was most effective when the situation was moderately favourable. If the situation was extremely favourable or unfavourable, however, the low LPC leaders tended to have the most effective groups. These relationships are illustrated in Exhibit 16.7. Although these results may look rather complex and difficult to understand, they seem plausible after a brief consideration. Relationship-oriented leaders (high LPC) tend to excel in situations of intermediate favourableness where concern for the group members is apparently a necessary prerequisite for motivating them to perform well. In these situations, people want to have leaders who care about them.

Task-oriented leaders (low LPC), however, are more effective when the situation is either very favourable or very unfavourable. In a highly favourable situation, the personal needs of members are apparently already satisfied and what is needed is a task-oriented leader to get the job done. In an extremely unfavourable situation, however, satisfying individual needs is probably impossible. A task-oriented leader who simply focuses on getting the work done is more effective than a relationship-oriented leader who spends time fruitlessly trying to build good relationships in an impossible situation.

Fiedler's theory has some interesting implications for the selection and training of leaders in organizations. Candidates for leadership positions should be evaluated to assess their basic orientations, and they should be placed in jobs consistent with their leadership orientation. The favourableness of a situation should be assessed before assigning a leader to that position. Leaders who are struggling may need to be placed in a different situation, or their current situation may need to be changed.

When leaders are not successful, it is tempting to suggest that they need to change their leadership orientation. Fiedler does not recommend this approach, however, and argues that the basic leadership orientation of an individual is a relatively stable personality characteristic that cannot be easily changed. Rather than changing the leader to fit the situation, Fiedler recommends changing the situation to fit the leader through what he calls job engineering. Job engineering consists of changing one of the situational factors to increase or decrease the favourability of the situation. For example, the task structure and power position can be effectively changed through job redesign programmes or changes in personnel policies.

The validity of Fiedler's contingency theory has been examined in numerous studies. Although most of the studies have been supportive, there have been enough contradictory findings for the model to remain somewhat controversial among leadership scholars. The most serious controversy about Fiedler's model concerns the LPC scale. Although the theory seems to predict leader effectiveness, the ambiguity over what the LPC score is actually measuring is disturbing.

Path-Goal Model

Another situational leadership theory is the path-goal model developed primarily by Robert House. This model is fairly well known because it is based upon a popular theory of motivation — expectancy theory. The path-goal model ex-plains how leaders can facilitate task performance by showing subordinates how their performance can be instrumental in achieving desired rewards. Expectancy theory explains how an individual's attitudes and behaviour are influenced by the relationships between effort and performance (goal paths) and the valence of the rewards (goal attractiveness). Therefore, individuals are satisfied and productive when they see a strong relationship between their effort and performance and when their performance results in highly valued rewards. The path-goal model claims that the most effective leaders are those who help subordinates folio's the path to receiving valued rewards.

Essentially, the model explains what leaders should do to influence the perceptions of subordinates about their work, the personal goals of subordinates, and the various paths to goal attainment. The model claims that leader behaviour is motivating and satisfying to the extent that it clarifies the paths to the goals and increases goal attainment,Leader behaviours. The path-goal model suggests that leadership consists of two basic functions. The first function is path clarification: the leader helps subordinates understand which behaviours are necessary to accomplish the tasks. The second function is to increase the number of rewards available to subordinates by being supportive and paying attention to their personal needs. To perform these functions, leaders may adopt a variety of leadership styles.

Four distinct leadership styles are explained in the model:

1. *Directive leadership:* tells subordinates what is expected of them and provides specific guidance, standards, and schedules of work.
2. *Supportive leadership:* treats subordinates as equals and shows con-cern for their well-being, status, and personal needs; attempts to de-velop pleasant interpersonal relationships among group members.
3. *Achievement-oriented leadership:* sets challenging goals expects subordinates to perform at their highest level, and continually seeks improvement in performance.
4. *Participative leadership:* consults with subordinates and uses their suggestions and ideas in decision making. Unlike Fiedler's model, which suggested that leadership style was resistant to change, the path-goal model suggests that these four styles can be performed by the same manager at different times and in different situations. In other words, the path-goal theory suggests that if a directive leader discovers the situation has changed and now requires a participative leader, it is possible. For the leader to change. The appropriate leadership style depends on the situation. Although the path-goal model does not explain how to identify the appropriate leadership leader style, the model does present a list of situational factors that need to be consid-ered.

Situational factors. Two types of situational factors are proposed—the char-acteristics of the follower and environmental factors. Three characteristics of the followers have been identified as significant variables determining the ap-propriate leadership style:

- *Locus of control:* Locus of control refers to the individual's belief concerning the determinants of reward. Individuals with an internal locus of control believe their rewards are based on their own efforts, while those with an external locus of control believe their rewards are controlled by external forces. Internals prefer a participative leadership style while externals are generally more satisfied oh are with a directive leadership style.
- *Authoritarianism:* Authoritarianism refers to an individual's willing to accept the influence of others. High authoritarian followers tend to be less receptive to a participative leadership style and more responsive to directive leadership.
- *Abilities:* The ability and experience of the followers will influence leader whether they are able to work more successfully with an achievement oriented leader who sets challenging goals and expects high perform-ance, or a supportive leader who is willing to patiently encourage and instruct them. The path-goal model identifies three environmental factors moderating the effects of leadership styles: (1) the nature of the task, (2) the formal authority system within thc organization, and (3) the group norms and dynamics. These environmental factors can influence the effectiveness of different leadership styles in a variety of ways. A highly structured task, for example, may reduce the need for a directive leader and even make a directive leader's attempt to pro-vide additional structure seem unwarranted and unwanted. However, a direc-tive leader would be more likely to succeed than a participative leader if the organization had a highly formal authority structure that followed a strict chain of command. Likewise, a concern for the personal needs of subordinates by a supportive leader may seem superficial and unnecessary in a highly cohesive work group. The basic elements of the path-goal model of leadership axe illustrated in Exhibit 16J. This model shows how leadership styles interact with follower-characteristics and environmental factors to influence the personal percep-tions and motivation of the followers. The perceptions of the followers concerning the situation and the followers' level of motivation determine their job satisfaction, performance, and acceptance of the leader.

Some simplified applications of the path-goat model are shown in Exhibit 16.9. In the first two situations, subordinates have an ambiguous job or they feel insufficiently rewarded. Both situations call for a directive leader who explains the job and helps subordinates know how to get rewarded for performing it. The next two situations, boring work and a lack of self-confidence call for a support- leader. Repetitive jobs are not as boring if a supportive leader helps subordi-nates see that their work is meaningful and significant. Likewise, a supportive leader can help subordinates feel greater self-confidence by coaching them and praising their accomplishments. In situation 5, subordinates are not challenged by the task. An achievement-oriented leader will set high goals and emphasize the intrinsic and extrinsic rewards from more effort. Finally, situation 6 in-volves a task that is unstructured and poorly defined, calling for participative leadership. By participating in the decision making, subordinates help to create an effective solution to the problem and, as a result of their involvement, feel committed to making it work.

Research on the path-goal model. The relationships specified by the path-goal model have been examined in a modest number of empirical studies. This research has tested the theory's predictions concerning the moderators of lead-ership effectiveness to determine whether the situational variables interacted with the leadership styles in the predicted manner. The evidence seems to indicate that the model does quite well in predicting how the situational variables and leader styles combine to influence individual satisfaction and group morale? However, the model has not been-shown to be a good predictor of individual or group performance. Perhaps the greatest disadvantage in trying to' validate the model empirically is that it contains too many variables and tries to explain too much. An experiment testing the full pat-goal model is difficult because too many variables have not been clearly identified and instruments -have not been developed to measure them. Nevertheless, the available studies tend to support the model, although they suggest that it understates the com-plexity of the situation. Furthermore, the research suggests that other variables, such as conflict and structure, also need to be incorporated into it.

Perhaps the major contribution of the path-goal model is that it provides a method for viewing leadership in terms of the rewards and punishments administered by the leader. The path-goal model explains why a particular style works best because of the reward contingencies determined by the environment and the leader's capacity to administer rewards and punishments. As more research accumulates, this type of explanation will have practical applications for those interested in the leadership process.

12

The Motivational Underpinnings of Charismatic Leadership

INTRODUCTION

To achieve frame alignment, charismatic leaders engage the self-concepts of followers in the mission articulated by the leader. Strong engagement of the self-concept of followers makes it cognitively dissonant for them not to behave in ways that further mission accomplishment. Charismatic leaders increase the intrinsic value of follower efforts in pursuit of mission accomplishment by linking effort and goals to valued aspects of the follower's selfconcept, thus harnessing the motivational forces of selfexpression, selfconsistency, selfesteem, and selfworth. Shamir *et al.* (1993) further argued that charismatic leaders change the salience hierarchy of values and identities within the follower's selfconcept, thus increasing the probability that these values and identities will be implicated in action. Finally, they argued that charismatic leaders increase selfefficacy and collective efficacy by positive evaluations, communicating higher performance expectations of followers, showing confidence in followers' ability to meet such expectations, and emphasizing followers' ties to the collective.

Shamir *et al.* (1993) specified communicative techniques that charismatic leaders employ to effect frame alignment and mobilize followers to action. They link present behaviours to past events by citing historical examples (Willner, 1984). They articulate an ideology clearly, often using labels and slogans. They provide a vivid and positive image of the future. Further, they amplify certain values and identities and suggest linkages between expected behaviours, amplified values and identities, and their vision of the future. By articulating an ideological vision and recruiting a number of followers who share the values of the vision, charismatic leaders provide for followers a sense of identity with the collective and a sense of efficacy resulting from membership in the collective. Articulation of high performance expectations, together with display of confidence in followers, results in enhancing both follower selfesteem and selfworth.

THE CHARISMATIC APPROACH TO LEADERSHIP

The trait approach to leadership began with the premise of the "Great Man Theory of Leadership." This theory claimed that there are certain people who appear to have special leadership skills that have seemed to set them apart from the average person. As discussed there, researchers' attempts to find traits that distinguished "born leaders" from everyone else were unsuccessful.

However, history is full of political and religious leaders such as Mohandas Gandhi and Martin Luther King Jr. who seem to fit the "Great Man" idea. Weber also worked on understanding the process by which some leaders can inspire such devotion and commitment from followers. Weber proposed the idea that some leaders are perceived by their followers to possess a trait he called "charisma." The term "charisma" was originally defined as the ability to perform religious miracles. Weber used the term to refer to leaders who appear to have exceptional, almost superhuman abilities to perform difficult feats and succeed in seemingly impossible situations.

Some theorists have extended the idea of "charismatic" leadership to the context of organizations. There have been well-publicized examples of organizational leaders who seem to arouse the same type of response in their followers as Gandhi and King did in theirs. Examples include Steven Jobs of Apple Computers, Lee Iacocca of Chrysler, and Mary Kay Ash of Mary Kay Cosmetics. Although there are differences among these and other cases, a few similarities are clear. In each case, the leader was able to inspire unusual effort and performance from their subordinates. Because of this inspiration, Jobs and Ash turned their ideas into corporations worth hundreds of millions of dollars, and Iacocca took a large corporation on the bring of insolvency and converted it into a large profit maker.

Many reports have been published listing the strategies and tactics of successful charismatic leaders. Sometimes these reports have implied that charismatic leadership is the key to organizational success. However, it should be clear from everything we have written about leadership that such sweeping generalizations are likely to be wrong. In many if not most cases, the success of charismatic leadership is short-lived. In fact, as we shall describe, the characteristics that can help make a person a charismatic leader often include the seeds of their eventual downfall. Lee Iacocca, for example, eventually became more concerned with improving his public image nationally than with the operations of Chrysler. As a result, Chrysler once again began struggling. Although Iacocca (and Chrysler) eventually righted themselves, there are many cases in which charismatic leaders have led once-successful corporations to ruin.

Having said this, research suggests that charismatic leadership can lead to organizational success. Bryman (1992) reported that measures of charismatic leadership tend to correlate with job performance at about.3. Although this is not a very high correlation, it must be considered that the success of charismatic leadership depends on the situation in which the leader and the members of the leader's group of subordinates are in. In fact, a number of theorists have proposed very similar theories of charismatic leadership. These theories are comparable to Fiedler's contingency theory of leadership in some ways. They propose that certain traits lead some people to adopt what could be called a "charismatic" style of leadership. There are certain situations in which this style leads to successful performance and some in which it backfires. However, this theory differs from Fiedler's in that communication is specifically described as part of the leadership process. Thus charismatic leadership theory fits the input-process-output model.

A THEORY OF CHARISMATIC LEADERSHIP

Leader characteristics. According to most theorists, charismatic leaders have a number of traits in common. First, they are high in the "Nepo," or "need for power" characteristic. Second, they have great self-confidence. Third, they are unusually willing to take risks. Fourth, they have a strong conviction in the correctness of their beliefs. Of course, having relevant traits is not enough. Advocates of the trait approach ignored the fact that leaders are most successful when performing tasks they are skilled in or knowledgeable about. Successful charismatic leaders generally have a great deal of experience in the organizational area in which they are managing. Lee Iacocca had many years of experience in the automobile industry before he took charge of Chrysler.

Finally, charismatic leaders have developed a "vision" of what their group or organization should stand for. This vision is often abstract, but must be simple enough for subordinates to understand. For example, Steven Jobs had a quest to improve education through making computers available to the average person. Mary Kay Ash wanted to help women learn to become independent and empower themselves.

Thus, charismatic leaders have particular traits, relevant experience, and a vision. Leader style. Charismatic leaders perform a number of characteristic behaviours that we can call a "charismatic" style of leadership. First, they are able to successfully communicate the content of their vision and confidence in their subordinates' ability to attain it. They do this through both verbally and non-verbally. Verbally, charismatic leaders tend to use a number of different strategies when addressing subordinates. Shamir, House, and Arthur (1993) have listed some of the strategies.

- They often refer to shared values and moral justifications. As discussed, Jobs described Apple's goal as bringing computers to schools and the average person. He also referred to Apple as if it were David taking on IBM as an evil Goliath. Thus the competition between the two multimillion dollar corporations was represented as a fight between good and evil.

- They tend to refer to distant goals rather than near ones. For example, Jobs was more likely to discuss what Apple Computer could eventually do rather than what would occur tomorrow.
- They tend to emphasize the collective identity of the subordinates. The needs of the corporation are always more important than the desires of its individual members for the charismatic leader.
- They tend to express high expectations for the subordinates. Their task is described as very difficult, and success as requiring great effort.
- They tend to show great confidence in the ability of their subordinates. No matter how hard the task as they have described, the subordinates have the "right stuff" to succeed.

Second, charismatic leaders deliver this content in an animated non-verbal style. They have great variety and dynamism in their voice, and use gestures, movements and eye gaze actively when talking.

In addition, the charismatic leader must "live" their vision. They must seem to practice exactly what they preach. If a charismatic leader expects their subordinates to put in sixty hour weeks, the leader should put in seventy. If the charismatic leader wants subordinates to look upon the organization as their family, they must take on the role of maintenance leader. If a charismatic leader wants the subordinates to trust their own abilities and judgements, the leader must trust the decisions and actions that the subordinates take.

Situational factors. This style of communicating and behaving appears to be successful only in the right situations. First, the circumstance should be particularly stressful or uncertain. This would occur either in a newly-formed organization or in an older organization that is having problems that threaten its survival.

Second, the subordinates need to be creative and dedicated. What can happen is that subordinates of this type who have become apathetic under other leadership styles are inspired when a charismatic leader takes over. Third, the leader must have the power to actually follow through on their vision. For example, if a middle-level manager has certain goals that those higher up in the organization do not value, then the manager will not be able to see their ideas through. Results. When a charismatic leader is able to communicate their vision and their confidence in their subordinates' ability to attain it, and when the situation is as we have described, the result in subordinates is

- Unusual confidence in and loyalty to leadership
- Strong identification with the organization and the leader's vision
- High motivation and commitment
- Increased self-confidence.

This can result in tremendous effort on the part of the subordinates and great success for the organization.

However, when the situation does not meet the requirements we listed above, the charismatic leader will not be successful. Further, although many of the traits of the charismatic leader are important in helping the leader succeed, they can and often do lead to eventual failure. Their high self-confidence and need for power can lead them to be extremely autocratic and self-serving. They can have little tolerance for subordinates disagreeing with them, and often blame others for their own errors. In the long-run, subordinates often tire of the charismatic leader, lose their dedication, and may even work to undermine the leader's authority. Further, if the charismatic leader has superiors in the organization, they often tire of the leader's style and become unwilling to tolerate any mistakes on the leader's part. There have been many reported examples of charismatic leaders who were not at the top of their organization being forced to leave the organization after only three or four years.

Explanation for the Effect

In attempting to explain why charismatic leaders succeed or fail, theorists have been influenced by the contingency view that leader characteristics and situational factors are input variables affecting the outcome of job performance. They also have also considered the process variables of communication and behaviour linking the input and output. In addition, they have described the importance of the subordinates' perception of the charismatic leader in a way reminiscent of the perceptual approach. In fact, they have used the same psychological factors in their explanations as the perceptual theorists.

Salience effects. As we have discussed, perceptual theorists stress the impact of the salience of a group member's behaviour on the odds that they will emerge as a group leader. Analogously, charismatic advocates talk about the importance of salience in the process by which a leader becomes viewed by followers as charismatic. The charismatic leader's animated communication style and inspirational communication content serve to catch the subordinates' attention, as does their attempts to behave consistently with their vision.

Implicit theory effects. We have also described the role of implicit theories in the process by which group member form leadership-relevant impressions of one another. One theorist, Conger (1989), has particularly emphasized the importance of the impression formation process on subordinates' evaluations of their leader as charismatic. After viewing the leader's salient behaviour, subordinates may then use their implicit leadership theories to develop a particularly strong and positive impression of the charismatic leader. Like the "ideal organizational leader," the charismatic leader may be viewed as confident, visionary, trustworthy, and expert. Analogously, if things start going bad, the subordinates might change their impression of the leader to include characteristics the "ideal leader" does not have. The charismatic leader might now be viewed as stubborn, dictatorial, and back-stabbing.

Although there is great agreement among scientists about this theory, much of it is speculative, and little of it has received research examination. A welcome addition to the work on charismatic leadership has come from two experiments testing it.

Howell and Frost study. Howell and Frost (1989) gave business students an individual task to perform in which each acted like a business executive making a decision. Two other confederates also "worked" on the same individual task side-by-side with the real participant. The task was described by a "leader" displaying one of the following leadership styles:

- Task-oriented. The leader described the task and told the participants to follow the instructions, show good judgement, and be methodical in their work. The task-oriented leader sat behind a desk to distance themselves from the participants, used a "moderate" tone of voice, intermittent eye gaze, and "neutral" facial expressions (no smiling or nodding).
- Maintenance-oriented. The leader described the task and told the participants to relax, work at their own pace, and not to worry about the outcomes. They sat at the front edge of the desk to lessen interpersonal distance, used a "warm" tone of voice, direct eye gaze, and "friendly" facial expressions (smiling and nodding).
- Charismatic. The leader described the task, emphasized the importance of the results to the future of the students' coursework, encouraged them to be creative, and expressed confidence in their ability. They alternated between sitting at the front edge of the desk and pacing around the room, used a "captivating" tone of voice, direct eye gaze and "animated" facial expressions.

Then the leader left and the task began. At one point, the leader returned and spoke again. The task-oriented leader reminded the participants to focus on the task, the maintenance-oriented leader thanked the participants for performing it, and the charismatic leader reiterated confidence in the participants' abilities to perform the task. At the end of the task, the participants reported their feelings about their experience on a questionnaire.

The findings showed support for the value of charismatic leadership. The charismatic leader condition was highest on task performance, with the maintenance leader condition lowest. Turning to the questionnaire measures, the charismatic and task-oriented leader conditions were highest on participants' satisfaction with their own performance and the charismatic and maintenance-oriented leader were highest on participants' satisfaction with the leader.

Kirkpatrick and Locke study. Kirkpatrick and Locke (1996) noted a weakness with the Howell and Frost study. Howell and Frost had the charismatic leader both exhibit a certain style of non-verbal behaviour and express a particular type of communication content. The results showed that this combination led to more satisfactory results for the charismatic leader conditions than for the task-oriented or maintenance-oriented. However, there is no way of knowing whether it was non-verbal style or verbal content that led to these findings.

Kirkpatrick and Locke then performed a study to distinguish between these two possible factors. They asked participants to perform a routine assembly task, in which they inserted pages into notebook binders according to a set of instructions. Before the task began, a leader either expressed a "vision" (commitment to quality) and confidence in the participants' abilities, or merely gave factual information about how paper is made. Half of the "vision" and half of the "factual" leaders used the charismatic non-verbal style as Howell and Frost had defined them. The other half used Howell and Frost's task-oriented non-verbal style. Kirkpatrick and Locke found that of the two possible factors, only the verbal expression of vision had an effect on quality of performance. This effect was indirect, working through changes in participants' goals and self-confidence.

A SEMIOTIC APPROACH TO STUDY CHARISMATIC EFFECTIVENESS

Though Lewin's theory provides a useful framework for integrating the motivational forces underlying charismatic leadership, it offers little guidance about how one might operationalize and test the theory's predictions. Since Lewin's theory addresses socially-constructed meaning, an appropriate tool for empirical investigation is semiotics - the science of signs.

Semiotics explicitly deals with the interface between individual and social values, the critical issue in effecting social change. As a formal mode of analysis, it identifies the rules that govern the construction and destruction of meaning in a particular social system. Like Lewin's (1951) field theory, it rests on the assumption that all meaning is contextualized and resides in a system of underlying oppositions. Semiotic analysis offers a systematic means of linking multiple surfacelevel expressions of opposition to the system of meaning that underlies them.

The Structure of Meaning

The units of signification in any communicative act express meaning through their differences (Eco, 1979). The social codes that regulate meaning arise from underlying oppositional structures. Two kinds of opposition interact to give meaning to a sign, or a unit of signification. For a given sign, the first opposition, called contradiction, expresses the total absence of the sign. For example, non-love contradicts love; non-conventional contradicts conventional. A sign can express either end of the contradiction, but not a combination (*e.g.*, one cannot express love and non-love at the same time). For a given sign, the second kind of opposition, called contrariety, includes another sign. The contrary sign, by social construction, also opposes the meaning of the original sign. For example, hate is contrary to love; innovation is contrary to convention. A given sign may have multiple contraries. Hate, loathing, and disgust each opposes love. Innovation, deviance, and spontaneity oppose convention. In contrast to contradictions, a sign may include combinations of contrary meaning or values. For example, one can express love and hate at the same time, though this combination expresses a complex and unstable condition.

Based on our theoretical framework, a charismatic leader performs the task of translating innovative ideas into socially conventional ideas, that is, translating a value into its contrary. Semioticians typically employ a visual representation of a value's contradictions and contraries. Figure depicts such a representation for the values of convention and innovation. Convention is contrary to innovation, and non-convention is contrary to non-innovation. Convention contradicts non-convention, and innovation contradicts non-innovation. This framework sets the stage for our subsequent discussion of leaderfollower interactions.

By practice, the dominant positive social value, in this case social convention, occupies the upper left corner of the semiotic square. Conventions represent socialized, institutionalized, and endorsed ideas or values, the frame through which most people experience their world. The contrary, innovation, occupies the upper right corner. The contradictions occupy positions diagonal to the values they oppose. The values depicted in a semiotic square relate hierarchically; the assertion of the dominant value presumes the negation of its contrary (convention presumes non-innovation). However, negation of the contrary only allows the possibility of the dominant value (non-innovation makes convention possible). Understanding the process by which one can effect change in social norms depends on this hierarchy.

Replacing one dominant value with another directly (*e.g.*, replacing convention with innovation), or shifting the balance of one in favour of the other, will lead to increasing tension that is likely to undermine change efforts (Lewin, 1951). According to Lewin, an effective change strategy begins by "unfreezing" the dominant value. Here, this means advocating its contradiction (*e.g.*, replacing convention with non-convention before advocating innovation. The terms and structural relations defined by a semiotic square can provide a theoretical starting point for identifying the components of meaning of any set of values within a social system. In this study, they depict values concerning leadership, values believed to both motivate leaders and to serve as standards by which society judges leader effectiveness.

The Social Structure of Values

Leaders operate and are judged within a social system whose values define what is "effective." Values associated with charismatic leadership imply rejection of the status quo and reliance on non-conventional solutions to existing social problems. These values oppose the socially-endorsed dominant cultural values represented by conventional leadership. Neither the conventional nor the innovative values contain "objective" content. Conventional leadership may mean one thing in the U.S., and something quite different in Cuba. Yet in a given social context, innovation/ non-convention always opposes convention/non-innovation.

Within such a meaning system, charismatic leadership, by definition, attempts to persuade society to embrace a contrary of a current social convention, that is, innovation. The logical relations depicted in the semiotic square imply that charismatic leadership is, at its essence, the contrary of conventions. As one adopts more institutionalized conventions, one appears less charismatic. According to this model, negation of existing beliefs is a fundamental characteristic of charismatic leadership.

The social structure of leaders' values identifies value components at a societal level. However, it does not reflect the personal values that motivate or predispose charismatic leaders to promote non-endorsed social values. Nor does it describe the personal value changes required when members of society follow the charismatic leader. Therefore, we need to more closely examine the personal value structure of leaders and of society's members.

The Personal SubStructure of Values

The two sets of motivators define individual human behaviour in relation to social values: desire and fear. The terms of the personal value system interact with the social value system to generate what one observes in human behaviour. Different value combinations lead to either conflicting or compatible relations. For example, desire that is, aspirations, intentions or a conscious impulse towards something positive interacts with endorsed social values to produce a compatible or balanced relation of personal and social values. Similarly, fear that is, the anticipation of danger or the impulse to avoid or overcome a negative combined with unendorsed social values (innovation), produces compatibility in personal-social values. Both relationships are stable over time, are deemed "effective" and represent "socialized" members of society.

On the other hand, people experiencing fear of society's conventions are unlikely to remain stable over time or to be "effective." Similarly, desire combined with socially unendorsed values (innovation) produces an unstable tension. Charismatic leaders represent this combination of tension – desire for innovation. Their leadership aims at replacing current social convention with their personal values in order to achieve a state of balance for themselves.

The charismatic leaders as having the power to modify the beliefs and preferences of individuals in order to create a new compatibility between personal and social values. Previous theory suggests that charismatic leaders effect such a change through frame re-alignment. Our analysis suggests that before followers will align around a new interpretive frame, they must reverse their previous relationship with the existing socially dominant values. As described below, this occurs through introducing conflict in a compatible convention-based structure and compatibility in a conflictive innovation-based structure.

THE FUNCTIONAL APPROACH TO LEADERSHIP

The functional approach to leadership first appeared at about the same period of time that scientists began questioning the trait and style approaches. Some scientists responded to the problems with the trait and style approaches by adopting the situational and contingency perspectives.

As you recall, each of these approaches has a unique perspective on leadership. For instance, the trait approach is concerned with the permanent characteristics of a leader. The style point of view maintains that the method a leader uses is most important. The situational perspective looks for differences in leadership style across different circumstances. Finally, the contingency approach examines leadership by looking at the association of trait and situation. These four points of view all have one thing in common, however. All of them, in the end, are concerned with a particular person in a leadership role.

The functional perspective, in contrast, in concerned with the behaviours of a group. Specifically, the functional approach examines the behaviours that allow the group to reach its goals. We discussed how behaviours serve functions that help a group solve its task and maintenance problems. Certain behaviours serve as leadership functions. For instance, leadership functions include actions that serve to help the group perform its task and clarify the group's goals. They also include behaviours that help the group interact effectively and give members social support.

The functional approach maintains that a group need not have only one particular member who performs these leadership functions. Any group member can perform them. This means that any member can lead. If we accept the functional perspective, we have the potential to uncover which behaviours help lead a group towards its goals. These behaviours help the group if at least one member performs them.

THE TRAIT APPROACH TO LEADERSHIP

The first time that researchers attempted to use a scientific method to study leadership was in the 1920s. Taken as a group, these early scientists worked with a basic hypothesis regarding who leaders were. They assumed that leaders were people with personal characteristics, or traits, that set them above and apart from non-leaders. This assumption was consistent with a philosophical view that was popular in the nineteenth century.

The "Great Man Theory"

The 1800s philosophical outlook that created the trait approach is known as the "Great Man Theory of Leadership." The theory states that certain people are born to be leaders. They have a special quality that sets them apart from "common" folk. The idea is that the great leaders of the world would have assumed a leadership role at any place or time in history. Thus, Julius Caesar or Napoleon would have been influential figures anywhere, at any time. Note that the "Great Man" title reflects the thinking of the times. Back then, most people did not consider women capable of possessing leadership qualities. We use the title here only because it is historically correct.

THE EARLY SCIENTIFIC APPROACH

Literal Approach

In the 1920s, various leadership researchers occasionally took the "Great Man" hypothesis literally. They searched for characteristics that differentiated between leaders and followers. They thought that there were certain qualities that only a leader could possess, such as charisma. Usually, however, the scientists looked at the characteristics that all people possess to some degree. They then would cautiously attempt to discover which traits were particularly evident in leaders. It was true that the idea that certain people would always be leaders, no matter what, intrigued researchers. However, it was not just the nineteenth century "Great Man" theory that caused scientists to examine leadership. In the 1930s, fascist governments in Europe and Asia grew increasingly belligerent. As they did so, the democracies of Europe and North America became fearful of impending war. In times of war, nations need leaders. They also need to find them quickly. Hence, these early scientists wanted to devise a psychological test that would allow them to recognize good leaders easily. If they could create such a test, countries could use it during the impending years of crisis. A leadership test would make it a relatively simple task for a country to place gifted people into the necessary leadership roles.

Early scientists created various types of leadership tests that they hoped would fulfill this need. Each test attempted to create a method to predict who would be a leader and who would not be. Before we describe the results of these tests, it is useful for us to discuss how the researchers performed their studies.

Methodology

These early researchers were interested in discovering which traits contributed to a person's degree of leadership. To do this, they decided to compare measurements of leadership scores with measurements of other traits. The scientists used a particular method to compare various measurements. This technique allowed the researchers to discover how the different measurements were related. We shall discuss their methodology step by step.

THE PERCEPTUAL APPROACH TO LEADERSHIP

One of the most important legacies of the emergent approach is the idea that a leader has successfully emerged from a group when the members of the group believe that person to be the group's leader. Thus, the emergent approach emphasizes the notion that group members' perceptions about leadership are critical to the process of leader emergence.

The perceptual approach to leadership grows out of that notion. It is an attempt to understand how the average group member judges the leadership abilities of other members. Hence, it focuses on an important aspect of the leader emergence process

The perspectives we have discussed differ mainly in only one point. This is in regard to which factors they claim are important. Respectively, we have seen approaches towards leadership that maintain that a leader's success is due to his or her traits, his or her style, or the situation of the group.

Further, we have discussed viewpoints that claim that the most important factors affecting leadership are the behaviours of all group members or the interaction between a leader's traits and the situation of the group. Despite these differences, scientists who advocate these approaches are united in their belief that they can objectively define "leadership" as a variable. Advocates of the perceptual approach do not share this belief. They believe that leadership exists primarily within the mind of each group member. Thus they believe that the way to study leadership is to examine what group members think leadership is.

IMPRESSION FORMATION PROCESS

The perceptual approach views leadership as an "impression formation process." We discussed the process by which personality impressions. Let's review it now. For example, Sue wants to form an impression of Charlie; so she watches how he behaves. Sue particularly notices attention-grabbing, or salient behaviour, on Charlie's part. Sue then decides whether his character is responsible for his behaviour or if he is just reacting to the situation. If she decides that Charlie is responsible for the way he acts, she forms an impression of him. This impression starts with a trait that describes the behaviour she has observed. The impression then builds, by adding other traits that Sue believes are associated with Charlie's first trait.

"Halo" and "Horns" Effects

If Sue observes something she believes is a "good" trait, she will tend to believe that Charlie has more "good" traits. Scientists call this tendency the "halo effect." If, on the other hand, Sue thinks Charlie has a "bad" initial trait, she will build up her impression by assigning more "bad" traits to him. This is the "horns effect." Finally, Sue will judge whether she likes Charlie based on her impression.

Biases enter into our impressions because of the halo and horns effects. As we have discussed, once we assign a trait to a person, we tend to further assign related traits. We can do this because we have a pre-existing idea of which traits are associated. Such a process of judgement often can be wrong. It is not always true that clumsy people are stupid, for example. We described how the halo effect often causes people to make "good" judgements about persons who are physically attractive. People tend to say that attractive people are intelligent, mentally stable, and so on, without seeing any relevant evidence that this is true. Clearly, attractive people are not always "good" in all ways.

IMPRESSION FORMATION PROCESS AND LEADERSHIP

The way in which we form impressions and make judgements about the leadership ability of our fellow group members works in the same way as any impression formation process. First, we watch the other members of our group to see which leadership behaviours they generally exhibit. We are particularly attentive to the most salient of those behaviours. Next, we decide whether each person's character is responsible for any leadership behaviours or whether the situation is responsible. If we decide that a person is responsible for his or her actions, we form an impression of the person as a leader. Our impression will include not only the behaviours we have actually observed but also the traits that we believe are associated with leadership.

For example, we see that Joan speaks her mind readily. We think that is what a leader should do. We then may come to believe that Joan also has integrity, spirit, organizational skills, and other traits that we think leaders should have, even if we do not see her exhibiting them. We may then decide that Joan is truly the leader of the group.

Behavioural Salience

We have noted that impression formation begins when an observer notices a particularly salient behaviour. Behavioural salience is an important part of the process by which group members come to judge one another's leadership. In fact, some of the variables involved in leader emergence work the way they do because they make a person's behaviour particularly salient.

Amount of communication. When someone is talking, we are likely to pay attention to them. Thus, the more a person talks during group discussion, the more attention they receive from the other members. Given this, it should not be surprising that talkative members are more likely to emerge as leaders than non-talkative members.

Further, anything that increases a talkative member's salience would increase the likelihood of that member emerging as group leader. For example, consistently with the material on deviance and minority, a small subgroup within the larger group is likely to gain the attention of the entire group if they are deviating from the group consensus. Thus, the behaviour of a talkative member of that subgroup would be particularly salient to the rest of the group, and especially likely to emerge as a leader. In their review of literature about the relationship between amount of talk and leader emergence, Mullen *et al.* (1989) found research evidence for this effect.

Seating position. One of the reasons that the ends or head of a table are the "leadership seats" is that a person who sits at one of those positions becomes perceptually salient to the other members of the group. Perceptual salience can increase the odds that a member will become group leader for two reasons. First, they are more likely to be in the normal line of sight of other group members.

The other group members are then more likely to direct their attention to them. Second, placing group members where they will receive the comments of other members is likely to lead them to talk frequently. As discussed, frequent talking will likely result in other group members judging them to be leaders.

Implicit Leadership Theories

As we have described, if an observer decides that a person is responsible for their behaviour, the observer begins to form an impression of the person. This impression begins with a trait that describes the observed behaviour, and then grows through the addition of other traits that the observer believes are associated with the first trait.

But where do these beliefs about the association among traits come from? They come from what researchers call implicit personality theories. An implicit personality theory is a person's beliefs about what traits and behaviours go together. For example, people's implicit personality theories usually associate "good" traits, such as intelligence and attractiveness, together. This is the reason why "halo effects" occur in impression formation. Similarly, implicit personality theories normally link "bad" traits, such as clumsiness and stupidity, with one another. This is the source of "horns effects" in impressions.

Research has shown that people have beliefs about the attributes that the "ideal leader" should possess. We can call these beliefs implicit leadership theories. Our own research (Pavitt and Sackaroff, 1990) has shown that implicit leadership theories tend to include traits such as "forceful" and "enthusiastic." These theories also include behaviours such as "states the group's procedure" and "encourages group member participation." Thus, these are included in the list of attributes that most people feel that the "ideal leader" should exhibit.

Group members use these implicit leadership theories when they form impressions of one another's leadership. For example, a group consists of Leon, Marvin, and Bram. Leon believes that an ideal leader who "encourages group member participation" is also "enthusiastic." He saw those two attributes as "going together" in an ideal leader. This judgement carries over into how Leon judges his fellow group members. For instance, if he were to think that Marvin exhibited a high level of "encouragement" behaviours, he would also judge Marvin as "enthusiastic." If Leon made a negative judgement about someone, he would connect similar negative attributes. If Leon judged that Bram exhibited a low level of encouragement behaviours, he would also think that Bram had low levels of the trait of "enthusiasm."

Leon is basing one judgement on another. He first observes Marvin and Bram and judges how much they encourage group members. As we have noted, Leon then believes that "encouragement" and "enthusiasm" go together in an "ideal leader." Therefore, he uses this belief and his previous judgement to decide how to assign the trait of "enthusiasm" to Marvin and Bram.

Further, group members use their implicit leadership theories as a basis for evaluating one another's leadership skills. If we form an impression of a group member that is similar to our preconceptions of the "ideal leader," then we would judge that group member to be a good leader. Analogously, if our impression is very different from our implicit leadership theory, then we would evaluate that member to be a poor leader.

We can use our example of Leon, Marvin, and Bram again to show this. Leon thought that Marvin had high levels of "encouragement" and "enthusiasm" attributes. Thus, Marvin's attributes were similar to those in Leon's vision of an "ideal leader." Hence, Leon evaluated Marvin as a good leader. In contrast, Leon thought that Bram had low levels of the attributes of "encouragement" and "enthusiasm." Thus, Bram was unlike Leon's vision of an "ideal leader." Accordingly, Leon, judged Bram to be a poor leader.

METHOD FOR ASSUMING LEADERSHIP

They wanted to know whether there are differences between groups whose leaders get their position in different ways. Does it matter whether leaders are assigned from the outside, elected by the members, or allowed to emerge from group discussion? Contrasting hypotheses could be proposed concerning this issue. It could be that groups with assigned or elected leaders perform better than groups with emergent leaders because emergent-led groups begin discussion without knowing who is in charge. It also could be that groups with emergent or elected leaders perform better than groups with assigned leaders because assigned-leader groups are not involved in the choice of leader and as a consequence are less satisfied with their leadership. Several studies have been performed that are relevant to this issue.

Mortensen study. Mortensen (1966) analyzed the leadership emergence process in six groups that met three times. Three of the groups had assigned leaders, and three did not. The three assigned leaders performed the most leadership actions during the first group meeting. However, by the third meeting, only one on the three was still leading his or her group. In the other two, the assigned leader had been supplanted by another member to whom the group had responded more positively.

Mortensen concluded that the group's approval of an assigned leader is important. Assigned leadership can help a person quickly assume the leadership role, but only if the group approves of him or her. In contrast, assigning a leader can slow down a group and make it difficult for a leader to emerge if the group disapproves of the assignment. In this case, leadership emergence would have been faster if there had been no leadership assignment.

Goldman and Fraas study. Goldman and Fraas (1965) found that the way in which a group acquires its leaders is important to the group's performance. They assigned leaders to groups through four methods. One way was that the group elected a leader by vote. The second method was that the experimenters selected a leader based on the person's ability. The third way was that the scientists arbitrarily chose a leader, and the last method involved groups that had no assigned leader.

The researchers then had the groups play "Twenty Questions." They compared the success rates of each group. The researchers found that groups with elected leaders performed the best. The performance of groups that had leaders appointed based on ability was close to the best success rate. Leaderless groups were a distant third. The groups with the worst scores were the ones with arbitrarily appointed leaders.

Hollander and Julian study. Hollander and Julian (1970) decided to compare the performance of elected and appointed leaders. The researchers told groups and the leaders of the groups that one of two criteria had determined leadership. They led their participants to believe that either the group had elected the leader or the experimenters had appointed him or her. In either case, the leader supposedly had important abilities for the position.

Hollander and Julian found that "elected" leaders had slightly more influence on their group's opinions than "appointed" leaders. They also were far more willing to deviate from their group's ideas. However, their position was far more precarious. Members lost confidence in "elected" leaders if they failed or if the group considered them incompetent at their task. In contrast, "appointed" leaders had to both fail and have the group consider them incompetent before the group would reject them.

Larson study. Larson (1971) compared nine groups whose members agreed on whom they felt had emerged as leader with five other groups whose members did not agree on who led the groups. Larson called the first nine groups "stable leadership" groups and the other five "unstable leadership" groups. The stable leadership groups spent more time on substantive issues and less time on procedural and irrelevant topics than the unstable groups. Further, the leader initiated the most substantive ideas in the stable groups. In addition, the stable groups spent more discussion time, per idea, on the topic that the leader had initiated, in comparison with topics the other members initiated. Thus, it appears that groups with stable leadership were more prepared to take on the their task than groups with unstable leadership.

Looking at these studies as a whole, it appears that competence and group acceptance are the most important factors in how a group will behave with a certain leader. It does not necessarily matter whether a leader is elected, emergent, or appointed. A group can behave well and be successful under any of these conditions. As long as the group accepts the leader and he or she is competent, the group can function well with the leader.

LEWIN'S RESEARCH

Methodology

In the late 1930s, Lewin and his students Lippitt and White performed a landmark study of the three leadership styles. They wanted to determine how each style would affect a group. The groups they chose to study were made up of 10-year-old boys. There were four groups with five members in each. The boys met to participate in arts and crafts activities or in similar hobbies. The groups experienced a succession of various adult leaders. These leaders were Lippitt, White, and two other coworkers. Each adult assumed a different leadership style. The study defined these styles in the following ways:

- Authoritarian leaders
  - These leaders determined all policies for the group members. They told the boys which projects to do.
  - They also dictated the methods and stages of goal attainment one step at a time. The adults would give instructions for a subsequent step only after the boys had completed the previous step. They did not give them all of the instructions at once at the beginning of a project. The researchers reasoned that the boys would have little understanding of the project as a whole if the leaders gave them instructions in this step-by-step manner. Without an understanding of the whole project, the boys would have little ability to make their own creative contributions to the assignment. This meant that the leader would have increased control over their activities. Remember that according to Lewin, the authoritarian leader wants group members to reach the leader's goals, not their own.
  - The authoritarian leaders also assigned work companions. They told the boys with whom they could work on their projects.
  - They further evaluated the boys individually. They did not judge the group as a whole. They expected that the approach would cause the boys to be concerned with their own tasks rather than with the work of the group as a whole.
- Democratic leaders
  - These leaders encouraged the group to make its own policy. They asked the boys which projects they wanted to do.

  - They also explained the stages of the project, along with the methods of goal attainment, in advance. This gave the boys the knowledge that they needed to take the initiative concerning how the group would perform its task. Remember that the democratic leader wants to help group members reach their own goals.
  - They further allowed the boys to choose their own work companions.
  - The democratic leaders evaluated the work of the group as a whole. They did not judge members separately. They expected that this method would influence the boys to be concerned with the whole group's efforts rather than with only their own work.
- Laissez faire leaders
  - Laissez faire leaders refused to help the group choose its policy.
  - They also never volunteered information on the stages and methods necessary to attain the group's goals.
  - Further, these leaders refused to help the boys choose their work companions.
  - They also did not evaluate any work. The laissez faire leaders only answered questions and provided work materials.

ADVANCE IN LEADERSHIP THEORY

As with the functional point of view, the emergent approach came to prominence in the late 1940s and early 1950s when the problems with the trait and style approaches became evident. As with the situational approach, advocates of the emergent perspective claim that the group's situation determines the group's leadership. However, whereas the situational approach is concerned with the style elected and assigned leaders should adopt in different situations, the emergent approach is concerned with predicting who will emerge as leader in a previously leaderless group and explaining why some people emerge rather than others.

Advocates of both the situational and emergent approaches understood that a situation consists of two parts. One part is the task that the group must perform. The other part includes the needs and desires of the group members themselves. Hence, they realized that group members themselves help to determine who their leader is.

This concept was a significant advance over earlier approaches to the study of leadership. Both the trait and style approaches did see that leaders influence group members. However, both ignored the possibility that members may influence their leader in return. Scientists who held the emergent point of view came to an even further realization.

They saw that even leaders with strong claims for power must receive their groups' approval in order to be effective. These claims for power include expertise, legitimacy, and the like. These realizations on the part of scientists who held the emergent viewpoint opened three new avenues of thought.

- Leader emergence. The trait and style approaches limited their enquiries to the ways in which appointed leaders affected group behaviour. In contrast, the emergent methodology shifted attention to the manner in which leaders emerge from previously leaderless groups. In other words, the researchers wanted to know the ways in which leaders gain influence over other group members.
- Method for assuming leadership. Research was performed to discover any differences between the behaviour of groups with assigned leaders, elected leaders, and emergent leaders.
- Deviance and leader acceptance. Theorists attempted to describe how a leader can still be accepted by a group after he or she has performed deviant actions.

  The research using the emergent approach involved all three of these issues.

LEADER EMERGENCE

The first research issue involved the ways in which leaders emerge from groups. To begin, it is clear that amount of communication is the most important factor in determining which group member will emerge. Most simply, the more a person communicates, the more likely it is that the person will emerge as leader.

Reviews of literature by Stein and Heller (1983) and Mullen, Salas, and Driskell (1989) found that the amount that a person talks in a group correlates with group member judgements of task leadership in the range of.5 to.7. It should be noted that the correlation between amount of talk and maintenance leadership is far lower, at about.15. In the Bales groups discussed under the functional approach, the biggest talker was judged as "group leader" 50 per cent of the time.

However, it stands to reason that what a person says should have as much impact on other group members' judgements of that person's leadership as how much that person talks. Surprisingly, many studies have found that the content of a person's talk has no effect on whether the person is judged to be a leader. However, most of these studies were performed in groups of students that were just formed into groups and were performing tasks that did not affect them, such as "Lost on the Moon" or a "human relations" problem.

Other studies have been performed using groups that had existed for many weeks or months and were performing tasks that did affect them, such as groups of students who were working on a class project for which they would get graded. In these studies, not only how much a member talked but also the content of their talk was related to whether or not they emerged as a leader.

There is reason to believe that members are particularly likely to be viewed as leaders if they perform procedural functions during group discussion. Recall that in the Bales groups, the member judged as "guidance" specialist was also judged as "group leader" 78.6 per cent of the time. Two other studies support this idea.

Baker study. Baker (1990) studied the first hour of discussion of eight groups of students in the process of performing two class assignments. She related the content of those discussions to judgements made by group members of who emerged as group leaders, who did not emerge as leaders but maintained high status within the groups, and who did not emerge as either leaders or high-status members. Baker concluded that emergent leaders tended to be concerned with procedural matters during discussion. Sometimes they also contributed ideas to the group, but they tended to not offer their opinions very often. In contrast, those who had high status but were not considered the group's leader concentrated on substantive issues; they contributed ideas and opinions. Finally, members who were neither leaders nor high in status concentrated on opinion giving.

Ketrow study. Ketrow (1991) videotaped a three-member "group" trying to solve a problem about white-collar crime. Each member of the "group" had a pre-assigned role in performing their task. One member specialized in procedural work, one in substantive, and the third in maintenance. One hundred fifty research participants watched the videotape and then made judgements about the members of the "group." Of these participants, 128 chose the procedural specialist as the group leader. Although the substantive specialist was chosen as the most influential member by 95 participants, only 17 chose that person as the group leader. Thus there is good reason to believe that verbal activity is related with emergent leadership. Of course, not every talkative person becomes a leader. As just described, the content of talk also has an impact on group member's judgements of one another's leadership. However, other factors may be involved. If verbal activity is associated with emergent leadership, perhaps non-verbal participation is too.

Baird study. Baird (1977) showed the plausibility of this proposal. He videotaped the interaction of 10 five-person groups. In doing so, he discovered that members' perceptions of leadership correlated with various non-verbal signals. With arm and shoulder gestures, the correlation coefficient was.45. In addition, the coefficient with vertical head movements was.27. There was a smaller correlation of.15 with shifts in posture, absence of horizontal or "no" head movements, and absence of frowns. Eye contact, smiles, and absence of hand or finger movement were also slightly related to leadership. These had a correlation of.09. Taken as a whole, it appears that groups judge people as leaders when their movement styles are active but not nervous. Also, group members believe that leaders give non-verbal signals that imply positive evaluations of the other group members.

Relevant Input Variables

The research we have discussed thus far shows that process (verbal and non-verbal communication) is related with output (leadership emergence). However, as we have discussed throughout this book, a valid theory of group discussion also needs to consider relevant input variables that affect group process. There are several input variables that can have an impact on the amount of leadership-relevant communication that occurs during group discussion. Next, we will consider three of these input variables; seating position, approval, and task-relevant knowledge.

Seating Position

Several studies have shown that seating position has an effect on emergent group leadership. For example, Strodtbeck and Hook (1961) performed research using 69 twelve-person mock juries. Those sitting at the ends of the jury table were the most talkative members of the groups, and were most likely to be chosen to lead the mock juries. Research has shown that people sitting in those positions also receive the most communication from other group members. It is clear that the ends or the "head" of a table are considered to be the "leadership seats" for a group discussion.

Seating position also has effects on the order in which group members speak. Steinzor (1950) examined the order in which members of two 10-member groups sitting in a circle spoke to one another. He found that, when a particular group member made a statement, the next statement tended to come from a group member sitting on the opposite side of the circle. Thus, comments are likely to go back and forth across opposite seating positions in the group.

Howells and Becker study. Howells and Becker used this idea in a study published in 1962. They reasoned that they could set up a "power differential" by placing fewer people on one side of a table than on the other side. They reasoned, as Steinzor had found, that comments go back and forth across a table. If this happens, the people on the less populated side proportionally receive and make more comments than those on the other side. The scientists formed 20 five-person groups. Two members, or 40 per cent of the group, sat on one side of the table. Three participants, or 60 per cent, sat on the other side.

If all else is equal in such a situation, we would logically expect that the number of leaders from each side should match their percentage in the group. Thus, among the 20 groups, 8 leaders should emerge from the less populated side of the table, matching the 40 per cent. Similarly, 12 leaders, or 60 per cent, should emerge from the more populated side. Did.this occur? No. Instead, only 6 leaders emerged from the more populated side. This was only 30 per cent. In contrast, 14 leaders came from the less populated side. This was 70 per cent, a great deal more than a logical prediction would have calculated.

Thus, the results supported the contention of Howells and Becker. They had been able to create a power differential. The less populated side did have participants who spoke more often than the other members. Consequently, the less populated side produced more leaders than a logical outcome would have predicted. Thus, research has shown that certain seating positions can make it more likely that a group member will become a leader. Other studies, however, have shown that this effect is weak and can be canceled by more powerful factors. For example, Bass and Klubeck (1952) found that seating position had no effect on leadership judgements in discussion groups with pre-existing status differences among members.

Approval

A second factor that can affect emergent group leadership is whether or not a member receives approval for what she or he says. A study by Pepinsky, Hemphill, and Shevitz (1958) shows this impact. Pepinsky, Hemphill, and Shevitz study. Pepinsky, Hemphill, and Shevitz conducted a study with four-person groups. The groups task was to build "products" out of tinkertoys that could be sold at a "buyer's table." The group had to purchase the tinkertoys, build the products and sell them at a profit at the buyer's table.

Each group included two confederates who acted in either of two different ways. In one condition, the confederates waited until the real participants had taken some leadership actions and then disapproved of what they had done. For example, they would say that they did not like bossy people who told them what to do. In the second condition, the confederates showed approval of the real participants' actions. For example they would say that they liked people who could get things going and come up with a good plan. The researchers found that the participants whose actions had received approval from the confederates performed many more subsequent leadership actions than the participants whose actions who had been rejected.

Task-Relevant Knowledge A third factor that affects emergent leadership is whether group members have knowledge relevant to the group's task. Hemphill (1961) reported an unpublished study by Shevitz that demonstrated this effect. Shevitz organized three-member groups with two "experts" and a third, non-expert member. One of the experts was a member of the local Amateur Radio Association, and the other had experience in statistics courses. The group had two tasks; assembling the components of a circuit from a schematic diagram, and a statistics problem. The "radio" expert performed the most leadership acts during the first task, while the "statistics" expert did the most during the second.

THE CONTINGENCY APPROACH TO LEADERSHIP

The trait approach was based on the idea that leadership can be predicted by considering the impact of one variable, the personality of the leader. The style approach was also based on the idea that leadership can be explained through the effect of one variable, the manner by which the leader leads. The situational approach was likewise based on the idea that the style that a leader should adopt is based on one variable, the situation in which the leader is in. The contingency approach to leadership is based on the idea that scientists can account for leadership by examining the ways in which two or more variables work together to determine leadership. As we have discussed, the various earlier approaches were unsuccessful in describing how leadership works. In contrast, there is some reason to believe that considering the impact of multiple variables simultaneously may lead to some success.

The most well known example of a contingency perspective towards leadership is Fiedler's "contingency theory" (1964, 1978). Fiedler's work involved not only the relationship between trait and situation, but also style variables. He thus incorporated into his theory all of the various approaches that we have discussed.

In the following section, we will describe Fiedler's theory in detail. We shall begin with his proposed leadership trait and its effect on leadership style. We will then turn to his typology of situations. We shall finish our discussion of Fiedler's work by examining his view concerning the manner in which trait and situation interact.

LEADER TRAIT - LPC

Fiedler devised a test that he used to help him determine what he could consider a leadership trait. Imagine that you are taking this test. You are given a questionnaire with the following opening instructions:

Think of all the people you have ever known or with whom you have worked. Describe the one person with whom it has been the most difficult to work. In other words, think of the person who has been your least preferred coworker. In order to describe the person, rate him or her on a scale of 8 (positive side) to 1 (negative side) on the following pairs of items:

Pleasant/Unpleasant	Friendly/Unfriendly
Accepting/rejecting	Relaxed/tense
Close/distant	Warm/cold
Supportive/hostile	Interesting/boring
Harmonious/quarrelsome	Cheerful/gloomy
Open/guarded	Loyal/backbiting
Trustworthy/untrustworthy	Considerate/inconsiderate
Nice/nasty	Agreeable/disagreeable
Sincere/insincere	Kind/unkind

According to Fiedler, your answers to this questionnaire indicate the degree to which you possess a certain trait. For want of a better name, Fiedler called this permanent characteristic the "Least Preferred Coworker" trait.

Scientists call it "LPC" for short. What is this characteristic? Fiedler would not necessarily agree with our interpretation of LPC, but the following discussion reveals how we believe LPC functions.

"High" LPC score. Suppose your answers on the questionnaire averaged 6 or higher on each item. This would give you a total score of at least 108 out of a possible total score of 144. With this high score, Fiedler would say that you are a "high" LPC person. What does this mean? As you recall, Fiedler's questionnaire asked you to describe the person you would least like to have as a coworker. A high score on this questionnaire means that you have judged this "least preferred coworker" to be, nevertheless, a pleasant, friendly individual. The evaluation may seem a bit of an inconsistency on your part.

However, what you have done is come to two separate conclusions about the person. On the one hand, you do not want to work with him or her. You have made a negative task-oriented judgement of the person. On the other hand, you think the person is relaxed, friendly, and so on. You have thereby made a positive social judgement of this person. Apparently, you are able to differentiate between how this least preferred coworker is as a worker and how he or she is as a person. In essence, you are able to separate the task and social aspects of the people around you. This ability makes you a high LPC person.

"Low" LPC score. In contrast, suppose your answers on each item on the questionnaire averaged 3 or lower. This would give you a low score, of only 54 at most, with 18 points being the lowest possible outcome. In this case you have judged your least preferred coworker to be an unfriendly, unpleasant person. This means that you give your coworker a negative rating for both task-oriented and social skills. The implication is that you cannot differentiate between the person's abilities as a worker and his or her skills as a person. You appear to be unable to separate the task and social aspects of people. This makes you a "low" LPC person.

LPC and leadership. How does the LPC trait affect a person in a leadership position? It appears that LPC has an influence on the leadership style that the person prefers to use. High LPC leaders like to follow a style that is maintenance oriented. When they feel pressured, they try to relieve the pressure by improving social relationships.

Low LPC leaders, on the other hand, prefer a task-oriented style. They receive their greatest satisfaction from the successful performance of a work assignment. When they feel pressure, they respond by working harder on the task than they had previously. In comparison with high LPC leaders, Fiedler has found that low LPC people tend to be more task-oriented during group discussion. They ask for and give more suggestions, demand greater member participation, and make negatively toned statements more often. The low LPC leaders also tend to be more active. They talk and interrupt more frequently and control the conversation to a greater degree than high LPC people do.

Finally, there is a third possible type of LPC trait. This is medium LPC. Medium LPC people have scores from each questionnaire item that average between 3 and 6, with total points ranging from 54 to 108. Fiedler finds that these people are socially independent. They are unconcerned with other people's evaluations of them and uninterested in leadership. Beyond identifying that they can exist, Fiedler ignores medium LPC people in his leadership theory.

GROUP SITUATION

One of the strong points of Fiedler's theory is the way in which he views the group situation. He does not present an unorganized list of possible circumstances. Instead, Fiedler has turned his attention to the features that make up a circumstance. This viewpoint has led to an orderly typology of group situations.

In general, Fiedler classifies situations according to their favourableness to a group leader. Different features within the circumstance can increase or decrease how favourable the circumstance is for a leader. Favourableness is the extent to which a leader can make decisions and take actions in his or her group. Further, it is the degree to which a leader can be confident these decisions and actions will lead to the outcomes that he or she intended.

Specifically, Fiedler defines situations in terms of the following three features:

- Leader-member relations. This is the most important feature. Fiedler defines it as the degree to which a leader has the support and loyalty of the other group members. He categorizes this feature as existing only at either end of the continuum. The continuum runs from "good" to "bad." If relations are good, the leader is confident that group members will follow his or her directions. According to our definition above of "favourableness," good relations are favourable to the leader. If relations are bad, a leader lacks confidence. This is unfavourable for him or her.
- Task structure. This feature is half as important as leader-member relations. Fiedler defines it as the extent to which the group can clearly specify the requirements for completing the task. The task structure also exists along a continuum. "Clear" is at one end of the continuum, and "unclear" is at the other end. A task structure is clear if the group members know the requirements for completing the task, if there is only one method for performing the task, if there is only one best solution, and if the group can verify whether a proposed solution is the best one. This is a favourable structure for leaders. In contrast, the task structure is unclear if the group members do not know the requirements for completing the task, if there is more than one method for performing the task, if there may be many "best" solutions, and if the group cannot verify which proposal is the best. Such a situation is unfavourable for a leader.

- Position power. This feature is half as significant for a group situation as task structure is, and thus one-fourth as important as leader-member relations. Fiedler defines position power as the extent to which a leader has legitimacy in a group. A leader's legitimacy is measured by the degree to which the leader has a position that allows him or her to reward and punish the other group members. The continuum for this feature runs from "strong" to "weak." A strong level of position power is favourable for a leader, whereas a weak level is unfavourable. A leader has strong position power if he or she has legitimacy as part of an organizational chain of command, as in the military. Position power is weak if a leader does not have such legitimacy.

13

Development of Achievement Motivation

ACHIEVEMENT MOTIVATION THEORIES

Current achievement motivation theories continue to emphasize children's beliefs, values, and goals as prominent influences on motivation. That is, many theorists adopt a social cognitive perspective on the nature of motivation. Central constructs of interest to motivation theorists include self-efficacy, perceptions of control, and other competence-related beliefs; the goals (both specific and general) children have for learning and other activities; children's interest and intrinsic motivation for learning; and children's valuing of achievement. Although the study of beliefs, goals, and values remains strong, self-determination theorists continue to emphasize the role of basic psychological needs and how they influence motivation.

As Eccles *et al.* (1998) did we organize our discussion of motivation theories and research around three broad motivation-related questions children can ask themselves: "Can I do this task?" "Do I want to do this task and why?", and "What do I have to do to succeed on this task?" The first two questions primarily are motivational, whereas the third merges cognitive and motivational variables crucial to the regulation of achievement behaviour. Some theories of course include constructs that deal with all of these questions, but even so we find these questions to be a useful way to organize the theories and constructs.

SELF-EFFICACY THEORY

Bandura's (1977, 1997) construct of self-efficacy is a major part of his broader social cognitive model of learning and development. Bandura defines self-efficacy as individuals' confidence in their ability to organize and execute a given course of action to solve a problem or accomplish a task. He emphasizes human agency and self-efficacy perceptions as major influences on individuals' achievement strivings, including performance, choice, and persistence. Bandura (1997) characterizes self-efficacy as a multidimensional construct that can vary in strength (*i.e.*, positive or negative), generality (relating to many situations or only a few), and level of difficulty (feeling efficacious for all tasks or only easy tasks).

An important distinction in Bandura's (1997) model is different kinds of expectancies for success. He distinguished between two kinds of expectancy beliefs: Outcome expectations, or beliefs that certain behaviours, like practice, will lead to certain outcomes, like improved performance, and efficacy expectations, or beliefs about whether one can perform the behaviours necessary to produce the outcome, (*e.g.*, I can practice sufficiently hard to win the next tennis match). Individuals can believe that a certain behaviour will produce a certain outcome (outcome expectation), but may not believe they can do that behaviour (efficacy expectation). Bandura therefore proposed that individuals' efficacy expectations rather than outcome expectancies are the major determinant of goal setting, activity choice, willingness to expend effort, and persistence.

Bandura proposed that individuals' perceived self-efficacy is determined primarily by four things: Previous performance (succeeding leads to a stronger sense of personal efficacy); vicarious learning (watching models succeed or fail on tasks); verbal encouragement by others, and one's physiological reactions (over arousal and anxiety/worry leading to a lower sense of personal efficacy). His stress on these four determinants reflects the link of this theory with both behaviourist and social learning traditions. In addition, Bandura acknowledged the influence of causal attributions on people's self-efficacy. However, Bandura argued that causal attributions only influence behaviour through their impact on efficacy beliefs. Bandura (1995) extended the self-efficacy model by discussing how collective efficacy along with individual efficacy also can be a strong influence on achievement strivings. The self-efficacy construct has been applied to behaviour in many domains including school, health, sports, therapy, occupational choice, and even snake phobia. By and large, the evidence is very supportive of his theoretical predictions with respect to efficacy's influences on performance and choice. For example, high personal academic expectations predict subsequent performance, course enrollment and occupational choice.

Bandura (1997) systematically discussed why he believes self-efficacy theory provides a fuller and richer depiction of the causal relations of self-beliefs to behaviour than do other theories focused on self-referent beliefs, including theories of self-concept, locus of control, effectance motivation, control beliefs, perceived competence beliefs, and possible selves, among others. He argued that self-efficacy is defined more precisely and is more task and situation specific than many of these other beliefs, and therefore should relate more strongly to behaviour. However, some of the distinctions among these constructs may be less clear than Bandura proposed. For instance, researchers measuring both self-concept and self-efficacy in the same study often have found it difficult to distinguish the two constructs empirically Skaalvik and Bong; 2003; Skaalvik and Rankin, 1996). Bong and Clark (1999) and Skaalvik and Bong (2003) provide a good discussion of conceptual and methodological similarities and differences between self-efficacy and self-concept. Like many social cognitive-based theories, self-efficacy theory can be criticized for its overly rational and information processing approach. How accurate are individuals at judging their efficacy, how do these calibrations vary over age, and how much are our decisions influenced by a rational judgement of our competence to do an activity? Further, the focus on one major variable as the major predictor of performance and choice perhaps is too limiting.

SOCIAL COGNITIVE THEORY

Albert Bandura's Social Cognitive Theory emphasizes how cognitive, behavioural, personal, and environmental factors interact to determine motivation and behaviour. According to Bandura, human functioning is the result of the interaction among all three of these factors, as embodied in his Triadic Reciprocal Determinism model. While it may seem that one factor is the majority, or lead reason, there are numerous factors that play a role in human behaviour. Furthermore, the influencing factors are not of equal strength, nor do they all occur concurrently. For example, employee performances (behavioural factors) are influenced by how the workers themselves are affected (cognitive factors) by organizational strategies (environmental factors). The figure below illustrates Triadic Reciprocal Determinism as portrayed by Wood and Bandura (1989).

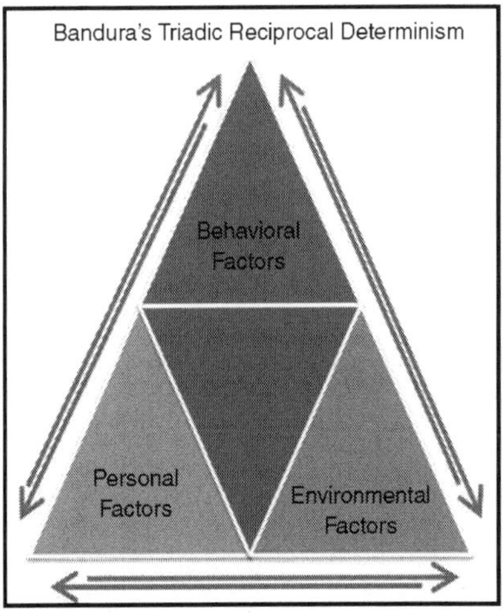

The Social Cognitive Theory is composed of four processes of goal realization: self-observation, self-evaluation, self-reaction and self-efficacy. These components are interrelated, each having an effect on motivation and goal attainment (Redmond, 2010). Self-observation– Observing oneself can inform and motivate. It can be used to assess one's progress towards goal attainment as well as motivate behavioural changes. There are two important factors with regards to self-observation: regularity and proximity. Regularity means the behaviour should be continually observed, whereas proximity means the behaviour should be observed while it occurs, or shortly after. Alone, self-observation is insufficient because motivation depends on one's expectations of outcomes and efficacy. Self-evaluation– Self-evaluation compares an individual's current performance with a desired performance or goal. It is affected by the standards set and the importance of the goals. Goals must be specific and important; therefore, goals such as, "do your best" are vague and will not motivate. Schunk and Zimmerman (1994) state that "specific goals specify the amount of effort required for success and boost self-efficacy because progress is easy to gauge." If one has little regard for his goal he will not evaluate performance. There are two types of self-evaluation standards: absolute and normative. For example, a grading scale would be an example of a fixed or absolute standard. A social comparison such as evaluating one's behaviour or performance against other individuals is an example of a normative standard. People gain satisfaction when they achieve goals that they value. When individuals achieve these valued goals, they are more likely to continue to exert a high level of effort, since sub-standard performance will no longer provide satisfaction.

Self-reaction– Reactions to one's performance can be motivating. If the progress made is deemed acceptable, then one will have a feeling of self-efficacy with regard to continuing, and will be motivated towards the achievement of their goal. A negative self-evaluation might also be motivating in that one may desire to work harder provided that they consider the goal to be valuable. Self-reaction also allows a person to re-evaluate their goals in conjunction with their attainments (Bandura, 1989). If a person has achieved a goal, they are likely to re-evaluate and raise the standard (goal); whereas, if a person has not achieved the goal, they are likely to re-evaluate and lower the standard (goal) to an achievable goal. Self-efficacy– One's belief in the likelihood of goal completion can be motivating in itself. "Self-efficacy refers to people's judgements about their capability to perform particular tasks. Task-related self-efficacy increases the effort and persistence towards challenging tasks; therefore, increasing the likelihood that they will be completed"

Beliefs in Self-Efficacy Theory

Self-efficacy beliefs are an important aspect of human motivation and behaviour as well as influence the actions that can affect one's life. Regarding self-efficacy, Bandura (1995) explains that it "refers to beliefs in one's capabilities to organize and execute the courses of action required to manage prospective situations". More simply, self-efficacy is what an individual believes he or she can accomplish using his or her skills under certain circumstances. Self-efficacy has been thought to be a task-specific version of self-esteem.

The basic principle behind Self-Efficacy Theory is that individuals are more likely to engage in activities for which they have high self-efficacy and less likely to engage in those they do not. According to Gecas (2004), people behave in the way that executes their initial beliefs; thus, self-efficacy functions as a self-fulfilling prophecy. For example, Employee A has high ability and a great deal of experience in creating graphs, but does not have confidence that he can create a high quality graph for an important conference. Employee B has only average ability and only a small amount of experience in creating graphs, yet has great confidence that she can work hard to create a high quality graph for the same conference.

Because of Employee A's low self-efficacy for graph creation, he lacks the motivation to create one for the conference and tells his supervisor he cannot complete the task. Employee B, due to her high self-efficacy, is highly motivated, works overtime to learn how to create a high quality graph, presents it during the conference, and earns a promotion. Self-efficacy has influence over people's ability to learn, their motivation and their performance, as people will often attempt to learn and perform only those task for which they believe they will be successful. Judgements of self-efficacy are generally measured along three basic scales: magnitude, strength, and generality.

- Self-efficacy magnitude measures the difficulty level (*e.g.* easy, moderate, and hard) an individual feels is required to perform a certain task. How difficult is my class work? Are the quizzes easy or hard?
- Self-efficacy strength refers to the amount of conviction an individual has about performing successfully at diverse levels of difficulty. How confident am I that I can excel at my work tasks? How sure am I that I can climb the ladder of success?
- Generality of self-efficacy refers to the "degree to which the expectation is generalized across situations.

The basic idea behind the Self-Efficacy Theory is that performance and motivation are in part determined by how effective people believe they can be. The theory is clearly illustrated in the following quote by Mahatma Gandhi:

- If I have the belief that I can do it, I shall surely acquire the capacity to do it even if I may not have it at the beginning"The basic idea behind the Self-Efficacy–Mahatma Gandhi

Bandura (1977) outlined four sources of information that individuals employ to judge their efficacy: performance outcomes (performance accomplishments), vicarious experiences, verbal persuasion, and physiological feedback (emotional arousal). These components help individuals determine if they believe they have the capability to accomplish specific tasks. Williams and Williams (2010) note that "individuals with high levels of self-efficacy approach difficult tasks as challenges to master rather than as threats to be avoided".

Performance Outcomes– According to Bandura, performance outcomes, or past experiences, are the most important source of self-efficacy. Positive and negative experiences can influence the ability of an individual to perform a given task. If one has performed well at a task previously, he or she is more likely to feel competent and perform well at a similarly associated task (Bandura, 1977). For example, if one performed well in a training workshop they are more likely to feel confident and have high self-efficacy in another training workshop.

The individual's self-efficacy will be high in that particular area, and since he or she has a high self-efficacy, he or she is more likely to try harder and complete the task with much better results. The opposite is also true. If an individual experiences a failure, self-efficacy is likely to be reduced. However, if these failures are later overcome by conviction, it can serve to increase self-motivated persistence when the situation is viewed as an achievable challenge (Bandura, 1977). Vicarious Experiences– People can develop high or low self-efficacy vicariously through other people's performances. A person can watch another perform and then compare his own competence with the other individual's competence (Bandura, 1977). If a person sees someone similar to them succeed, it can increase their self-efficacy.

However, the opposite is also true; seeing someone similar fail can lower self-efficacy. An example of how vicarious experiences can increase self-efficacy in the work place is through mentoring programmes, where one individual is paired with someone on a similar career path who will be successful at raising the individual's self-efficacy beliefs. An example of how the opposite can be true is in a smoking cessation programme, where, if individuals witness several people fail to quit, they may worry about their own chances of success, leading to low self-efficacy for quitting.

Verbal Persuasion– According to Redmond (2010), self-efficacy is also influenced by encouragement and discouragement pertaining to an individual's performance or ability to perform; such as a manager telling an employee, "You can do it. I have confidence in you." Using verbal persuasion in a positive light leads individuals to put forth more effort; therefore, they have a greater chance at succeeding. However, if the verbal persuasion is negative, such as a manager saying to the employee, "This is unacceptable! I thought you could handle this project" can lead to doubts about one self resulting in lower chances of success. Also, the level of credibility directly influences the effectiveness of verbal persuasion; where there is more credibility there will be a greater influence. In the example above, a pep talk by a manager who has an established, respectable position would have a stronger influence than that of a newly hired manager. Although verbal persuasion is also likely to be a weaker source of self-efficacy beliefs than performance outcomes, it is widely used because of its ease and ready availability (Redmond, 2010).

Physiological Feedback (emotional arousal)– People experience sensations from their body and how they perceive this emotional arousal influences their beliefs of efficacy (Bandura, 1977). Some examples of physiological feedback are: giving a speech in front of a large group of people, making a presentation to an important client, taking an exam, etc. All of these tasks can cause agitation, anxiety, sweaty palms, and/or a racing heart (Redmond, 2010). Although this source is the least influential of the four, it is important to note that if one is more at ease with the task at hand they will feel more capable and have higher beliefs of self-efficacy.

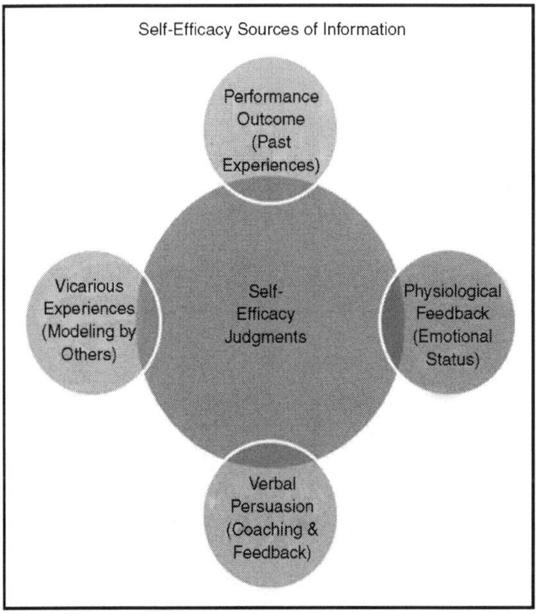

Self-Efficacy and Related Ideas

Personality Traits - Personality is considered a fairly stable pattern of psychological behaviour (thoughts, feelings, and actions) and influences how one will act in response to diverse circumstances (Quinn, Faerman, Thompson, and McGrath, 2003). Personality does not determine behaviour; behaviour arises in a context, such as work. According to Berens *et al.* (2001), "personalities reflect the requirements of the contexts as well as our innate tendencies and how we have adapted to these contexts over time". In other words, an individual's behaviour is determined by the requirements of the situation. "Efficacy beliefs do not share the major properties ascribed to personality traits" (Bandura, 1997). While self-efficacy is not considered a personality trait, it is considered a situation-specific construct.

This is context dependent and functions as, a "cognitive mediator of action" (Bandura, 1982). "Self-efficacy is a related but subtly different personality characteristic. Self assessments of ability contribute to self-efficacy but so does the individual's personality". For example, an employee may have a high self-efficacy for performing a job, but due to a personality trait such as shyness has low self-efficacy for training a new employee to do the same job. According to the self-efficacy theory, the employee would exert more effort on performing the job them self than on training a new employee on how to perform the job. Bandura (1977) upholds that efficacy beliefs can be changed and that, "psychological procedures, whatever their form, serve as a means of creating and strengthening expectations of personal efficacy". An efficacy expectation is defined by Bandura (1977) as, "the conviction that one can successfully execute the behaviour required to produce the outcomes."

Self-esteem - Self-esteem and self-efficacy are often thought of as synonymous, however they vary greatly. Self-efficacy differs from self-esteem in that it's a judgement of specific capabilities rather than a general feeling of self-worth (Beck, 2008). For example, an employee may have low self-efficacy for training a new employee, but this will not cause any ill feelings of perceived self-worth. Even though the two concepts are different, they are connected. The philosophy behind Bandura's Triadic Reciprocal Determinism is that all determinants of motivation are functionally dependent, interacting and influence one another (Bandura, 1997).

Therefore, an individual who has high self-efficacy and is successful in most of the tasks he/she undertakes will most likely build a high self-esteem. Vice-versa, self-esteem could also influence self-efficacy. "It is true, however, that people tend to cultivate their capabilities in activities that give them a sense of self-worth. If empirical analysis are confined to activities in which people invest their sense of self-worth, they will inflate correlations between self-efficacy and self esteem, because the analysis ignore both domains of functioning in which people judge themselves inefficacious but could not care less and those in which they feel highly efficacious but take no pride in performing the activity well because of its socially injurious consequences" (Bandura, 1997).

Equity - Self-efficacy theory utilizes an important construct of equity theory. Like equity theory, motivation can be influenced by how an individual perceives themselves when compared to another. The difference between the two theories is equity theory illustrates that an individual's motivation is influenced by the perceived equality of input/output ratios of the comparison-other, where in contrast, self-efficacy theory predicts an individual's motivation can be influenced by the positive/negative vicarious experiences of the comparison-other. In truth, both theories have been proven to be correct.

VIE theory - The expectancy theory, also known as the VIE (expectancy, instrumentality, and valence) theory, is based on the beliefs that an individual's effort will lead to performance, which in turn, will lead to a specific outcome. Comprehensively, self-efficacy is based on an individual's belief about their ability to perform specific behaviours. Expectancy theory explores how rewards affect motivation, whereas self-efficacy explores how beliefs about capabilities affect motivation.

According to Bandura (1997), "People take action when they hold efficacy beliefs and outcome expectations that make the effort seem worthwhile. They expect given actions to produce desired outcomes and believe that they can perform those actions." To successfully achieve the desired outcome, individuals must possess the necessary skills as well as a buoyant self-belief that they are capable of controlling the specific situational factors (Bandura, 1989). People with high self-efficacy are more likely to respond with renewed effort (expectancy) when feedback shows that they are not reaching their goals by developing more successful strategies.

However, individuals with low self-efficacy, given the same circumstances, may perform poorly because their low self-efficacy impairs their motivation and effort. For example, an employee with high self-efficacy and ability for performing a job, but low self-efficacy for training a new employee will most likely be an inadequate trainer. On the whole, perceived self-efficacy can be distinguished as being competence-based, prospective, and action-related as opposed to related ideas that only share some these elements (Bandura, 1997).

The Interaction of Self-Efficacy with the Environment

According to Bandura (1997), two levels of efficacy (low and high) interact with two types of environment (responsive and unresponsive) to produce the following four predictive variables:

- Success (H, R) - A person with a high level of self-efficacy in a responsive environment will be successful. Their positive attitude towards their abilities coupled with environmental change promotes success and improves long-term motivation.
- Depression (L, R) - A person with a low level of self-efficacy in a responsive environment may fall into a depressed state. They know the environment will change but their lack of belief in their own abilities stops them from trying and succeeding.
- Apathy and helplessness (L, UR) - A person with low self-efficacy and an unresponsive environment will feel helpless and decide that all efforts are pointless thus causing them to be completely inactive.

- Effort intensification or change of course (H, UR) - A person with high self-efficacy in an unresponsive environment will either increase their efforts towards change or decide they need to change their goals.

Attributes of Self-Efficacy and Social Cognitive Theories

Constructive Attributes:

- When faced with a difficult task, people who have high self-efficacy will face the challenge as something to be learned and mastered. Their interest and motivation in mastering the task will drive them to succeed in their difficult, yet approachable goal. This can be seen within the academic domain due particularly to the theory focusing on task and situational specific instances.
- While striving to complete a challenging task or difficult goal, individuals with high self-efficacy may face failures or setbacks, but they will not give up. Where people with low self-efficacy may decide the task is impossible, people with high self-efficacy strive to develop a higher amount of knowledge and increase their effort in order to overcome their failures and setbacks.
- People with high self-efficacy are more likely to set more challenging goals for themselves and be more committed to the goal, which enhances self-efficacy (Bandura, 1995).
- Researchers have demonstrated the positive effects of self-efficacy beliefs on effort, persistence, goal setting, and performance).

"People who regard themselves as highly efficacious act, think, and feel differently from those who perceive themselves as inefficacious. They produce their own future, rather than simply foretell it" - Albert Bandura

Potential Detrimental Attributes:

- Very high self-efficacy can sometimes lead to degradation in performance of a particular task. This is because high self-efficacy can lead to overconfidence in one's aptitude, which creates a false sense of ability. Overconfidence can lead to employing the wrong strategy, making mistakes, refusal to take responsibility for mistakes, and rejecting corrective feedback (Clark, 2001). Overconfidence can also result in lower effort and attention being devoted to the task.
- Verbal and tangible rewards can have both positive and negative effects on self-efficacy depending on the context and environment in which the reward or praise is delivered.

Application of Self-Efficacy and Social Cognitive Theories in the Workplace

Self-efficacy and social cognitive theories both provide a number of suggestions that can be applied in the work setting. They can be used in almost any work environment, with any task, and any demographic of individuals.

These theories can be applied in a basic form or specific to an employer's leadership style. They are cheap, easily attainable, and can be used outside the workforce as well. Efficacy beliefs can be changed, depending on the particular circumstance, the task, or an individual's prior experience (Bandura, 1977). This can be attractive to organizations because it can be applied to any type of individual regardless of background or work history.

Self-efficacy theory suggests that increasing the self-efficacy of employees will boost motivation and performance. This basic idea behind this theory is that motivation and performance are determined by how successful people believe they can be (Bandura, 1982). This is extremely useful in the workplace because employers can develop and improve self-efficacy beliefs in their employees by focusing on the four primary sources. Utilizing the sources of self-efficacy (performance outcomes, vicarious experiences, verbal persuasion, and emotional arousal) can improve employee's effort, persistence, goal setting, and performance on specific tasks. Applying vicarious experiences can be as simple as a waitress shadowing another experienced server or an apprentice learning his trade. Verbal persuasion can be used by showing praise for a job well done or by giving positive feedback on a specific task. Verbal persuasion can be used at any time and requires almost no effort.

According to Bandura's social cognitive (learning) theory, an important source of motivation comes through the many links between goal setting and self-efficacy. Managers can begin by setting up small, basic goals leading up to larger, more difficult ones in order for the employee to develop beliefs of efficacy as each one that is successfully completed (Bandura, 1982). For example, if a new employee is assigned an extremely difficult task, the employee will likely experience self-doubt, stress, and threat of performing an unfamiliar task, resulting in an unsuccessful performance. However, if they are assigned a simple task and are able to experience initial success, with more difficult tasks being introduced slowly they are building high self-efficacy along the way (Bandura, 1982). These tasks are examples of performance outcomes, which are the most significant sources, used to develop self-efficacy. As stated by Bandura (1988), competencies are superbly developed when, "modeling is combined with guided practice and success experiences".

According to Bandura (1982), self-efficacy affects both learning and performance in employees in the following three ways:

- Self-efficacy effects the goals that employees choose. For example, employees with low levels of self-efficacy are more likely to set lower goals for themselves than employees with higher self-efficacy.
- Self-efficacy impacts learning as well as the effort that employees exert on the job. For instance when an employee has high self-efficacy they are more likely to work harder to learn a new task as they will be more confident in their abilities than an employee with low self efficacy.

- Self-efficacy will influence the persistence for which a person will attempt to learn a new and difficult task. Employees who are high in self-efficacy are thought to be more confident and therefore will persist in their efforts when learning a new task even when encountering a problem.

Support of the applicability of self-efficacy to work motivation has been established by numerous studies performed in organizational settings. The following section highlights only a few of the studies performed:

1986: Effects of Employees' Self-Efficacy Beliefs on Productivity

P. Christopher Earley has conducted a study of employee beliefs in their capabilities, and the affect on their productivity in manufacturing organizations in the United States and in England. Earley found that when employees are taught better production techniques and are given production goals, their belief in their capabilities increases. Consequently, as an employee increases his/her self-belief of efficacy, he/she more robustly accepts the production goals and has a higher level of productivity.

1987: Effects of Self-Regulation Training on Absenteeism

Research by Frayne and Latham (1987) on employee absenteeism led to the development of a programme to reduce employee absenteeism. Groups of employees who often missed work were taught how to more effectively manage their motivation and behaviour, in addition to strategies to overcome obstacles that prevented them from attending work.

The study found that as individuals raised their self-efficacy, their work attendance also increased. In addition, by setting short-term goals for work attendance, individuals increased their work attendance and were personally rewarded.

1988: Effects of Self-Efficacy Beliefs on Organizational Productivity

Wood and Bandura (1990) conducted a series of simulated studies on the level of organizational productivity as a function of managerial perceived self-efficacy. In a simulation organization, MBA graduates assumed manager positions and were tasked with matching employees to sub-functions, motivating the employees, and establishing and applying rules. The study found that perceived self-efficacy and personal goals have a direct effect on organizational performance.

In addition, challenging goals have a positive effect on performance in a low complexity organization, but not in a high complexity organization. Furthermore, the study confirmed that, "the interaction of cognitive and motivational processes is important to an understanding of how managers approach the daily stream of decisions that must be made in complex and uncertain decision environments".

1993: Effects of Training on Self-Efficacy Beliefs

A study by Eden and Aviram (1993) to evaluate the effects of training intended to boost self-efficacy on reemployment. The training provided unemployed workers intensive workshops and job search training, as well as the opportunity to build positive performance outcomes. The study found that individuals with low self-efficacy were able to build higher self-efficacy through training.

As a result, these individuals were equally successful in finding jobs as the individuals who began the training with high self-efficacy. Furthermore, the treatment increased reemployment among the individuals who began with low self-efficacy, but did not increase reemployment among the individuals who began with high self-efficacy. This study demonstrates the importance of self-efficacy and shows that self-efficacy perceptions can be changed (Redmond, 2010).

1999: Effects of employees' self-efficacy on working in a team; and the satisfaction with teams and individual performance

Application of self-efficacy theory in the workplace is evidenced in a case study conducted by Sanjib Chowdhury and Thomas Lanis at East Central University in 1999. This case study examined the relationship between employees' self-efficacy of team membership, their satisfaction in regards to this membership and individual performance. The study demonstrated dependencies on the teams' performance. The subjects of the case study were junior and senior students enrolled in a business course that required team projects that were similar in nature to workplace projects.

2003: Task Control, Breadth of Training Raise Self-Efficacy

Research by Axtell and Parker (2003) prove that increasing task control (autonomy) and training phases of increasing generalizability increase the transfer of self-efficacy to the workplace. The study also finds that job enlargement can lower self-efficacy if task control is not also increased.

Measuring Self-Efficacy

There are many ways to measure self-efficacy. One such scale is the Skill Confidence Inventory scale (SCI). The SCI scale measures perceived confidence to successfully complete several tasks, activities, and coursework. The SCI scale measures self-efficacy in the vocational domain and is used in career counseling. The SCI is usually combined with the Strong Interest Inventory scale (SII). The SCI consists of six 10 item General Confidence Themes (GCT scales) (sixty items total). Each 10 item scale is scored by taking the mean of responses of each scale. GCT scales measure perceived level of confidence and range from 1 to 5; 1= No Confidence and 5= Complete Confidence. A score of 3.5 or higher implies a high skill confidence for that scale.

The SCI scale is written in an eighth grade reading level and can be administered to high school students, college students, or working professionals. The SCI is offered in pencil and paper format via mail in tests, and in the Entrepreneur Report. The SCI is also available via the internet through the Consulting Psychologists Press.

Self-efficacy is described as domain specific. Indeed the SCI measures self-efficacy for the vocational domain. Another such example of a scale that measures self-efficacy in a specific domain is the Mathematics Self-Efficacy Scale (MSES). The MSES measures self-efficacy in the domain of math. This is the most commonly used scale to measure self-efficacy in math related tasks. It was created by Betz and Hackett (1983). The scale ranges from 0 to 9; 0= Not at all difficult and 9= Extremely difficult.

Another interesting measurement of self-efficacy is the Generalized Self-Efficacy scale (GSE). One could say that it measures self-efficacy in adaptation, optimism, and coping in regards to facing adversity or everyday problems. The purpose of the GSE is to measure confidence in goal setting, effort, and persistence. The complete guide to GSE is located below:

Research of Self-Efficacy and Social Cognitive Theories

Extensive research on self-efficacy has been well tested and well supported in many different aspects of self-efficacy, from self-efficacy in the workplace to self-efficacy in nursing (Bandura, 1997; Berends, *et al.*, 2001; Van der Bijl, *et al.*, 2002). One example of research performed recently is a study by Roach *et al.* (2003), which examined the impact of self-efficacy on weight loss. The study included 66 male and female participants, ranging in ages from 18 to 23.

The participants were randomly placed in either a control group or an intervention group. Based on a programme developed by US Air Force personnel, the study consisted of 12 weekly, one-hour sessions. The sessions for both groups included information on nutrition and healthy eating habits. The intervention group, however, was also educated on activities to promote self-efficacy. Results of the programme were recorded throughout the entire 12 weeks. At the end of the 12 weeks, results showed that both groups did have some improvement in dietary intake, weight status, and self-efficacy. The intervention group, however, showed a slightly higher improvement in eating behaviour than did the control group.

This research supports the theory that self-efficacy has an impact on how individuals perceive themselves. Supported by education on how to increase self-efficacy, the intervention group was able to apply their new knowledge on reducing weight and improving eating habits. As a result of their self-efficacy increasing, their belief and motivation in attaining their goal increased as well.

In another study, Teti and Gelfand (1991) examined whether maternal self-efficacy beliefs moderate parenting behaviours caused by "depression, perceptions of infant temperamental difficulty, and social-marital supports". The subjects in the study were 38 non-depressed and 48 clinically depressed mothers with infants 3 to 13 months of age. The mothers were observed interacting with their infants, in their homes, by two female research assistants who were unaware of their mental status. The subjects completed questionnaires during the visits that obtained from them information concerning "demographics and maternal psychosocial functioning". The research assistants observed the interactions between the mothers and their children during a ten minute feeding and play session which included three colourful toys, and the observed amounts of maternal sensitivity, warmth, flatness of affect, disengagement, and anger were rated by the assistants and recorded.

After analyzing and compiling the results of the study, Teti and Gelfand (1991) concluded that maternal self-efficacy is a "central mediator of relations between mothers' competence with their infants and factors such as maternal perceptions of infant difficulty, maternal depression, and social-marital supports". Support for this conclusion was based on the finding that maternal self-efficacy was strongly associated with maternal capability. In addition, maternal self-efficacy was the factor most strongly related to parenting behaviour, and it remained that way when all other predictors were controlled for. Beliefs regarding infant difficulty, which are related to maternal ability, were also strongly associated with self-efficacy when demographic variables were controlled. The authors found that depression affected maternal competence only in that it affected maternal self-efficacy.

These findings support the premise of Self-Efficacy Theory, which is that beliefs regarding one's abilities are strongly associated with the amount of motivation and resulting performance. The mothers who had high maternal self-efficacy felt more competent as a result of their confidence and displayed positive parenting behaviours during the study. There were many variables analyzed and discussed in this study, but it illustrates well how important self-efficacy is in parenting.

Additional research findings in support of self-efficacy:

- High self-efficacy individuals persist longer in the face of difficulty and are extremely resilient in the face of failure.
- High self-efficacy individuals are generally more content with their work and lives (Judge, Locke, Durhamn, and Kluger, 1998; as cited in Redmond, 2010).
- High self-efficacy individuals set higher goals for themselves (Bandura and Cervone, 1986; as cited in Redmond, 2010).
- High self-efficacy individuals are more committed to their goals (Locke, Frederick, Lee, and Bobko, 1984; as cited in Redmond, 2010).
- High self-efficacy individuals generate more effective task strategies to facilitate goal attainment and respond more optimistically to negative feedback than low self-efficacy individuals.

- Strengthening self-efficacy augments goal attainment motivation.
- Feedback and self-efficacy are necessary for effective goal-setting.
- Self-efficacy has been found to lead to higher performance (McIntire and Levine, 1991; Mathieu, Martineau, and Tannenbaum, 1993; Eden and Zuk, 1995; Locke and Latham, 1990; Stajkovic and Luthans, 1998; as cited in Redmond, 2010).
- High self-efficacy individuals succeed often and better than individuals with low self-efficacy (Mitchell, Hopper, Daniels, George-Falvy, and James, 1994; as cited in Redmond, 2010).
- High self-efficacy individuals habitually work harder and persevere while low self-efficacy individuals frequently quit (Bandura, 1986); as cited in Redmond, 2010).
- Individuals who perform well develop high self-efficacy (Davis, Fedor, Parson, and Herold, 2000; as cited in Redmond, 2010).

Criticism of Self-Efficacy

Criticism of Self-Efficacy Theory

Eastman and Marzillier (1984) outlined three main criticisms to Bandura's Self-Efficacy Theory. The first was ambiguity and lack of definition in self-efficacy. The second included methodological deficiencies which could cast doubt on the "published relationship between the empirical findings and self-efficacy." The third stated that claims and conclusions made by Bandura were not adequately evaluated, and more precise definitions and modification of assessment procedures are needed.

In regards to the conceptual problems of self-efficacy, it was thought that "efficacy expectations were definite in such a way that included within them expectations of outcome, and thus could not be regarded as conceptually distinct". Bandura had sought to make a distinction between self-efficacy and outcomes but others found some of his statements to be misleading in this regard. One specific statement, "the conviction that one can successfully execute the behaviour to produce the outcomes," was the focus of much criticism and debate over the true difference between outcomes and efficacy. Kazdin (1978) found the concepts of self-efficacy and outcome expectations to be "very closely related." Bandura has replied to this criticism by stating that the outcomes are conditional upon the behaviour and that the critics were "misreading the definition of efficacy." (Bandura, 1978)

SELF-CONCEPT AND SELF-WORTH THEORIES

Harter presents comprehensive reviews of the work on self-concept, and so we only include a brief discussion of it here. Work on self-concept is relevant to this section of the chapter in two main respects. First, many of the most widely used measures of self-concept, such as those developed by Harter

(1982) and Marsh (1989) assess perceived competence as the major dimension of self-concept. Thus essentially self-concept as measured by these instruments is beliefs about one's competence in different areas.

Second, a variety of researchers have examined the relationship between self-concept and achievement, one of the outcomes of great interest to motivation researchers. For many years researchers debated about the causal direction between self-concept and achievement, with some proposing that growth in self-concept produces growth in achievement, and others proposing just the opposite. Many of the studies that purportedly tested these relations used designs that were not adequate to test fully either position. Recently a number of researchers utilizing longitudinal designs found that relations between self-concept and achievement are reciprocal. These reciprocal relations have been observed in studies of children of different ages, including children as young as seven. These findings (finally) move the field away from the seemingly intractable question of "which causes which" to the more reasonable conclusion that each variable has causal influence on the other. Such findings provide support for the important role of social cognitive and behavioural variables in the study of motivation.

Self-worth, or one's overall evaluation of one's worth as a person, continues to be an important variable relevant to motivation as well. Covington and his colleagues provide the most complete motivational analysis of self-worth, arguing that individuals have a strong desire to protect their self-worth in achievement settings. Schools often focus on the demonstration of relative competence, and Covington argued that to maintain self-worth in school children must protect their competence. Children who do less well than their peers are most at risk for losing self-worth, and so can develop strategies such as not trying or procrastinating as a way to try to protect their sense of competence. These strategies may provide some short-term benefits with respect to self-worth protection, but over the long run actually work against children. Covington and his colleagues have written about ways in which school environments can be changed to lessen the emphasis on relative competence of children, thereby allowing more children to maintain a sense of self-worth in school.

Researchers also continue to study other self-processes that guide, direct, and motivate behaviours in ways other than self-worth maintenance (*e.g.*, Garcia and Pintrich, 1994; Markus and Wurf, 1987). For example, Markus and her colleagues discuss how "possible future selves" motivate behaviour. Possible selves, the vision individuals have of themselves in the future, include both hoped-for and feared (I will not pass geometry) components. Because possible selves are not identical to one's current self-concept, they motivate the individual by providing goals that the individual tries to attain and outcomes that the individual tries to avoid in order to achieve one's image. Whether or not the possible self is attained depends on many things, one of which is the individual's current perceived competence.

BELIEFS ABOUT INTELLIGENCE AND ABILITY

Attribution theory concerns individuals' explanations (or attributions) for their successes and failures and how these attributions influence subsequent motivation. Weiner and his colleagues identified the most frequently used attributions (ability, effort, task difficulty, and luck), and classified these and other attributions into the different causal dimensions of stability (stable or unstable), locus of control (internal or external), and controllability (under one's volition or not). For instance, ability is classified as internal, stable, and uncontrollable. Each of these dimensions has important psychological consequences that influence subsequent motivation and behaviour.

The stability dimension relates most directly to expectancies for success and failure, locus of control to affective reactions to success and failure, and controllability to help giving. For instance, attributing failure to lack of ability leads to lowered expectancies for success, and negative affect like shame for more detailed review). Attribution theory was quite dominant in the motivation field for many years, but its influence has waned to an extent recently. Despite this, there still is great interest in the motivation field in perceptions of ability and also of effort. Indeed, some theorists (most notably, Carol Dweck) working in the attribution tradition have become interested in individuals' beliefs about the nature of ability and the implications of these beliefs for their motivation and effort.

Dweck and her colleagues posited that children can hold one of two views of intelligence or ability. Children holding an entity view of intelligence believe that intelligence is a stable trait. Children holding an incremental view of intelligence believe that intelligence is changeable, so that it can be increased through effort. Note that this differs from the traditional attribution theory view, which is that ability is a stable characteristic. In Dweck's work there is more than one way to view one's ability.

Dweck and her colleagues have discussed how children's conceptions of ability and intelligence can have important motivational consequences. Dweck (2002) argued that children holding an entity theory of intelligence are motivated to look smart and protect their sense of ability. Children believing intelligence can change focus on learning and improvement. When children do poorly, believing that one's ability has a limited capacity means that failure is more debilitating. Some children holding this view will believe they have little chance of ever doing well, because their ability cannot be improved. Children holding this belief can become learned helpless in achievement settings; we discuss learned helplessness later. In contrast, believing effort can improve performance in important ways can mean that children will continue to try even if they are not doing well on a given task.

Dweck and Leggett (1988) tied children's beliefs about intelligence to their achievement goals. Children holding an incremental view of intelligence tend to have mastery or learning goals, whereas children holding an entity view have performance goals. Further, Dweck and Leggett broadened their analysis to other domains, contrasting the relative benefits of incremental vs. entity views about social relationships, and moral development. In each case they argued that the incremental view has many benefits to children.

CONTROL THEORIES

Building on the seminal early work of Rotter (1966) and Crandall, Katkovsky, and Crandall (1965) on internal and external locus of control, theorists have elaborated broader conceptual models of control. Connell (1985), for example, added unknown control as a third control belief category and argued that younger children are particularly likely to use this category. He developed and validated to a scale to assess external control (in terms of "powerful others,"), internal control (in terms of effort and ability), and unknown control for cognitive, physical, social, and general activities.

Connell and Wellborn (1991) then integrated control beliefs into the self-determination framework that proposes the fundamental psychological needs for competence, autonomy, and relatedness. They linked control beliefs to competence needs: Children who believe they control their achievement outcomes should feel more competent. They hypothesized that the extent to which these needs are fulfilled is influenced by the following characteristics of their family, peer, and school contexts: the amount of structure, the degree of autonomy provided, and the level of involvement in the children's activities.

Ellen Skinner and her colleagues (*e.g.*, Skinner, 1995; Skinner, Chapman, and Baltes, 1988) proposed a more elaborate model of control beliefs. This model includes three critical control-related beliefs: strategy beliefs, control beliefs, and capacity beliefs. Strategy beliefs concern the expectation that particular causes can produce certain outcomes; these causes include Weiner's various causal attributions and Connell's (1985) unknown control. Control beliefs are the expectations individuals have that they can produce desired events, and prevent undesired ones. Capacity beliefs are the expectations that one has access to the means needed to produce various outcomes. Skinner (1995) proposed that control beliefs are a major determinant of actions, leading to outcomes that are interpreted by the individual and subsequently influence their control beliefs, starting the cycle again.

Skinner distinguished her position from self-efficacy theories by noting that self-efficacy theorist discuss connections between agents and means primarily in terms of expectancies that the individual can produce some outcome; thus outcomes are contingent on one's responses. In contrast, she argued that her capacity beliefs relate to potential as well as actual means. Further, an individual can have strong capacity beliefs for different means without believing that any of the means are necessarily effective. Finally, Skinner, Connell and their colleagues have broadened their discussion of perceived control and its influences by developing a model of the relations among context, the self, action, and outcomes (*e.g.*, Connell, Spencer, and Able, 1994; Skinner and Wellborn, 1994). They proposed when contexts are set up in a way allows the needs of competence, relatedness, and autonomy to be supported, then individuals will be engaged more fully in activities, which leads to positive developmental outcomes.

Contexts not supportive of these needs lead to disengagement. that the ways in which these needs are fulfilled determine engagement in different activities. When the needs are fulfilled, children will be fully engaged. When one or more of the needs is not fulfilled, children will become disaffected. Connell, Spencer, and Abler (1994) and Skinner and Belmont (1993) conducted studies in classroom settings that supported these linkages. We discuss the implications of these findings in the section on how school contexts influence children's motivation.

Modern Expectancy–Value Theory

Modern expectancy value are based in Atkinson's (1957, 1964) original expectancy–value model in that they link achievement performance, persistence, and choice most directly to individuals' expectancy-related and task value beliefs. However, they differ from Atkinson's theory in several ways: First, both the expectancy and value components are more elaborate, and linked to a broader array of psychological and social/cultural determinants. Second, they are grounded more in real-world achievement tasks than the laboratory tasks often used to test Atkinson's theory. We focus here on the ability and expectancy portion of Eccles and her colleagues' model; see Eccles *et al.* (1998) for review of some other modern expectancy – value models.

The Eccles *et al.* expectancy–value model. Eccles (Parsons) and her colleagues elaborated and tested one expectancy–value model of achievement-related choices. This model focuses on the social psychological influences on choice and persistence. Choices are seen to be influenced by both negative and positive task characteristics and all choices are assumed to have costs associated with them precisely because one choice often eliminates other options. Much of their work focuses on individual differences and gender differences in decisions regarding which courses to take, what careers to seek, and what activities to pursue.

THE DEVELOPMENT AND REMEDIATION OF MOTIVATIONAL PROBLEMS

Many children begin to experience motivational problems during the school years We focus on three motivational problems that have received the most attention in the literature: test anxiety, learned helplessness, and apathy. The first two of these problems are tied to beliefs about not being able to do different activities, whereas the third emerges when children devalue achievement related activities.

ANXIETY

Anxiety, and its close cousin test anxiety, is estimated to interfere with the learning and performance, particularly in evaluative situations, of as many as 10 million children and adolescents in the USA (Hill and Wigfield, 1984; Tobias, 1985; Wigfield and Eccles, 1989), and this problem likely will get worse as evaluation and accountability become more emphasized in schools. Anxiety often is conceptualized as having two components, worry and emotionality, with worry referring to cognitive ruminations and emotionality referring to physiological reactions. Researchers have focused on the cognitive/worry aspect of anxiety because worry is more strongly and negatively related to performance than emotionality.

Researchers postulate that high anxiety emerges when parents have overly high expectations and put too much pressure on their children, but few studies have tested this proposition. Anxiety continues to develop across the school years as children face more frequent evaluation, social comparison, and (for some) experiences of failure; to the extent that schools emphasize these characteristics, anxiety becomes a problem for more children. With a few important exceptions, work on anxiety has diminished. One reason for this is the argument that anxiety is simply the flip side of negative judgements about one's ability and efficacy. For instance, Nicholls (1976) concluded that many items on one of the major scales used to measure anxiety, the Test Anxiety Scale for Children, refer to negative ability beliefs. When he separated the ability and anxiety items, the ability items related more strongly to indicators of achievement than the anxiety items. Second is increasing interest in other kinds of emotions and their relations to motivation and achievement.

Anxiety Interference Programmes

Many programmes have been developed to reduce anxiety. Earlier intervention programmes, emphasizing the emotionality aspect of anxiety, focused on relaxation and desensitization techniques. Although these programmes did reducing anxiety, they did not always lead to improved performance, and the studies had serious methodological flaws. Anxiety intervention programmes linked to the worry aspect of anxiety focus on changing the negative, self-deprecating thoughts of anxious individuals and replacing them with more positive, task-focused thoughts. These programmes have been more successful both in lowering anxiety and improving performance.

Learned Defencelessness

"Learned helplessness... exists when an individual perceives the termination of failure to be independent of his responses". Eccles *et al.* (1998) reviewed the early work (primarily by Dweck and her colleagues) on how helpless and mastery oriented children differ in their responses to failure.

When confronted by difficulty (or failure), mastery oriented children persist, stay focused on the task, and sometimes even use more sophisticated strategies. In contrast, helpless children's performance deteriorates, they ruminate about their difficulties, often begin to attribute their failures to lack of ability. Further, helpless children adopt the "entity" view that their intelligence is fixed, whereas mastery oriented children adopt the incremental view of intelligence.

As noted earlier, the "optimism to realism" pattern of change in children's ability-related belief led some researchers to conclude that helplessness is less likely to occur in younger children. Dweck and her colleagues' more recent work shows that in fact some young (5 and 6 year old) children respond quite negatively to failure feedback, showing the helpless pattern and judging themselves to be bad people. Indeed, they proposed that young children's helplessness is based more on their judgements that their worth as persons is contingent on their performance than on having a mature entity view of intelligence. This work by suggests an important developmental modification to Dweck and Legget's (1988) model of learned helpless versus master oriented motivational styles that is based in beliefs about intelligence and goals.

What else influences the emergence of individual differences in learned helplessness in children? Dweck and Goetz (1978) stressed the importance of whether children receive feedback that their failures are due to lack of ability or lack of skills and effort from parents and teachers. In support, Hokoda and Fincham (1995) found that mothers of helpless third grade children (in comparison to mothers of mastery-oriented children) gave fewer positive affective comments to their children, were more likely to respond to their children's lack of confidence in their ability by telling them to quit, were less responsive to their children's bids for help, and did not focus them on mastery goals. Recently Dweck and Lennon (2001) found that students' perceptions that their parents had entity views of intelligence (measured in terms of the kinds of feedback they would provide their children about different achievement outcomes) predicted their own views of intelligence. For instance, students perceiving their parents had an entity view were more likely themselves to have an entity view.

Alleviate Learned Helplessness

Various training techniques (including operant conditioning and providing specific attributional feedback) have been used successfully to change children's failure attributions from lack of ability to lack of effort, improving their task persistence, and performance (*e.g.*, Andrews and Debus, 1978; Dweck, 1975; Forsterling, 1985). Two problems with these approaches have been noted. First, what if the child is already trying very hard? Then the attribution re-training may be counter productive. Second, telling children to "try harder" without providing specific strategies designed to improve performance is likely to back fire if the children increase their efforts and still do not succeed. Therefore, some researchers advocate using strategy re-training in combination with attribution retraining in order to provide lower achieving and/or learned helpless children with specific ways to remedy their achievement problems. Borkowski and his colleagues, for example, have shown that a combined programme of strategy instruction and attribution re-training is more effective than strategy instruction alone in increasing reading motivation and performance in underachieving students (*e.g.*, Borkowski, Weyhing, and Carr, 1988; Paris and Byrnes, 1989).

Student Indifference

Apathy has more to do with students' sense of the value of participating in different activities rather than their beliefs about whether they are capable of accomplishing the activity. Children who are apathetic about learning or participating in other activities do not find much worthwhile to do in school or in other situations, and may even be so alienated from these activities that they actively resist attempts to get them involved. Brophy (2004) contended that apathy is the most serious motivational problem that teachers most contend with in their students, more serious than learned helplessness or anxiety. The apathy construct has some overlap with the construct of amotivation in SDT.

There has not been a lot of research on the development of apathy, but different researchers have discussed possible reasons for it. These range from broad social and cultural explanations to more psychologically oriented ones. Ogbu's (1992) discussion of why some minority children do well in school and others do not is an example of a broad cultural approach to this issue. Children who believe their ethnic or racial group is excluded from meaningful participation in the economic structure of this country may find little reason to engage in the school activities said to be needed to obtain good occupations. Ogbu has argued that such children often become oppositional to participation in school activities, resisting attempts of teachers to engage them in learning activities. We return to this issue later. A more psychological perspective on apathy can be drawn from Markus and Nurius's (1986) work on possible selves. Markus and Nurius argued that possible selves provide an important motivational force for engagement in different activities such as school or sport activities. If children do not see much of a future for themselves in these or other domains they likely will not see much reason to be involved in school or other activities designed to prepare them for the future, and so may be very apathetic about becoming involved in such activities.

We noted that apathy stems from the de-valuing of different kinds of activities rather than from children's perceptions of their competence to accomplish them, but the interplay of competence beliefs and values may play a crucial role in the development of apathy. Recall our earlier discussion of how children maintain their self-worth by valuing those activities at which they are competent, and de-valuing activities where they are doing less well. Children doing poorly at school may begin to de-value school achievement, as a way to protect their self-esteem. This de-valuing could lead to apathy, again as a self-protective mechanism. Engaging in learning has risks, particularly for students not doing well, and one way to protect against those risks is to be apathetic about learning.

Finally, there likely are different developmental trajectories for the development of apathy. We noted two major possibilities to this point, children who perceive few opportunities for themselves or for their group and so come to de-value school, or children who begin to do poorly in school and so begin to de-value it as a way to protect their self-esteem. We use school activities to illustrate these points, but it should be noted that these patterns could occur for other kinds of activities as well.

Another trajectory occurs for students doing well in school during the early school years and who come from backgrounds and cultural groups who generally have succeeded in our society, but who decide (for a variety of reasons) to no longer engage in school. These children may become alienated from school and therefore apathetic about participating in school activities. To date there is little developmental work on any of these trajectories, and that should be undertaken.

THE DEVELOPMENT OF GENDER DIFFERENCES IN MOTIVATION

GENDER DIFFERENCES IN MOTIVATION AND ACHIEVEMENT

Despite recent efforts to increase the participation of women in advanced educational training and high status professional fields, women are still under-represented in many fields, particularly those associated with technology, physics and applied mathematics and at the highest levels of almost all fields. Efforts to understand these persistent sex differences in achievement patterns have produced a proliferation of theories and research. Eccles and her colleagues originally proposed their expectancy - value model of achievement choices as an effort to organize this disparate research into a comprehensive theoretical framework.

This model predicts that people will be most likely to enroll in courses and choose careers that they think they will do well in and that have high task value for them. Expectations for success depend on the confidence the individual has in his/her intellectual abilities and on the individual's estimations of the difficulty of the course or activity. These beliefs have been shaped by the individual's experiences with the subject matter, by the individual's subjective interpretation of those experiences (*e.g.*, does the person think that her/his successes are a consequence of high ability or lots of hard work?) and by cultural stereotypes regarding both the difficulty of the course and the distribution of relevant talents across various subgroups. The value of a particular course is also influenced by several factors including the following: Does the person like doing the subject material? How well does the course fit with the individual's self-concepts, goals, and values?

Is the course seen as instrumental in meeting one of the individual's long or short range goals? Have the individual's parents or counselors insisted that the course be taken or, conversely, have other people tried to discourage the individual from taking the course? Does taking the course interfere with other goals and values activities? Existing evidence, reviewed next, supports the conclusion that gender-role socialization and internalization are likely to lead to gender differences in each of these broad motivational categories, which, in turn, could contribute to the under representation of women in many high achievement-oriented occupations and activities.

Causal Attributions, and Control Beliefs

Gender differences, often favouring males, in competence beliefs are often reported, particularly in gender-role stereotyped domains and on novel tasks, and these differences are apparent as early as kindergarten or first grade, if not before. For example, gifted and high achieving females are more likely to underestimate both their ability level and their class standing. In other studies, the gender difference depends on the gender-role stereotyping of the activity.

For example, boys hold higher competence beliefs than girls for math and sports, even after all relevant skill-level differences are controlled; in contrast, girls have higher competence beliefs than boys for reading and English, music and arts, and social studies. Recent work shows that the gender differences in competence beliefs in math narrow during adolescence, but those in English remain. Further, the extent to which children endorse the cultural stereotypes regarding which sex is likely to be most talented in each domain predicts the extent to which girls and boys distort their ability self-concepts and expectations in the gender stereotypic direction. However, these sex differences are generally relatively small when they are found.

Gender differences are also sometimes found for locus of control, with girls having higher internal locus of responsibility scores for both positive and negative achievement events and the older girls had higher internality for negative events than did the younger girls. These two developmental patterns resulted in the older girls accepting more blame for negative events than the older boys. Connell (1985) found that boys attributed their outcomes more than girls to either powerful others or unknown causes in both the cognitive and social domains.

This greater propensity for girls to take personal responsibility for their failures, coupled with their more frequent attribution of failure to lack of ability (a stable, uncontrollable cause) has been interpreted as evidence of greater learned helplessness in females. However, evidence for gender differences on behavioural indicators of learned helplessness is quite mixed. In most studies of underachievers, boys outnumber girls 2 to 1. Similarly, boys are more likely than girls to be referred by their teachers for motivational problems and are more likely to drop out of school before completing high school. More consistent evidence exists that females, compared to males, select easier laboratory tasks, avoid challenging and competitive situations, lower their expectations more following failure, shift more quickly to a different college major when their grades begin to drop, and perform more poorly than they are capable of on difficult, timed tests.

Gender differences also emerge regularly in studies of anxiety. However, Hill and Sarason suggested that boys may be more defensive than girls about admitting anxiety on questionnaires. In support of this suggestion, Lord, Eccles, and McCarthy (1994) found that test anxiety was a more significant predictor of poor adjustment to junior high school for boys even though the girls reported higher mean levels of anxiety.

Closely related to the anxiety findings, Spencer *et al.* (1999) documented another motivational mechanism likely to undermine females' performance on difficult timed tests: stereotype vulnerability. They hypothesize that members of social groups (like females) stereotyped as being less competent in a particular subject area (like math) will become anxious when asked to do difficult problems because they are afraid the stereotype might be true of them. This vulnerability is also likely to make them respond more negatively to failure feedback, leading to lowering their expectations and their confidence in their ability to succeed. They gave college students a difficult math test under different conditions: (1) after being told that males typically do better on this test, or (2) after being told that males and females typically do about the same, or (3) gender differences were not mentioned. The women scored lower than the males only in the first condition.

When gender differences emerge on competence-related measures of motivation, they are both consistent with gender-role stereotypes and are likely mediators of gender differences in various types of achievement-related behaviours and choices.

GENDER DIFFERENCES IN ACHIEVEMENT VALUES

Eccles, Wigfield and their colleagues have found gender-role stereotypic differences in both children's and adolescents' valuing of sports, social activities, and English that begin quite early in the course of children's development. In Eccles *et al.* (1993), girls also valued instrumental music more than boys. Earlier work showed gender differences in math value favouring boys emerging during adolescence, but more recent studies show that boys and girls value math equally during adolescence. Although boys and girls now appear to value math equally, girls are less interested in science (with the exception of biology) and engineering than are boys, and enroll much less frequently in these majors in college. Eccles *et al.* (1998) reviewed the work on the psychological processes that underlie some of these sex differences in children's achievement values.

Disidentification. Earlier we discussed the relationship between values and competence-related beliefs. Drawing on the writings of William James (1892/1963), we suggested that children will lower the value they attach to particular activities or subject areas if they lack confidence in these areas in order to maintain their self-esteem.

Spencer *et al.* (1999) suggested a similar phenomenon related to stereotype vulnerability. They hypothesized that women will disidentify with those subject areas in which females are stereotyped as less competent than males. By disidentifying with these areas, the women will not only lower the value they attach to these subject areas, they will also be less likely to experience pride and positive affect when they are doing well in these subjects. Consequently, these subjects should become irrelevant to their self-esteem. These hypotheses need further testing.

APPROACHES TO MOTIVATION

Whether the approach is from the point of view of the educator or the point of view of the learner, consensus, is that motivation is an important factor in learning. Part of that consensus is the notion that it is both internally and externally generated and that it is a quality that is found in differing and varying degrees in everyone. Internally generated motivational forces are usually referred to as intrinsic motivation.

Naturally, influences external to and acting on the subject in ways that change behaviour are connoted by the term extrinsic motivation. Simply speaking, intrinsic motivation is different from extrinsic motivation according to its source. In the former case, the stimulus for the behaviour affected originates from within the individual, and in the latter, the stimulus originates, conversely, from without. This distinction should be taken free of any value judgement regarding kinds of motivation at this point.

TOWARDS A DEFINITION OF MOTIVATION IN EDUCATION

As a model of motivation we turn to the successful learner and what he or she does to affect that success. The more successful learner brings to the task a certain awareness of his or her own drives and a certain state of mental cognition. These qualities enable further success in every stage of development, whether it be as a person or as a learner (to make a perhaps unnecessary clarification here, the person and the learner are not divisible but both exist dependent on the other). The modern educator should recognize the importance of the concept of self-awareness of drives. This is reflected in the concern with the needs of his/her students. In modern theory, these needs have been reformulated as goals, a concept which has gained vital recognition by most theorists connected with motivation. Goals will come under discussion later; what is important at this point is the significance given to the cognitive state of the subject; the individual's thoughts, beliefs, and emotions.

While the concept of motivation is ubiquitous in discussions of academic success, the meaning, or rather definition, remains vague otherwise. It has met with numerous and varied definitions while at the same time, remaining the center of a certain degree of disagreement as to its nature.

Part of that nature has been summed up quite well by Pintrich and Schunk (1996) when they note that motivation is a process rather than a product. In this sense we recognize motivation more by its effects than by anything else, and this is usually the common understanding of motivation. We would not hesitate to add that it can also be said to be a condition rather than a cause. We would further emphasize that it is in all probability a necessary but not sufficient condition for achievement associated with success.

The influence of Maslow, in this area has been of extreme importance. The modern trend of so-called student-centred learning owes its respects however directly or indirectly to the self-actualization model of human drives proposed in the 70s. Maslow's development of a "third force" in psychology created an alternative to the existing schools of psychology (psychodynamic psychology and behavioural psychology being the other two forces) giving rise to social cognitive theories. A further refinement of this type of division reveals that these three forces can be reformulated into two basic orientations of theory with the schools of psychodynamic and behavioural psychology on the one hand and social cognitive theories on the other. This distinction has been referred to by Deci and Ryan as mechanistic and organismic, respectively:

Mechanistic theories tend to view the human organism as passive, that is, as being pushed around by the interaction of physiological drives and environmental stimuli, whereas organismic theories tend to view the organism as active, that is, as being volitional and initiating behaviours.

Motivation expresses itself in all aspects of life, but what is of concern here is the social and psychological context in which learning takes place. It is here where our activities take place and here where motivation seems to lend itself to influential change. Since "...motivation is indeed the foundation on which learning and skill development must be built...", we must keep in mind the basic principles that are likely to have an effect on the behaviour of our students. Some of these principles are that, "[individuals] with interpersonal problems generally experience difficulty in life including diminished motivation, academic performance difficulties, and social maladjustment".

Van Lier also emphasizes the importance of motivation in education by noting that, "[experts] and amateurs alike agree unanimously that motivation is a very important, if not the most important factor in language learning", and quotes Pit Corder as saying that "given motivation, it is inevitable that a human being will learn a second language if he is exposed to the language data". (emphasis mine) However, this should not be taken to mean that motivation is wholly sufficient as mentioned above.

While this is not adequate as a definition of motivation other than pointing out its importance, Ford offers a definition within the framework of his Motivational Systems Theory (Ford 1996:3), precisely because of its importance. In general terms, he describes motivation as an "...integrated patterning of a set of intimately related processes". More specifically, he defines motivation as, "the organized patterning of three psychological functions that serve to direct, energize, and regulate goal-directed activity: personal goals, personal agency beliefs, and emotional arousal processes," none of which are exclusive of any other.

Emotional arousal process may or may not hinder personal goals just as personal agency beliefs may or may not conflict with emotional arousal processes, & tc. He then lays out these processes in their relationship with one another in the following formula:

Motivation = Goals x Emotions x Personal Agency Beliefs Rosen characterizes motivation differently from, but not necessarily in opposition to, Ford in that he argues that achievement motivation (in his definition the drive to excel) "..should be distinguished from achievement values and that achievement motivation will only lead to educational success and social mobility when associated with these values".

In contrast to Ford's three psychological functions, Rosen characterizes the values that make up motivation as achievement-oriented preferences, and orientations. One preference is for the active desire to manipulate one's environment, and this to the advantage of the individual. Another preference is towards planning for the future with an acceptance of the deferment of gratification. The orientation that he mentions is the striving towards independence from primary social groups. This reverberates of the self-actualization hypothesis of Maslow (1970).

What has been discussed so far, are ongoing developments in the field that offer a valuable source for further consideration and modification of thought concerning motivation. What these theories, and others as we shall see further, have in common has been put as precisely as possible by Child when he says, " working definition of motivation would be that it consists of internal processes which spur us on to satisfy some need" (1993:35). As vague as that may seem, it suffices to encompass a range of outlooks wide enough to be of value or this discussion. This will be the definition accepted here allowing for further development and interpretation.

With that in mind, it is the intention of this author to attempt to clarify in this chapter what some of the motivational factors in learning in general, and in Second Language Learning (hereafter SLL) in particular, are. As these are the driving forces of students' capabilities, the ultimate purpose of this chapter is to explore how they can be capitalized upon. The focus will be on how they affect learning a foreign language in the classroom environment. Finally, it is my aim to develop methods that are applicable and discuss how to take advantage of the principles of motivation in the teaching situation.

Social Motives Theory

One facet of motivational theory is that which deals with social motives. As an aspect of needs theory, recognition is given to the interplay between the organism as acting upon inner forces that may have stimulation and nurture from outside sources. The concern of this area of thought is "...the effect that culture patterns might have on the rearing of children and the subsequent behaviour patterns which arise from these motivational precursors" (Child 1993:37).

While using Cattel's theory to point out that some of these motives include (but are not limited to), and are generated by, "self-sentiment (the desire to maintain a favourable image in the eyes of oneself and significant others, and comparable with the 'self-concept), superego (rule-abiding and maintaining a 'moral; reputation), career, boy- or girl-friend/spouse, parental home, religion and sport..." and their relationships. Child emphasizes their importance by noting, "[r]ecent developments and applications to education indicate that self-sentiment, superego and a high, positive sentiment (attitude) to school correlate with achievement in school subjects" (1993:41). (my parenthesis)

It is without a doubt, (whatever the source) that learning in humans takes place in a social context. Needs in humans and their behavioural manifestations are inextricable from social situations. Even basic survival needs meet satisfaction through others as mediators, and this goes on from infancy throughout adulthood. As Davidoff (1987:312) puts it, "...all human motivation can be considered social... [with] even the most basic human drives [being] influenced by culture".

One person prominent in Social Learning Theory is Rotter who laid out four basic variables that comprise social learning: behaviour potential (the probability that an individual will act in a certain fashion relative to alternatives based on the understanding that these behaviours include both observable and covert acts), expectancy (an individual's belief concerning the likelihood that a particular reinforcement will occur following a specific behaviour), reinforcement value (how much an individual values a particular outcome relative to other potential outcomes), and the psychological situation (the importance of the context of behaviour). The view here is that behaviour is situation specific, but expectancies for reinforcement can generalize to similar situations.

Rotter's theory usually comes to us as expectancy-value theory that posits the importance of the context of behaviour. The belief system of the individual receives emphasis under this theory. The individual is instrumental in determining the value placed on likely social effects of behaviour. Moreover, for a behaviour to take place, and it should be stressed, the individual must believe that the valued outcome will occur.

Following Rotter, expanding on his theory, and equally prominent in the field, Bandura developed the theory of triadic reciprocality. It would be better to let him speak for himself to describe this framework: In the social cognitive view, people are neither driven by inner forces nor automatically shaped and controlled by external stimuli, Rather, human functioning is explained in terms of a model of triadic reciprocality in which behaviour, cognitive and other personal factors, and environmental events all operate as interacting determinants of each other.

Social cognitive theory makes a distinction between learning and the performance of learned actions. Skills that people learn may lie dormant (even at the time of acquisition) for quite a while. What is needed is the motivation on the part of the individual to display them. This comes about through the belief system of the person that the skills are appropriate to the situation and that they meet the requirement that the display will lead to positive consequences.

Those optimistic consequences seem to occur mainly in the social milieu and this is especially true concerning education and the learning mechanism. Learning and the acquisition of knowledge may be intrinsically rewarding to the individual and an end in itself. For the most part, however, the instigation for learning lies mainly in our active participation in society. Cavalli-Svorza (1995:195) puts it in stronger terms than this author would, but the drift is the same when he asserts that, "[a] suitable social context is imperative to activate the innate learning mechanism."

Social learning theory rests on two proposition. One, that it is possible for people to learn merely through observation. The other is that people are able to learn new behaviours without the benefit of reinforcement. It is the first consideration that impacts on this research, because this type of observational learning (that on which the educational principle of role-modeling is based) relies on the fact that people imitate the behaviour of others they hold in high esteem. This is not to discount reinforcement as an educational method. In fact, according to Lefton and Valvatne, "...observational learning combined with traditional classical and instrumental conditioning approaches can account for nearly all learned behaviour" (1983:107). The important point here is the emphasis on learning by observation as dependant to a certain degree on the cognitive recognition of role models as attractive or worthy of imitation by the learner.

There is a slight (and sometimes not so subtle) relationship between what the individual does for him/herself under the influence of intrinsic drives vis a vis what is done under the influence of extrinsic forces. Our experiences in society act upon our personal beliefs and influence the choices we make by modifying, and at times transforming our value system. It is our personal value systems which engender the goals that we find intrinsically pleasing or rewarding. Oftentimes there is a congruence between the behaviours that society is willing to reward and to which degree, and the goals that we find self-satisfying or worthy. Our personal belief systems, of which goals form a part, depend on our personal knowledge systems. These in turn are formed under the influence of those around us. Or as Cavalli-Svorza (1995:209) puts it:

- We constantly alter our personal knowledge system on the basis of what we learn not only from our own experiences but also, and above all, from the experiences of others — from the body of information, received in the form of orders, advice, or potentially useful ideas. Consciously or subconsciously, we use this knowledge system to guide our behaviour."

One model posits that goals which spring from social motives, or are somehow socially motivated, have mainly to do with either performance or learning in their orientation. In the performance paradigm the goal is "...to gain positive judgements/avoid negative judgements of social attributes". Within the goal orientation of learning (development) the goal is to increase social competence, and (in order to?) develop relationships. Accordingly the outcome, in terms of behaviour patterns is that of helplessness (avoiding risk; low persistence) in the former case and mastery oriented behaviour (seeking challenge; high persistence) in the latter.

Dweck and Leggett address the question of the predictability of goal orientation within this framework. Specifically, they ask if social goals are predictive of motivational patterns. Hesitant to draw a direct connection, while at the same time pointing out the need for more research in this area, they note that, "children of low sociometric status are more likely to formulate or endorse "avoidance" goals — performance goals in which the concerns center around avoiding negative outcomes". They further stipulate that one orientation will, more likely than the other, yield the behaviour it is associated with within their paradigm. In other words, performance goals are more predictive of the helplessness pattern than a learning orientation which, in turn is more predictive of mastery-oriented patterns of behaviour.

However in either case, under theories of this sort, analysis is made within the framework of an analysis of behaviour that views people as being pushed, pulled, and energized by internal and external forces. Further, in both cases part of the makeup of these forces include and, which in turn are directed towards, the social milieu; that is, other people. This is typically reflective of considerations of theories of motivation within the cognitive framework. As such, cognitive theories assume a power of decision making in humans concerning how and when they will behave.

To recapitulate, "[a]ccording to the cognitive view, humans make decisions about what their goals are and how they should achieve these goals.

The emphasis is on active decision-making and the unique human qualities of abstract thought processes. Achievement theories are cognitive in nature because they rely on a person's expectancy for success or failure; choices are made".

Extrinsic and Inherent Motivators

Education owes a great debt to behaviourism, which, through the research dealing with reinforcement theory, has contributed much to the understanding of extrinsic motivators. Among the extrinsic motivators known as incentives we find commonly accepted labels and characterizations, such as knowledge of results, reward and punishment, and coöperation and competition.

Of these incentives, knowledge of results is the most discussed in modern times in the field of human resources and has come to us in the popular parlance as feedback. With the knowledge of how successfully one is performing a given task, high levels of motivation can be achieved. Of course, on the other hand, when met with successive failures, deleterious avoidance patterns can develop. Therefore, it is suggested by the behaviourists that the setting of small incremental tasks likely to meet with success is one way to avoid negative effects while at the same time accentuating successful motivation. This point will be touched upon later.

The most commonly understood application of extrinsic motivators, especially as concerns operant conditioning, is in reward and punishment. In a ground-breaking study done by Hurlock in 1925 a control group of learners were matched with three other groups; (1) a group that received praise regardless of their level of performance., (2) a group that where chided for poor work, careless mistakes or lack of improvement, (3) and a group that was neither praised nor reproved but who witnessed the interaction of the teacher with the other groups. This study found a marked difference for the better in the scores of the group that received praise. The other groups, in descending order of improvement; reproved, and control (ignored) showed clear differences in performance. There are implications of this finding that obtain their effect in terms of general education procedures, and by extension, in the SLL classroom.

While both coöperation and competition seem to be valid motivators in and of themselves, there remains the dilemma of developing methods that encourage both. It seems that neither coöperation nor competition produces the more effective mode for heightening learning. However, they are both quite important, singularly and in tandem, in that it is through them that opportunities for social development are provided. Placing value on one has a detrimental effect on the other, and it has yet been shown that one yields more effective learning than the other (Child 1993:49).

Again, it is Maslow to whom we owe the debt of enhanced understanding when it comes to how needs theory relates to intrinsic motivation. Some of the needs he laid out coincide with what may be called intrinsic motivators.

Through curiosity, exploration and manipulation the human as a phenotype is able to enhance his/her condition and validate one's drive towards life; in other words meet with actualization. Humans, like any other living creature, strive towards life and engage in life-affirming activities. The drive towards life has as a contingent parallel, the drive towards success. We avoid failure in many ways.

In any of the life-affirming behaviours [as in the case of the basic physiological needs] failure to succeed in obtaining, for example, food, liquid, oxygen, etc., can have dire consequences for the organism. It is the same with any of the so-called levels of Maslow's hierarchy up to and including self-actualization. Failure to satisfy deficiencies, lead to stagnation. It may sound trite, but life is change. The human organism realizes this not only on the instinctual level but is cognitively aware, for the most part, that homeostasis is a state that needs monitoring and that appropriate changes need take place to maintain it. Whether this is true at the cognitive level for other animals is neither here nor there, for our purpose at hand. For human beings, some of the tools for this monitoring can be said to be the attention needs of curiosity, exploration and manipulation.

Motivation involves some kind of state of tension as its driving energy. Curiosity, exploration and manipulation are ways of generating tension in order to maintain a certain level of arousal. They are means of gathering from the environment the agencies of growth and familiarity with the environment which provides safety. They are self-satisfying to the individual and do not require instigation from outside sources for their manifestation. As a matter of fact, as Flavell points out, motivation is an important aspect of cognitive functioning that leads us "...to master problematic situations, to be effective with respect to [our] environment, to be competent...." So much so that, "...this aspiration towards mastery, effectiveness, and competence is an important part of the cognitive system's power source".

A common misconception is to view extrinsic and intrinsic motivation as polar opposites, however a more useful view might be to view them as contextual with the dynamic being the level of intensity. There are many combinations to be had: high on both, low on both, medium on both high on one and medium on the other, et cetera. Being contextual, the same activity can be extrinsically motivating for one person and intrinsically motivating for another and moreover, with intrinsic motivation in particular, there is the possibility of change over time.

An interesting relationship between the two has been brought out in a study by Lepper, Greene, and Nisbett. Subjects were put into three groups. One group (Expected-award group) was told they could get a reward by engaging in an activity and received such after the activity. Another group (Unexpected-award group) were not told they would be given a reward but did receive one. The last group (No-award group) were neither told they would receive a reward nor given one when the activity was complete. The group that ended up spending less time on the activity with a deterioration in the quality of work in the post-experimental phase was the expected-award group. This lead Lepper *et al.*, to conclude that rewards can have a detrimental effect on intrinsic motivation. Or as Pintrich and Schunk put it, "...engaging in an intrinsically interesting activity to obtain an extrinsic reward can undermine intrinsic motivation".

MOTIVATION IN SECOND LANGUAGE LEARNING

Motivation is the psychological quality that leads people to achieve a goal. For language learners, mastery of a language may be a goal. For others, communicative competence or even basic communication skills could be a goal. In linguistics, sociolinguistics and second-language acquisition, a number of language learner motivationmodels have been postulated. Work by Gardner, Clément, Dörnyei, Usioda and McIntyre are perhaps most known if not all accepted.

Language is a communication coding system that can be taught as a school subject; an integral part of the individual's identity involved in almost all mental activities; the most important channel of social organization embedded in the culture of the community where it is used.

Socio-Educational Models

Gardner's Socio-Educational Model

While Gardner (1982) identified a number of factors that are involved when learning a second language (L2), it was earlier work by Gardner and Lambert (1959) of second-language acquisition: the social and cultural milieu, individual learner differences, the setting and context. In Gardner's model, one of the most influential in second-language acquisition are the four individual differences: intelligence, language aptitude, motivation, and situational anxiety.

Revised Socio-Education Model

Gardner (2001) presents a schematic representation of this model. There are four sections, external influences, individual differences, language acquisition contexts, and outcomes. In the socio-educational model, motivation to learn the second language includes three elements. First, the motivated individual expends effort to learn the language. Second, the motivated individual wants to achieve a goal. Third, the motivated individual will enjoy the task of learning the language.

Role of Motivation in Language Learning

Integrative Motivation: Crookes and Schmidt (1991) identified as the learner's orientation with regard to the goal of learning a second language. It means that learner's positiveattitudes towards the target language group and the desire to integrate into the target language community. Instrumental Motivation: Hudson (2000) characterised the desire to obtain something practical or concrete from the study of a second language. Instrumental motivation underlies the goal to gain some social or economic reward through L2 achievement.

Another kind of motivation is when the learner feels motivated by the engagement they feel in the activity itself, when it is at the exact level of difficulty that they feel that they can cope with.

Integrative Motivation from the Socio-Educational Model

The one who is integratively motivated to learn the second language has a desire to identify with another language community, and tends to evaluate learning situation positively and accurately.

PERSONALITY FACTOR AND MOTIVATION

Motivation seems to be a highly generalizable personality factor. The focus of which, in SLL has been on its internally generated origins. However, that research itself, as van Lier notes, "has been hitherto partial, even though a promising agenda can be constructed for future research in this area. It is particularly important to broaden the social-psychological outlook which has predominated with information from psychology and education......and in line with Crookes and Schmidt, to broaden the research agenda...". Schmidt himself finds it remarkable, "that theories of foreign language learning have been generally silent about how motivation works, in terms of the mechanisms of acquisition" (Oxford 1996:17). He goes as far as to say that, "[it] is equally remarkable that there has been so little research exploring the links between motivation and cognitive processes".

This limitation, however, is not due solely to the nature of SLL. In the field of psychology in general, "...[we] are as ignorant of the nature of memory and the forces controlling behaviour in general as we were about the nature of genes some fifty years ago". The focus of the rest of this chapter will be upon these forces, their measurement, and their effect, as pertains to second language learners.

The state of the cognitive existence and activity of the learner is brought under discussion by such statements that, "...learning style, such as field dependence-independence, analytic-global orientation, or the judging-perceiving mode, has a strong effect on the strategies that language learners use" (Oxford 1990:13). While this seems to focus on the choice of strategy made by the learner, Oxford goes on to qualify the choice of strategy as being motivationally based by noting, "[more highly motivated learners use a significantly greater range of appropriate strategies than do less motivated learners". She goes even further in narrowing down the state of mind of the learner vis a vis motivation and the driving force thereof, by stating quite explicitly that, "[motivation] is related to language learning purpose", with examples of how purpose might influence the choice of [successful or otherwise] strategies. By no means does this focus preclude an examination of external influences that are brought to bear. In fact, this is one direction in which I intend to take this discussion

Placed in a taxonomy of factors influencing SLL, I venture that it is safe to say that motivation would fall into the category subsumed under affective factors (in this chapter affective refers to emotions, attitudes, motivations, and values). This complicates the matter of definition, considering that, "the affective domain is impossible to describe within definable limits" (Brown 1987). However, placing it within this framework highlights the relationship between emotions and motivation. The strong expression of this relationship would be a statement to the effect that that which controls emotions is also that which controls motivation. One of the strongest of these controlling influences upon motivation may be attitudes themselves. Accordingly,

- Attitudes are strong predictors of motivation in any area of life, and especially in language learning. Just as attitudes affect motivation, attitudes and motivation work together to influence language learning performance itself—including both global language proficiency and proficiency in specific language skills, such as listening comprehension, reading comprehension, and oral production".

It is useful to keep in mind that the realm of affect (or emotion), at least according to Vygotsky, has as its manifestation, the volitional side of human nature. Accordingly, Klinger gives pride of place to affect, asserting that:

- There is growing reason to believe that affective response forms the core of evaluation. The most fundamental role of cognition in evaluation, then, is to transform perceptual input into a form. capable of eliciting in the individual one or another kind of affective response (Ford 1992:147).

Crookes and Schmidt use Keller's definition as the current guide for thinking about motivation:

- Motivation refers to the choices people make as to what experiences or goals they will approach or avoid, and the degree of effort they will exert in that respect.

In setting out a formula for success in SLL that relies on the individual learner, Spolsky (1989) mentions three conditions that facilitate success. These are aptitude conditions, exposure conditions, and motivation conditions. It is debatable whether teachers have the power to influence aptitude and exposure as these are more or less pre-determined values.

In the case of aptitude, the powers of (sound or tone) discrimination, effective memory, and grammatical sensitivity, are all values that lie within the learner. It is uncertain whether any influence the educator has can be brought to bear to change these inherent values in any significant way. It is also uncertain whether exercises meant to heighten these aptitudes are language-learning specific or whether they develop generalizable skills.

Exposure refers to the time spent in contact with the language in a learning situation. There are two aspects of exposure: what the teacher provides and what the student does whether in the classroom or on his/her own. Formally, the teacher can make available instruction and language data only in the time limited by allotment in the classroom. Of course, this can be extended by outside assignments, such as homework and so on, but still on a limited basis.

On the other hand, the amount of time devoted to learning a language, in and outside of the classroom, rests with the learner. The amount of contact with the second language depends on the individual learner's level of motivation.

Drawbacks of Training Theories

Personal knowledge systems and personal belief systems are the foundations of cognitive theories concerning motivation as a human mental activity. In line with Piaget's conceptualization of the learner as a mentally active entity, the approach here is that learning is an active, experience-seeking dynamic. The present examination of motivation and personality stems from a goal-oriented, social-cognitive approach. This approach assumes an interest on the part of the researcher in "...[identifying] major patterns of behaviour and link them to underlying psychological processes".

This is in contrast to conditioning theories or drive theories that attempt to explain behaviour disregarding (which may be too strong a word) volition on the part of the learner. Conditioning theories, drive theories and the approaches developed from them, while important, have a different focus than that which the cognitive approach enjoys. Part of this difference seems to stem from the fact that the behavioural approach does not speculate about the underlying processes of learning and especially learning a language:

A problem with an adherence to operant-conditioning theories of learning is the failure to recognize that much of human cognition (this of course includes the learning and use of language) have three conditions that place it beyond the control of straight forward stimulus-response methods. These essentially important properties are that [parenthesis mine]:

- It is innovative and potentially infinite in scope.
- It is [therefore] free from stimulus control.
- It is appropriate to the situation.

Because their focus is situationally appropriate behaviour, and because learning takes place in the classroom, what is elicited (or perhaps rather, rewarded) is behaviour appropriate to the classroom. This approach, then in turn, relies (unstated) on the ability (an underlying process, hence not measured) of the learner to extrapolate or make analogies with new situations outside of the classroom. The same rewards and incentives that are experienced in the classroom may not have the same meaning or may not be available in the 'real world'.

In other words, one of the basic planks in the platform on which operant conditioning rests, comes into play; that of extinction. Connections between stimulus and response can be extinguished by the removal of the reward which accompanies the response. There is no assurance that the rewards for a certain behaviour will take the same form or be so finely directed to the individual outside of the classroom. In the absence, or perceived absence of such rewards as have been learned, and without consideration of the underlying processes of motivation, there seems to be nothing compelling or sustainable of learned behaviour.

A drawback in controlling students' behaviour with rewards and punishments is that the effect is temporal. The immediacy of both the reward and the desired behaviour is a condition that must be met. In other words, the balance of time spent away from the reinforcing situation is overwhelmingly against any long term effect of conditioning. In any case, theories about motivation must, in my opinion be able to recognize the limitations of conditioned response theories in relation to meaningful learning.

Another weakness that Child (1993:36) points out is that, "[human] beings do not display stereotyped patterns of unlearned behaviour." In other words, responses to any given stimuli are so wide and varied as to preclude a real prediction of a definite controlled behaviour resulting from any given stimulus. An important development of instinct theories are the ideas of imprinting and critical periods. The relevance to language learning is well accounted for in the literature and a critical period is postulated for the ease and instinctual nature that characterizes first language learning.

Above and beyond these considerations is the fact that operant conditioning theories, since they do not speculate about the underlying processes or motives of learning, are limited in the sense that they do "...not distinguish motivation from learning but rather [use] the same principles to explain all behaviour". While instinct based conditioning theories have their applications, in SLL we cannot rely on instinctive behaviour as the agent of success. This type of motivation may play an important role in learning one's first language, however there is a different type of motivation in effect when we consider learning a second language.

Adults especially are seen as more than "passive agents responding to biological or social stimulation...." with "...some actions performed for their own sake......in which humans are active agents..." (Child 1993:36). Also, as Ford (1992) points out, theories that rely on instinct as an explanation of human behaviour confound motivation and action and hence find themselves lacking in predictive or explanatory value. These theories tend therefore, to create a label for each new class of behaviour. Ford repeats a common complaint that: If he goes with his fellows, it is the "herd instinct" which activates him; if he walks alone, it is the "anti-social instinct";...if he twiddles his thumbs, it is the "thumb-twiddling instinct"; if he does not twiddle his thumbs, it is the "thumb-not-twiddling instinct." Thus everything is explained with the facility of magic—word magic (Ford 1992:9). Conditioning theories rely in part on instinct as an explanation for their effect. Here we might take Pavlov as an example of a developer of conditioning theories with some very basic limitations. "Although Pavlov believed that conditioning occurs with repeated Conditioned Stimulus/Unconditioned Stimulus pairings, research shows that conditioning is not automatic but instead depends on cognitive processes".

In developing his operant conditioning theory, Skinner relied on external variables as the determiners of behaviour. His theory does not take into account and in effect, negates the effects of internal processes on behaviour. Behaviours evinced by the subject depend on, and manifest themselves from the reinforcement history of the subject. This presupposes that there are reinforcers in the environment. In other words, this type of theory is based on extrinsic factors as the main mitigating factors determining behaviour. The cognitive theory that I speak of accepts the value of extrinsic motivators, while at the same time attempts to understand and exploit the functional autonomy of intrinsic motives and their concomitant goals.

It may be possible when dealing with first-language learning to assume that instincts play a major role. However, one common feature of SLL is that it is normally done through social interactions. It would be a futile exercise to postulate instincts for the infinite variety of social situations. Furthermore, "...labeling a behaviour as instinctive does not explain it. A complete theory of motivation must be able to explain what causes an action, what factors interact with it, and how it can be modified". This in no way should be taken to mean that we should not consider as useful the principles of approach to the positive and avoidance of the negative. On the contrary, a more robust approach or analysis recognizes the ability that people have in regards to cognitive control over their actions to approach or avoid outcomes.

Finally, in common with conditioning theories, a characteristic of drive theories is the aspect of reinforcement. For example, Mowrer "postulates that behaviours are motivated by emotions that become conditioned to cues." The problem with this approach is that these theories "can account for the performance of established behaviours but not the instigation of new behaviours" (ibid. 41). This is further highlighted by the observation that "...individuals of equal ability... show marked performance differences in response to challenge" (ibid. 41).

On Dimension of Motivation

Considering that motivation, as mentioned above, is viewed as an affective factor in human behaviour, one question soon arises: If motivation is a factor in learning in general, and second language in particular, and it is of an emotional, affective nature, is it possible to measure? The hint to the answer of this question was expressed in the discussion of considering motivation as a factor of cognition. In the behaviourist construct, the answer is that it is not necessary to measure motivation. It is enough to measure the effects that motivation has on behaviour without dealing directly with motivation, as an emotional state, itself.

It is questionable whether behaviourist methods of measurement may be useful for the purposes of assessing motivation. The standard position of these theorists is an approach to personality assessment that, in effect, measures the behaviour of people in various situations. The techniques employed are usually observational, giving us the common term for the tool of behavioural observation. This sort of measuring device requires that the observer make "...precise counts of particular acts that occur during pre-established time periods". Typically, observers tally the number of times a specified act occurs in a given situation. For example, in a situation measuring sociability or friendliness, the observer notes how many times a child initiates conversation with another.

In more complex situations, more complex models are necessitated. Some situations require a number of observers. This is quite obviously true in the case where the actions being measured are different. Even in the case where what is being measured is the same, at times multiple observers act as a control of reliability of each other. Reliability and precision can be had using this method, however the many drawbacks make it questionable that this type of measurement can be used for the purposes put forth in this chapter. Some of those drawbacks, as noted are logistical. The observers are limited as to the number behaviours to be observed. The situations also can not vary greatly from one instance to another to maintain comparability. This results in a "...very small number sample of the subject's behaviours in a very small number of situations" (ibid. pg. 346). Ultimately, what we are left with is a limited view of the subjects' behaviour, and to the extent that it is measured by using these methods, personalities.

The cognitive construct is that, if it can be measured, the best approach may be to measure it within the cognitive framework of the subject him/herself. In this way the cognitive approach that I have outlined here recognizes in, and attributes to, the learner a certain power of self-awareness. A self-awareness that is not a consideration to the behaviourists.

The recognition of this type of self-awareness goes back to the James-Lange Peripheral Response Theory, where it is the act of reflection that determines feelings. In other words, we have certain sensate experiences, experiences that, in our homeostatic model, create a feeling of satisfaction and upon reflection we label that as a fulfilled desire. It may be that this reflection takes place consciously at times and subconsciously at other times. In either case, it is the cognitive standpoint that we have the facility to recognize our feelings and the effect they have upon us. As a tool of assessment, self-report was the foundation in a recent study of motivation done by Schmidt et. al. (Oxford 1996 - henceforth Schmidt will refer to Schmidt et.al.), to identify the components of EFL motivation. Schmidt conducted a 100-item questionnaire based on existing questionnaires in use, concepts of motivation found in the literature of psychology, and discussions with teachers, administrators, and students. Their questionnaire focused on three aspects of student cognition: motivation, preferences for instructional activities, and cognitive strategies employed by learners.

INTRINSIC MOTIVATION THEORIES

INTRINSIC MOTIVATION

Some theorists (*e.g.*, Combs, 1982; Purkey and Schmidt, 1987; Purkey and Stanley, 1991) maintain that there is only a single kind of intrinsic motivation, which can be described as a motivation to engage in activities that enhance or maintain a person's self-concept. Most theorists define the term more broadly.

Note that even though the following pages will describe intrinsic motivation ashighly desirable, most of the activities in which teachers, students, and other human beings engage are most directly influenced by extrinsic rather than intrinsic motivation. For example, most people use a knife and a fork in a certain way or follow conventions in a restaurant not because they find knife and fork use to be intrinsically motivating, but because the correct use of these utensils leads to such intrinsic benefits as a good meal or the respect of people we care about. This is not a serious problem, unless the person feels coerced or in some other way alienated by having to use the utensils.

However, extrinsic motivators may lead to merely short-range activity while actually reducing long-range interest in a topic. If this does not happen, the result is likely to be areduction in the very behaviour we want to promote. One of the most frequent failures in education is that students rarely say that they find studying to be intrinsically rewarding. This is a critical problem. One of the most straightforward conclusions of research from the past two decades is that extrinsic motivation alone is likely to have precisely the opposite impact that we want it to have on student achievement.

FUNDAMENTAL DISTINCTION IN THE MOTIVATION

There is a fundamental distinction in the motivation literature between intrinsic motivation and extrinsic motivation. When individuals are intrinsically motivated they do activities for their own sake and out of interest in the activity. When extrinsically motivated, individuals do activities for instrumental or other reasons, such as receiving a reward. There is continuing debate about the pros and cons of intrinsic and extrinsic motivation, and a growing consensus that these two constructs should not be treated as polar opposites. Rather, they often both operate, and may even form a continuum.

Much of the work on intrinsic motivation stemmed from White's (1959) seminal article on effectance motivation, in which he argued persuasively that both people and at least some animals are motivated by curiosity and interest in developing their competence, rather than just by rewards or the satisfaction of basic bodily needs. This influential article had a strong influence on the views of Edward Deci and Richard Ryan, whose self-determination theory of intrinsic motivation is the main focus in this section.

Self-determination theory. Deci, Ryan, and their colleagues' self-determination theory (SDT) is an organismic theory of development that has a particular focus on the role of motivation in development and learning (*e.g.*, Deci and Ryan, 1985; 2002a; Deci, Vallerand, Pelletier, and Ryan, 1991; Ryan and Deci, 2000a). Broadly, self-determined behaviour is behaviour that originates from the self and, results from the individual utilizing his or her volition. Deci, Ryan, and their colleagues suggest that when individuals' behaviour is self-determined they are psychologically healthier, and tend to be intrinsically motivated. Indeed, they make a specific link between intrinsic motivation and self-determination, arguing that intrinsic motivation is only possible when individuals freely choose their own actions; that is, they are self-determined.

A fundamental aspect of this theory is that Deci, Ryan, and their colleagues propose that there are three basic or fundamental human psychological needs: the need for competence, the need for autonomy, and the need for relatedness. In order for healthy development to occur these needs must be met. Further, these needs are a basis for motivation. For instance, the need for competence is the major reason why people seek out optimal stimulation and challenging activities.

The need for autonomy refers most directly to volition and self-determination; Deci and Ryan argue that this sense of volition is necessary for optimum motivation. Ryan (1992) discussed the importance of distinguishing between competence and autonomy. He argued that models that focus primarily on competence, like self-efficacy theory, do not make this distinction clearly enough. Individuals can act competently and demonstrate their competence but still be doing so under the control of others. Ryan compared such actions to those of a robot, rather than a self-determined individual, and argued that intrinsic motivation only occurs when individuals are both autonomous and competent.

As we will see, the proposal that autonomy is a basic human need has led to much interesting research on topics such as choice and how providing children and adults with choice influences their intrinsic motivation. Relatedness refers to the need to be connected with others. This need was added to the theory after the other two, and reflects Deci and Ryan's beliefs that individuals must have strong connections to others for optimum development to occur. In their view autonomy does not imply total independence; connections with others are key to optimum development.

Deci, Ryan, and colleagues go beyond the extrinsic - intrinsic motivation dichotomy in their discussion of internalization, the process of transferring the regulation of behaviour from outside to inside the individual. They developed a taxonomy to describe different types of motivation involved in the process of going from external to more internalized regulation of motivation. This taxonomy forms a continuum. At one extreme is amotivation, which as the name implies means an absence of motivation to act. Next are several types of extrinsic motivation that range from least to most autonomous.

In order these are external, or regulation coming from outside the individual; introjected, or internal regulation based on feelings that he or she should or has to do the behaviour; identified, or internal regulation of behaviour that is based on the utility of that behaviour (*e.g.*, studying hard to get grades to get into college), and finally, integrated, or regulation based on what the individual thinks is valuable and important to the self. Each of these levels also is associated with different kinds of motivation. For instance, extrinsic rewards are most salient for external regulation, and at each subsequent level motivation become more internalized.

Deci, Ryan, and their colleagues have developed scales to measure these different levels of regulation They have tested their continuum idea by looking at how related the different kinds of motivation are. For instance, Ryan and Connell (1989) assessed children's external, introjected, identified, and intrinsic reasons for doing schoolwork, and found that these correlations formed a simplex pattern. That is, the levels of regulation closer to one another in the continuum were more highly related than those further apart, which they took as evidence for their placement on the continuum. Further, they found that the more extrinsically motivated the students were the less invested they were in their schoolwork.

One major focus of Deci, Ryan, and their colleagues' research and theorizing has been how extrinsic rewards can undermine intrinsically motivated behaviour. They call this portion of their theory Cognitive Evaluation Theory. They and others described different conditions under which rewards can be undermining; the most notable is when rewards are controlling, which reduces the individual's perceptions of autonomy over their own learning. When rewards provide individuals with information about how they are doing rather than focus on controlling them, the undermining effects do not occur.

In 1994 Cameron and Pierce published a meta-analysis of this research in which they questioned the strength of these undermining effects, arguing that they occurred only in very limited circumstances if at all. This article led to a series of commentaries and reactions and further meta analyses of the findings regarding the undermining effects of rewards on intrinsically motivated behaviour, with many claims and counter-claims about the adequacy of the meta-analytic techniques used and ways of parsing the findings. We believe that Deci, Ryan, and their colleagues have replied effectively to Cameron and Pierce's various arguments against the undermining effects of extrinsic motivation. Yet this debate was useful because it served to clarify the conditions under which extrinsic motivators do undermine intrinsically motivated behaviours, and so moved the field ahead in important ways.

SDT has been a dominant theoretical model and one that has generated a great deal of research. It is a broad model that encompasses a variety of constructs, and integrates many important issues with respect to the development of motivation. The theory, however, has been the subject of some criticism.

A number of questions have been raised about Deci and Ryan's contention that there are three basic psychological needs. Other questions have been raised about the universality of these needs and whether they operate similarly in different cultures. For instance, in cultures defined as less individualistic and more collectivist does the need for autonomy take on the same importance? This question currently is the focus of a great deal of research. There also has been debate within SDT on the role of choice in helping children fulfill their need for autonomy. Finally, although the continuum from extrinsic to intrinsic motivation is intriguing, there is some concern that intrinsic motivation as defined in this way only describes a very limited set of activities that people do in the normal course of their daily lives. This perhaps constrains intrinsic motivation too much.

Flow theory. Csikszentmihalyi (1988) discusses intrinsically motivated behaviour in terms of the immediate subjective experience that occurs when people are engaged in the activity. Interviews with climbers, dancers, chess players, basketball players, and composers revealed that these activities yield a specific form of experience - labelled flow - characterized by: (1) holistic feelings of being immersed in, and of being carried by, an activity, (2) merging of action and awareness, (3) focus of attention on a limited stimulus field, (4) lack of self-consciousness, and (5) feeling in control of one's actions and the environment.

Flow is only possible when people feel that the opportunities for action in a given situation match their ability to master the challenges. The challenge of an activity may be something concrete or physical like the peak of a mountain to be scaled, or it can be something abstract and symbolic, like a set of musical notes to be performed, a story to be written, or a puzzle to be solved. Further research has shown that both the challenges and skills must be relatively high before a flow experience becomes possible.

At first sight, the theories of Deci and Ryan and Csikszentmihalyi seem to be very different. Deci and Ryan (1985, 2002a) explain intrinsic motivation by assuming innate, basic needs, whereas Csikszentmihalyi stresses subjective experience. We suggest, however, that this difference reflects two sides of the same coin. As Schneider (1996) has argued, one has to distinguish between immediate reasons (*e.g.*, enjoyment) and ultimate reasons of behaviour (*e.g.*, survival). Intrinsically motivated behaviour can be conducive to ultimate goals even though the actor is only motivated by immediate incentives. A typical case is exploratory or play behaviour. Both types of behaviour help to increase an individual's competence but they are usually performed because they are exciting, pleasurable, or enjoyable.

This distinction between immediate and ultimate causes of behaviour makes it possible to reconcile the positions of Deci and Ryan and Csikszentmihalyi. Deci and Ryan (1985) focus on ultimate reasons of behaviour, whereas Csikszentmihalyi (1988) focuses mainly on immediate reasons. Csikszentmihalyi and Massimini (1985) have suggested that the experience of flow is a reward that ensures that individuals will seek to increase their competence. According to Csikszentmihalyi, the repeated experience of flow is only possible when individuals seek out increasingly challenging tasks and expand their competencies to meet these challenges. Thus, the experience of flow should reinforce behaviours underlying development.

Individual difference theories of intrinsic motivation. Until recently intrinsic motivation researchers like Deci and Ryan and Csikszentmihalyi have dealt with conditions, components, and consequences of intrinsic motivation without making a distinction between intrinsic motivation as a state versus intrinsic motivation as a trait-like characteristic. However, interest in trait-like individual differences in intrinsic motivation has increased recently, particularly among educational psychologists.

These researchers define this enduring intrinsic motivational orientations in terms of three components: (1) preference for hard or challenging tasks, (2) learning that is driven by curiosity or interest, and (3) striving for competence and mastery. The second component is most central to the idea of intrinsic motivation. Both preference for hard tasks and striving for competence can be linked to either extrinsic or more general need achievement motivation. Nonetheless, empirical findings suggest that the three components are highly correlated.

In addition, evidence suggests that high levels of trait-like intrinsic motivation facilitate positive emotional experience and well-being, self-esteem, high academic achievement (Cordova and Lepper, 1996; Schiefele and Schreyer, 1994), creativity, self-regulation and persistence (Cordova and Lepper, 1996; Pelletier, Fortier, Vallerand, and Brière, 2001; Pintrich and Schrauben, 1992; Schiefele and Schreyer, 1994). As a consequence, many have suggested that the development of an intrinsic motivational orientation should be fostered in the home and the classroom (*e.g.*, Brophy, 1999; Dewey, 1913; Lepper and Chabay, 1985).

INTEREST THEORIES

Closely related to the notion of intrinsic motivation is work on the concept of "interest". Hidi and Harackiewicz (2001) propose that interest is more specific than intrinsic motivation, which is a broader motivational characteristic. Researchers studying interest differentiate between individual and situational interest. Individual interest is a relatively stable evaluative orientation towards certain domains; situational interest is an emotional state aroused by specific features of an activity or a task. Two aspects or components of individual interest are distinguishable: feeling-related and value-related valences. Feeling-related valences refer to the feelings that are associated with an object or an activity itself - feelings like involvement, stimulation, or flow. Value-related valences refer to the attribution of personal significance or importance to an object.

In addition, both feeling-related and value-related valences are directly related to the object rather than to the relation of this object to other objects or events. For example, if students associate mathematics with high personal significance because mathematics can help them get prestigious jobs, then we would not speak of interest. Although feeling-related and value-related valences are highly correlated, it is useful to differentiate between them because some individual interests are likely based primarily on feelings, while others' interests are more likely to be based on personal significance. Further research is necessary to validate this assumption.

Much of the research on individual interest has focused on its relation to the quality of learning. In general, there are significant but moderate relations between interest and text learning. More importantly, interest is more strongly related to indicators of deep-level learning (*e.g.*, recall of main ideas, coherence of recall, responding to deeper comprehension questions, representation of meaning) than to surface-level learning. Findings by Ainley, Hidi, and Berndorff (2002) and Hidi (2001) suggest that attentional processes, affect, and persistence mediate the effects of interest on text learning.

There is also ample evidence that subject matter interest is positively related to school achievement. Recent studies suggest that interest particularly predicts achievement when there is a context that allows for choice. Specifically, Köller, Baumert, and Schnabel (2001) found that interest in mathematics predicts achievement only at higher grade levels when students have a choice between more or less advanced courses. The "effect" of interest on achievement was partly mediated by choice of course level. However, there was also a direct path from interest to achievement even when controlling for prior achievement.

Most of the research on situational interest has focused on the characteristics of academic tasks that create interest. Among others, the following text features were found to arouse situational interest: personal relevance, novelty, vividness, and comprehensibility. Empirical evidence has provided strong support for the relation between situational interest and text comprehension and recall.

Goal Theories

Work on achievement goals and goal orientations has flourished since the publication of our previous chapter. This work can be organized into three relatively distinct areas. One group of researchers has focused on the properties of goals for specific learning activities. These researchers focus on goals' proximity, specificity, and level of challenge and have shown that specific, proximal, and somewhat challenging goals promote both self-efficacy and improved performance. A second group of researchers defined and investigated broader goal orientations students have to their learning, focusing primarily on three broad orientations: a mastery or learning orientation, an ego or performance orientation, and a work avoidant orientation.

These orientations refer to broader approaches children take to their learning, rather than goals for specific activities, although of course goal orientations can also influence the approach one takes to a specific task. A third group focuses on the content of children's goals, proposing that there are many different kinds of goals individuals can have in achievement settings, including both academic and social goals. We focus in this section on the work of the latter two groups.

Goal orientation theory. Researchers initially distinguished two broad goal orientations that students can have towards their learning. One orientation, called a learning, task involved, or mastery goal orientation, means that the child is focused on improving their skills, mastering material, and learning new things. Questions such as "How can I do this task?" and "What will I learn?" reflect task-involved goals. A second goal orientation, called performance or ego orientation, means that the child focuses on maximizing favourable evaluations of their competence and minimizing negative evaluations of competence. Nicholls and his colleagues and Meece (1991, 1994) also have described a work avoidant goal orientation, which means that the child does not wish to engage in academic activities.

The different terms used to label these goal orientations occurred because different researchers were working on them simultaneously, with each having a somewhat distinctive view of each orientation. For instance, Dweck and Leggett (1988) proposed that children's goal orientations stem from their theories of intelligence that were described earlier. Children believing intelligence is malleable tend to hold a learning (mastery) goal orientation, and children adopting the entity view take on performance goals. By contrast,

Ames (1992) focused primarily on classroom antecedents of these goal orientations, rather than characteristics of children, which implies that goal orientations are more a product of context rather than the person, and so may vary more widely across different achievement situations. We acknowledge that the different terminology used by these theorists reflects some important distinctions in the conceptualization of these" goal orientations, but also believe that the similarities are stronger than the distinctions between them. We will use the terms mastery and performance goal orientations in this chapter.

One of the newer directions in goal orientation theory is further differentiation of these two broad goal orientations into approach and avoidance components. This occurred first for the performance goal orientation, beginning with work by Elliot and Harackiewicz (1996) and Skaalvik (1997), among others. These further distinctions emerged for two main reasons. Empirically, findings concerning the outcomes of having a performance goal orientation were somewhat contradictory, leading researchers to wonder why this occurred. Theoretically, Elliot and Harackiewicz noted that traditional achievement motivation theories, such as Atkinson's (1957) expectancy-value model, included both approach and avoidance motives. By contrast, most modern theories focus primarily on the approach aspect, thus overlooking the importance of avoidance motivation.

Therefore, Elliot and Harackiewicz (1996) proposed approach and avoidance aspects of performance goals, as did Skaalvik (1997). Performance-approach goals refer to the students' desire to demonstrate competence and outperform others. Performance-avoidance goals involve the desire to avoid looking incompetent. Researchers began to disentangle the effects of these two kinds of performance orientations.

As we will see later, there is evidence that performance-approach goals can have a positive impact on different outcomes such as grades, whereas the impact of performance-avoidance goals is nearly always negative. Elliot and Pintrich (2000c) proposed that the mastery goal orientation also may be divided into approach and avoid components. Elliot and McGregor stated that the assumption likely was made that mastery goals always referred to approach situations, rather than avoidance situations, which they believe does not provide a full characterization of situations to which mastery goals apply. They argued that mastery-avoidance goals include such things as working to avoid misunderstanding, or the use of standards to not be wrong when doing an achievement activity.

As Elliot and McGregor and Pintrich both note, perfectionists may be characterized as holding mastery avoidance goals. Elliot and McGregor (2001) developed items to assess mastery avoidant goals, and found (in a study of college students) that these items factored separately from items measuring the other three kinds of goal orientations. The antecedents (as perceived by the participants) of mastery-avoidance goals were not as positive as antecedents of mastery-approach goals. These results are intriguing, but much more work is needed to establish the meaningfulness of this new category.

There is a growing body of research documenting the consequences of adopting one or the other of these goal orientations. Researchers have used a variety of methodologies in this work, including classroom observations, interviews, and questionnaire-based studies, often using Midgley and her colleagues' Patterns of Adaptive Learning Scale (PALS). Experimental manipulations of students' goal orientations also have been done, by introducing achievement tasks in a way that fosters either mastery or performance goals. The results concerning mastery orientation are quite consistent and positive.

When children are mastery oriented they are more highly engaged in learning, use deeper cognitive strategies, and are intrinsically motivated to learn. Elliot and McGregor (2001) found that mastery-avoidance goals are associated with a mixture of outcomes, including subsequent test anxiety, mastery-approach goals, and performance-approach goals. Based on this and other work researchers have proposed that schools should work to foster mastery goal orientations rather than performance goal orientations, and school reform efforts to do just that have been undertaken.

As noted above the research on performance goals is somewhat less consistent, in part because of the methodological confounding of performance avoidance and approach goals. When these two aspects of performance goals are unconfounded, researchers find that performance avoid goals have negative consequences for students motivation and learning. Performance approach goals relate positively to academic self-concept, task value, and performance (at least in college students), but not to intrinsic motivation to learn.

The distinction between performance approach and avoid goals, and evidence showing that performance-approach goals relate to positive motivational and achievement outcomes, led Harckiewicz, Barron, and Elliot (1998) and Pintrich (2000a,c) to call for a revision of goal theory that acknowledges the positive effects of performance-approach goals, and also the need to look at how different goals relate to different outcomes. Traditional (or normative, to use the term adopted by Harackiewicz et al) goal theory argues for the benefits of mastery goals and the costs of performance goals. Pintrich (2000b) studied 8th grade students' goal orientations, and identified four groups of children crossing high and low mastery and performance goal orientations.

He found that students with a combination of high mastery and high performance-approach goal orientations were similar with respect to a variety of motivational outcomes to a group of students who were high in mastery but low in performance goal orientations. This finding does not support the normative theory view that only mastery goal orientations lead to positive developmental outcomes, and was one impetus for the call for a revised goal orientation theory.

Midgley *et al.* (2001) disputed these claims, arguing that the costs of performance avoidance goals are clearly documented and that the benefits of performance approach goals are not as clearly established in the literature. They also noted that performance approach goals may benefit some students (boys, older students) rather than others (girls, younger students), and that we do not yet have enough information about how performance-approach goals operate in other groups of children. They also pointed out that benefits of performance goals identified by researchers may be in part due to the focus of our educational system on standards, assessments, and performance rather than effort and improvement, which they argue is a better approach to schooling.

In response, Harackiewicz *et al.* (2002) argued that the evidence for the positive effects of performance-approach goals is clearer than Midgley *et al.* stated that it was, and continued to propose the multiple goal perspective (that both mastery and performance goals can benefit different educational outcomes) is the more viable approach to goal orientation theory. They noted a number of areas of research that now are needed to assess each of these perspectives.

In a final response Kaplan and Middleton (2002) took a broader perspective and focused on what the purposes of schooling should be. In their view the purposes of schooling should be knowledge growth and the fostering of a love of learning, rather than performance *per se,* and thus for them a mastery orientation continues to be more desirable, even if performance-approach goals relate to some positive educational outcomes in our current educational system. So this debate appears to be at different levels. At one level is the concern for how the specific goal orientations relate to different kinds of outcomes within our current educational system.

The second level concerns what that system should focus on, rather than an acceptance of the current system and its strong performance emphasis. This healthy debate among goal orientation theorists should move the field ahead, as more research is done to look at the benefits and costs of different kinds of goal orientations, and as we consider further the nature and purposes of schooling and their influence on the development of students' motivation.

We believe the move beyond the perhaps too simplistic two-goal orientation theory is welcome, but acknowledge that more work is needed both on performance approach and (especially) mastery-avoidance goals to evaluate their effects, and in the case of mastery-avoid goals, document their existence. Work on achievement goal orientations also needs to look more carefully at how different achievement domains (math, science, English) might impact achievement goal orientations and their effects. The goal content approach: Academic and social goals.

Building on Ford's (1992) work defining a taxonomy of human goals, Wentzel has examined the multiple goals of children in achievement settings. Her view on goals differs from the goal orientation theorists in that she focuses on the content of children's goals to guide and direct behaviour, rather than the criteria a person uses to define success or failure (*i.e.*, mastery versus performance). In this sense, these goals are like the goals and self-schema that relate to attainment value hierarchies in the Eccles *et al.* expectancy value. However, she does view these goals as contributing to children's competence in particular situations. Wentzel primarily has focused on academic and social goals and their relations to a variety of outcomes.

Wentzel has demonstrated that both social and academic goals relate to adolescents' school performance and behaviour (Wentzel, 2002b). For instance, she found that the goals related to school achievement include seeing oneself as successful, dependable, wanting to learn new things, and wanting to get things done.

Higher-achieving students have higher levels of both social responsibility and achievement goals than lower achieving students. Similarly, Wentzel (1994) documented the association among middle school children's pro-social goals of helping others, academic pro-social goals like sharing learning with classmates, peer social responsibility goals like following through on promises made to peers, and academic social responsibility goals like doing what the teacher says to do. Pro-social goals (particularly academic pro-social goals) related positively to peer acceptance. She also found positive relations between prosocial goals and children's grades and even IQ scores.

While it appears valuable to have multiple goals, Wentzel (2002b) discussed the difficulty some children may have coordinating these multiple goals. Can students manage a variety of social and academic goals? This question also applies to the multiple goal perspective in goal orientation theory. Having multiple goals may be especially challenging for younger children, whose resources to manage such goals may be limited.

THE DEVELOPMENT OF MOTIVATION: WITHIN-PERSON MODIFY AND COLLECTION DIFFERENCES

Developmental and educational psychologists have focused on two major developmental questions: (1) How do the different beliefs, values, and goals defined in the different theories develop during childhood and adolescence? and (2) What explains the emergence of individual differences in motivation? Different sources of influence have been considered: Within-person changes resulting from growth and maturation in cognitive processing, emotional development, or other individual characteristics; and socially-mediated developmental changes resulting from systematic age-related changes in the social contexts children experience at home, in school and among peers as they grow up; and socially-mediated influences that differ across individuals and contexts. Of course, these different sources often interact with one another but the nature of this interaction is rarely studied.

Consequently, we have organized our discussion of the development of motivation and of individual differences in motivation around these broad categories of influence. First, we present work on within-person changes, beginning with work on children's early self-evaluations, and then describe the work on within-person changes in the constructs discussed thus far. We also include a consideration of the development of certain motivational problems. Also discussed in this section are the development of sex and ethnic differences in children's motivation. We include this work in this section because they emerge over the course of children's development. The next major section then considers how various socialization agents influence children's motivation.

WITHIN-PERSON MODIFY IN MOTIVATION

Early Development of Self-Evaluation During the Preschool Years

Some researchers have looked at very young children's reactions to success and failure, reactions which likely provide the foundation for the development of the different motivational beliefs, values, and goals discussed in this chapter. Heckhausen (1987) found that children between 2 1/2 and 3 1/ 2 years start to show self-evaluative, non-verbal expressions following a successful or unsuccessful action.

The earliest indicators of achievement motivation were facial expressions of joy after success and sadness after failure. The experience of success (around 30 months) preceded the experience of failure (around 36 months). Several months later children showed postural expressions of pride and shame following success and failure. When competing with others, three and four year old children initially showed joy after winning and sadness after losing.

It was only when they looked at their competitor that they expressed pride and shame. Stipek, Rechchia, and McClintic (1992) identified three stages of development in young children's self-evaluations: The children younger than 22 months were neither concerned with others' evaluation of their performance nor self-reflective in their evaluations. However, they did show positive emotional reactions to accomplishing a task and negative emotions when they did not.

Thus, unlike Heckhausen, Stipek *et al.* found that reactions to success and failure occurred at the same time in development. Two -year-olds reacted more to others' evaluations by seeking approval when they did well and turning away when they did poorly. After age 3, the children were able to evaluate their own performance, without needing to see how adults reacted to that performance, and engaged in more autonomous self-evaluation. Children three and older also reacted more strongly to winning and losing than did younger children. Dweck and her colleagues (*e.g.*, Burhans and Dweck, 1995; Heyman, Dweck, and Cain, 1992; Smiley and Dweck, 1994; see Dweck, 2002, for review) also have done interesting work on young children's reactions to failure; we review this work more completely later when we discuss the development of learned helplessness. Generally, their findings show that some preschool children already react quite negatively to failure, reactions that may lead to later learned helplessness in response to failure.

Taken together, these studies show that reactions to success and failure begin early in the preschool years, likely laying the groundwork for the development of motivation in the middle childhood years and beyond. The results concerning children's reactions to failure are particularly important because they suggest that children are more sensitive to failure in the preschool years than was once believed.

The Development of Competence-Related Beliefs

Much of the work on the development of children's achievement-related beliefs has looked at the development of children's ability and expectancy-related beliefs. We discuss three kinds of changes in these beliefs: change in their factorial structure, in mean levels, and change in children's understanding of them.

The factorial structure of children's competence-related beliefs. Eccles *et al.* (1998) reviewed factor analytic research showing that children as young as five or six appear to have distinctive competence perceptions among different academic and non-academic domains of competence. Since that review researchers have looked at even younger children and found that these children also have differentiated competence-related beliefs (Mantzicoupolus, French, and Maller, 2004; Marsh, Ellis, and Craven, 2002). This does not mean, however, that there is no change or refinement in children's beliefs from kindergarten through high school. The pattern of correlations of self-concept factors differs in meaningful ways for younger and older children. Younger children use fewer of the scale points when responding to the items on the questionnaires, and their responses correlate less well with both their teachers' and their parents' estimates of their competencies.

Eccles and Wigfield (1995) and Eccles *et al.* (1993) also have used factor analytic strategies to access whether children's competence beliefs and expectancies for success are distinct constructs. Analyses of both children's and adolescents' responses indicate the ratings of one's current competence, expectancies for success, and perceived performance load on the same fact or, suggesting that these components comprise a single concept for children age 6-18.

Change in the mean level of children's competence-related beliefs. Another well-established finding in the literature is that children's competence beliefs for different tasks decline across the elementary school years and through the high school years. Many young children are quite optimistic about their competencies in different areas, and this optimism changes to greater realism and (sometimes) pessimism for many children.

To illustrate, in Nicholls (1979) most first graders ranked themselves near the top of the class in reading ability, and there was no correlation between their ability ratings and their performance level. By contrast the 12 year olds' ratings were more dispersed and correlated highly with school grades (.70 or higher). Recently, researchers in the U. S. have examined change over the entire elementary and secondary school years in children's competence beliefs for math, language arts, and sport (Jacobs, Lanza, Osgood, Eccles, and Wigfield, *et al.*, 2002; Fredericks and Eccles, 2002;), and Watt (2004) looked at change across middle and senior high school in Australia.

Jacobs *et al.* examined change in children's competence for math, language arts, and sports across grades 1 through 12. Children's perceptions in each area were strongly positive early on. However, the overall pattern of change was a decline in each domain. There were some differences across domain with respect to when the strongest changes occurred, particularly in language arts and math. In language arts the strongest declines occurred during elementary school and then little change was observed after that. In sports the change accelerated during the high school years. The decline in math competence beliefs was steady over time. Frederick and Eccles and Watt also found declines over time in competence beliefs and values, although the specific trends were somewhat different across these studies.

One caveat about this general "optimism early and realism later" pattern should be noted. As just discussed, researchers observing children's reactions to failure find that some preschool children already reacted negatively to failure. Dweck notes that during the preschool years children likely do not have a clearly defined notion of what ability is. So these earlier negative reactions to failure may not mean that children doubt their ability, as their views of ability still are taking shape. But the connection between these reactions and level of ability beliefs likely begins to develop early in the school years, and children reacting negatively to failure early on may be more likely to be pessimistic about their abilities later.

In summary, children's competence beliefs and expectancies for success become more negative as they get older. The negative changes in children's competence-related beliefs have been explained in two ways: (1) Because children become much better at understanding, interpreting, and integrating the evaluative feedback they receive, and engage in more social comparison with their peers, children become more accurate or realistic in their self-assessments, leading some to become relatively more negative; (2) Because school environment changes in ways that makes evaluation more salient and competition between students more likely, some children's self-assessments will decline as they get older. We return to this issue of how school environments influence children's motivation later.

There are two important limitations to this work on mean-level change in the development of competence beliefs. First, most of it is normative, in the sense that researchers report overall mean differences in their studies. We thus know less about patterns of changes within different groups of children and adolescents, although there is some information about this. Wigfield *et al.* (1991) found that this pattern of change varied somewhat for children high or low in math ability. Second, the measures used in this work either are at the school level or (more frequently) at the domain-specific level. It is possible that children's beliefs about their competence for more particular activities may show different patterns of change, and we know little about this. We also know little about how children arrive at judgements of their competence in something as broad as "reading" or "science"; do they simply average their performance in a variety of different relevant tasks, or use a more elaborate strategy.

Finally, one other set of findings relevant to the issue of mean-level change should be mentioned. Longitudinal studies looking at relations of children's competence beliefs over time show that these beliefs become increasingly stable as children get older. Even by the middle of the elementary school years children's competence beliefs correlate quite highly across a one-year period, with the correlations reaching as high as.74. Thus by early adolescence there is much stability in these beliefs, even though the overall pattern of change is the decline just discussed.

The implication of these findings is that individuals tend to maintain their relative position in their group, even as the group's mean declines. Changes in children's understanding of competence-related beliefs. The research on both the structure of and mean level differences in children's beliefs does not tell us about children's understanding of these constructs, because the questionnaire methodology used in these studies requires children to respond to researcher-defined constructs rather than generate their own definitions of a given construct. But it is important to understand how children conceptualize the different constructs in order to interpret comparisons of different-aged children's beliefs meaningfully.

Dweck (2002) described important developmental changes in children's understandings of ability. During the preschool years and into kindergarten children do not have a clear sense of ability as a characteristic that determines outcomes, but as discussed earlier they do react to success and failure experiences. Part of this reaction is to think they are good when they do well and bad when they do poorly; indeed, Dweck argues that conceptions of goodness and badness are primary at this time. During the early school years concepts of ability begin to emerge, and children see ability as distinct from other qualities and also differentiate their ability across domains. They often think of ability as changeable, and use normative rather than comparative standards to judge ability, but some children begin to see ability as a stable characteristic.

As children move through these ages social comparison takes on increasing importance, however. Children's beliefs about ability also become more accurate, in the sense of correlating more strongly with performance measures. Between ages 10 and 12 children differentiate more clearly ability, effort, and performance, and also see how they interrelate. These children more often use comparative standards in judging ability. More children come to view ability as capacity (or take an entity view of intelligence, to use Dweck's term), which means they are less likely to believe that with increased effort their ability will improve.

Researchers have investigated children's understanding of ability, effort, task difficulty and intelligence. Nicholls and his colleagues found a developmental progression between ages 5 and 12 with respect to children's beliefs about ability, effort, and performance. They found four relatively distinct levels of reasoning. At level one (ages 5 to 6), effort, ability, and performance are not clearly differentiated in terms of cause and effect. At level two (ages 7 to 9), effort is seen as the primary cause of performance outcomes. At level three (ages 9 to 12), children begin to differentiate ability and effort as causes of outcomes, but they do not always apply this distinction. Finally, at level four, adolescents clearly differentiate ability and effort, and understand the notion of ability as capacity. They also believe that ability can limit the effects of additional effort on performance, that ability and effort are often related to each other in a compensatory manner, and, consequently, that success requiring a great deal of effort likely reflects limited ability.

As we will discuss in more detail later in the section on learned helplessness, these different views of ability and intelligence have important implications for children's reactions to success and failure, particularly their reactions to failure. As Dweck and her colleagues have discussed, children with an entity view of ability are more likely to give up following failure, because they are less likely to believe that additional effort will improve their performance, because their ability is fixed. By contrast, children with an incremental view are more likely to continue to strive after failure, because they think their ability can change.

Pomerantz and Saxon added another distinction to this discussion. They distinguished between (in their terms) "conceptions of ability as stable to external forces", and "conceptions of ability as stable to internal forces." Stability of ability with respect to external forces "is the view that ability is unlikely to be influenced by forces external to the individual possessing the ability (*e.g.*, situational changes)". Pomerantz and Saxon argued that as children get older they increasingly hold this view about ability and a number of other characteristics, with the implication that children see individuals' behaviours as relatively consistent across types of activities and over time. Pomerantz and Saxon see conceptions of ability as stable to internal forces as analogous to Dweck's (2002) entity theory of ability. One reason they see these is similar is that Dweck and her colleagues operationalize the entity view of ability as the belief that ability is not under one's own control. For instance, one item from Cain and Dweck's measure of views of intelligence is " You're a certain amount smart, and you can't really do much to change it" (p. 153). That is, the individual cannot do much to change his or her ability. Pomerantz and Saxon proposed that the latter but not the former conception about the nature of ability could have negative consequences for motivation and achievement.

They studied these two conceptions of ability in a sample of fourth through sixth grade children. Concepts of ability as stable to external forces were measured by the researchers describing to participants another child as either smart or not very smart at schoolwork, and then having children rate the other child's ability at four time points and in four situations. Similar procedures were used to measure social ability. Differences between children's ratings of the other's ability and the initial description were used to determine how much children believed that the other children's ability was stable with respect to external forces.

Ability as stable with respect to internal forces was measured using Cain and Dweck's (1995) scale. Results showed that the two kinds of conceptions were inversely (but weakly) related. Children's beliefs that ability was stable with respect to external forces increased over time, and their conceptions of ability as stable with respect to internal forces decreased over time. Believing that ability is stable with respect to external forces correlated positively with the importance children attached to being competent, a preference for challenge, positive perceptions of competence, and academic performance. The opposite pattern of relations occurred for perceptions that ability is stable with respect to internal forces. It should be noted that both sets of correlations were relatively weak.

Pomerantz and Saxon (2001) concluded that seeing ability as stable, at least with respect to external forces, actually is a positive belief for children to have, because of the pattern of its relations with other motivational beliefs and performance. By contrast, believing that ability is stable with respect to internal forces has negative implications for motivation and performance. Thus it is not stability *per se* but the type of stability that is crucial. Further, they noted that viewing ability as stable with respect to external forces was a more stable belief over time than was viewing ability as stable with respect to internal forces. These intriguing findings provide a more subtle representation of the impact of having "stable" beliefs on motivational and performance outcomes. However, because many of the observed relations were rather weak (albeit significant) this potentially important distinction requires further research. Further, both Dweck's work and Nicholls' work suggests that children increasingly view ability as stable as they get older, whereas Pomerantz and Saxon found just the opposite with respect to beliefs about stability of ability with respect to internal causes. This apparent contradiction needs to be resolved.

In sum, work on children's understanding of ability converges with the factor analytic work in the sense of showing that young children differentiate ability into different areas. However, this work shows that younger and older children have different ideas about the nature of ability and its relations to effort, other achievement beliefs, and performance, which means we must take some care in how we interpret the factor analytic findings. Using the same scales to measure perceived ability at different ages may be problematic given the apparent differences in how younger and older children understand ability.

EXPANSION OF EFFICACY BELIEFS

There has not been extensive research on the development of efficacy beliefs *per se*, although the work on ability beliefs and expectancies is directly relevant. Instead, research on children's self-efficacy has focused primarily on interventions to enhance the self-efficacy and school performance of low achieving children. Extant work on the development of efficacy shows that children's efficacy beliefs increase across age.

Shell, Colvin, and Bruning (1995) found that 4th graders had lower self-efficacy beliefs for reading and writing than did 7th and 10th graders, and the 7th graders efficacy beliefs were lower than 10th graders beliefs. The inconsistency of these findings with those on children's competence beliefs just discussed likely reflects the self-efficacy measure used by Shell *et al.* Their instrument measured children's estimates of their efficacy on specific reading and writing skills rather than more general beliefs about competence reading and writing,; the more specific beliefs should be higher among older children. Also, efficacy beliefs usually are not measured comparatively, whereas many measures of competence beliefs include comparisons of one's ability with that of others. The latter kind of measure may be more likely to show declines over age.

Bandura (1997) and Schunk and Pajares (2002) discussed factors influencing the development of self-efficacy. They proposed that children who have mastery experiences in which they exert some control over their environments develop the earliest sense of personal agency. Through these experiences, infants learn that they can influence and control their environments. Parents and other adults can facilitate the growth of this sense of agency by the kinds of experiences they provide children. If parents do not provide infants with these experiences, they are not likely to develop a strong a sense of personal agency. Second, because self-efficacy requires the understanding that the self produced an action and an outcome, Bandura argued that a more mature sense of self-efficacy should not emerge until children have at least a rudimentary self-concept and can recognize that they are distinct individuals, which happens sometime during the second year of life. Through the preschool period, children are exposed to extensive performance information that should be crucial to their emerging sense of self-efficacy.

However, just how useful such information likely depends on the child's ability to integrate it across time, contexts, and domains; Schunk and Pajares discuss the challenges children face in doing so. More work is needed to understand how children become able to integrate diverse sources of information about their performances (*e.g.*, information about their own performance, social comparison information, etc.) to develop a stable of self-efficacy. Schunk and Pajares also discuss the crucial role peers can play in the development of self-efficacy, or its demise.

Finally, Schunk and Pajares (2002) and Bandura (1997) stressed the importance of school environments for developing and supporting a high sense of efficacy, or possibly undermining it if support is not provided. We return later to a discussion of how this can occur.

Growth of Control Beliefs

Work done on perceived control done in the 1980s and 1990s showed that there are developmental patterns in these beliefs. Weisz (1984) found that younger children actually believe they have greater control over chance events than do older children. Similarly, Connell (1985) found a decrease in the endorsement of all three of his locus of control constructs (internal control, powerful others control, and unknown control) from grades 3 through 9.

Like Weisz's findings, the unknown belief results suggest that older children have a clearer understanding of what controls achievement outcomes. However, the older children also rated the other two sources of control as less important, making interpretation of these findings difficult. Skinner examined age differences in both the structure and the mean levels of means-ends beliefs, and found the factor structure becomes increasingly complex as children get older.

She also found the largest mean-level differences on some of the means-ends beliefs. At all ages between 7 and 12, children believe effort is the most effective means. In contrast, older children are much less likely to believe that luck is an effective means than younger children. As in Connell (1985), belief in the relevance of unknown control and powerful others also decreased across age levels.

In a landmark three-year longitudinal study, Skinner, Zimmer-Gembeck, and Connell (1998) assessed the development of perceived control in children and early adolescents and how it predicted student engagement in school. Their cohort-sequential design encompassed third through seventh grade children. Skinner *et al.* measured overall control beliefs, beliefs about the strategies needed to do well in school (including the strategies of effort, ability, powerful others, luck, and unknown), and beliefs about capacity to access one's effort, ability, powerful others, and luck. They also measured children's engagement in school, and their perceptions of the structure and involvement provided by teachers, and examined predictive relations among these variables.

Skinner *et al.* (1998) found that perceived control showed a curvilinear pattern of change, being stable at first, increasing slightly through 4th grade, and then declining after 5th grade. Student engagement declined during middle school, as did students' perceptions that teachers provided structure and were involved with them. Changes in perceived control related to changes in engagement, and change in the teacher context variables predicted change in perceived control. Specifically, children initially either high or low in perceived control decreased in their control perceptions if they perceived that teachers were providing less structure and were less involved with them. A number of interesting age differences in the predictors of engagement and control emerged.

Younger children's beliefs about their capacity to exert effort were a stronger predictor, whereas for older children it was their beliefs about their ability. Grades predicted perceived control more strongly for older than younger children. Skinner *et al.* also suggested that the context provided by teachers may provide a stronger role in the development of perceived control for younger than for older children. Skinner *et al.* also examined how the constructs they measured varied across different subgroups in their sample, and thus went beyond the normative approach often taken in this area.

This fascinating study provides a rich depiction of the development of perceived control, and how it relates to students' engagement in the classroom. While rich in many respects, the measures of both academic performance and perceived control were done at the general level. Based on work we reviewed earlier, these beliefs (and certainly performance) likely varies across different areas. The measure of teacher context also focused on just a few features of the classroom context. Nevertheless, the study provides a model for how to study the development of motivational processes.

In overall summary of this section on competence-related beliefs, there are numerous changes in children's competence and control beliefs. These changes include structural change, mean level change, and change in children's understanding of the constructs. We need more complex longitudinal studies such as those of Jacobs *et al.* (2002) and Skinner *et al.* (1998) to examine these changes over time, for different groups, and in relation to other contextual and psychological factors.

Growth of Children's Goal Orientations

There still is not a large body of work on the development of children's goals and goal orientations. Instead, most of the work has focused on relations of goals to ability beliefs, and how different instructional contexts influence achievement goals. For instance, Dweck and her colleagues looked at relations of children's beliefs about ability and their goal orientations, and found that performance goal oriented children only show mastery behaviour when their perceived ability is high. By contrast, mastery oriented children engage in mastery-oriented behaviour irrespective of their perceived ability. Butler and her colleagues have done an elegant series of studies in which they have shown how different learning conditions (competitive or non-competitive; performance or mastery focused) influence children's subsequent motivation, and found quite interesting differences in motivation depending upon these conditions.

Maehr, Midgley, and their colleagues conducted a number of studies looking at how classroom instructional practices relate to children's goal orientations and how these relations may change over time. L. Anderman and E. Anderman (1999) reported that adolescents endorse performance goals more than mastery goals. A major reason for this likely is that schools increasingly emphasize performance goals as children get older. One clear example of this is how evaluations of different kinds proliferate, and have stronger consequences for adolescents' futures. Midgley and their colleagues work (Midgley, 2002) has shown two major things with respect to this point: 1) elementary school teachers focus on mastery oriented goals to a greater extent than do middle school teachers, and 2) middle school students perceive school as more performance-oriented than do elementary school students. Thus any observed changes in children's goal orientations seem very bound up in changes in the school goal culture. We return to this issue in a later section.

Goal orientations often are studied at a relatively general level, but some researchers have looked at goal orientations towards particular school activities. Meece and Miller (2001) studied the development during elementary of students' goal orientations in reading and writing, looking at performance goals, mastery goals, and work avoidant goals. The found that children's goal orientation were reasonably stable over a one-year period; the lagged correlations were.44 for task mastery goals.58 for performance goals, and.45 for work-avoidance goals.

With respect to change over time, following prediction children's mastery goals decreased over time. Contrary to prediction, performance goals did as well. The pattern of change in work avoidant goals was less consistent. There is much less work on the development of the content of children's goals. Thus, we know very little about how the contents of children's goals vary across age and context.

Development of Self-Regulation and Volition

Eccles *et al.* (1998) reviewed work establishing two general developmental points concerning self-regulation. First, children's ability to self-regulate increases dramatically across the toddler period due to increases in ability to focus on both the outcomes of their behaviours and the behaviours themselves, increases in understanding of the self as a causal agent, and increases in both the ability and desire to evaluate the success or failure of one's achievement efforts. Second, parents play a critical role in the extent to which children regulate their own behaviour. For instance, both the ways parents define and organize tasks for the children, and the control strategies they use, have a big impact on very young children's ability to regulate their behaviour.

From the self-determination theory perspective, development involves the process of internalization, where children take increasing control over their own behaviour and thus become more self-determined. Grolnick and her colleagues (2002) discussed the important role of autonomy support in the development of self-determination and intrinsic motivation. They reviewed research showing that when parents and teachers support children's autonomy children have more positive competence beliefs, greater intrinsic motivation, and higher self-esteem. Along with autonomy support Grolnick *et al.* stressed the roles of affective support, involvement in children's lives, and the provision of adequate structure in children's environments as fostering the development of self-determination.

Turning to self-regulated learning, Zimmerman (2000) proposed a four-step developmental sequence of self-regulation. Children first learn effective strategies by observing successful models and focusing on process goals. Second, children imitate the strategies, following what the model did relatively closely. Third, they learn to use the strategies apart from the model; Zimmerman called this self-controlled learning. Although children do the strategies on their own, they still are dependent on the model. Finally, in the self-regulated phase children begin to both use the strategies in different situations and tailor them to their own purposes. They also focus more on outcome goals. Research is beginning to show that individuals' ability to learn different behaviours relates to the kind of regulatory training they experience. Kitsantas, Zimmerman, and Cleary (2000) found that novice learners learned best when learning from models rather than simply receiving performance feedback on their own performance. Zimmerman and Kitsantas (1999) found that as students moved through the levels of regulatory skill they learned more efficiently when focused on outcome goals rather than process goals, because the former matched more clearly their level of self-regulation.

Pintrich and Zusho (2002) also discussed the development of self-regulation, discussing both phases of self-regulation like those we discussed earlier and different areas that need to be regulated (cognition, motivation, behaviour, and context). Like Eccles *et al.* (1998) they noted that children become more efficient at regulating their cognition and behaviour, and possibly their motivation, as they get older. They also discussed, however, that older children may know how to regulate these areas but oftentimes do not, reflecting the pervasive competence/performance distinction that occurs in many areas of psychology.

Pintrich and Zusho reviewed specific aspects of cognition and motivation that relate to the ability to self-regulate learning and behaviour. With respect to motivation, one's level of efficacy, degree of interest in the activity, and goals for it all relate to children's self-regulation. When children are efficacious, interested in the activity they are doing, and hold learning goals, they are more likely to regulate their behaviour to accomplish a certain activity. Further, there are potentially interesting developmental issues with respect to each of these motivational constructs. For instance, younger children's competence and efficacy beliefs relate less closely to their actual behaviour, and (particularly with respect to competence beliefs) often are overly optimistic, which may mean that younger children do not see the need to carefully regulate their actions to produce an outcome. As competence beliefs and performance become more closely calibrated this likely changes. With respect to goal orientations, if mastery goals become less prevalent and performance goals more prevalent then self-regulation may decline (but see Pintrich, 2000b, on multiple pathways to different outcomes).

With respect to the use of different self-regulatory strategies, Zimmerman and Martinez-Pons (1990) found a complex pattern of differences across age in use of these strategies by older children and adolescents. Researchers have not yet systematically tested how strategies, goals, and self-efficacy interact to influence the regulation of learning in different-aged children. Additionally, it would be useful to compare Zimmerman's model with Deci and Ryan's discussion of the development of internalized regulation. There is some developmental work on volitional strategies. For example, Kuhl and Kraska (1989), in German and Mexican elementary school-aged children, found increases in children's ability to use all of the strategies except for emotion control. But more developmental work is needed here as well.

Growth of Subjective Task Values

Eccles, Wigfield, and their colleagues examined age-related changes in both the structure and mean levels of children's valuing of different activities. In Eccles *et al.* (1993) and Eccles and Wigfield (1995), children's competence-expectancy beliefs and subjective values within the domains of math, reading, and sports formed distinct factors at all grade levels from first through twelfth. Thus, even during the very early elementary grades children appear to have distinct beliefs about what they are good at and what they value. The distinction between various sub-components of subjective task value appear to differentiate more gradually. Children in early elementary school differentiate task value into two components: interest and utility/importance. In contrast, children in grades five through 12 differentiate task value into the three major subcomponents (attainment value/personal importance, interest, and utility value) outlined by Eccles *et al.* (1983). These results suggest that the interest component differentiates out first, followed later by the distinction between utility and attainment value.

As with competence-related beliefs, studies generally show age-related decline in children's valuing of certain academic tasks. Jacobs *et al.* (2002), in the study described earlier in the section on the development of competence beliefs, found that children's valuing of the domains of math, language arts, and sports declined. As was the case for competence beliefs, children's valuing of language arts declined most during elementary school and then levelled off. By contrast, children's valuing of math declined the most during high school.

Researchers have not addressed changes in children's understandings of the components of task value identified by Eccles *et al.* (1983), although there likely are age-related differences in these understandings. An eight year old is likely to have a different sense of what it means for a task to be "useful" than an 11 year old does. Further, it also is likely that there are differences across age in which of the components of achievement values are most dominant. Wigfield and Eccles (1992) suggested that interest may be especially salient during the early elementary school grades with young children's activity choices being most directly related to their interests. Young children likely try many different activities for a short time each before developing a more stable opinion regarding which activities they enjoy the most. As children get older the perceived utility and personal importance of different tasks likely become more salient, particularly as they develop more stable self-schema and long-range goals and plans. These developmental predictions need to be tested.

A related developmental question is how children's developing competence beliefs relate to their developing subjective task values. According to both the Eccles *et al.* (1983) model and Bandura's (1997) self-efficacy theory, ability self-concepts should influence the development of task values. In support of this prediction, Mac Iver, Stipek, and Daniels (1991) found that changes in junior high school students' competence beliefs over a semester predicted change in children's interest much more strongly than vice versa. Does the same causal ordering occur in younger children? Bandura (1997) argued that interests emerge out of one's sense of self-efficacy and that children should be more interested in challenging than in easy tasks.

Taking a developmental perspective, Wigfield (1994) proposed that initially young children's competence and task value beliefs are likely to be relatively independent of each other. This independence would mean that children might pursue some activities in which they are interested regardless of how good or bad they think they are at the activity. Over time, particularly in the achievement domains, children may begin to attach more value to activities on which they do well for several reasons: First, through processes associated with classical conditioning, the positive affect one experiences when one does well should become attached to the activities yielding success. Second, lowering the value one attaches to activities that one is having difficulty with is likely to be an effective way to maintain a positive global source of efficacy and self-esteem.

Thus, at some point the two kinds of beliefs should become more positively related to one another. In partial support of this view, Wigfield *et al.* (1997) found that relations between children's competence beliefs and subjective values in different domains indeed are stronger among older than younger elementary school-aged children. Recently, Jacobs *et al.* (2002) found that changes in competence beliefs predicted changes in children's valuing of the activities, accounting for as much as 40 per cent of the variance in change in children's valuing of the activities. This suggests that the causal direction in this relation goes from competence beliefs to values, but more longitudinal work is needed to assess this possibility.

Growth of Interest and Intrinsic Motivation

Eccles *et al.* (1998) summarized work on the early development of children's interests, which shows that children have general or universal interests at first, which become more specific relatively quickly. Todt (1990) argued that this early differentiation eventually leads to individual differences in interests in the social versus the natural sciences. The next phase of interest development - between 3 and 8 years of age - is characterized by the formation of gender-specific interests.

According to Kohlberg (1966), the acquisition of gender identity leads to gender-specific behaviours, attitudes, and interests. Children strive to behave consistently with their gender identity, and, thus, evaluate activities or objects consistent with their gender identity more positively than other activities or objects. As a consequence, boys and girls develop gender role stereotyped interests.

At the next stage (ages 9 - 13) - the emerging self-concept is assumed to be linked more directly to social group affiliation and cognitive ability, leading to occupational interests consistent with one's social class and ability self-concepts. The final stage (occurring after age 13 or 14) is characterized by an orientation to the internal, unique self leading to more differentiated and individualized vocational interests, based on abstract concepts of self (*e.g.*, of personality). Thus, the development of vocational interests is a process of continuous elimination of interests that do not fit the self-concepts of one's gender, social group affiliation, ability, and then personal identity (Todt, 1990). This process is assumed to depend mainly on the general cognitive development of the child or adolescent. It is also likely that changing needs or motives across the life span can influence the development of interests. A good example is the increasing interest in biology and psychology during puberty. The need to know oneself and to cope with rapid bodily and psychological changes seems to foster interest in biological and psychological domains of knowledge at this age (Todt, 1990).

Consistent with studies of American children (*e.g.*, Eccles *et al.*, 1993; Gottfried *et al.*, 2001; Harter, 1981; Wigfield *et al.*, 1991), several European researchers have found that that interest and intrinsic motivation in different subject areas school decline across the school years. This is especially true for the natural sciences and mathematics and particularly during the early adolescent years. Pekrun (1993) found that intrinsic motivation stabilized after eighth grade, and Gottfried *et al.* (2001) reported surprisingly high stability coefficients for intrinsic motivation measured across a one year period for children ages 13 and above.

Baumert (1995) argued that the decline in school-related interests during adolescence reflects a more general developmental process in which the adolescents discover new fields of experience that lead to new interests and reduce the dominant influence of school. In contrast, other researchers have suggested that changes in a number of instructional variables like clarity of presentation, monitoring of what happens in the classroom, supportive behaviour, cognitively stimulating experiences, self-concept of the teacher [educator vs. scientist], and achievement pressure may contribute to declining interest in school mathematics and science.

Index